D1603633

In the Name of Love

In the Name of Love
Romantic Ideology and its Victims

Aaron Ben-Ze'ev
Ruhama Goussinsky

OXFORD
UNIVERSITY PRESS

Great Clarendon Street, Oxford, OX2 6DP,
United Kingdom

Oxford University Press is a department of the University of Oxford.
It furthers the University's objective of excellence in research, scholarship,
and education by publishing worldwide. Oxford is a registered trade mark of
Oxford University Press in the UK and in certain other countries

Published in the United States of America by Oxford University Press
198 Madison Avenue, New York, NY 10016, United States of America

British Library Cataloguing in Publication Data
Data available

Library of Congress Cataloging in Publication Data
Data available

ISBN 978–0–19–856649–6

Cover image: ericsphotography/iStockphoto.com

For my brother Yehuda, who knew so well what love is, but did not get the chance to enjoy it for very long. ABZ

For Raanan, with love. RG

Contents

Introduction

'I want to know what love is'

Love – such an abundant source of vitality; it encases an explosive and releasing power that excites the body and soul alike, mixing creation and conception with ancestral chaos. Love makes a man stand tall and look straight. The contact between woman and man unleashes an internal strength, through the fusion of the sexes, through their unconquerable desire to copulate and become one, to pierce the outer shell that separates a man from his wife, distancing one from the other. Is there a greater or more powerful urge than this? Is there any other power that can thus astonish humans, freeing them from their bonds of distress?

> From a diary written by Yehuda Ben-Ze'ev, on 21 November, 1966; he was killed in 1967 in the Six Days War, at the age of 32.

My intuition is that there is a new category of women: the victims of the Symbolists – like the victims of the Romanticists – like Madame Bovary was a victim of romanticism. Women are not literature, they are life. The sadness of love, like the sadness of life, stems from having to make concessions. One can only say to his beloved: you have given me a portion of the beauty the world has to offer – whereas one dreams of possessing all of beauty and all potential lives encapsulated in one single woman and one single life. But one comes to terms with his love, just as one does with his life.

> From a letter written by Alain-Fournier to his friend on 11 October 1906; he was killed in 1914 in World War I, at the age of 28

We all want to understand what constitutes romantic love and to some extent, in different ways, most of us know quite a lot about love. We all yearn to feel love, and most of us have loved someone. Nevertheless, for the majority of people love remains a mystery, and they feel that they have not achieved it in the way in which they want to. This book is about our ideals of love, our experiences of love, and the disparity between the two. (Unless otherwise indicated, 'love' refers to romantic love.)

We yearn to experience the idealized love depicted in so many novels, movies, poems, and popular songs, all of which help to form what this book will refer to as 'Romantic Ideology'. The basic tenets of this ideology, discussed in Chapter 1, include the following beliefs: The beloved is everything to the lover and hence love is all you need; true love lasts forever and can conquer all; true lovers are united – they are one and the same person; love is irreplaceable and exclusive; and love is pure and can do no evil. According to this Romantic Ideology, love is comprehensive-there are no boundaries to such love; uncompromising – nothing can dilute or impede such love; and unconditional-reality is almost irrelevant to love and has scant impact on it. This ideology is quite evident in heterosexual love and some of its features can also be found in homosexual love.

A major case study in this book concerns men who have murdered their wives or partners allegedly 'out of love'. It is estimated that over 30 percent of all female murder victims in the United States die at the hands of a former or present spouse or boyfriend.[1] How can murdering a beloved be associated with love? Can the desire to hurt a loved one emerge out of love itself? Love is generally considered a moral, altruistic, and well-intentioned emotion; however, this idealized notion of love is far from realistic. Not only is love intrinsically ambivalent, but it can also give rise to dangerous consequences.

In this book, we argue that Romantic Ideology implies extreme behavior: After all, the expressions 'all is fair in love and war' and 'love will always prevail' are often used to identify 'true love'. Furthermore, this ideology, which promotes problematic notions like eternal love ('true love can never die') and dangerous notions like self-sacrifice and unlimited justification ('love can do no evil'), is also used to legitimize whatever is done 'in the name of love'. Since we are so deeply influenced by prevailing cultural precepts about love, these beliefs have become rooted and are treated as self-evident truths. The content of the assumptions underlying Romantic Ideology, like the content of many religious ideologies, is highly moral and compassionate. However, when such content is placed within a rigid and uncompromising framework and when it lacks a proper regard for reality, it can give rise to extreme and appalling behavior. People have committed the most horrific crimes in the name of the altruistic ideals of religion and love.

Romantic Ideology does not impact only on murderers. Most, if not all, of us have been occasional victims of this ideology, quite often without being aware of it. As Lynn, a divorcee in her late 40s, admits, 'In the past I have definitely been a victim of romantic ideology and I have even gone so far as to buy the story that love has to be difficult and painful'. Although the act of intimate murder is an extreme example of the dangers inherent in certain perceptions of love, the state of mind of such a murderer can be similar to that of other victims of Romantic Ideology. Killing the one you love is not an example of 'loving too much' but of how love can go wrong when totalitarianism and extremism, rather than compromise and accommodation, are the guiding principles. The murderous dictator who proclaims that he 'loves his people too much' fits neatly into this category.

Our analysis of wife-killing deviates from the prevailing popular understanding and scientific explanations of this phenomenon in two major respects: (a) we believe that in an important sense, these murders are committed out of love, so that an understanding of which components of love play a role in these murders would increase our understanding of the phenomenon of wife-murder; and (b) we believe that whereas wife killing is undoubtedly the most extreme manifestation of male violence, it is not a 'natural' continuation of that violence, nor is it the 'inevitable' end of a path of male violence, and it thus should be understood as a phenomenon that is separate to other forms of male violence. These claims offer a new perspective on this terrible phenomenon.

Chapter 2 discusses the meaning of separation and love in the face of romantic rejection. Whereas the popular media consistently reminds us that love is all we need, statistics concerning the rate of depression and suicide after divorce or the breakup of intimate relations remind us what might happen if 'all that we need' is taken away. We argue that what is perceived to be the ultimate expression of romantic love – 'I can't live, if living is without you' – is in fact a state of mind that turns the partner, who is perceived to be the sole supplier of meaning, into a hostage. We further analyze the behavioral patterns and the emotional state characteristic of the rejected partner in general and its manifestation among men who killed their wives in particular.

Chapter 3 explains the ambivalence and danger of love. We argue that it is the idealization of love that, ironically, gives it such destructive power. However, the dangers inherent in love do not lie in these romantic conceptions per se, nor are they related to the inevitable disappointment in the face of the actual experience. Love becomes dangerous when its fulfillment – often formulated in an extreme and deceptive manner – becomes the ultimate, most significant symbol of our lives. We argue further that typical romantic love seems to entail not only jealousy, but possessiveness as well. The chapter ends by examining whether we can hate the one we love.

Chapter 4 analyzes the act of wife killing. We propose to understand a murder as (a) rooted in a unique constellation of factors and circumstances, (b) an act in which the perpetrator intends to cause his wife's death, rather than one in which he temporarily loses control, and (c) the climax of a dynamic and gradual process culminating in an emotional experience in which one person seeks to destroy the other even at the cost of self-destruction. This approach suggests that the dynamic underlying wife murder is different from that which characterizes other manifestations of violence against women.

Romantic Ideology has not been extinguished; in fact, the desire to fulfill it may be increasing. However, the likelihood of realizing such love, in particular within the framework of a committed, long-term relationship, grows ever slimmer. For most people, such ideal love remains beyond their reach. The gap between what we want from love and what we actually achieve is increasing and the resulting dissonance gives rise to mounting dissatisfaction with our love lives. In Chapter 5, we begin the discussion of ways in which we can cope with this gap by examining the crucial role that imagination plays in creating our personal ideals and boundaries.

One of our greatest advantages over animals is our capacity to imagine circumstances that differ from our present ones. However, the capacity to imagine, which unchains us from the present, chains us to the prospects of the possible. Imagination is a two-edge sword: It is a gift, but one that bites. The great human blessing – that is, our capacity to be aware of possible scenarios – is also our fundamental curse, as it affords us realization of our profound limitations as well as our imminent death. When Engelbert Humperdinck asks, 'Please release me, let me go, for I don't love you any more', he refers to the chains of the present. Granting his request is easy these days, as there are fewer formal, social, and practical bonds to impede departure. A more profound difficulty lies in the chains of the possible: We have become slaves to many tempting romantic options available in modern life – the Internet, business trips, and cell phones all facilitate various romantic and sexual possibilities. The chains of potential possibilities prevent us from enjoying or even being comfortable with the present and are often harder to escape from the chains of the present. We tend to get used to the chains of the present, as we really have no other choice. It is much harder to cope with the chains of the possible, as this realm, bounded only by our imagination, is extremely exciting and can prevent us from being happy with our present lot. The present may make us somewhat sad, but the realm of the possible makes us restless and continually disappointed. Coping with the mixed blessing of the possible requires us to establish a normative order of priority in the form of ideals and boundaries. As we establish a set of normative priorities, we shall often find ourselves giving up an ideal or violating a certain boundary. We also show that romantic love is rife with the difficulties associated with fulfilling ideals and maintaining boundaries.

In Chapter 6, we explain the way in which these difficulties gain additional weight in romantic love by examining the nature of our emotional system and the prevailing norms in modern society. We indicate that since emotions are generated when we perceive a significant change in our situation, emotional intensity decreases as familiarity increases. The difficulties of fulfilling those postulates of Romantic Ideology that refer to the exclusiveness of the beloved and to the eternal nature of true love (summed up in the vow: 'Till death do us part') are amplified in light of two major developments in modern society: (a) the lifting of most of the constraints that once prevented long-term committed relationships, such as marriage, from dissolving, and (b) the apparent presence of so many attractive alternatives that offer the promise of replacing any given committed romantic relationship. Staying within a committed relationship has become a choice that requires us to constantly reexamine its value in light of, among other issues, the presence of love.

Given the above circumstances, the need for compromise has become urgent in the romantic domain. Using the word 'compromise' in the same breath as 'love' may appear a contradiction in terms—you cannot tell your beloved that you are madly in love with her, even though she constitutes some kind of compromise for you. We distinguish here between compromises and accommodations: When we compromise, we accept certain behavior that we still evaluate as negative, whereas when we accommodate, we change our attitudes so that we no longer consider this behavior to be negative. In Chapter 7 we indicate that if one wishes to avoid the very high cost of invasive romantic partnerships, one needs to make compromises and accomodations that are in fact already widely practiced in mordern society. Examples include postponing romantic gratification, declining romantic intensity, reducing the exclusive nature of the romantic relationship by enlarging the scope of activities that are not restricted to the beloved, serial monogamy, and loving more than one person at the same time. The presence of such compromises and accommodations is expressed in the generation of new terminology. Thus, instead of the highly negative terms of 'adultery' and 'betrayal' some people use the more neutral term of 'parallel relationship'. People in love should recognize that a loving relationship has limitations; we can call this 'bounded love'.

Throughout the book, we emphasize the need of most people to find an alternative to Romantic Ideology. These are indeed hard times for lovers. Is there anything we can do to alleviate this suffering? Chapter 8 presents an initial outline for an alternative, which we term the 'Nurturing Approach'. Although developing the details and consequences of such an approach requires a whole book in itself, we hope that providing an initial conceptual framework will benefit our understanding of love and of how to maintain long-term romantic love. At the basis of this approach lies the assumption that in order for romantic love to be nurtured, the lover should not merely seek to ensure that the beloved feels good; it is imperative, too, that the lover is profoundly satisfied with the way in which the relationship enhances her own development and satisfaction. The emphasis is shifting here from a model based upon other-validation to one of self-validation. Only a deeply satisfied person can provide love and happiness to another. The self-validated model is by no means a matter of egocentrism. It is not egocentric to attempt to nurture your capacities and genuine needs, while at the same time developing a loving equal relationship with another person. Moreover, the nurturing aspect also refers to nurturing the other. We also argue that in romantic love, uniqueness is more significant than exclusivity. Uniqueness focuses on greater nurturing of ourselves and others, while exclusiveness entails curtailing or obstructing others' decisions or pursuits. Accordingly, we argue that in love, caring is more significant than prohibiting various types of sexual practices.

Our analysis indicates that the decrease in marital constraints and the increase in the presence of tempting alternatives have enhanced the role of love in our life. Despite greater sexual freedom, genuine love and aspirations for long-term commitment have not disappeared. On the contrary, we are witnessing an impressive comeback of romantic love, which makes it difficult to ignore the whole issue of what we mean by love and how we deal with it. The good news is that nowadays love is everywhere; the bad news is that we cannot run away from it. Like the passionate Hotel California, described by the Eagles, in love 'You can checkout any time you like, but you can never leave!'

This is not a book of advice on how to love properly; rather, the book analyses love, its hurdles, and its challenges. Nevertheless, our analysis may help people to discover a way of loving that is more suitable for them. We illustrate and clarify our claims by referring to many sources, such as formal interviews with murderers, informal conversations with people, and popular songs. Needless to say, citations from these references do not intend to prove our claims, but are offered in order to illustrate them and to give them, in addition to the conceptual analysis and available empirical evidence, further support.

Data about the murderers were collected by means of in-depth, semi-structured interviews, followed by content analysis. The eighteen men interviewed were Israeli prisoners convicted of murder (15) or attempted murder (3) of their female partner. Twelve men were sentenced to life imprisonment, and six to prison terms ranging from 9 to 14 years. Most were high-school graduates. Eleven of them are Jews, three are Muslim, two are Druze, and two are Christian. At the time of the crime, eight of the interviewees were in their twenties, four in their thirties, four in their forties, and two were over fifty years old.

All the cited murderers are men, whereas most of the informal talks were with women (who seem to be more open about their emotional attitudes). We find striking similarities in the perception of love expressed by the murders and those found in the various cultural expressions of Romantic Ideology.

When referring to popular songs, we indicate the name of the performing artist who is commonly associated with the song in the public perception, rather than the lyricist, who is usually unknown.

The conceptual foundations for the analysis of emotions used here are based on Aaron Ben-Ze'ev's book, *The Subtlety of Emotions* (2000), and on a detailed analysis of the impact of the Internet upon romantic relationships, presented in Ben-Ze'ev's book, *Love Online: Emotions on the Internet* (2004). The analysis of the murderer's perspective is based on research conducted by Ruhama Goussinsky, *Was the Handwriting on the Wall?! The Meanings Perpetrators Attribute to Intimate Murder* (2002). Aaron Ben-Ze'ev is President, and Professor of Philosophy at the University of Haifa, Israel, and Ruhama Goussinsky is a Lecturer, at the Human Service Department in Emek Yezreel College, Israel. We thank the editor and publisher of *Philosophia* for the permission to use materials from Ben-Zeév's article, 'Hating the one we love' (2007).

We are grateful for many people who have helped us in forming the ideas presented here. In particular, we would like to thank John Portmann and Andrew Ortony with whom we have conducted many fruitful conversations on issues related to the book and who sent us extensive and helpful comments on various parts of the manuscript. We would also like to express our profound gratitude to the following people who have read various portions of the manuscript and provided us with insightful suggestions: Nira Adler, Shulamit Almog, Wered Ben-Sade, Avinoam Ben-Ze'ev, Ruth Ben-Ze'ev, Nili Cohen, Ronald de Sonsa, Irwin Goldstein, Eva Illouz, Hara Estroff Marano, Ariel Meirav, Orit Razy, Lilli Rosenberg, Rivka Shtatfeld, Saul Smilansky, Michael Strauss, Naomi Sussmann, and Yoram Yovell. We are profoundly grateful to Alex, Alexandra, Andrea, Ariel, Bernard, Barbra, David, Diana, Elena, Esther, Eva, Grace, Hazel, Iris, Laura, Lisa, Lori, Lynn, Mark, Nadia, Nancy, Naomi, Natalie, Nina, Robin, Rosa, Ryan, Shirley, Sandra, Sarah, Susan, Teresa, Tiffany, and Yadin (fictional names, but real people) and to many other people who talked with us about their romantic experiences. The men who were formally interviewed for this book have all been convicted of appalling crimes. Their stories are often horrific and we appreciate their willingness to discuss their experiences with us.

We are thankful for our family members, Ruth, Dean, and Adam Ben-Ze'ev and Raanan Goussinsky, for their patience and love during the years of writing this book.

Without all the above people we would have been unable to understand '*this thing called love*' (Queen).

Chapter 1

Romantic ideology
'If you love someone'

Only you can make this world seem right …
Only you and you alone.

The Platters

You are all that I am living for.

Elvis Presley

In this chapter we present Romantic Ideology alongside a description of the attitude towards this love demonstrated by those who committed the most horrible crime connected with love: men who killed their wives (or partners) out of love. We begin with a brief discussion of the nature of ideologies, followed by an analysis of the major components of Romantic Ideology and how they are expressed in the beliefs of many, including murders. Finally, we conclude the chapter with a comparison between Romantic Ideology and religion.[1]

Love and ideology – 'You're the nearest thing to heaven'

With your unparallel love you were my life, you were my everything… our wondrous love for each other will go on into eternity.

Subscription in Brompton Cemetery, on the grave of
Terence J. Feeling (1928–2000), written by his wife

Without your love I'm nothing but a beggar.

Aerosmith

She was everything for me.

A murderer

Romantic love has always played a central role in human life: it is a central theme in many works of art and we are still excited by reading what people from various cultures wrote about it at different periods. Although the term *romantic love* has been used in various manners and it is known to refer to a complex set of features, its general meaning is typically understood. Therefore, we shall not try to define here this term but rather examine a prevalent use of it, and then offer certain revisions.

In light of the centrality of love in our lives, it is no wonder that cultures all over the world have depicted an ideal form of romantic love towards which all of us are supposedly striving. Although this ideal may vary from one culture to another or within a single culture at different times, it nevertheless is grounded in many cultures and appears to be present, in various formulations, in many periods. We term the basic features of this ideal, 'Romantic Ideology'. This ideology is common in the novels we read, the movies we see, the songs we hear, and in many other aspects of our culture. Romantic Ideology is part and parcel of the education our children receive from a very early age, when they begin to watch Disney's movies and listen to fairy tales. It continues to pervade their adulthood and culminates in their vow to live together, happily ever after. Indeed, according to a 2003 Harris Poll, nearly 50 percent of the male and female teens are likely to identify television as their chief source of information about romance, although they undoubtedly heard romantic fairy tales (such as *Cinderella* and *Sleeping Beauty*) when they were younger.[2]

The juxtaposition of the terms *ideology* and *love* may be considered suspect; although it may sound a bit provocative, it is nevertheless adequate. The common dictionary definitions of *ideology* are (a) a system of ideas and ideals forming the basis of a theory (usually, an economic or political theory); and (b) a set of beliefs characteristic of a social group or individual. Both definitions are in accordance with our use. Romantic Ideology is indeed a system of ideas and ideals forming a kind of theory about love, and it is also a set of beliefs characteristic of an individual, and often also of society. Like other ideologies, also Romantic Ideology is characterized by being comprehensive, uncompromising, and having little regard for reality. Romantic Ideology is also similar to other ideologies in that it creates self-fulfilling prophecies, at least for some of its believers, in the spirit of 'If you don't believe in miracles, then you aren't realistic'. In fact, researchers argue that while extreme romantic beliefs generally tend to engender unrealistic standards for relationships, a certain degree of romance is necessary to sustain relationships. Those who follow the tenets of Romantic Ideology are more likely to experience a more intense love and to be more committed. However, it is still unclear precisely to what extent this ideology is related to the stability, satisfaction and quality of romantic relationships.[3]

As in the case of other ideologies, the romantic one also plays a central role in the life of its believers and especially in determining their happiness: certainly when we're in love, other problems become insignificant.[4]

Many cultures have indeed considered romantic love to be crucial for personal fulfillment and a happy life. However, romantic love is also a major factor in people's misery, as it involves many disappointments and unfulfilled hopes. It has been claimed that Western culture has no history of happy romantic love within marriage.[5] Love may be 'many splendid things', but love also hurts a lot, can be dangerous, and may lead us to foolish deeds. Committing suicide because of unrequited love is not an unusual story; it is even regarded as a perfect instance of true love. In light of its central place in our happiness, love has often been described in extremely idealized terms.

Despite such prevailing descriptions of love, most people are aware of the great difficulty in fulfilling this love. The encouragement to seek ideal love and the sober belief that this is an almost impossible task are intertwined in our paradoxical thinking about love. As Lynn says:

> I am a victim of romantic ideology – I can feel the tendency toward shame knowing that I am so much like these descriptions. Even though I know that I have been seduced by songs, movies, and the pervasive, powerful, and influential messages about how love should look and feel, I believe I am now much more realistic than that. I see now how so much of the time I am not ... and I have allowed myself to be seduced.

Nevertheless, Lynn still believes in the great value of Romantic Ideology, which 'like The North Star guides us through choppy seas and from distant shores, never to be reached, but valuable nonetheless'.

Characteristics of ideal love – 'To live without your love is impossible'

> Don't you know that you are all my life to me? ... My whole being, my love ... I cannot think about you and about myself separately. You and I are one to me.
>
> Vronsky to Anna, in Tolstoy's *Anna Karenina*

> When a man loves a woman, can't keep his mind on nothin' else.
>
> Percy Sledge

> I only had love for a single woman, even though I had so many girls. This means that for me, she was the one, the only one. To this day I say that there is only her, and there will never be another, even if I get out of prison, no, not in my life, never.
>
> A murderer

The prevailing Romantic Ideology can be found in various forms, yet it seems that there are certain basic elements that are common to most of its manifestations. We present here the basic characteristics of Romantic Ideology, arranged in three major groups, as they relate to the profundity, the uniqueness, and the purity of love.

The profundity of love: The profundity of love in Romantic Ideology relates to three major aspects: its profound significance, its ability to prevail, and long duration. Accordingly, love gives meaning to our life ('You are everything to me'), love can overcome all obstacles ('True love will find a way'), and love aims at the eternal (we shall love each other 'forever and a day').

The uniqueness of the beloved: The two lovers are fused into a unique entity ('We are soul mates who are meant for each other'), the beloved is irreplaceable ('There is only one true love'), and exclusive ('Millions of people go by, but they all disappear from view – because I only have eyes for you').

The purity of love: Love is morally good ('Love can do no evil'; 'I am in love with an angel').[6] Love and the beloved both have their own intrinsic value and are morally pure.

Underlying the above features of ideal love is its total (in the sense of comprehensive), uncompromising (in the sense of inflexible), and unconditional (i.e., unaffected by the conditions of reality) nature. Totality refers to the fact that all aspects of the beloved and the loving experience are part of this optimal state. The uncompromising aspect of ideal love refers to the lover's own attitude toward the beloved: this attitude cannot accept 'maybe', 'to a certain extent', or 'gradually' as adequate loving terms. Ideal love is unconditional in the sense that reality cannot change it; accordingly, it disregards reality and considers love to be beyond the reach of mundane altering events. It is also unconditional in the sense of willingness to give everything to the beloved. These attitudes are expressed by so many lovers, fictional and real. Lynn, a divorcee, said 'when in love I know that I will do anything for this person – love is unconditional'. Flora, a married woman in her early 40s who is involved in a long-term loving relationship with a married man, says:

> He magnetizes all my thoughts, all my feelings, and he does it all the time. Our love does not depend on any external circumstance, nor can it ever be threatened by them, which is the whole miracle of it. I love him so romantically and wildly, and I love him without limits, for everything he is and everything he does. All external circumstances are completely against it, but we can continue to develop our love, no matter how difficult the circumstances are. I am his, and his alone; now and forever.

We turn now to describe the basic features of ideal love and to indicate a striking similarity between the way songs, poems, and other major means of cultural expressions describe this love and the way men who killed their wives describe their attitude. We shall argue that this similarity is not accidental, as those men believed in the reality and validity of ideal love.

Romantic Ideology describes love as profound in three basic senses: it gives meaning to our entire life; it can overcome all obstacles; and is eternal. In this sense, love functions as the ultimate significance, the irresistible and eternal force of our lives. Accordingly, love is considered to be the essence of life and should be our top priority. Let us analyze in more detail the basic components of ideal love.

Love as a source of meaning and needs – 'You are everything to me'

I am my husband's life as fully as he is mine.

Charlotte Bronte, *Jane Eyre*

You are everything I hoped for, you are everything I need.

Joe Cocker

He's all I've got, he's all I've got in this world.

Whitney Houston

I felt as if she was my air, as if she was the only thing that sustained me.

A murderer

In ideal love, the beloved's value is profound in the sense that the beloved provides the whole meaning for the lover's life. When the beloved is around, life is meaningful and when clouds cover the horizon of love, life begins to lose its meaning. Actually, there is no life without the beloved, implying, as one person said to us, that 'anything without her couldn't be life at all'. And Grace, a married woman in her mid-50s, says about her married lover:

Since and only since I met him I know why I have come to this world. Before, I felt no meaning in anything, and just pain. Now I feel that everything is so much more meaningful, and joyful, also all the little things. Every single time with him is like coming to life again, being born again.

Ideal love is described as not merely giving meaning to our life, but it creates a whole meaningful new world, a world that can be known only to lovers. Hence, statements like 'The world has changed, everything is different now', 'Loving him is wonderful; my whole being expands into unprecedented realms', are common among lovers.

People in love often feel as though they are starting life all over again, like having, as one man said, 'the first-ever impressions of a newborn infant', and like experiencing 'the purity and innocence of virginity'. They say that their new loving experience is so new and exceptional to them that they do not know how to handle it, as it takes them through previously unknown heights and terrains. This newness may confound, but it also surely adds to the intoxication of the experience of being 'swept away', so central to the great Romantic poets. This profound meaning overshadows all others, such that equating love with life comes naturally. Thus, the all-encompassing quality of love is expressed in statements like 'I am surrounded by nothing but you'. And indeed when love is essential in our life and everything is smiling upon us, the world is 'Shining, shimmering, and splendid' and is seen from 'a new fantastic point of view'. This unique experience makes lovers wonder whether a love as wonderful as theirs is possible at all. Although many love songs describe this experience of love, lovers still wonder whether other people have ever experienced such love. As Flora states:

> I do wonder if there are other people who may have experienced a love like mine with my lover; I think that this would be completely impossible, and that only we experience such a love, beyond anything that can ever be described.

And so idealized love can alienate us from everyone else – everyone, of course, but the object of our profound affection.

Identifying love with life gives firm grounds to the extreme claim arguing that 'all you need is love'. The move from 'you are the sunshine of my life … you are the apple of my eye' to 'you are everything I need', cannot be taken lightly: it is a move from the subjective way we perceive the world to an objective statement of 'fact', supposedly unrelated to the subject's point of view. Fulfilling one's needs is essential; it is not merely a matter of subjective interpretation such as that of rendering meanings to things: on the contrary, it typically involves more objective processes.

Claiming that love is all there is to life enhances the importance of love, but is exaggerated. It may be the case that 'as long as we're in love, we're in life', but this merely indicates that love is necessary for a profound meaningful life, it does not entail that love is identical to a meaningful life nor that is even a sufficient condition for such a life. Similarly, there are certain needs, such as the biological needs of eating, breathing, or sleeping, which can be met without a noteworthy contribution by a unique lover (though, of course, one can sleep better and have a better appetite while being in love). Romantic Ideology may refer to psychological needs, which are often claimed to be fulfilled in the optimal manner by the beloved. Those include needs such as psychological support, emotional intimacy, sexual satisfaction, social companionship, intellectual curiosity and spiritual fulfillment. Romantic Ideology postulates that all these needs should be met by the beloved; however, this may considerably reduce the complexity and quality of our life, as very few people can excel in all realms. The one who provides the most profound psychological support or financial assistance to a certain person is not necessarily the one who is the best partner for satisfying intellectual curiosity, generating the most profound spiritual fulfillment, or being the most desirable sexual partner.

Love will conquer all – 'Gladly move the earth for you'

There ain't nothing in our way baby,
Nothing our love couldn't raise above.

Celine Dion

Ain't no mountain high enough.

Diana Ross

I said to myself: I will fight in the army … I will fight against everyone, but I will take her. No one will take her from me, and this is what I did.

A murderer

A central feature of ideal love is its ability to overcome various difficulties; hence, no mountain is high enough to stop love. Powerful love can overcome – 'against all odds' – all major obstacles. A true lover can do anything for his beloved. In the words of Frank Sinatra (in 'Until the real thing comes along'), the lover is ready to do all sorts of things for the beloved: 'move the earth', 'tear those stars down from the sky', 'walk on burning coals', 'punch out Mr. T', 'rob, steal, beg and lie', and, of course, 'die for you'. In Fisher's survey of lovers, over 65 percent of them agreed that they never gave up loving their beloved, even when things were going poorly.[7]

Ideal love is perceived as an overshadowing force, stronger than a person, with which one must abide (no wonder people equate love with the divine). Love can cope with all obstacles, not merely in the sense that it can solve all difficulties, but in the more profound sense that such difficulties, even if they continue to exist, are of lesser importance. If I love you, I can 'fly on the wings of love', and then the earthly difficulties seem so far away and insignificant. The ascribed ability of ideal love to conquer all is compatible with the total nature of such love and the justification for disregarding reality. Even if reality may pose some obstacles to love, love can overcome them. The belief that 'love overcomes all' is similar (in its optimistic nature) to the notion that 'justice prevails'.[8]

The claim that love can overcome various obstacles does not mean that such a task requires no effort. Yes, love at first sight may spontaneously, effortlessly lead to an intimate relationship, but even in such cases, appearances may be deceiving, and we still struggle to maintain such love. In many other cases, even the first stages of love involve the investment of much effort in order to overcome various obstacles. It is often the case that such efforts can strengthen love – the resulting love is sweeter for the struggle it required. This has become known as the 'Romeo and Juliet effect': if real impediments exist, such as a family feud or loving a married person, our love is likely to intensify. Think of Erich Segal's *Love Story* – in which a fatal illness can intensify love as perhaps nothing else. 'Playing hard to get' is certainly a most effective strategy for attracting a partner. Playing hard to get forces the other person to make significant investments and ensures that indeed this person is ready to make a commitment to an enduring relationship. Indeed, Hollywood films portray genuine love as a culmination of a difficult journey; love in this sense must be 'earned' and 'proved', often by enduring the pain of separation.[9] Just as the will to sacrifice is portrayed as an expression of genuine love, so is the will to fight against love's enemies. It is struggle that authenticates love as true. For in fact how can we cling to the whole ideal love – to the belief in 'the right one', one true love, its enduring quality and immortal nature – if surrendering to difficulty is an option? Therefore, it cannot be an option. Obstacles are only tests one must endure and successfully pass; for love is proven in the defiance of external forces and constraints, which are merely attempts to shatter it.

It is surely the case that love places us in a good and optimistic mood, enabling us to function better and to meet the severe obstacles and mundane demands of everyday life. However, functioning better and being able to better confront difficult obstacles is a far cry from dismissing the significance of such obstacles. There are many obstacles that love cannot overcome; hence love is uncertain and fragile.[10] The assumption that love can conquer all gives no weight to changing personal and contextual features, and may be a source of a disappointment and distress, since people may blame themselves or their beloved for the relationship failing or even for having a relationship that is short of perfect. Assigning blame may also become a prophecy that fulfills itself, and hence endangers healthy relationships. As Rosa, a single mother in her fifties, says:

> I am looking for perfection and I have been mistaken in my choices. I turn down opportunities to be with men because I judge these men as far from perfect. As I get older, I seem to be softening, but I also seem to be getting clearer on what I like and want. I don't want superficiality – but for the first time in my life, I am considering having sex with someone I don't see as partner material!

A total and uncompromising attitude toward reality and the beloved may terminate many relationships, which are, in this sense, doomed from the start. In the words of Jim Croce, 'you wanted a martyr, just a regular guy wouldn't do'.

Eternal love – 'Till death do us part'

You will always be my endless love.

Lionel Richie

Forever, and ever, you'll stay in my heart.

Aretha Franklin

With you eternally mine, in love there is no measure of time.

Barbra Streisand

For me, love has no end.

A murderer

For 20 years, was it the same love? Even today, it's the same love. For another million years, even when I'm dead, it will be the same.

A murderer

The profound nature of love is also expressed in the temporal dimension: 'true love never dies', 'I will always love you for the rest of your life', and 'I'll be yours through all the years, till the end of time'. The ideal is that true love lasts forever: love is not real unless it is eternal and enduring. Although it is extremely difficult to fulfill this ideal, and romantic love often recedes with time, there are people who are madly in love with each other for a very long time, sometimes till death comes and parts them.

The brevity of our existence always hovers over our hopes for life. One way of coping with this anxiety is to bestow significance upon everyday events. This type of diversion and magnification is taken to the extreme in Romantic Ideology. While being in such love we do not merely change the relative weights we assign to various components in our everyday life, we take our loving experience to be totally unaffected by our immediate surrounding; it is considered to be as eternal as death, something that even death cannot destroy. As Flora says about her married lover: 'he will be my great and greatest love until I die, and much, much beyond'.

The temporal dimension pertaining to the continuation of genuine love is also expressed in the fact that implicit in Romantic Ideology is the notion that the lovers constantly think about or are occupied with their beloved, even to the point of obsession. As Eva, a married woman in her mid-40s, says about her married lover:

I think of him all the time. I can do nothing without thinking of him. There is not a single moment he is not with me and there is not a single thought that is not about him. I have never experienced such intense and impatient longing in my life, and I neither sleep nor feel a sense of calm until I finally fall into his arms.

It is not merely that genuine love is supposed to last forever, but that it is assumed to occupy every minute of our day.

There is a price to pay for entering the gates of eternity: a substantial disregard for reality. In reality, events have a beginning and an end and their nature changes over time. In Romantic Ideology, transient, everyday events are perceived to be so insignificant that they have no impact upon love. As it is written in the Song of Songs: 'Many waters cannot quench love, neither can the floods drown it'. If in fact love is perceived as eternal no matter what we do, people may believe that once we enjoy true love, we have to do nothing to maintain it, and nothing we could do could harm it. This is obviously an illusion, and maintaining our love depends upon our behavior and many other factors.

Modern society has witnessed an increasing discrepancy between the desire for enduring romantic relationship and the probability of its fulfillment. Breakup, rather than marriage, is the norm in dating relationships, and even concerning marriages: the likelihood that first marriages will end in divorce is around 50 percent; this estimate increases by approximately 10 percent for second marriages.[11] Breakups are common despite their distressing consequences. Some of the mentioned factors that can explain this phenomenon include changes in economic conditions (e.g., increased affluence), societal circumstances (e.g., increased number of working women, personal freedom, and social and geographical mobility, reduction in external barriers for dissolving marriages), and values (e.g., greater sexual freedom, increased privacy and autonomy, erosion in religious beliefs, and greater acceptance of violating normative boundaries). Those factors are believed to have a significant impact upon our psychological satisfaction from current romantic relationships.[12] Social statistics underscore the puzzle of romantic love today: shouldn't we know better than to believe in romantic love? And yet we persist.

Love as a perfect union – 'We are soul mates who are meant for each other'

> I am Heathcliff – he's always, always in my mind – not as a pleasure, any more than I am always a pleasure to myself – but as my own being.
>
> Catherine, in Emily Bronte's *Wuthering Heights*

> I've got you so deep in my heart, that you're really a part of me.
>
> Frank Sinatra

> I felt as if she was my air, as if she was the only thing that sustained me.
>
> A murderer

> I couldn't live, I couldn't function without her… I believed that I couldn't function if I wasn't with her.
>
> A murderer

The uniqueness of love, as postulated in Romantic Ideology, manifests itself, among other ways, by depicting the two lovers as a unique, single entity.

The two lovers form a profound union (or fusion) as if they were two faces of the same coin. The desire to be with the beloved, so typical of love, often becomes a desire to fuse with the beloved and in a sense to lose one's identity. Such a union is often understood to involve a joint identity. Plato claims that love is essentially the process of seeking our missing half. In the same vein, the psychoanalyst Eric Fromm argues that erotic love 'is the craving for complete fusion, for union with one other person. It is by its very nature exclusive and not universal'.[13] Likewise, Robert Nozick says that in romantic love, 'it feels to the two people that they have united to form and constitute a new entity in the world, what might be called a *we*'.[14] The notion of unity may be associated with the fact that in sexual intercourse, corporal penetration literally fuses the two bodies.

The wish to fuse with the beloved and to form a single unit is understandable in light of the greatest fear of lovers: separation. The solution for preventing the separation from the beloved is that of making the beloved an inseparable part of the lover. As Zygmunt Bauman nicely puts it, 'Wherever I go, you go; whatever I do, you do … If you are not and cannot be my Siamese twin, be my clone!'[15] David Schnarch also argues that we have embraced a Siamese twin model of intimacy, where every single movement of one of them would require consensus. If you didn't have your twin's validation and acceptance, you are in trouble. In this model, the more your spouse becomes her own person, the more you would feel controlled and torn apart.[16] The Siamese model is indeed quite common among lovers. Consider, for example, the following typical statements of lovers: 'we think alike, dream alike, wish alike, and love alike', 'I can't be a second without him', and 'I never want to be separated from him ever again, I want him to be deep inside me for the rest of my life'. 'While I am myself I am also him. I feel one with him in every cell of my longing heart and body, every minute of my life'. Lisa, a married woman in her late 50s, describes her feeling toward her married lover in this way:

> I so want him to feel and know every single one of my thoughts and dreams; I never want to hide anything from him, I so want him to be one with me, as he is part of myself.

In accordance with the wish for unity, lovers are often described as 'soul mates', 'meant for each other', two who always 'want to be in the arms of each other'. It is no accident that the two lovers are together: 'we didn't make it by chance, and there is someone belonging to someone'. Indeed, 'All of my life I been looking for someone to carry my love away', and 'There's no one I could love more' (Bee Gees). This type of predetermined connection makes the romantic relationship very unique and strong. Lovers often feel that meeting their beloved is the end of an epic quest. They can finally end the exhausting wandering and come home to someone they long dreamt about. As Lisa describes how she feels toward her married lover:

> For all my life I thought I was not on this earth to enjoy love, and then he walked into my life, and changed everything. Now I know that I was sent to this world to find him. He is all that I have always been waiting for. I knew he was somewhere, and I never stopped searching for him. It is such a heavenly destination that we met in such circumstances; I immediately had this urgent feeling that this could change my life.

The notions of 'the right person' and 'the perfect match' are central in this perception of love. As Lisa further argues: 'I have never known anything more gratifying, heightening, fulfilling and joyful than the love he gives me. I have never been so happy in my life'. This view implies that when something goes wrong in your romantic relationship, it is because you attached yourself to the wrong person. The perfect union can be achieved once the right person is found.

In light of the uniqueness of such intense love, it is sometimes hard for lovers to believe in the reality of their love and beloved. They cannot believe that such a perfect human being, as their beloved is, love them, of all people. Nina, a married woman in her early 40s, confesses that only now after meeting her lover:

> I know that what I imagined to be true in novels only has become true for me ... More often than not, I do not believe that all this is really true. He is the love of my life, my one and only, and most heavenly treasure, who – and this is still the most unbelievable to me – truly exists.

Lovers may therefore say that before meeting the beloved, they were convinced that 'a person like this does not exist as it is a contradiction in terms'. The uniqueness of such love is also expressed in using words related to miracles and magic: 'you put a spell on me', 'you are my magic magician', and 'our love reverses nature's laws'. For this reason, the beloved is often described as 'exceptional' or as the only human being who ever really understood the lover. It is easy to understand here how love is associated with the divine – a miracle of sorts.

The experience of exceptionality is so profound that people clearly distinguish it from their previous loving experiences as if those were not instances of 'true' love at all. It's as if all of one's past life were nothing but a dull dream, as if one has only now become truly alive, for the first time. Hence, there will never be further need to be in a romantic or sexual relationship with other people. Grace, a married woman, describes her attitude toward her married lover:

> This hot passion and desire only exists and has only existed for him. I really cannot imagine being touched by any other man ever again. I was never mentally in

the arms of anyone, as I felt so uncomfortable there; only now with him, I can feel what true love is and I will never have anyone else. Throughout my life I have been thinking that men and women never match because they are so different. And now I think that nobody has ever been a better match with me than him. Nothing in this universe has ever touched and will ever touch me as deeply as his words, caresses, and love. It is incomparable to anything else, not even 'unique' or 'special' come close to describing it.

Lovers consider their love as exceptional not only in the sense that they fit each other in a perfect manner, but also in the sense that such a perfect union and sublime passion are not to be found elsewhere: there is no need to wonder whether life with another lover might be more exciting, as no more exciting lover could possibly exist. Statements such as 'I believe that no one has ever experienced feelings of such magnitude', are common among lovers. The loving experience is perceived to be so thrilling that in the whole universe it is rare and hard to find. Although there are many stories, poems, movies about profound love, the lovers still consider their own particular case as one of its kind. No wonder that lovers are so proud of their love. Consider the following sentence that Alex, a married man says about his lover: 'I would like everybody to know what a treasure I own. I am so in love, I am so proud, I am so immensely happy, because she is my wonderful love'. The following state-ment by a man who killed his wife illustrates a similar attitude concerning their relationship: 'I wanted to show that in love, I was more than Romeo and Juliet. That isn't love for me. Love is something that didn't exist before. That no one ever did before'.

It is indeed the case that in love, the self and the other are in a sense mentally overlapping. Thus, rating a relationship in terms of the degree of overlap of two circles, which represents the inclusion of other in the self, functions as an effective measure of closeness.[17] Love revolves around including each other in each other's self and even body. This is expressed in the Biblical story of the creation of the first woman. God created a woman out of the man's rib, and therefore 'shall a man leave his father and his mother, and shall cleave unto his wife: and they shall be one flesh'.[18] Lovers begin to develop similar preferences, for example, to enjoy music to which they were previously indif-ferent, or even to wear similar clothes. Such lovers often testify that they frequently have similar thoughts or that they understand each other even before words are spoken.

As the notion of unity is so crucial for Romantic Ideology, we shall point out some of its difficulties in this early stage of our discussion. It is evident that total unity (and of course, fusion) is impossible in light of the physical separateness of the two lovers. However, even mental unity is hard to imagine, and the nature of the psychological process underlying the creation of the assumed perfect unity is not clear.[19] It is not obvious whether the idealized unity involves the loss of the unique identity of each lover or rather it involves finding the one and only person who is completely compatible with us. Both options are problematic, as one cannot completely lose one's identity, and likewise, there is no perfect compatibility. It is probably the case that people adjust to each other in a loving relationship, but such adjustment is always partial and leaves room for various incompatibilities, which prevent the perfect unity and gives rise to the possible temporary nature of the relationship. Although closeness is indeed essential for love, perfect unity is impossible. Lovers may give up a lot for their beloved, but they cannot completely disappear from view in the attempt to retain a loving relationship – one has to go to work, for example, and earn a living.

For many people, the constant search for the perfect union or the belief in the existence of such a union is a major obstacle to a loving relationship. It is unfeasible to find a perfect union; rather, it is possible to achieve a good-enough compatibility within your loving relationship. Since life is dynamic, and people regularly change their attitudes and wishes, achieving such compatibility is not a one-time accomplishment but rather an ongoing process, whose success requires loving attitudes. Perfect compatibility then is not a precondition for love; love may assist in increasing the compatibility.[20]

The notion of unity may be dangerous to a loving relation, as every small movement of one of the lovers may have an exaggerated impact upon the other, and hence upon the relation itself. When some distance between two lovers exists, it can absorb certain shocks. The distance has a somewhat similar function to the cartilage in our bones: it protects the bones from rubbing against each other too much. In a similar manner, when we place the object right next to the eye itself, we do not see the object. We need some distance in order to achieve a perspective that encompasses the multiple aspects of the object and thereby to really see it. This perspective is also required in love, otherwise our perception of the partner will be quite fragmented. However, keeping a distance is contrary to the involved and intimate perspective typical of intense love. In many cases, the lover is unable to detach herself from the beloved in such a way that a more complex perspective can be achieved. Although complexity governs human relationships, Romantic Ideology is simplistic and one-dimensional. The lack of a complex and broad perspective, which enables the lover to focus upon the beloved and to generate a more intense emotional attitude, signals the danger of blind attachment to the beloved, which can even lead to inflicting self-harm.

The irreplaceabilty and exclusivity of the beloved – 'Only you and you alone'

Love is not love
Which alters when it alteration finds
Or bends with the remover to remove
Oh no! It is an ever fixed mark
That looks on tempests and is never shaken.

Shakespeare

When she decided that she didn't want any part of me anymore, I was left with nothing.... I used her as a source of existence, because I had nothing else.

A murderer

I started to see life all clear, with one goal, and it was her. I forgot everything around me. I forget everything. Only she was in my head. People might say, there's happiness, and I'd tell them, it's her. People might say there's enjoyment, and I'd tell them, it's her. People might say there's a world, and I'd tell them it's her. My life is a black curtain. Just her.

A murderer

An important issue in the characterization of love and sexual desire is whether their objects are (a) replaceable, and (b) non-exclusive. 'Replaceable' is used in a diachronic sense: replacing the object after a certain period of time; 'non-exclusive' is used in a synchronic sense: having different objects at the same time. In Romantic Ideology, a lover wants to be unified with the beloved in the sense of being together 'for ever' and in the sense that the beloved is 'the only one'.

The belief that love is irreplaceable is related to the assumed eternal nature of love: if genuine love lasts forever, and if we assign this love a unique status, it is plausible that genuine love cannot be replaced. This is compatible with the basic belief of Romantic Ideology, which assumes that the beloved is the one and only person who gives meaning to the lover's world.

It is problematic to assume that the object of our romantic love is irreplaceable since people's attitudes may shifts as occur in their reality and in themselves. As Rosa, a single mother, says:

I thought I believed that love is enduring – and that it only gets covered over or obstructed – just as clouds can block the sun, but we know it is still there even on a dark day. But now I wonder if it isn't something that needs to be learned and grown and intentionally cultivated.

While it is certain that we would not describe every love affair as genuine love, there is no reason to suppose that one can only experience a single instance of genuine love in a lifetime. Many people could be loving spouses for any individual. There is no reason to assume that one cannot find a new and more compatible partner. After all, Adam and Eve are the only couple who were truly made for each other. It is even more obvious that the object of sexual desire is both replaceable and non-exclusive. We are sexually attracted to different people in the course of our lifetime, and we may also be attracted to several people at the same time.

The replaceability of the beloved does not deny the existence of cases in which one has only one genuine love throughout one's life. The replaceable nature of love does not mean that the beloved should be replaced. On the contrary, people who are rapidly replacing their partners often lack an ability to form loving relationships. Romantic love is replaceable, though not as replaceable as sexual desire. Replacement of a partner may take place because of the following (and other) reasons: (a) knowing our partner better and consequently realizing that the partner is not as valuable as previously considered; (b) finding someone who has higher emotional value for us; (c) changing our evaluative patterns. The object of romantic love may be replaceable, but to deliberately search for someone with 'better' characteristics is not compatible with romantic love. If there is readiness for a change, it should appear in the form of an improvement in one's mate, not via a mere replacement with someone else.[21]

In addition to the assumption concerning the irreplaceability of the beloved, Romantic Ideology assumes that love is exclusive. In light of the totality of ideal love and the perfect unity between the two lovers, there is no place for another person in this relationship, and hence the exclusive or partial nature of love is central in Romantic Ideology. We cannot love anyone; we can, however, learn to love people with whom we do not fall in love at first sight. We cannot love everyone; our romantic love must be directed at a few people. Since romantic love, like other emotions, necessitates limiting parameters such as time and attention, the number of its objects must be limited as well. We have greater resources to offer when we limit the number of emotional objects to which we are committed. In the words of Susan Orlean (Meryl Streep), in the movie *Adaptation*, 'I was starting to believe that the reason it matters to care passionately about something is that is whittles the world down to a more manageable size'. The beloved has emotional significance no other person has; the beloved fulfills much of our emotional environment. The exclusivity of the romantic relationships is indeed a central feature of love. In Fisher's survey of people in love, over 80 percent of the people agreed that being sexually faithful is important in love.[22]

Exclusivity, which is an essential characteristic of emotions, has a few important practical roles in love, for example, to ensure high confidence in paternity and to ensure mutual commitment. Furthermore, since romantic love requires many resources, such as time and attention, its objects must be limited. One does not have enough free time and attention to love many people simultaneously. Parental love is less replaceable than romantic love. Parents' love for their children is usually maintained as long as they live, and is less exclusive than romantic love: the number of children a parent can love simultaneously is greater than the number of people a person can love simultaneously in a romantic manner. However, in both romantic and parental love there is a limit to the number of intimate relations one can maintain at a given time without reducing the quality of each relationship. Sexual desire, which is typically an important component in romantic love, is a major factor opposing the tendency to make romantic love exclusive and irreplaceable.

It is not only the case that romantic love is narrowly focused; it is also experienced from a very personal and egoistic perspective. Our personal perspective may also include consideration of those related to us, who are like extensions of our egos; their emotional weight, however, is typically of a lesser degree. Such an extension is particularly evident in the case of parental love. The egoistic aspect in romantic love is evident in the common attitude of 'I want you, my love, to be happy, but only with me'.

A total, uncompromising love implies an absence of ambivalence: there is no equivocation in the lover's wholehearted devotion to his beloved; this love is solid and secured.[23] In such love, all resources are directed at one person and there are no other resources left for anything else. The following experience is typical to lovers: 'You are so deep inside my heart, mind and body that there isn't the slightest room for anything else'. However, such a total focus and lack of ambivalence are possible only if one completely disregards reality and its constant changes in the environment around the lovers and in the lovers themselves, as is the case in ideal love. Only in such artificial, invented circumstances can the object of love always be utterly exclusive and irreplaceable. Thus, we see again the impracticality of Romantic Ideology.

The purity of love – 'Love can do no harm'

Hatred stirs up strife, but love covers all crimes.

Proverbs 10: 12

If I give all I possess to the poor and surrender my body to the flames, but have not love, I gain nothing. Love is patient, love is kind. It does not envy, it does not boast, it is not proud. It is not rude, it is not self-seeking, it is not easily angered, it keeps no record of wrongs. Love does not delight in evil but rejoices with the truth. It always protects, always trusts, always hopes, always perseveres.

The Apostleship of Paul, Corinthians 13: 3–7

Whatever is done from love always occurs beyond good and evil.

Friedrich Nietzsche

I started to ask myself: What should I accuse myself for? Am I guilty for going and loving her? That I loved the girl? ... What did I do, after all? I loved her. She broke me.

A murderer

Love is typically evaluated in very positive terms. However, as there are various kinds of love, some of them – especially the romantic or erotic one – have been frequently criticized. The different views of love can be extreme; thus, while some people consider love to be a supreme source of moral value and strength, others regard it to be a kind of disease, perversion, or destructive intoxication, which tears people away from their moral values. Let us elaborate more about the first stance, which is the one taken by Romantic Ideology. Aristotle's view may be a good starting point.

Aristotle takes love to be a wish for good things to happen to another person, with no benefit for the subject. This wish is accompanied by the desire to have the power to produce these 'good things'.[24] The lover wishes the other's benefit for its own sake, without calculating whether there is any personal benefit to be drawn. Thus, love is not measured in terms of its practical value as a means to achieve certain ends. For instance, loving someone as a means to satisfy one's sexual desire or to become rich, is partial and transient; the moment the end is achieved, or a better means is found, love disappears. Disinterested care is not the same as indifference. Disinterested care implies that the beloved is evaluated as having intrinsic worth and not as something that may give us some future benefits. Harry Frankfurt argues that when a man tells a woman that loving her is for him the only thing that makes living worthwhile, she clearly understands that what he is saying implies that he values her for herself, and not merely as a means to his own advantage. The fact that loving her is so important to him is entirely consistent with his being unequivocally, wholeheartedly, and selflessly devoted to her interests. This position is plausible once we assume the identification of the lover with the beloved. In such a case, the interests of the beloved are not actually other than those of the lover, and protecting the beloved's interests is necessarily among the lover's own interests.[25]

The wish to benefit the other is not merely reactive, but proactive as well. The lover does not merely wish to prevent current harm from coming upon the beloved but to actively promote the beloved's development and flourishing. Although in Aristotle's view the essence of love is in its characteristic of caring for the other, love is not an entirely selfless emotion. Aristotle argues that the good things an individual wishes for other people are the same things he wishes for himself. So in a sense, our activities for promoting the good things for the beloved will in fact bring good things for us as well. Aristotle also emphasizes the importance of reciprocity in love, as a lover is someone who loves and is loved in return. Accordingly, although Brian wants Anna's good for Anna's own sake and not for his, he is more likely to pursue his love if Anna wants his own good as well.[26] If indeed love is seeking the good of the beloved for its own sake, then unlike other emotions, genuine love cannot be criticized, since it has intrinsic value involving disinterested care for the beloved. Thus, we do not ordinarily criticize a man who profoundly loves a certain woman just because we think he could have done better.[27]

The virtuous aspect of love is emphasized in many cultures that consider true love to be modeled on God's bestowal of love on humans: an unconditional act that lacks any association with deservedness. It is a kind of gift the beloved receives. Hence, 'The world always welcomes lovers'. Erich Fromm defined love as 'the active concern for the life and the growth of that which we love'.[28] True love has less to do with the lover's own needs and more with concern for the other. Accordingly, love has often been considered to be pure in the moral sense: love involves merely good deeds and 'can do no evil'. Hence, it has been claimed that those who fail to love should be considered sinners.[29] Romantic Ideology even upgrades the moral status of love and considers it to be a moral seal of approval, a synonym for purity of intention. Therefore, everything that is done for the sake of love, because of love, and in the name of love is justified precisely for that reason. As Esther, a widow in her late 50s, who had many affairs with married men, says: 'I really, truly believe that all love is good wherever you find it – independently of what status your lover is'. In such a view, love is considered an ultimate justification for either self-sacrifice or for evil; thus, it can even be considered worth dying or killing for.

The above view has more than a grain of truth in it, but its conclusions should be restricted, since there are some significant personal benefits for the lover, without which love will not be sustained. The attitude of a lover toward his beloved cannot be entirely disinterested, as the lover's own happiness is the product of such attitude. Although romantic love encompasses genuine care for the beloved, it is not a general concern for the beloved's happiness in all circumstances. Typically, the lover desires the beloved's happiness only insofar as the lover is either a part or the cause of this happiness. The spouse can be an extension of our self only in a conditional manner: the condition is being connected to us. In particular, we do not want our beloved to be sexually happy with another person. Pablo Picasso expressed this concern in a rather extreme manner when saying 'I would prefer to see a woman dead than see her happy with another man'. The egoistic nature of romantic love generates an inherent contradiction: whereas romantic love expresses great concern for the beloved, it cancels the beloved's autonomy. Moreover, the lover's care for the beloved may focus on those aspects that the beloved does not consider to be significant.

Only a small minority of people can actually be happy in their beloved's happiness if it is unrelated to them. Rosa says about her current boyfriend: 'My love is pure in the sense that I truly do want what is best for him – and for him to be happy regardless of whether I am in his life or not'. This attitude expresses the uncompromising and total nature of romantic love: no matter what reality is, love does not and should not bend. It can be postponed, but never compromised. Bending or compromising is an unfamiliar attitude to such true lovers. It is common to find lovers who have been waiting for a long time for their beloved to reappear, even though the prospects for this are dim. Generally, one can be happy with the beloved's happiness, even after a separation, as long as this happiness concerns the beloved's general well-being, success, health, and so forth. It is much harder to be happy when the beloved is romantically and sexually happy about being with another person. Emotions are not detached theoretical states; they address a practical concern from a personal perspective.

Romantic ideology and reality – 'Just the two of us'

All of you, your body and soul ... I want everything.

Julio Iglesias

Without you darling my arms would just gather dust.

Elvis Presley

The various related aspects of ideal love – its being total, uncompromising, and unconditional – as formed by Romantic Ideology indicate the extreme nature of that ideology. When ideal love is total, then it suffuses all aspects of the beloved's life. Love pervades all of life's components in an uncompromising manner. In this sense, the beloved is all the lover needs; true love lasts forever and can conquer all; the two lovers are totally united; love is totally irreplaceable and exclusive; and it is totally benign, as it can do no evil.

As the break with the real world so thoroughly characterizes Romantic Ideology, we shall now return to the way in which love compels us to ignore what we know to be true, compels us to live an illusion. Due to love's uncompromising nature, it is also unconditional, in the sense that it prevails regardless of external conditions or circumstances. As Lisa, a married woman, describes her new lover, 'everything is possible since I am in love with him; my immense love for him depends on nothing other than he himself'. In such circumstances, reality is of no concern to her. The beloved becomes the whole world to the lover, a world that the lover has never known before, and there is no room in such a world for anyone else but the beloved. Regardless of where she is and what she does, the beloved is on her mind. Given that, on the one hand 'reality can be cruel' (Bee Gees), and on the other hand love is such a valuable experience, disregarding reality can be valuable from time to time. In fact, this observation can be a great motivator for generating and maintaining love. Sometimes disregarding reality can indeed be advantageous, as it increases our chances of creating a self-fulfilling prophecy. Just as saying to my beloved that my love for her will decrease as time goes by may very well diminish the likelihood of the relationship's survival, the promise of everlasting love has the function of encouraging lovers to believe in the feasibility of enduring love. However, the unrealistic nature of Romantic Ideology may also impede coping with real problems surrounding intimate relationships. It can be of some relevance to mention that it has been known for a long time that more prostitutes fly into a town during Republican conventions than during Democratic ones.[30] In other words, those who attempt to project an ideal image of the family (also part of Romantic Ideology) have a greater tendency to transgress moral rules than those who are more flexible in regard to the ideal. Although there may be some benefits in intentionally overlooking certain difficulties, turning a blind eye and a deaf ear to our environment and personal limitations can hardly be advantageous.

While in the grip of Romantic Ideology, we all overlook various common hurdles of love, yet we are all painfully aware of the many cases of love failing. Our cultural and personal experiences are replete with references to cases of a love turned sour. It seems that there are as many (and even more) stories of failed love experiences as there are of ideal love, and often the two are related to the same person. Love can disappear, either because it has faded away (often in a gradual manner), or because one or even both of those who believed they would love each other for ever, have found a new love, making them realize that their 'eternal' love no longer exists. Nonetheless, many of those who experienced the shattering of their ideal love do not blame the ideology; they still seek ideal love again, believing that only adverse circumstances or an unsuitable partner prevented them from attaining and maintaining it.

It appears that the closest people get to experiencing ideal love is at the opening moments of a romantic relationship, at the stage of infatuation, when they first fall in love. Some people distinguish infatuation from romantic love; however, it seems that infatuation is a typical example of emotions, in general, and of romantic love, in particular. Infatuation expresses romantic love at its very peak, and while it cannot last forever, it is something people long for.

The mythical power of love is expressed in the description of 'falling' in love, an act that occurs unintentionally. We say that we are 'falling in love', or getting 'turned on', as if is something that is forced upon us and we are simply helpless, almost victims of this act. This is emphasized in the myth about Cupid: this god is blind and his arrows force us to fall in love. Accordingly, it is not up to us whether or not we fall in love, nor with whom it happens. In this sense, romantic love involves a feeling of profound surrender.[31] Along the same line, Connie Francis sings: 'I got the feeling I'm falling, Like a star up in the blue … And it's all because of you'. In another song, she states: 'I'm a puppet and I just can't seem to break the string'.

At the basis of romantic love there is a profound positive evaluation of one or a few of the beloved's qualities. This qualitative evaluation is typically associated with a comprehensive quantitative evaluation, whereby the positive evaluation is extended to include many additional characteristics. In this case, love is not based primarily upon the value of the specific characteristic, but upon its association with what we love. By giving a significant weight to various characteristics of the beloved, lovers do not necessarily distort reality, nor are they completely blind to the beloved's faults; they just do not consider such faults to be significant. Indeed, in Fisher's survey of people in love, about 60 percent agreed to the statement that they love everything about their beloved and that the beloved has some faults but those don't really bother them.[32] This view of romantic love, as basically attributing significance to one or a few of the beloved's characteristics, enables ideal love to last longer. Thus, becoming madly in love for an extended period of time does not require the lover's blindness to the beloved's actual characteristics or to reality. The act of assigning specific importance to a quality is not a cognitive task which can be true or false, but an evaluative task that has in it a significant subjective element that refers to what the lover wants and needs. Needless to say, this evaluative task is less sensitive to being refuted by reality.

Does the unfortunate situation of lovers these days stem from the abandonment of Romantic Ideology by so many people, or is it rather because people still hold this unrealistic ideal? Although the chances of entirely fulfilling Romantic Ideology are next to nil, and most people are aware of its difficulties, many people still believe that this ideology expresses what love should be and wish their own love to be just like this. If Romantic Ideology is responsible, at least in part, for the hard times lovers have nowadays, we may want to revise this ideology.

The extreme claims made by Romantic Ideology place a great deal of responsibility upon the shoulders of the lovers. They cannot take love slightly and they cannot treat love as another insignificant item in life. Love, in this ideology, is our life and the fate of our love is the fate of our life. This identification makes lovers disregard life – as long as they are considered in love, there is nothing else to consider. Lovers feel that their love lets them experience life again, and this time from a new promising perspective. It is no wonder that lovers often say to their beloved something to the tune of: 'You have given me a new life again. This must be reincarnation', 'You have changed everything for me. You have taught me about true love, passion, and happiness', 'You have made me the happiest person in the universe', and 'I can't live without you any more'. In this ideology, love is taken seriously, while life – as much as it concerns other aspects beside love – is taken lightly. When love disappears there is no sense of living anymore or even of letting others live on. There is no doubt that love is central to our lives, but should it be so central? Would we not feel more fulfilled and profoundly happier if love would not be so central? Would we not give love a better chance, if it were considered less profound and central?

We shall refer to these questions later in the book. Now we turn to the impact of Romantic Ideology upon one group of people – men who murdered their wives out of love. Through this unusual category of lovers, previously neglected by most scholars, we shall get a much more vivid sense of the problem with Romantic Ideology. Through the murderers, we shall get a better sense of how mundane, common disappointments do much more than disillusion us about love: such disappointments may become lethal.

The love of wife-murderers – 'It enters the heart, it doesn't leave'

At the end of a highway, there's no place you can go, but just tell me … you are only mine, and our love will go on 'til the end of time.

Earl Grant

Love is everything … Love enters the heart, it doesn't leave. What happened doesn't interfere with love.

A murderer

In this section, we describe Romantic Ideology as perceived by men who killed their wives; we shall see that it is perceived in a manner similar to the one described above.

In analyzing the interviews with the murderers, we must remember that what they actually say may or may not describe what has actually happened.

Certain questions would be relevant in the search for historical truth, in a process intended to determine the man's guilt, such as: whether or not the woman betrayed the man; whether she said the words attributed to her; whether the man is telling the truth when he claims that he was not violent prior to the murder; whether he testified truthfully in claiming that he did not go out to look for her on the day of the murder, but that he met her by chance. However, these questions are not at issue in a study that emphasizes the essence of the subjective experience. The meaning of the woman's distancing and separation cannot be revealed in a context other than that of reality as perceived by the murderers. Nevertheless, one must constantly recall that the only objective truth about which there is no controversy, and which is not subject to negotiation, is the fact that the woman who was murdered was once the wife of the man who killed her. Some of the historical truth was buried with the dead woman and the living person also buries part of it.

Although there are differences among the motives of the love of men for the wives they killed, almost all of them describe their love using terms such as profound, unique, eternal, irreplaceable, and characterized by purity of action. The woman who will never return is also the one and only true love that will never return.

> She was for me ... she was everything for me. I knew her since I was 15.... We got engaged when she was 16-and-a-half. Eleventh grade. She was like someone you grow up with very slowly ... as big as you may get, as old as you get, in your head you'll always think that you grew up with that person, that you got used to that person. You won't forget her all your life. No matter what. I grew up with her. I loved her. She was the first one that I said, 'I love you', to. I grew up with her.

The fact that she was also the first woman in his life is significant. His love for her is characterized by motifs of uniqueness. The uniqueness of love derives from its being the first. The first love is endowed with virtues that make it into an irreplaceable love, putting it in a special, unforgettable place. The motif of growing up together, which he repeats several times, expresses a process of cohesion and interweaving. He grasps the two of them as joined together in a common process of growing up, and their fates are interwoven. The process of growing up together is slow. For that very reason, the relationship can spring roots that forge a deep and unseverable connection. In the process of growing up together, he came to love her, became used to her, until he considered her a part of him. Because she was part of his self and his past, she will always be part of his future, too.

Unlike the previous example, in which the uniqueness of the beloved was related to her being the first woman in his life, the next interviewee attributes the uniqueness to a woman who was not the first. He notes his first love only as a reference for comparison:

> I only had love for a single woman, even though I had so many girls. Maybe some were prettier than her. I was always with good lookers, good lookers, and when I ran into her, I already had a girlfriend, who was beautiful … then I ran into her, and the first one became nothing to me then, that was the end of her. Only this one, this new one. Like a kid you give a doll to, and then later you give him something else, and that 'new something' becomes everything to him. He doesn't want anything anymore…. That's first love. I had a lot of girls before her, sure, no less beautiful than her, but she's the one I loved. I remember all the girls. I had a lot of girls. But I loved her more than all of them. That means that for me, she was the one, the only one. To this day I say that only her, and there will never be another one, even if I get out of prison, no, in my life, never.

In this case, profoundness of this love does not derive from the innocence that characterizes first love. On the contrary, the profoundness is based on the comparison: because she was not the first woman in his life, he was able to recognize the profoundness of his emotions toward her. There were a lot of girls, but none was like her. The story of his successes with other women shows something about him, but it shows even more about her role in his life, as someone who overshadowed all the others. Whereas the use of the motif of 'there were a lot of girls' helps bring out her uniqueness for him, the image of the child with the doll indicates exclusiveness as well. From the moment she appeared in his life, he knew two things for certain: that he wanted her, and that he did not want anyone but her.

The past has implications for the future. His love for her is unique and therefore eternal as well. For him she was the first, last, and only love. That is to say, love is separated from the object of love. The woman may die, but love for her cannot perish: 'Even today, it's the same love. For another million years, even when I'm dead, it will be the same'. He claims that not only did 20 years of marriage not diminish the power of his love, but that neither will her death. Love, from his point of view, is raised above all the actual people who played a role in his reality. Love is above and beyond time and events. It exists as an idea more than as an emotion subject to influence. As an idea, it is immune to the effects of time and events. Therefore, the death of love is not bound up with the woman's death. Entertaining the possibility of the existence of another woman in his world is like forfeiting his eternal love for the dead woman. She is defined in many places in the interview in terms of his self: 'She was everything for me. She was my soul'. If she was his soul, she cannot be replaced. Therefore, there will never be another woman, and his love for her is firm and abiding.

The following interviewee exemplifies profoundness as the force which rebuilt his personality. His wife succeeded where no other woman before her had succeeded. She made the leopard change his spots – marrying someone is a fateful, life-transforming choice:

> Look, from the moment I met her, I changed 180 degrees. I stopped screwing other women. Suddenly I learned what a washing machine was. Something I never knew in my life. Suddenly I knew what a supermarket was. Something I never knew in my life. Suddenly I discovered the market, something I never knew in my life. Do you understand? Suddenly I opened up my closet and took out clothes. Suddenly I knew how to iron, something I never knew in my life. Do you understand? I changed completely. Imagine that. I go to Club Med with some friends, and all of them are screwing, and I just sit around. They say 'Danny can't get it on. What's the matter with him?' I'm not interested. I go with her brother to Vegas a lot of times, and he screws, and I don't want to screw. I don't want to screw. He says, 'What? What did she do to you? Tell me, what's so special about my sister?' Do you understand? I changed. And I was with seven thousand women. Not with one woman. What you could call a professional. Like they say, I fell in, hook, line and sinker!

In this case, the profoundness is rooted in the ability to establish a new self. The meaning of the woman for him and the meaning of his love for her are concretized through his contemplation of himself. She is the turning point between the man and his opposite, as though she had cast a magic spell. The magic lies in the drastic change between his self-images, the huge gap between the dissolute and irresponsible philanderer, unconstrained by social mores, and the faithful husband. The surprise expressed by his brother-in-law conveys information about the man he once was and the man that he became. This surprise indicates the great gap between the identities. The voice that asks, 'What's so special about my sister?' reflects his conception of her uniqueness in his life, uniqueness exemplified through the new self it created.

The profoundness of love and its uncompromising nature is expressed by yet another man:

> A. She's my wife. I love her. What happened, happened, but I love her. That remains in place. I love my wife.
>
> Q. You loved her despite everything that happened?
>
> A. I loved her till the end. I can't do anything about it. Love is something else. Even when there are problems, they don't interfere with love. Why? It's not in the head. It's in the heart. It's in the heart. Do you have children? A sister? Do you love the sister? Even if she messes things up for you, because she's your sister, you love her.
>
> Q. That means, because she's your wife, you love her?
>
> A. I can't talk now, because it's in the heart. First of all, if you're not in love, you don't marry. I got married – that means I was in love.
>
> Q. And it couldn't be that people stop loving each other?
>
> A. Love is everything, children. When a woman has children, more love. The more children, the more the husband loves. That's not in the head, it's not in the eyes, it's in the heart. It enters the heart, it doesn't leave. It isn't just me. It's that way with

everyone I think, but they won't admit it. A lot of men are that way, but they won't admit.

Q. What won't they admit?

A. People love, but they don't talk. It's in the heart. They don't admit it. There are many men, I've seen them, I'm 38 now. There are men in the prison now. Their wives threw them into prison. They went to the police and talked, saying he did such and such, but I see that they're in love. They love, and because of some mistake ... what happened doesn't interfere with love.

This scenario of love begins in the first person but moves beyond a personal definition, because, from his point of view, he is unusual not in his conception of love but in his willingness to admit to it. His central claim is that love is not responsible for the joining of two people, but rather the opposite: the connection and the feeling of ownership are responsible for the appearance of love. For him, what is true of familial love – love for those family members that one does not choose – is also true of couple's love. The use of the example of siblings shows a view of love in which the other is considered a part of you. Love, in his scenario of life, does not depend on its object or on transient circumstances in reality: 'what happened doesn't interfere with love'. Love stems from the inseparable connection between the two. This connection can take the form of ownership, but it can also be a unity of equals. When this bond grows stronger – as when children arrive – love intensifies as well.

In light of such insensitivity to reality, love is of eternal and invulnerable nature. Love is presented as an overshadowing, infinite force that cannot be impaired. Love is invulnerable because it is 'in the heart and not in the head' – it is not based on any logic. Rather, it is based on the other's being part of you. Because such an experience cannot change, nothing can impair love. It is an irreversible emotion: 'it enters the heart and doesn't leave'. From the moment it comes, it is destined to remain forever. The argument that 'love is something else' seeks to distinguish between love and other emotions. Unlike other emotions, which come and go, love never disappears: 'it remains in place'.

The conception of the loving heart as rigid and unchangeable derives from the identification of the two lovers as one entity. Once such a unity is created, the claim for belonging and ownership can be established. His brother cannot stop being his brother. His sister will always remain his sister. By virtue of such an identity, he will love her without considering her actions or the type of person she is. Moreover, he will continue to love his brother even if his brother does not love him. That means that reciprocity is not part of the conditions of love. His wife is like his brother and his sister: he loves her because she is his wife, and he will continue to love her without any connection to events or to her feelings towards him. Love does not demand reciprocity or even a good relationship or a positive view of the beloved person. All that is needed for love is unity and, hence, ownership. Ownership, like love, cannot be impaired. Therefore, in the scenario of his love, love is forever. It cannot be that one stops loving. His love for her is a love for what is his. What is his cannot become what is not his. Conquered territory can never be liberated.

Legitimacy is claimed for this interpretation of love by presenting it as normative, and commonly accepted. 'It is not just I', he says. 'Everyone is like that'. The bond between the two is unique, and no one else can replace it, but this should be the case with all other people. The need to identify himself as part of the general community, to present his love as part of a normative scenario, most likely derives from the need to justify the behavior, which, in the end, brought him to the place where he is. He feels a need to justify his way of loving, because it became the motive for murder.

Violent men, according to his conception, made mistakes and were sent to prison. The view of violence against women as an error greatly reduces the guilt of violent men, for people make mistakes unintentionally. No one purposely makes a mistake. A mistake is accidental and can be corrected. Love, in contrast, endures. It is stronger than any error, unconnected to what transpires between the spouses, in terms of either time or intensity. Love is profound, stable, and cannot be impaired.

He claims that, unlike the other men around him, he admits his love. The notion of admission suggests something of which one might be ashamed. It would appear that in his case, the shame does not stem from the significance inherent in love; rather, it is related to the contrast between love and rational logic. Perhaps because love is 'in the heart', it might embarrass men who wish to view themselves as acting according to rational logic, not the dictates of the heart. The fact that he emphasizes the heart in this context might indicate a feeling of shame as a function of the opposition between emotions and masculinity. Unlike the 'others', he is not ashamed. He loves her 'to the end', and her end comes to her precisely for that reason.

The conception of love as something enormous, which is borne beyond the dimension of time and events is also reflected, though in a more minor fashion, in the words of the following interviewee:

> It's hard to explain love. What can I tell you? It's connected to lots and lots of things, like the food that she makes for you, everything that you touch of hers – that's part of love. She pours a cup of coffee – you love that cup of coffee. It's hard for me to explain what love is. It's something gigantic!
> I loved her for many years. I never had a bit of anger against her. Anger passes. It comes and goes. But it goes. But, in fact, our tempers stay in a corner. Anger builds up, but in the end it goes. Anger is something that passes, not like love, which is a big thing.

The conception of love as something 'great' or 'gigantic' expresses not only the intensity of the emotion, but also its being a kind of envelope for life. Love is an overshadowing power. It colors everyday life and the little details that comprise it (a cup of coffee, food). It leaves a mark on the entire space of shared existence (everything of hers, anything she touches).

Love is characterized as a stable, profound, and continuous emotion. He emphasizes: 'I never had a bit of anger against her'. He quickly corrects himself by explaining that anger is a temporary emotion, 'It comes and goes'. It cannot replace or impair the profound and continuous emotion that is love. Anger ends, whereas love is a strong, stable, and invulnerable core. When anger builds up, it is still not as powerful as love. That is to say, although it builds up, 'in the end' it falls away.

For yet another man, love is an ideal of constant excitement and an uncompromising emotion. Love knows no varying degrees and never has to compromise; love is everything, love in its entirety is pure ('white'):

> For me, love has no end. Love is every day, to feel it anew every day. To feel every day 'I love him for the first time'. I let her feel that, and I wanted her to let me feel that. Love is ... for my point of view, love – it has no end. Love ... it's a feeling, it's hard, very hard to explain it, how I understand it in my head. Love, it's like a flower. I see flowers, and I see love ... it is not only sex. Okay, I love you, fine, let's go to bed. This is not love for me. We sleep together, we have children, and that's the end of it. No, love has no end ... I don't want love to be out of my life.

On the lesson he learned for the future, he says:

> A. I will see her once a week, I'll be angry at her. I'll say things to her. Like any woman. But inside me I know – that isn't love. Love, for me it's either black or white. That's love for me. I just want love in my life all the time, without any arguments.
>
> Q. Everything has to be white?
>
> A. White, everything.

The text describes ideal love as a continual tempest of emotions, a total and uncompromising feeling that cannot include within it lulls or any stains on the purity of love, in the form of anger or arguments. When 'Love has no end', it tries to turn falling in love from a temporary, powerful emotion into a permanent experience. Absurdly, it seeks newness every day (To feel every day 'I love him for the first time'). The totality embodied in the conception of love as endless is multifaceted. It has no end in the sense that it must persist with great force all the time, that it has to be expressed at every moment, and that no stain can mar it. In the ideal love that he describes, love is new every day. It cannot grow old or 'be out of my life', or even change its aspect. His utopian love must invent itself every day again, continually.

The separation of sex from love is the separation of the physical from the spiritual. Love rises above its physical expression – 'Love is a flower'. A flower is delicate, pure, and fragile. A flower arouses admiration. Sex, in contrast, is contaminated with earthliness, which does not arouse respect. The interviewee expresses the lack of respect in a contemptuous tone: 'Okay, I love you, fine, let's go to bed'. Sex diminishes love. Therefore the two have to be distinguished. Moreover, sex not only fails to arouse respect, but it is also trapped within boundaries. A sexual episode has a beginning, middle, and end: 'We sleep together, we have children, and that's the end of it'. Love cannot be identified with sexual relations, because 'love has no end'. From the interviewee's point of view, love is not an extended, dynamic emotion, with highs and lows, characterized by times of turmoil along with times of tranquility. Love must not diminish, as it is not influenced by transitory events in reality. Unlike sexual relations, it has no boundaries.

According to the interviewee, love is total and uncompromising, and therefore it necessitates behavioral dictates that are also uncompromising: on the one hand, it requires the lover to express his love at every moment; on the other hand, it forbids him to behave in any way that would express any emotion that might impair that utopian perfection. It is defined in polar terms of black or white, with no intermediate situation between what is experienced as love and its opposite. The possibility of movement between the poles is not part of the meaning attributed to love. Therefore, there is no place for an emotion like anger, which is liable to deflect the emotional focus, even for a short time. The commandment to feel love all the time, at every single moment, cannot permit the entry of emotions that deflect attention from love (but inside me I know – that isn't love).

The course of love according to the scenario described here is a course of fantasy, an irresponsible one that disregards actual circumstances. Love 'that has no end' is placed within the boundaries of an illusion. Here a trap is created. The 'white' color that the interviewee seeks cannot be part of reality. Lacking intermediary hues, reality, any reality, will necessarily be grasped as the opposite of 'white'. This love is good, with the possibility of evil. The problem is that what is grasped as right, as 'white', what is experienced as 'this is love for me', cannot exist in the real world, as it derives from an illusion. The transition to the concrete sphere necessarily destroys the fantasy: then it is no longer love. The color black replaces white.

Practically speaking, his love takes on the guise of clinging, without leaving room to breathe:

> I used to come to her every day from work. I wouldn't go home. I couldn't stand being away from her. I couldn't stand that … I forgot work. I forgot everything. Nothing

mattered to me. I wanted to see her day and night. I wanted her to feel that … for me love has no end. That's why I used to pursue her.

He tries to give practical expression to the meaning that he attributes to love by demonstrating behavior that seeks to devour the woman. His world is emptied of all meaning that is not connected to her. From his point of view, this is the reality of a fantasy: he wants her 'to feel that it's love'. That is to say, he behaves according to the dictates of the scenario that he himself developed. Love that has no end is translated into pursuit. Pursuit and his unwillingness to leave her alone are justified by love ('Love has no end. That's why I used to pursue her'). He wants to fuse with her.

From his point of view, her behavior must follow his own interpretation of the meaning of love. The subject dictated this impossible scenario of love not only to himself but also to his girlfriend ('I let her feel that, and I wanted her to let me feel that'). However, because the scenario derived from an illusion, the woman's 'failure' was quick to arrive. This was a predictable failure. It was implanted in the illusory expectations. When she cannot stand the burden, he accuses her of wanting to ruin the love.

> Once she said to me: you love me too much, and I don't like that. You invest so much. You're making me into something that no one here makes a girl into. And I don't like that. Let me feel…. Be strong with me a little. But five minutes later she says no don't be strong with me. She wanted to ruin the love.

From the interviewee's point of view, there is only one correct way of loving. The option of love that she offers him – relations with boundaries and breathing space for both parties – does not fit his fantasy. His is the dream of melding with the other side. Bounded love destroys the dream.

Even today, this person is not willing to acknowledge anything but that fantasy as the meaning of love. Therefore, the lesson that he draws from relations of love that ended in murder of the beloved wife involves only a change of tactics. He concludes that he must change the outer expressions of love. If he ever finds love again, he will act conventionally, 'though inside me I know   that isn't love'. He will change his behavior, but not his conception, and not his interpretation of the concept of love: 'In the future, if I ever have love again, I won't relate like in the past. In my heart I'll relate like in love, but I won't show it'. The rigidity and uncompromising totality of this view of love is also expressed in his unwillingness to give up love when it becomes one-sided. When the interviewee was asked whether his wife wanted to leave him, he answered: 'I, from my point of view, wasn't willing to give her up'. That is to say, her wishes are of no importance. The reciprocity of love is not a condition for prolonging the relationship.

Demanding permanence while ignoring the desires of the other party is also reflected in another interviewee's testimony, as he indicates his unwillingness to accept his wife's refusal to come back and live with him: 'Look, I never went out with any other girl before her. That's what I knew, and I said, you marry once and you die once'. When he expresses unwillingness to recognize the possibility of change in those aspects of reality consisting of marriage, life with one woman, and death, he creates a world in which only his desires and his needs are important. The answer to the question of why he wanted to go back to her is based on the motif of primacy (she was his first woman) and habit (that is what he knows). That is to say, he views his aspiration for the known and his need for the security given by familiarity as sufficient reason to force her to live with him. His aspiration for familiarity finds support in the adoption of a view of marriage as a step from which there is no going back. The parallel between death and marriage – as phenomena that take place just once in a person's life – nullifies the possibility of divorce, on the one hand, and creates the identification of separation with death, on the other. The worldview that says 'you marry once and you die once' dooms the woman to captivity. Only death can free her from marriage.

We turn now to discuss in some detail the murders' attitude toward another major aspect of ideal love, that is, the purity of love. It is precisely because love is considered to be so pure, that people cannot believe that such horrible murders are associated with – not to mention generated from – genuine love. The following testimonies present these murders' perceptions of this type of association.

Here is how an interviewee explains the fact that even after he was removed from the house by a court order, he did not leave his wife alone and tried to force her to take him back:

> Yes, I still wanted. I loved her. What can I do? Love, how do people say: love is as strong as death. That's also written in the Song of Songs. I'm not the one who wrote it. King Solomon wrote it. The wisest of the wise men.

Love, for him, is sufficient justification for his actions. He uses it as a magic charm that can justify his behavior, including ignoring his wife's wishes. When he says: 'I loved her. What can I do?' he is portraying himself as helpless in the face of a power stronger than he is: love, which is 'as strong as death'. By basing his opinion on authority ('King Solomon wrote it. The wisest of the wise men'), he reinforces the idea that a power greater than him left him helpless, as it were, with no alternative. For what can he do against a power 'as strong as death'? Indeed, by presenting love as an entity outside of man, a very powerful force that deprives a person of the power of choice, he attributes to love the ability to purify every abomination: his blindness and deafness to his wife's desires, as well as his violent efforts to force himself upon her. The place of the other party, the beloved person, in the mosaic of relations is derived entirely from the lover's needs.

Here is another example of the way love functions as a place of refuge:

> I started to ask myself: 'What should I accuse myself for? Am I guilty for going and loving her? That I loved the girl?' I stood in front of three judges, looking backward, I remembered two years ago. A soldier, a brave guy, I got to know a girl. How did I sin in life? I loved her. She made my life a living death. Today I'm a dead man. Today I'm a man without any feelings. I'm telling you the truth. What did I do, after all? I loved her. She broke me. I told them that I made a mistake by loving the girl. What's the matter with you?

From the point of view represented in the testimony, you cannot accuse the lover, because his love defends him. Subject to the belief that love bears the stamp of moral approval, and for that reason it cannot contain guilt or error, he claims he is innocent. Can you find a lover guilty for loving or claim that he was wrong in loving? As a proper and valued social ideal, love becomes the modern equivalent of the corners of the altar, which provided asylum. It cancels guilt, expunges sins. It is a defensive wall and a city of refuge. The person who acts for love automatically receives immunity.

The moment that love becomes a 'city of refuge' is naturally the moment when a person is called upon to account for his actions. In practice, we must emphasize, he did not use love to justify his actions to the judges, because at that stage he had not yet admitted guilt. However, love serves him in the trial he holds for himself. When he examines his actions ('I started to ask myself: "What should I accuse myself for?"'), love is the means for expunging guilt and bridging between identities. The discrepancy between 'a soldier, a brave guy', and the identity of a murderer, this gap that was opened by love, is also bridged by love. The halo of love, as a moral, noble emotion, that can do no evil, offers him moral defense and helps him avoid recognizing his identity as a murderer.

He goes further, trying to reverse the situation. In fact, he is the only dead person mentioned in his testimony: 'I loved her. She made my life a living death.... Today I'm a dead man'. Love serves two purposes for him: on the one hand, it defends him from guilt; on the other hand, it is a means for portraying himself as a victim. Love is a Moloch (a Semitic God to whom children were sacrificed): any sacrifice is viewed as a worthy one. One such worthy sacrifice, for example, is a person's life. Thus, love is identified with the acceptance of self-sacrifice:

> I thought of committing suicide, I did. When you die, they cover the dead body with white, I brought it to her father, the shroud, I wrote him a letter, so that people would know what love is. I wanted to commit suicide to show her how much I loved her.

That way I wanted to show that for me love was something special. How do they talk about Romeo and Juliet? I wanted to show that in love, I was more than Romeo and Juliet. That isn't love for me. Love is something that didn't exist before. That no one ever did before. Something rare, nothing like it, nothing. But there was no woman to give it. They caught me. Her father came: 'What are you, crazy?' They convinced me. I wanted them to write on my gravestone, that I loved, that I love you. I dreamt about it. To this day, I dream about it. I'm ready, just so that someone will love me the way I loved her. Why? Love is something rare for me. And they couldn't overcome me.... I'm sorry it didn't happen. I would have died of joy, of love. And she would be alive. I don't know. Maybe she'd be alive, maybe she'd be dead. But people would have talked about love. I'd let people know what it is, why love has no limit, it has no limit.

Acting on the idea about which he dreams today was never a real option. In fact, he made do with the symbolic act of giving the shroud to his father-in-law. The failure to carry out the act is rationalized in contradictory ways: on the one hand, he was 'convinced', which should imply that he changed his mind; on the other hand, he simply had no weapon, suggesting that he did not change his mind, but lacked the means to fulfill his dream. Undoubtedly, at the time, he had no intention of carrying out the suicide scenario. However, this scenario is embedded in his dreams today. Now he fantasizes about the way things could have been different. The difference between reality and dream is not in death but in the identity of the dead person. Both in reality and in his dream, death is the end of love, but the identity of the victim has changed. Had he possessed the courage to carry out his idea, he would have been the one to die 'of joy, of love'. She would be alive, but, even more important is the mark of love, as something special, rare, that 'didn't exist before'. It would have remained alive after him, as a legacy and a message to the entire world.

The expressions of regret, sorrow, and longings intermingled in his testimony are due to his realization that this great and powerful love did not manage to remain permanent and leave its mark on human history as a love previously unparalleled. Given that the proof of love is in the death of the lover, he uses the story of Romeo and Juliet as an ideal love and a model for imitation. It was the couple's death that kept their love eternal, just as it was at the moment of death. They never arose from their graves to spoil it with the realistic demands of life. Their love remains an image reflecting an entity vast and pure. His death at the altar of love would have made him into a mythological figure, greater than Romeo and Juliet. He is sorry because he did not manage to become a legend. He is sorry because he did not manage to turn his interpretation of love into a model and an ideal of romantic love, which would have replaced that of Romeo and Juliet, and would have been spoken of by everyone ('People would have talked about love. I'd let people know what it is').

A common motif in many of the murderers' testimonies is the claim that love is a willingness to sacrifice oneself for the beloved. Self-sacrifice takes on a number of meanings, from giving everything and dedicating oneself solely to the relationship, through risking one's life, to actual death. Self-sacrifice is supposedly the ultimate offering of love. The declared desire to give the ultimate gift sounds like cruel mockery given that it was the wife's life that was sacrificed. In fact, today these speakers are judged by what they took, not by what they gave. Nevertheless, what their declarations and actions have in common is extremism and totality, which are so typical of Romantic ideology. Although giving everything and taking everything are as distant from one another as possible, what is common to them is their position at the extreme end of the scale. The two possibilities join the extremes. The danger lies in extremist attitudes.

Romantic Ideology as religion – 'I'm truly blessed for everything you give me'

Heaven on earth that's what you've made for me since the day we met.

The Platters

I lost my faith, you gave it back to me I was blessed because I was loved by you.

Celine Dion

Maybe I wasn't good before God. Maybe I was a sinner. I was trapped by her. What is that trap? It's love.

A murderer

Love plays a central role in many religions. We can see a parallel between Romantic Ideology and Jewish, Christian, and Muslim devotion to God. The Hebrew Bible, home to Jews, Christians, and Muslims alike, seems to require a kind of perfect romantic love for God. The major Jewish pray of *Shem'a*, requires: 'Thou shalt love the Lord thy God with all thy heart, with all thy soul, and with all thy might'. Such a central role is emphasized in many religions, but it is particularly significant in Christianity. The first encyclical letter of Pope Benedict XVI to his bishops, priests, deacons, and lay believers, given on December 2005, was about love. He opens his letter by citing the First Letter of John, which clearly expresses the central place of love in Christianity: 'God is love, and he who abides in love abides in God, and God abides in him'.[33] Both love and religion are perceived to be central to human life.

In many respects, Romantic Ideology resembles a kind of religion. Both are similar in that they dictate basic beliefs, demand a high moral standards, and bestow this high moral status upon their objects. Like faith, love is regarded as an expression of profound, unique, and morally pure attitudes. The basic assumptions underlying Romantic Ideology can indeed be found in many monotheistic religions. Like many religions, Romantic Ideology is basically characterized by its comprehensive and uncompromising nature. Not unlike the function of religion, love is considered to give meaning to life, to overcome all obstacles, and to provide a share in eternity.

The comparison of love to religion is made explicit by lovers. Thus, the following line, which is common in one version or another in prayers directed at God, is also often used to describe the attitude toward the romantic beloved: 'You are the only one that can give me comfort; you touch my heart in such a way that all I can do is cry your name'. Some even replace God with the beloved: 'I do not wish God to aid me nor to give me joy and happiness except through you'.[34] Consider also the following lines from a letter written by John Keats:

> Love is my religion – I could die for that – I could die for you. My creed is Love and you are its only tenet – You have ravish'd me away by a Power I cannot resist: and yet I could resist till I saw you; and even since I have seen you I have endeavoured often 'to reason against the reasons of my Love'. I can do that no more – the pain would be too great – My Love is selfish – I cannot breathe without you.[35]

It is indeed common to find in romantic conversations expressions such as, 'Heaven has sent you to me', 'I was quite sure that love as we are experiencing it right now only existed in the imagination of some people', and 'our love is a dream come true'.

The attitude of many religions, and in particular Christianity, to romantic love and especially to its sexual aspect, is mixed. Whereas sometimes romantic love is included in the Christian love, it is also regarded as inferior to other types. The Christian tradition has considered a central aspect of romantic love – that is, sex – as degrading and therefore marriage was widely acknowledged to be fundamentally flawed and, accordingly, inferior to chastity. The main value of marriage, in this view, is making sex tolerable and preventing the greater sin of sex among unmarried people. For people who considered themselves married to Christ or to the Church, any sexual temptation was often considered to be almost as sinful as fornication. It is useful to mention that the biblical tradition, where polygamy was widely accepted and adultery was allowed under certain circumstances, was not so uniformly sex-hating, as implied in the Christian tradition.[36]

The relationship between God and His people has been described in the bible and elsewhere in romantic terms, such as betrothal and marriage. When the people of Israel followed their idols, they were like an unfaithful partner – their activities are described as betraying God and as committing adultery and prostitution. God is described as jealous of the people of Israel. Jeremiah complains in the name of God that 'like a woman betraying her lover, the House of Israel has betrayed me', and Ezekiel compares Israel to a whore.[37] The romantic lines of the Song of Songs have been described as ultimately depicting God's relation to man and man's relation to God. As Pope Benedict put it, 'Corresponding to the image of a monotheistic God is monogamous marriage. Marriage based on exclusive and definitive love becomes the icon of the relationship between God and his people and vice versa'.[38] The fidelity to God and marital fidelity are celebrated as the utmost human accomplishments.

Monotheistic religions often consider the sins against God as similar to those prevailing in marriage. The original sin, which is the source of all the miseries in the world, is that of disloyalty: the first man and woman disobeyed God their creator. In the same way that the scriptures demand that people prefer the monotheistic God over all other Gods, God sometimes chooses one person or one people over the rest. Regina Schwartz argues that the belief in scarcity is common to monotheistic assumptions about God and women. God is monotheistic 'not only because he demands allegiance to himself alone but because he confers his favor on one alone'. The biblical God did not allow multiple allegiances 'neither directed toward the deity nor, apparently, emanating from him'.[39] The first murder in the bible, in which Cain murdered his brother Abel, was done because Cain felt that God preferred Abel over him. Cain felt outcast and he killed the one God preferred. Schwartz further claims that we are the descendants of Cain because we too live in a world where some are cast out and scarcity prevails. Cain's sad tale is retold in the bible with another set of brothers, Jacob and Esau. There is not enough favor and blessing for both of them: when Jacob steals his brother's blessing, there are no blessings left for Esau, and again the outcast feels the need to murder.[40] Also the men who killed their wives felt outcast by a woman who excluded them and preferred to look somewhere else for love. Unlike Cain, who could not kill the one who excluded him and therefore killed his rival, those men did kill the person who excluded them from her favors.

The similarity between Romantic Ideology and religion is also expressed in the resemblance of the beloved to God. The beloved is often characterized as 'the sweetest angel in heaven and on earth', and as a 'divine gift'. The beloved is perceived to be a perfect person whose existence cannot be comprehended. The beloved may be described with phrases like, 'the most genius creation on earth'. Hence, loving the beloved is often claimed to be so easy, since, unlike other people who are always found inadequate in something, the beloved is perfect and complete. Moreover, our inability to find the perfect mate may be compared to our inability to meet God: the fact that we have not found one does not imply that one does not exist.

In light of these similarities, love may take on some of the functions attributed to God: love may provide the comfort zone that enables us to escape existential anxieties and everyday fears. The loss of a lover is therefore the loss of the meaning of life. In order to prevent such a loss, love, like religion, contains elements such as self-sacrifice, devotion, the experience of the sacred, and means to attain spiritual perfection.[41] Indeed, textual analyses of popular films and findings that emerge from of a series of interviews with couples have shown that love is characterized by achieving a transcendent emotional state. In fact, the emotional state that indicates 'true' love must be one that is irresistible and uncontrollable.[42]

The identification of love and religion with moral deeds is so profound that every major religious tradition has encouraged morally good behavior, and the association between love and morality is very common. Love and religion, as well as the beloved and God, are perceived by devoted lovers and believers to be morally pure: they are considered major factors leading one to choose a moral life. However, despite their profound moral value, both love and religion have been used as an excuse for justifying immoral deeds, which can become global scale atrocities, as in the example of religious wars, or personal atrocities, as in murdering the beloved in the name of love. This trend of taking an ideal to such extremes that it engenders actions that contradict its own spirit may seriously question the value of the ideal itself. Indeed, a survey conducted recently in Britain indicated that the majority of people polled thought religion causes more harm than good.[43] Ronald de Sousa nicely describes this problematic aspect of love:

> It is a commonplace that love motivates some of our worst behavior, ranging from dishonesty to murder.... But what is most astonishing is that we regard love as a justification for treating people far worse than we would ever condone treating a stranger.[44]

After describing Romantic Ideology in this chapter and showing its presence in the views of the men who killed their wives, we turn in the next chapters to examine other salient behaviors typical of romantic love and the way they are present among these murderers.

Chapter 2

Love at breaking point
'What have I got to do to make you love me?'

I thought you loved me, you said you loved me …
The dream has ended, for true love died.

Nat King Cole

I must let you know tonight that my love for you has gone …
For tonight I wed another, Dear John.

Pat Boone

Once she said to me: you love me too much, and
I don't like that … She wanted to ruin the love.

A murderer

Romantic Ideology describes the best case scenario that only very few people will ever experience – certainly, as a lasting experience. A much more common experience in the romantic realm is that of separation which is often interpreted as rejection. The essential role of love in our life, and our profound personal involvement in love, makes such separation very painful – particularly so when separation involves rejection and the people involved adopt Romantic Ideology. This is the case of the men who killed their wives.

Love and reciprocity – 'Will you give me love in return?'

It feels so right, so warm and true, I need to know if you feel it too.

Foreigner

I can't keep on loving you one foot outside the door.

Brandy

When a girl is with me, when I love her, I'm afraid of everything there is for her. I'm willing to risk my life for her. I'm willing to do anything for her. As long as she loves me and respects me.

A murderer

The issue of reciprocity is central to love. Mutual attraction is for both sexes the most highly valued characteristic in a potential mate.[1] People like to hear that they are desired. The lover wants to be loved in return, to be kissed as well as to kiss. The lover is ready to be committed, but expects to find similar commitment in the beloved's attitude. Assuring reciprocity, for example, by repeatedly declaring their love for one another, or by mutual praise, is crucial to lovers. The lack of reciprocity, that is, the knowledge that you are not loved by your beloved, usually leads to a decrease in love intensity, and ultimately, to humiliation. This decrease does not tend to be immediate; the one suffering from unrequited love persists in trying to win the other's heart. Indeed, many books and movies feature as their theme aspiring lovers persisting doggedly to win the hearts of their beloved. In some cases, love may even briefly intensify while one tries to win the other's heart.

In light of the reciprocal nature of love, a major characteristic of love is the lack of indifference. Indifference expresses the absence of evaluative preference and hence the absence of emotional sensitivity. Therefore, people in love prefer to be hurt by the beloved rather than treated indifferently. The person in love 'prefers the anguish which her beloved causes her to painless indifference'.[2] Similarly, the saying goes that it is better to break someone's heart than to do nothing with it. In her song 'A second-hand love', Connie Francis says 'I'd rather have this kind of (second hand) love than not see you at all'. Concerning those who are near and dear, we even prefer anger to indifference, as anger implies caring about the other person.

The nature of the reciprocity required in love is not self-evident. In this regard, a distinction can be made between profound and superficial aspects of the loving relationship. Aristotle defines love as the desire to do 'what is good for the other not for one's own sake, but for theirs'.[3] Since Aristotle considers acting for the good of someone else to be central to love, love is essentially connected to friendship and kindness. As people may be wrong about what is good for them, the kindness involved in love is not equivalent to doing what the other person wants; it is rather associated with what is good and suitable for the other person. Hence, love may involve going against your partner's wishes, because fulfilling these wishes may be pleasant in the short run but harmful in the long run. Love is concerned with the profound good of the other, rather than with the other's superficial wishes.[4] In genuine love, the lover encourages the beloved to develop his or her unique capacities. The quest for the beloved's happiness is essential in love. It should be noted, however, that one person cannot ensure the happiness of another, since one's happiness is not determined by other people's attitudes; rather, one's happiness is more likely to be determined by one's own virtues, attitudes, and ways of coping with various circumstances. Doing what is good for the beloved, rather than following the beloved's wishes, may be interpreted as abolishing the central role of reciprocity in love. It seems, however, that sometimes, the lover is in a better position to judge the well-being of the beloved and in light of the profound trust between the two, letting the lover lead the way is a valuable option.

Regardless of one's understanding of the idea of reciprocity between lovers, unrequited love is a painful experience that significantly damages our self-image. When the romantic rejection is perceived as irrevocable, it is a humiliating blow to our self-esteem, as it reflects a significant negative evaluation of our worth.[5] We deeply want someone, but this person does not care for us. Someone who we believe is extremely good and suitable for us does not think that we are good enough. Romantic rejection involves not only the frustration of an unfulfilled desire, but also an impoverished and ravaged self-esteem. The act of rejection is perceived as a demonstration of the beloved's blindness to our needs and desires. The essential aspect of reciprocity is evidently absent.

Love is risky, as lovers are vulnerable to profound frustrations, unexpected misfortune, or dishonest behavior. To avoid such distressful situations lovers should be careful (which is obviously contrary to the disregard for reality characteristic of Romantic Ideology).[6] Precautions intended to mollify the painful nature of romantic rejection can include fear of commitment, which may be expressed as a preference for the risk-free environment entailed in being alone over the uncertainty of romantic relationships, or maintaining multiple relationships simultaneously in order to have a default option: should your lover hurt you, there will be others to lean upon.

People look for a heavenly haven in love. The intensity of love and the perceived unity of the lovers create the illusion of security; in fact, underlying romantic love is the desire to live happily ever after in the safety of the beloved's arms. However, love is not safe, but rather risky. Lovers are quite vulnerable to the risk of being separated from the object of their love. The dynamic and changing nature of love constantly threatens its existence: 'The lover builds the castles of romance as if they would last forever, knowing fully well they are fragile, transitory structures'.[7]

Adhering to Romantic Ideology further complicates and intensifies the painful situation of the rejected person. In such a case, it is harder to interpret romantic rejection as a normal behavior which could happen to anyone. There is no evaluative (or ideological) framework in which the rejected lover can find consolation. On the contrary, the framework they believe in denies such an option, as the Carpenters ask about the reason why the sun goes on shining and the sea rushes to shore: 'Don't they know it's the end of the world, because you don't love me anymore?'

The conception of love as eternal, not susceptible to waning, and invulnerable to any threat is contrary to the wife's intention of leaving. Indeed, the love of the men who have murdered their wives is a treasure trove of contradictions: the ideal of love is in a constant clash with the reality of love. The pain of romantic separation is exacerbated by the feeling of personal failure, because of the expectation that it should be otherwise (even when the current divorce rate is quite high).[8] This may explain why people take romantic separation, and in particular romantic rejection, in such a harsh manner. It is evident that the separated or rejected lover can find another lover who may even be more suitable; nevertheless, some lovers cannot stand the separation or rejection and commit suicide or kill their beloved.

The meaning of separation – 'Love of my life don't leave me'

I'll never know what made you run away …
I only know there's nothing … in this wide world, left for me to see.

The Brothers Four

Every time we say goodbye, I die a little.

Ella Fitzgerald

When she decided that she didn't want any part of me anymore, I was left with nothing… I used her as a source of existence, because I had nothing else.

A murderer

The painful experience of rejection or separation is evident in the case of those men who killed their wives. Most cases of such murder or attempted murder took place against the background of the woman's intention to leave the man and put an end to the relationship. The meaning of the woman's intention of leaving the man can be summed up in the words of a popular Israeli song that places a huge burden on the woman: being the man's whole world and the condition of his existence: 'Without you I'm half a man, without you I'm really nothing'. If the man's ability to keep on viewing himself as a human being depends on the woman's being part of his life, how can he let her go? Thus, the dark side of the ultimate expression of love turns the woman into a hostage – a hostage to the man's life, and, therefore, puts her life at risk. The words of such songs may be no more than superficial clichés about love, but when these clichés are adopted wholeheartedly, love becomes a knife. Although, at their best, conjugal relationships join two people in a harmonious framework, the consciousness that identifies her as 'without you, I'm nothing' revolves solely around the man's self-identity. The woman as a person, with her virtues and weaknesses, actions and failures to act, is not the focus of this consciousness. Paradoxically, the enormous importance attributed to the object of love is bound up with the object's lack of importance, in the sense that the woman's self, her character and personality, desires and feelings, play no role. She becomes one-dimensional: her only role is to exist for the sake of this other consciousness. She becomes an entity only when she threatens to relinquish this role. Her refusal to exist for him is what brings her into focus.

The following testimonies present various observations regarding the meaning of separation for the man.

> I believe that what happens with this whole story of murder for love, it isn't so much love, although people think it's love. In my case, even though for many years I thought I loved her, and it was because of love, today I don't believe that at all. It was more an obsession. It was a dependency. At least I really developed dependency. The moment she wanted to break off the relationship, I felt as if the air was being taking away from me. I was so dependent that I simply couldn't live without her. That's how I felt. An erroneous feeling, and incorrect, but …

Elsewhere the same interviewee says:

> After we had already separated, one day she told me that was it, she couldn't stand it any more, she couldn't stand me any more. That was a process that went on.… All the time fewer and fewer meetings. And all in all, what we used to do when we met was argue, until she told me she was fed up. I was completely broken, totally. I felt as if she was my air, as if she was the only thing that sustained me. I expected it to happened, but I wasn't ready for it. I wasn't ready to accept it. No way. And certainly not in the situation I was in.… I felt like I wasn't a person, that if I was without her, I didn't exist, that there was nothing like myself. I'm nothing.

The metaphor of air that he uses repeatedly emphasizes the concept of separation as the end of life. The end of life functions as the end of existence and the end of a familiar identity, and the two are one and the same, because a condition for continuing to exist is the ability to grasp yourself as somebody, as something, as a person. The woman's being is not only the most important thing in the man's world, but also the only thing in his world, and because she is the only thing, her importance for him does not derive from who she is. It derives from the fact that she exists. The woman does not compete with other suppliers of meaning. She is alone there, endowed with great power. By her will she gives life and by her will she kills. Involuntarily, she holds infinite power. His fate is in her hands.

In such circumstances, separation, which is predictable, is also inconceivable. This is an idea which, from his point of view, cannot come into being, because its meaning is death. His unwillingness to separate has a double meaning: one is that of lack of psychological preparedness, which, paradoxically, conflicts with the fact that he expected it to happen, because their relationship had been expiring for a year. The second meaning is that of unwillingness to accept it. He is not prepared to be reconciled with the possibility of separation. He cannot permit her to go.

Beyond her desire to leave him, the woman is absent from the equation. She is present because she wanted to depart. This is the sum of her function in the scenario. In fact, because this interviewee, unlike most of the others, points an accusing finger at himself, as a man who developed an obsessive dependence and not as the object of the dependence, her existence throughout the interview was only marginally alluded to and without depth. He seldom mentioned her, spoke little about her actions, behavior, or personality. She was a presence only in terms of her absence. The shift to himself and away from her suggests the most exact reflection of 'without you I'm nothing'. His choice of words, in the text at hand as well, is cautious and demonstrates her lack of guilt: he says that when she wanted to break off the relationship, 'I felt as if the air were taken from me'. She was not the one who took away his air: she was responsible for her desire to part; however, she was not responsible for what he experienced afterward.

His avoidance of the explanation of love ('it isn't so much love, although people think it's love') is also a repudiation of the typical justification murderers offer for what they did. When he disavows love, he also disavows the legitimacy that love could offer for the lover's desperate deeds. When he proposes the explanation that it was not love but rather obsession and dependence, he transfers the framework to a non-normative area. Whereas love is desirable and cannot be regarded as a defect (and therefore actions motivated by love are justifiable), obsession can only be regarded as a defect. With the new way of seeing the world that he has constructed, he can no longer say to himself: 'I loved her, and it was because of love'. Were he to say that, he would be trying to justify his actions – the murder and the behavior that preceded it. His new interpretation of the murder undermines any possibility of justifying it, and at the same time it allows the existence of a world where love is possible, where he himself could love – according to his definition – without fearing the results of love.

His demonstrated unwillingness to use the woman, her personality or her actions, as a means of obtaining sympathy and understanding is relatively rare. Nevertheless, the attitude that emerges from the interview with the man quoted below is similar:

> I never had such deep insecurity before, so that I was really in need, addicted to the relationship with that woman.... I couldn't live, I couldn't function without her....

what was interesting in our relationship, that there is always ... because I killed her, there is always a framing like that of a man who abused his wife, but in this case, unusually enough on the emotional level, she was the more stable person. She came from a more stable environment, and I was the one who was emotionally dependent on her. I was the one who enslaved myself ... to that kind of situation ... that I believed that I couldn't function if I wasn't with her.

Elsewhere in the interview he says:

I had nothing to lose. The only thing I had to lose was her. And I lost that, and that's it. And I didn't want anything else ... and when she decided that she didn't want to be part of me anymore, I was left without anything ... I used her as a source for existence, because I didn't have anything else.

The extreme feeling of dependence expressed in this interview reflects exclusivity on the one hand, and need on the other. In his world, there is nothing except her, and he cannot live without her. The two facets of his dependence also function as both the cause and the result of his predicament: because the woman was grasped as the sole source of existence, she became a precondition for the man's existence, and she was experienced as a physical need for the purposes of his survival.

The image of the interviewee that emerges from this description is that of a man who is 'addicted' to the woman he killed. The addiction is revealed through loss. Being addicted means being unable to do without. Understanding the existence of the need arises from the disappearance of the source of its satisfaction ('I couldn't live, I couldn't function without her'). The notion of one's source of existence, therefore, bears a meaning similar to that of air – understanding that one cannot do without it arises not from its existence but rather from its absence. Hence, the test of addiction is the absence of the object of dependency, when the elixir of life is gone, when the man experiences the inability to live, to function, the greatness of the dependency and the depth of the need suddenly become patent. The motif of need shows that separation from her has the meaning of death.

The conception of the woman as the sole source of meaning and existence is usually formulated in a context of loss, that is, the woman becomes a source of existence when other sources of meaning are lost. In that situation, her multidimensional value – that which is attributed to her by virtue of being who she is – changes nothing. She becomes his grip on life only because she is the only thing left.

As someone who has murdered his wife, the interviewee assumes that he is already labeled as violent man, an abusive man. He recognizes that in most cases abusive relations assume the woman's weakness and the man's strength. However, his definition of power is not physical; rather, it relates to the strength that a person draws from himself and from the supportive resources in his environment. From his point of view, she was solid ground, and he was a fluttering floating leaf. Her resources of strength made him dependent on her; he was in servitude to her because of everything that he derived from her: confidence, strength, and a feeling of value. When she left, all of that departed with her. Hence, he understood that he could not live without her.

This testimony, like others, brings out the circumstance of being rootless, which places the woman in a position of having a function; her importance for the man derives from her functionality in the context of loss. Separation is a type of death, because everything that is drawn from her and makes the man into what he is departs with her. 'Without you, I'm really nothing', say the words of the song. These testimonies exemplify well the essence of the 'nothing' that threatens to emerge with the woman's disappearance. On the one hand, the perception of the woman as the sole source of meaning and, on the other hand, the notion of life being without content in her absence form a cognitive reality in which separation is grasped as an impossible option, as the loss of the source of existence, as the absence of any other source of life.

Here is how another interviewee describes his love for his wife: 'Look, I loved that woman more than my own soul, more than myself, more than everything, more than anything in the world'. He describes her death, after being hospitalized in a coma for a year, as his own death:

> I knew that she was dead, I knew it, I knew, I, as much as I love her and I was connected with her, she was a vegetable for a year, she died one day before I got the sentence. Pay attention to what I'm saying, I got the sentence ... let's say the day that she died, the next day I got the sentence of life in prison. And why, why am I telling you this? Because she always used to say, 'You don't love me, you don't love me', and she knew that I loved her more than anything. 'If I die, the next day you'll marry another woman. Why, because you have so many good looking girls here, and stuff'. I used to tell her 'If you die, the next day I'll die'. She died one day before I got the sentence. So my mother said to me,'Why are you so angry? You said it. She died one day before you. You're also dead. You're also a dead man'.

The view that emerges from his words to her, that is, his inability to live with-out her, equates the woman with a vital need such as air, his source of existence. The association between the visible and the latent, which we have noted in others' testimonies, appears here too: the connection between love and threat. On the one hand, in the explicit statement, he offers her what should be considered the greatest gift of love: he promises her eternal exclusivity – she will always be the only one in his life, because without her he is dead. On the other hand, the implicit message is the mandate to continue to exist in his life. She is his hostage. In the orchestration of his allegorical death – in the form of life imprisonment, which in the course of a single day coincides with his wife's physical death, he sees the precise fulfillment of his prophecy. In his view of himself, as suggested through his mother's voice, he is a walking dead man. When he sentenced her to death, he sentenced himself as well. According to his construct, she could not die without his dying, and therefore it was predictable that he would learn about the moment of her death (even after a year of living as a vegetable), at the time of his sentencing, for it was his death, too. The woman is not only part of him, she is his very self.

The meaning of separation from the wife cannot be understood in isolation from the context that created it. Making the woman the sole supplier of meaning, which is so typical of Romantic Ideology, is a phenomenon that takes place within a steadily depleting reality: deprived of other goals, other sources of meaning, and a reason to live, the man latches on to the beloved. An inherent part of the construct that claims, 'without you I'm nothing', is that of nothing – the presence of a vacuum within.

Behavioral patterns – 'No white flag above my door'

How am I supposed to carry on, when all that I've been living for is gone?

Laura Branigan

What have I got to do to make you love me …
What do I say when its all over?

Elton John

It didn't pass through my mind exactly in that way, like 'I'll never let her go', but that I'd do anything so that she wouldn't leave me. And I was really willing to do … I don't know, anything.

A murderer

In the case of romantic rejection, the relationship is being 'robbed' of the element of reciprocity. The mixture of despair and hope that ensues can activate what are otherwise unthinkable behaviors, such as stalking, surveillance, intimidation, harming oneself, and verbal and physical abuse.[9] Despite their obvious negative aspects, these kinds of behavior are in accordance with the unwilling-to-give-up response that is so positively evaluated in Romantic Ideology. Interviewed college students reported employing the following behaviors when they were rejected: more than half of the sample reported waiting outside for the person who rejected them, more than 20 percent reported calling and hanging up and following the person. Even intimidating behavior was found to be relatively common, with 30 percent of men reporting such behavior. Verbal aggression was reported by a quarter of the sample, and physically violent behavior was reported by over 10 percent of both of men and women. More extreme acts of aggression were much less common, but none of the behaviors listed in the survey received a zero response.[10]

These kinds of behaviors cannot then be considered as characterizing merely a small portion of behavioral responses; rather, the unwilling-to-give-up response is found to be a normative one. When love becomes one-sided, it appears that social conventions are cast aside and overruled. Studies have shown that not only do people engage in a wide range of stalking-related behaviors when responding to romantic rejection, but in fact the line between normal persistence and obsessive behavior, that is, between what is acceptable behavior within the context of love and what should be defined as illicit stalking, is becoming blurred.[11] As a result, stalking proved to be an elusive phenomenon to define. While it is generally defined as a pattern of harassing or threatening behavior, it also seems to include anything from benign attempts at courtship to assault and murder. Thus, it can be seen as a part of a spectrum of activities that merges into normal behavior, often around the aspiration to reestablish a relationship.[12]

The stalking-related behaviors may vary in nature and severity, but they all share a common motive: an oblivious attitude to the other person's desires, interests, and emotions. As indicated above, being oblivious to reality is indeed a characteristic of Romantic Ideology. When reciprocity is eliminated from romantic love, the selfish – rather than selfless – side of love becomes prominent and explicit. In the glorified ideology of love, there is the belief that 'if you love someone you merely care about his or her happiness'. Following this tenet would lead us to let go; however, the more emotional characteristic of love motivates us not to give up. Persistence rarely receives social disapproval; in fact it is more often glorified: countless books, movies and songs have suggested that persistent efforts are eventually rewarded by success. Armed with several dozen such stories, the lover knows not to give up on love. So they keep on trying.[13]

So did the men who murdered their wives. Typically, the dread of separation is bound up with two patterns of behavior: one is characterized by coercion, stalking, harassment and violence, while the second is characterized by appeasement and obedience, which are often experienced as self-effacement. Although these two patterns of behavior appear to be opposites, both – the imposition of oneself and the willingness to efface oneself – are provoked by one motivation: when the woman is viewed as someone who holds the man's fate in her hands, he will do anything to assure her presence in his life. Coercion has multiple facets, some of which are harmless. The degree of using force, intimidation, and coercion may vary, but not their purpose.

Between innocent surveillance and physical violence, a range of behaviors exists, including harassment, threats of self-injury, actual self-injury, verbal violence, threats of murder, intimidation, and terrorization. Pursuit may take on various guises, but only seldom are they criminal and justify police involvement or arrest. Nevertheless, fundamentally they all embody a single essence, for they are all means of coercion directed to take by force what is not given willingly.

Unwillingness to give may reflect, in some cases, rigidity of personality, which expresses itself by unwillingness to let go of lost goals, and stubborn clinging to a vision of the way things 'ought' to be. Rigidity rejects alternatives and shades of gray, ignores risks, and refuses to revise dreams in response to a changing reality. It is not perseverance but rather the ignoring of the reality in which it takes place that makes behavior non-adaptive. Here is how one interviewee explains himself:

> Look, I have this problem … I have to bang my head against the wall, I don't know what it is to stop. So that's part of the problem…. This guy doesn't want to stop. He just wants to keep going, that's all. Because that's how I am … and gradually I started to think that way about her, too. That's it. I have to have her. I started to relate to her that way, too. That's it. I have to be with her.

For this man, unwillingness to give up is considered to be an aspect of his personality, whereas for most men, persistence is a matter of obeying the code of masculine identity, which commands the man to fight for what is his: 'A man is someone who is willing to die for what's his. That's a man for me'. For this interviewee, the identity of a man and the identity of a warrior are combined. Both reject surrender. Both demand achieving the goal even at the cost of life. Giving up, therefore, is not an option:

> Up there, at my base, among the officers, there is someone from my village. He told her, 'Look, we know him. He'll get into more trouble. You're making him do it. Everybody knows that you're making him do it, and he won't give you up. He has to come and see you. For that he'll fight against the whole world. I suggest that you leave the north and go to a place where he won't know where you are. Why, because he'll get to you. He loves you, and he wants you, and no court is going to help you'.

The interviewee uses another man's voice, while emphasizing familiarity between him and that man in order to establish credibility and validate his self-presentation as someone who would never give in until he attained his goal. By so doing, he also validates his identity in terms of manhood, which commands a man to fight for what is his. The external voice also serves as an arbitrator and a moral judge: the corroborative testimony confirms the woman's guilt and the man's innocence. Even though it is the behavior of the interviewee himself, that will make him get into 'more trouble', the guilt rests with her. If 'she made him' behave in a way that would get him into trouble: what happened later was her fault.

In some cases, the traces of forcible coercion stand out, characterized by violence, threats, pursuit, and terrorization. Some men described breaking into the woman's home despite a restraining order; another person cut himself in front of her; others chose to wait for her outside her home; and some used violence. But whereas physical violence and explicit threats set the institutional mechanisms of enforcement in motion, most manifestations of coercion and harassment are neither violent nor criminal. Indeed, frequently they are interpreted merely as signs of love.

Patterns of behavior that mark the man's unwillingness to give up the woman's presence in his life end up trapping the woman in a nightmare world, in which life-threatening behaviors are defined as love. Only a very thin line separates what can be interpreted as courtship behavior from harassment. Significantly, that line is not connected to the act itself, but to the interpretation that accompanies it. Naturally, the interpretation depends on the eyes of the beholder. Very frequently, it is not the content that makes the difference between what can be interpreted as a courtship or as a threat, but rather the form in which it is presented. Thus, for example, the following statement made by one of the men to his girlfriend, 'I told her, even if you marry someone else, I'll still be with you', may not be interpreted as threat. Nevertheless, it does imply a far-reaching and fateful threat, for he tells her that regardless of what she does, he will always be around her. He will not allow her to live her life without him. On the day of the murder, she wanted to talk to him:

> Q. Do you think she just wanted to end things with you, to separate?
>
> A. I, from my point of view, I wouldn't give her up.

Typically enough, there is not a shred of interest for the woman's attitudes and desires; nothing interferes with the stubborn persistence of the man's unwillingness to give her up. The woman's existence as an object of desire paradoxically is bound up with her absence as a human being.

The second pattern of behavior, which is born of the dread of separation, is placation. This pattern includes giving, which the giver ultimately interprets and conceptualizes as an act of exploitation and an expression of self-effacement, self-abasement, and inferiority. The episodes described by men share one motive: the women were asking for something and they rushed to obey, no matter how inconvenient and humiliating it was for them. They felt exploited, but nevertheless they could not refuse, for the threat of separation places the man in a situation in which he is prepared to do anything in order to get her back. In such circumstances, pleasing gestures are not a result of good will but of the circumstances in which the possibility of refusing does not appear to exist. The essence of altruism that is perceived as imposed is nothing but submission.

The loss of self-esteem, which is probably one of the most painful recollections of the rejected lovers, is exacerbated by the lover's acceptance of indignities during the attempts to win the other person's heart. Thus, 'one's own actions may aggravate the loss of self-esteem, insofar as one humbles oneself and sanctifies dignity on the altar of love'.[14] While force and coercion may characterize the typical response to rejection, the inner experience has nothing to do with power and everything to do with weakness. In the eyes of these men, the man is the one being controlled and the so-called 'bully' is no more than a limp rag.

The humiliation of the rejected – 'Merely a rag'

Why don't you love me like you used to do,
How come you treat me like a worn out shoe?

Hank Williams

It was shame, shame.... I came from the heights and I reached the depths. Everybody pointed at me ... Then you turn into a rag ... I'm talking about inside me, inside me I was a piece of rag.

A murderer

In a relationship where one party wants to prevent the other from leaving, the allocation of power and weakness is inevitable; the weakness of the party vulnerable to being abandoned is built in, inherent in the situation. Therefore, although the interviewees present their place in the relationship from various points of view, they do share one significant common feature: the self-identity within the relation is that of the weak party. The loss of power is experienced in terms of a blow to honor and a blow to masculine identity. It is interwoven with shame, humiliation, and anger. Consider the following statement by one of the men who killed his wife:

A. I was young. I was a kid at that time. Maybe because she was my first love. I ran after her. I wasn't a man with her. I wasn't a man at all. I think about myself, how I reacted, I was like ... like a rag, a rag, a real rag. I wasn't a man, not at all a man. I don't know who I was. I don't know what I was at that time. Not the man people know, not this person. What happened to me? I don't know. Today that's the way I see it.... If I went back to the beginning, I wouldn't let that happen again.

Q. Why not? What would you change?

A. First thing, I wouldn't be a rag. She would see me once a week. I'd get angry at her. I'd say some things to her. Like with any woman ... I didn't want to upset her, get her angry. That was my problem, my mistake ... Listen, I know, women don't like men who love them too much.

The behaviors that construct the meaning of 'not being a man at all' include both self-effacement and his forcing himself on her. His silence, on the one hand, and his pursuit of her, on the other, establishes the identity, which is worthless in terms of loss of honor and loss of masculinity. Masculinity and honor are complementary essences. The loss of one is also the loss of the other. The self-abnegation that colors that memory is now a source of shame. Therefore, although only five years have passed between the time when the murder was committed – he was only 20 – and the time of the interview, he makes use of the forgiveness awarded to youth to shelter himself from the shame that he feels today.

Power and weakness are a zero-sum game: the power of one side is equal to the weakness of the other. The view proposed by the following interviewee focuses on the woman's power. If she had pushed him to get treatment, says this interviewee, it is likely that the murder would have been prevented:

> I think that in my case, if she had done it, if she had pushed me, because she had the power in that situation … because in fact whatever she said, I would do. That's actually the case.

The essence of their relationship, claims the interviewee, was around the imbalance of power. In 'that situation,' marked by dependency and willingness to do anything to keep her from leaving him, she had all the power and whatever she said he would do.

Common to many of the interviewed murderers is their willingness to bear the burden of choice. They do not experience themselves as if their hands had been forced and their power or virility stolen. When the loss of power is constructed in terms of sacrifice, the man's weakness becomes a source for justifying the murder.

In the following testimony, justification of the murder is built into the perception of the self as being diminished within the relationship. The identity of the rag serves the interviewee in two ways: it helps him position himself as a victim, and it allows him to point out the woman's guilt, since she wielded the power in the relationship. His position in the relationship is portrayed in two voices: his own voice and the one he attributes to her. From his own point of view he chose behavior that would serve him, he assumed, in attaining his goal:

> I have always been tolerant. I always diminished my ego. Because I wanted that. I wanted that connection. It was right for me to be with her. I loved her. I loved her look. I loved her personality. I loved her body. I loved her food. I loved everything in her. Everything.

In his love for her and in being vulnerable to her ability to leave him, he was weak, and because he was weak, he had to behave in a way that he interprets as canceling his ego. His behavior diminished him, he gave in; he forfeited his honor. From his point of view, he was 'tolerant'. But from the point of view attributed to her, he was nothing:

> She used to tell her friends: 'Him?! I can buy him with a lollipop'. She didn't expect behavior like that from me, I think. She used to say: 'He can't do anything'. Because that was me, someone who couldn't do anything … I was like dice in her life. She didn't believe that I would get up on my own two feet, as people say.

The use that he makes of her voice, her words, her thoughts, and the feelings that he attributes to her are intentional, because through this use of her voice he construes the justification of the murder. The point of view that he attributes to her creates his humiliation, his diminished self-image, which reflects a combination of innocence and stupidity (someone who can be bought for a pittance), helplessness and lack of personal worth (unable to do anything), lack of importance (dice in her life), and lack of independent existence. Hence, the presentation of the woman's voice, with the contempt and scorn woven into it, serves as his narrative of justification. His humiliation is also his justification for the murder: 'As a result of my innocence and afterward because of the blow to my honor, a situation from which there is no returning, I became what I became'.

His injured honor is the sword brandished over her. The blow to his honor cannot be rehabilitated: 'a situation from which there is no return'. The blow to his honor demands revenge. His placing himself as the victim of innocence and humiliation necessarily places the other side as the aggressor. Through the eyes of the victim, the murder was committed against the injuring side, as retaliation for the humiliation and in revenge for lost honor. The rag, on the one hand, and the murderer, on the other hand, meet in an act to balance the forces. The murder was a demonstration of strength and capability enacted by someone who was robbed of these qualities and needs to come back and prove them. He did not rise against her from a position of strength but from a position he assumed is weakness in her eyes. She (supposedly) regarded him as worthless, and he stood up and proved the extent of her error to her. The person who 'can't do anything' showed his ability to take away her life. She believed, so he claims, that she controlled him and that he was a plaything in her hands, but the ultimate power was in his hands.

The meaning of his feelings of weakness, humiliation, loss of power and control should be understood in the context of masculinity, which he perceived as a compound of strength, determination, honor, and control. All of these are components in the definition of masculine identity. For example:

> As hard as it was for me, and as much as she stepped on me, and whatever her parents and the whole world did to me, I never showed her for a tiny moment that

> I was broken.… I showed her that … you've got to know when you go with a man, not with a girl, and if you go out with just a rag … I told her, 'See me as a man all the way, not just a man inside, but a man outside, too'.

Masculinity is *a* façade of power and vigor. What a man experiences within him is far less important than what he presents to the world. The power and vigor that are displayed to the world are the constructs of his social identity and function as a calling card for the person who wants to call himself 'a man'. To show that things are hard for you is to be a 'rag,' 'a sissy' – all of these fit the anti-masculine image.

The following two quotations reflect another aspect of masculine identity: the need to control. The interviewees offer an explanation for the fact that most murders committed by spouses are those of wives by husbands:

> I spoke about the relationship in two senses: she was the only thing I had, and she was the only thing I could control. I couldn't control anything else in my world – in my studies, at work. In a relationship, a man feels that he is part of something, and usually he has a conception, whether it's right or not, that he controls the relationship. Very sad to say, but that's the problem men have. When I can't control anything, it's only logical that I should look for something that I can manage, and I thought that was the relationship with her.

Another interviewee says, in this context:

> I don't think it's so strange. I think that it's some desire to control. Men always have some need to control. There is always some desire to control. The moment you don't control the situation, the wheel starts to spin.

The concept of masculine control, as reflected in these quotations, bears a broader meaning than the control by a man of his wife. The need for control relates to the need to direct what happens to you, to grasp the reins of life. As a need, it is not limited to relationships alone. One motif of this attitude is that masculinity involves the need to control life. A second motif is that of justification, based on the disappearance of personal responsibility. For both motifs, control is the essence of masculine identity. The interviewees corroborate their statements by referring to the masculine majority, which 'always' or 'usually' seeks control. The generalization creates a norm. The person himself, the individual, is not deviant or exceptional. Identification of masculinity with the need to control helps diminish personal responsibility. Since people are part of the gender identity to which they are born, they are forced into patterns of thought and behavior. Just as a person does not choose his gender, he does not choose the meaning of belonging to a certain gender. Arguments that give a kind of identifying mark of belonging to a certain group serve to exonerate the individual. A man obeys the biological or social commands that shaped him into what he is. The behavior is cast within him almost like a physiological trait. Collective masculine identity is therefore a kind of safe haven. When the interviewee says, 'When I can't control anything, it's only logical that I should look for something that I can manage', it is 'only logical' in the context of his identity as a man, since the desire to control is part of who he is.

His construction of a psychological reality in terms of extreme dependence, which necessarily places him in a position of weakness, functions as the backdrop to the murder. However, desperation is also a position of power. A person who has nothing left to lose is stronger than someone who has something. The person who has lost everything has an advantage over the person who still has something to lose. Thus, weakness is also a source of power. The deeper the desperation is, the stronger the power that desperation gives. From this perspective, the ultimate exercise of force – murder – is depicted as a mere expression of his state of complete weakness and submission, the weakness that gives a person greater strength, the strength of someone who has nothing to lose.

From the context in which the words were said – to explain why the massive majority of people who have murdered their spouses are men – it can be concluded that from the point of view of two of the interviewees, the path to the act of murder can be traced back to the loss of control. 'The moment you don't have control,' says one of the interviewees, 'the wheel starts to spin'. The spinning wheel is offered as an image for what cannot be halted. That is to say, when control is lost, a scenario begins to be written, the end of which is known in advance. The image of the spinning wheel works to free the man from responsibility for the results, for, from the moment that the process began, there was no way of stopping it. With the desire to control as a background, the feelings of dependence and need become the proverbial loaded gun: its presence is intimated in the first act, it is ignored and supposedly forgotten in the second, and fired in the third and final act. The horrible end is, as it were, foreshadowed from the start. It is the fact that both the unraveling of the situation and its horrible end were foreseeable that makes the murder a tragedy.

Emotional states – 'At a certain point, you're just ready to die'

Since my baby said good-bye …
All I do is sit and sigh.

Hank Williams

I was really broken. Completely … Depression, really … I sat at home, shut up in a room, didn't go out to eat.

A murderer

The loss of a love relationship is a major source of negative emotions (or more precisely, affective state). Loss, however, only partially accounts for the emotions raised in the face of romantic rejection. The typical emotions experienced by the rejected lovers, such as anger, shame, jealousy, depression, despair, humiliation, and feeling deceived, illuminate the two aspects of the emotional responses: one focuses on the hurting self, while the other is directed at the one blamed for hurting. The emotions that focus on the self, such as depression, shame and humiliation, revolve around issues of self-identity and self-esteem, as well as the meaning and the significance of life. These kinds of emotions are responsible for the behavior that sometimes is associated with the experience of abandonment and loss of love – namely, suicide. It is interesting to mention that men often take romantic rejection in a more dramatic manner than women: men are three to four times more likely than women to commit suicide after a love affair has decayed.[15] However, it is not depression alone that characterized the rejected lover's typical response. Jealousy and anger, which are directed at the other person, are no less prominent and much more dangerous. In fact it is the combination of anger and depression that was found to be the most common predictor of violent behavior.[16]

Most of the interviewed murderers reported that the period preceding the murder was replete with prolonged affective states such as despair, anxiety, and depression as well as with emotions such as jealousy, humiliation, anger, hope, and fear. The despair, anxiety, and depression continued for months and were accompanied by such physiological symptoms as weight loss, thoughts of suicide, inability to function, efforts to flee, separation from the world, withdrawal and seclusion, and sometimes by the use of addictive substances such as drugs and alcohol. Here is how an interviewee describes the period of separation from his wife:

> I was really broken. Completely. Just when that happened, I was working, and I stopped. The one who helped me was my brother. He took me and tried to help me a little. He saw that the situation was really bad. Depression, really. I sat at home, shut up in a room, didn't go out to eat. All kinds of things like that. Depression. I didn't weigh anything at all. Then, according to my mother's stories, I didn't want to get up in the morning in the two months we were separated, at all … I got even thinner. I thought about suicide. … One of the thoughts that preoccupied me a lot was to run away from everything. I just wanted to leave Israel, to go as far away as possible.

Mourning for the expected loss before the separation, and for the actual loss after it, took on a form that was interpreted as depression, because the man was living as though he wanted to die. Unlike many of the other men, there was no aggression, anger, or accusation. There was a sadness that went very far and very deep in its length and force, a sadness that became depression accompanied by loss of motivation for life. Depression is a kind of withdrawal and immersion in pain. The physical and psychological withdrawal is accompanied by severance from the framework of the outside world: from work, family, and friends. Thus a situation of total and sweeping mourning is created, with no way of escape or relief.

The interviewees whose testimonies are presented below describe despair and depression as a situation of disintegration of the self, until it reaches loss of sanity. For both of them, depression was accompanied by many other emotions such as shame, humiliation, and anger, as well as the desire to die, efforts to flee, separation from the world, inability to function, and the use of addictive substances:

> I was a man on the brink of madness, and I didn't get any help. I couldn't function, and I didn't function. To go to the drugstore and buy, to order, to get pills, no! I sent a taxi to bring me the pills.... What I wanted, and all the time there were masses of pills next to me, was to take them and finish myself off, from the shame. Because everybody predicted the results. Everybody predicted the results, where I would get to. It was shame, shame. My thing was shame. I began at the highest height and I reached the depths. Everybody pointed at me. Everybody warned me. And I kept on. I caused families to break up – do you understand? Suddenly it came true. Then you turn into a rag. You're ashamed to go out into the street. That's what happened to me. I'm completely serious, I tell you, you just don't pick up the phone, you shut yourself up in the house, you don't work. You feel a decrease in the tension in your body. To get up and take a shower, you need to drag yourself. Your feet won't walk. You feel dread, fear. You start to sweat. You have chest pains, headaches. You're mixed up. At a certain stage, you just want to die. You're ripe for death. I was helpless. That brought me to the situation. I'm talking about inside me; inside me I was a piece of rag. I couldn't even brush my teeth.... I was helpless in a frightful way.... It's impossible to describe it. It's impossible to convey it in words.

By separating the picture of depression into its physical, behavioral, emotional, and cognitive elements, the construction of 'the brink of madness' takes on palpable form. The loss of the motivation to live, the inability to function, helplessness, seclusion, immersion in pain, desire for death, and physical symptoms – all of these come together to create an understanding of depression as an experience so harsh and powerful that life in its shadow is seen as impossible. The meaning of the term *brink* also includes the threat of going over the edge. Standing at the brink of madness is like standing at the edge of a chasm, temporarily. The brink is a sign of transition. It refers to a situation on the seam between sanity and madness. Hence, it is possible to either fall into the chasm or to return to the bosom of safety. The interviewee claims that, had he received help at that juncture, he might not have crossed the line. The claim that he did not receive help expresses a kind of unfocused accusation. In fact, he did consult a neurologist, who prescribed antidepressants.

The shame, to which he ascribes the depression, reflects his view of his responsibility for the ruin of his life. By not listening to the warnings, he brought disaster upon himself with his own hands. The accusing finger can only be pointed at him, not to any other person, nor to his own innocence. From his point of view, he knew what was going to happen and, nevertheless, did what he did. The power of shame that caused him to shut himself up in the house and hide from the world derives from the multitude of prescient eyes before which he must account for his actions – all those who warned him, who pointed, who showed him the future.

He attributes his depression to shame. He also attributes the brink of madness to it, and to the lack of certainty that he experienced as a result of her behavior.

> She sat on my brain and dripped. The uncertainty, that's what killed me.... That uncertainty. You have days when you feel like you're going crazy, you're losing your mind, that you don't know where you are with yourself. That she doesn't let you take a single step. She won't leave you. She won't let you alone. She put me in uncertainty. She said this and that, yes and no, yes and no, yes and no. And in the psychological state of the person I was, that shook me more and more. That made me more of a rag.

Uncertainty is a major factor in generating emotions. The more we are certain that the eliciting event will occur, the less we are surprised at its actual occurrence and the lesser the emotional intensity accompanying it. Spinoza emphasizes this point, arguing that the wise man:

> who rightly knows that all things follow from the necessity of the divine nature and happen according to the eternal laws and rules of nature will surely find nothing worthy of hate, mockery or disdain, and no one to pity.17

Certainty is a salient feature in the total and uncompromising nature of ideal love, which is eternal, can overcome all obstacles and provides for all your needs.

The above interviewee presented himself as preferring certainty – the meaning of which can be life or death – or at least preferring to put an end to the vacillation. He accuses her of forcing the uncertainty on him: she did not tell him decisively and unequivocally that their relationship was over. However, the power that he accords her, the power to end the vacillation, is power that he could have taken himself. The complete cessation of their relationship was equally in his hands, and in this sense he could have created certainty for himself. However, he refrained from doing so, because to do so would have meant actively destroying any hope for continuing the relationship and to create this kind of certainty was also to create the possibility of death. He demanded certainty from her because he wanted to preserve hope: 'You say to yourself, wait a moment, on the other hand, maybe it'll come back, maybe it will be again, maybe this is it'. He did have the ability to grant himself only one kind of certainty, obtainable by removing himself from her, and putting an absolute end to the relationship. He chose hope. But hope, being an emotion associated with the future, is also the essence of uncertainty.

The following interviewee describes the period preceding the murder as marked mainly by loss of identity. In the interview, he reports in great detail his 'psychological situation', as he calls it, during which he perceived that he was unable to function and cope, and which was accompanied by suicide attempts, disappearances and flight, substance abuse, outbursts of anger and violence, and a feeling of loss of sanity. At the same time, he was boycotted by his family, entangled in debts that he could not repay, and entirely subject to his love for the girl who wanted to leave him:

> I got into a very difficult psychological situation. A very very difficult situation. At that time, I wasn't sane within myself. I would do things outside of awareness. I entered the situation, you know, somehow my head was spinning a little from all the pressure. Like an idiot, like a madman, I started to do crazy things. I tell you that I would beat up people in the street. I would take someone and hit them, explode, anger … for no reason, from my craziness. People took me to a doctor. They said 'the guy is totally lost'. I stole. I tell you that there came a time when I wasn't sane within myself. I didn't eat. I didn't do anything. All I did was smoke, drink vodka, drink whiskey, and I was as stupid as you can be. Whoever saw me would run away from me. From being a good guy, I became a bad guy, as evil as can be. And all of that was because of her. And she was still in my head.

The parallel between madness and violence introduces the justification for what was later to happen. From a point of view that he attributes to other people, the person who is 'out of his mind,' says the interviewee, behaved toward the people around him in a way that had to be interpreted as 'madness'. However, madness indicates lack of control over what happens, because the person behaves in a way that does not suit his character and cannot be explained. In contrast, his own testimony suggests that he was in full control, as he made sure that no expression of his inner feeling of crisis would get out. The dictates of masculine identity guided his powers to guard against any outwardly expression of loss of power and control:

> I swear to you by my life that I used to feel … from the outside I would show them that I was king. I lied about myself all the time. I lied to everybody all the time. For who? I said, 'look at me. I'm a man. Everything's perfectly fine'. But inside I was eating myself up. That's the only expression I would play with: look at me from the outside. Everything is whole. But inside, I'm destroyed…. I'm with myself, with my truth from inside. I was in conflict, in conflict with my soul. I started with myself. Mixed up with myself. I couldn't sit alone for two minutes. 'Let's get going. I feel like getting up. I feel like doing something. I feel like doing anything at all'. I got to a situation of confusion. Everything was black.

Because he understands masculinity as an essence that cannot contain breakdown, weakness, difficulty, or distress, he invests effort in hiding his distress and in keeping up a strong front. The result is a torn and divided identity that exists in a dichotomy of black and white, wholeness and destruction. Not only is his strength usurped by the erosion of his whole self, undermining his efforts to cope with the tasks before him and with the impending inner destruction, but his struggle to preserve the façade keeps information from reaching the people around him and thus deprives him of resources of external support. By containing rather than exposing his distress, he increases it. His unwillingness to show weakness inevitably imprisons him in the world of lies that he himself constructed. At the same time as he endeavors to preserve his social identity (Look at me. I'm a man. Everything's perfectly fine), on the inside the feelings of distress, confusion, and anxiety were constantly building up.

Chapter 3

The ambivalent nature of romantic love
'What is this thing called love?'

Some say love, it is a river that drowns the tender reed.

Betty Midler

It's hard to explain love.

A murderer

The emotional upheaval and ambivalence associated with periods of romantic separation are not limited to the periods of romantic separation, but are rather typical features of romantic relationships in general. Hence, romantic love may entail negative emotional states and types of behavior. We begin the discussion of romantic ambivalence by describing what constitutes a typical example of romantic love. Then we shall discuss some typical features of love such as its being dangerous, a kind of sacrifice, and its uncontrolled nature. Then an analysis of the murderers' emotional states will be provided. The chapter will end by examining the issue of whether you can hate the one you love. These discussions will be helpful for understanding significant features in the lovers' behavior.

Typical ambivalent love – 'It breaks my heart loving you'

Angel in disguise she was but somehow you fell for her until she broke your heart.

Brandy

I love the girls who don't.
I love the girls who do.
But best, the girls who say, 'I don't …
But maybe just for you'.

Willard Espy

It's either black or white. That's love for me.

A murderer

Confusing descriptive terms, such as 'common' and 'rare', with normative terms, such as 'typical', 'extreme', and 'pathological', is extensive. To speak of what is 'common' is to refer to the most frequent and widespread cases of a category. 'Typical' cases are those exhibiting significant characteristics of a category. Thus, an instance is typical of a category if it has the essential features that are shared by members of that category and, conversely, does not have many distinctive features that are not shared by category members.[1] However, to speak of 'extreme' elements in a category is to refer to those that have an excessive measure of a property that is by and large considered a diagnostic feature of the category, but usually appears in a much more moderate form. Typicality tends to co-vary with frequency: common instances are generally more typical than unusual instances. A warm and sunny day is both typical and frequent in the summer. Similarly, the typical and common American family has two children. There are, however, circumstances in which typicality is at variance with frequency. This occurs when referring to an excessive measure of a highly diagnostic attribute: an excessive manifestation of the typical attribute means that it appears less frequently within the category and therefore it is no longer typical nor common. For example, in one experiment, most people stated that it is more typical (or, rather, representative) for a Hollywood actress 'to be divorced more than four times', than 'to vote Democrat'. However, most people from another group stated that, among Hollywood actresses, there are more 'women who vote Democrat' than 'women who are divorced more than four times'. Multiple divorce is more diagnostic of Hollywood actresses than voting Democrat, but it is less common.[2]

Quite often, extreme cases constitute the public image of a category: they are mistakenly perceived to be both typical and frequent, because, like other abnormalities, they are more noticeable than the typical or the common. Indeed, the media are more interested in unique, abnormal cases than in common, normal ones; only the former are exciting to most people. The tendency to confuse extreme with typical attitudes is more prominent when dealing with attitudes that are perceived as morally negative, such as hate, anger, pleasure-in-others'-misfortune, jealousy, gossip, or revenge, than with perceived positive attitudes, such as happiness, gratitude, or friendship. The reason may be that an excess of negative attitudes is more threatening to the individual and to society than an excess of positive attitudes; hence, it is more noticeable. Nevertheless, the fusion of the extreme with the typical is quite common in love as well. This may be an expression of the importance of love in our lives.

Perceiving love in the idealized manner involves the widespread confusion of the extreme with the common and the typical. The typical, common case of

Romantic Ideology excludes from love diverse phenomena and deeds that often occur in romantic relationships. These include, for example, decline in sexual desire over time, decentralization of love when faced with everyday difficulties and chores, taking one's partner for granted, and so forth. Perceiving of love as extremely pure and good prohibits any association between love and wife killing. Love in this perception is pure and uncontaminated by any ambivalence – it is entirely good. Any negative aspects that might be found in love are explained as stemming from negative emotions, such as jealousy, hate, or from morbid and pathological types of behavior. Love precludes any association with negative aspects, in general, and with killing, in particular. Accordingly, the literature dealing with wife killing adds adjectives such as 'extreme', 'morbid', or 'pathological' to the terms 'jealousy', 'possessiveness', or 'need for control'. Most causal factors used for explaining this phenomenon are transferred from realm of the normal to the deviant one, to an arena where the only players are those with extreme, morbid, or pathological personalities. These adjectives, which serve to locate the murder in the context of the deviant and extreme, function to create a safe – albeit illusionary – distance from the people who commit the ultimate crime. This explanation, which provides love with a safe distance from such horrible deeds, is too simplistic, as is Romantic Ideology. Ironically, it may be the idealization of love that arms it with its destructive power. As in the case of religion, some of the worst evils have been committed in the name of love.

Least of all are we willing to admit that love entails an evil intention. Love is supposed to be a pure, well intended, altruistic emotion. Evil intentions are rejected and denied: 'what's love got to do with it?' As long as 'it' refers to an evil deed, the prevailing answer is 'nothing'. Precisely at this point, the non-love explanations are presented as an appropriate substitute from which we are required to choose: 'it is not love; it is an obsession/possessiveness/pathological jealousy'. It is not love as we want to treasure and preserve it, but rather a deviant behavior mistakenly called love, stemming from the altogether unhealthy personality of the actor. So, love is held responsible for whatever is moral and selfless, while jealousy, envy, anger and hate are considered responsible for whatever is nasty, harmful and selfish.

While most attempts to account for the phenomenon have focused on the role of sexual jealousy in triggering lethal attacks upon female partners,[3] the role that love plays in the murder has been largely overlooked. Jealousy, especially when defined as extreme, morbid and pathological, is perceived to be capable of inspiring pursuit, injury, and murder. However, this is not true of love. Thus, love is ignored, as if it were not part of the emotional backdrop, as if it had nothing to do with sexual jealousy and possessiveness.

By adapting the 'either/or' attitude (either love or pathological jealousy), two goals are achieved simultaneously: the preservation of the concept of love as a moral and pure emotion, and the perpetuation of the 'somewhat pathological non-normative personality' of the murderers as the definitive explanation.

The concept of romantic love, and especially that of idealized love, is saturated with positive rhetoric. Thus, it is usually believed that the central features of love, in terms of concept and experience, include trust, honesty, respect, warmth, joy, happiness, good communication, shared thoughts, sexual desire, acceptance, and personal sacrifice.[4] Sternberg's well-known Three-Component View of romantic love, which speaks about intimacy, passion, and commitment, refers to a content world very similar to that mentioned above, embodied by noble attributes such as respect, support, trust, understanding, sacrifice, selflessness and totally devoted love.[5] In fact, the most prototypic features of love are equated with selflessness and bliss, while the most non-prototypical features of romantic love were perceived to involve behaviors such as possessiveness, submission/ obedience, controlling, selfishness, and negative experiences, such as accelerated heart rate, anxiety, vulnerability, insecurity, loss of freedom and regret, depression, deception, or submission.[6] The equation of love with personal happiness rejects not only pain but even a shred of negative insinuation, such as vulnerability. In idealized love there is no room for ambivalence.

In the face of rejection, however, the rhetoric of love is utterly transformed. Both the rejecter and the rejected lover use the vocabulary of romance and love to account for coercion, stalking, even violence[7]. Love is no longer a selfless, all giving, and well-intended emotion. Now it turns to be an evil, selfish emotion which legitimizes whatever is done in its name. Moreover, persistence, which sometimes takes the shape of persecution, stalking and violence, seems to be what 'true love' is all about. In fact 'the core dynamics in relational stalking – persistence in seeking a relationship in the face of continuing rejection – mirrors in extreme and dogged pursuit of "true love" idealized in the culture and media'.[8] Although possessiveness, dependency, submission/obedience, controlling, vulnerability, insecurity, loss of freedom have all been considered to be the essence of what love is not, they are all embodied, in fact, in the one central desire characteristic of romantic love: the desire to include each other in each other's self.[9] We may label it closeness and intimacy, and by so doing we load this desire with connotations of warmth and happiness; however, at the core of such a union and merging of identities is dependency, entailing risk and insecurity. Attempts to control the beloved are driven by fear of loss, reflecting efforts to minimize the lover's insecurity.

Romantic beliefs are not merely abstract ideas; they intervene and color the practice of love. They become standards by which people interpret their experiences of love and guide their own behavior.[10] If love is compared to a religion, the stored cultural knowledge about love can be compared to some kind of bible. It tells us what love is and what it is not. It functions as a guideline. Not surprisingly, given the lack of ambivalence in romantic beliefs, they were found to encourage greater commitment.[11] Thus, it is expected that people who believe strongly that love can find a way to overcome obstacles and who believe strongly in a one and only true love are apt to work hard to maintain their relationship in the face of difficulties.

The fact that love is included in the rationalization of such diverse attitudes, from purity and altruism to selfishness and persecution may lead both aggressive lovers and victimized beloveds to conflate love with violence. This can explain why over one quarter of the victims of violence and almost a third of the aggressors, interpreted abusive behaviors as meaning 'love'.[12]

When love becomes one-sided, the very non-prototypic features of love mentioned above, selfishness, negative emotions, and abusive behaviors are presented as the very essence of love, or better yet, as the very essence of true love. Knowledge about love is thus saturated with contradictions. Paradoxical expectations and conflicting beliefs flourish side by side. Here are a few examples that have emerged from our discussion.

- Love has been described as involving genuine and disinterested care for the beloved, that is, care which does not consider the lover's benefits. However, should the beloved wish to be happy with another person, most lovers, in their distress, would quickly abandon that definition of care and attempt to prevent the fulfillment of this wish.

- Romantic love is perceived as the fusing of two individuals into a single, united entity. Such a fusion implies not merely loss of freedom but also loss of one's identity. Yet neither loss can be typical of love, which is supposed to provide the optimal circumstances for personal development and freedom. In this sense, love contradicts the value of individualism.

- Love is perceived to be a highly moral emotion, which becomes the symbol for peace and nonviolence. Yet love has become a viable causal explanation for both ethically venerable and ethically questionable actions.[13]

- Love is perceived to be irrational and uncontrollable, but the idea of finding the 'right one' implies a rational and controlled choice. The dictate 'to follow your heart and not your head', thus, is opposed to the rationality required in the task of choosing the beloved, which must be based on the unsurpassed virtues of the beloved. [14]

The above (and other) related incongruities and contradictions stem from the problematic subject–object relationship in love. Love is central for the lovers' happiness; hence, the lovers' own attitudes are profoundly affected by love. However, such happiness also depends on the beloved's happiness in general, and on the beloved's attitudes toward the lover, in particular. In a relationship of idealized love, however, one is encouraged to demonstrate unselfish sacrifice, selfless concern for the happiness of the other, and lack of concern for one's own personal needs. Thus, Romantic Ideology seems to require the unity or fusion of identities, practically contradicting the very essence of individualism. Individualism is correlated with personal autonomy, self reliance, independence, and selfish pursuit of one's personal happiness, which occasionally is achieved and expressed by lack of concern for others.[15] In actuality, the lover and the beloved are two independent individuals; therefore, there are bound to be individual differences, and certain events will enhance the happiness of only one of them. This situation contradicts the tenets of Romantic Ideology and thus is considered as paradoxical.

The presence of contradictory features in the experience of love is related to the assumed crucial role of love in promoting meaning in life. Given love's huge positive significance, rejection or unrequited love is experienced as extremely painful. The contradiction between the attitudes prevailing in idealized love and the ones common in cases of rejection demonstrates the genuine difference between the two lovers. These differences cannot be erased by the ideal of mutual unity. It is the presence of two genuinely different perspectives that enables opposite types of behavior, such as devotion, caring, and commitment, on the one hand, and harassment, abuse, and violence, on the other hand, to be interpreted as concurrent aspects of love. Coercion, controlling behavior, and jealousy can all be taken as a demonstration of possessiveness, but also as an expression of caring, devotion, commitment and love.

The dangerous aspects of love – 'A beautiful disaster'

The adventure and risk of love, its tempestuous force and its activating power can shatter us if it does not find a suitable object. And who can tell us men where to find a safe and loyal support for our love? When is the yearning heart's cry real? And when will we be greeted by the true, and honest, echo of love's call? When does the response resonate falsely, and when does our call fall on deaf stone cliffs? How often do we cut ourselves against its jagged edges that come up to greet us, sharp and cruel? Their points spear and slash us to the end.

Yehuda Ben-Ze'ev

One early and erroneous theory maintains that violence and love cannot coexist, although the fact of their joint existence is perhaps the most secret, subversive, and insidious aspect of the phenomenon.

Richard Gelles

Love makes a person stupid. Or maybe, maybe it's not worthwhile loving a woman so much. Maybe you have to love less, less madly, that's the madness of love.

A murderer

What makes love dangerous does not lie in Romantic Ideology per se, nor is it related to the inevitable disappointment in the face of the actual experience. What makes love dangerous lies in its deceiving nature once it came to be 'a central symbol of ultimate significance ... and eventually almost a religion in its own right'.[16] For unlike God's love, a human's love is selfish, conditional and mortal. It may die and vanish. Its devotion requires rewards. Its sacrifices call for compensation. Much like the faith in God, it is treated not only as the ultimate significance but also as the ultimate justification. Love made me do it – these are the magic words that win social applause. Love seems to be the only ideal that is not controversial. As long as it endures mutually, its demons remain dormant.

Love can be dangerous for both the lover and the beloved. People may be addicted to love in the way they are addicted to drugs. Love may disable the lover from functioning properly and generate depression and despair.[17] In this sense, love can be regarded as a serious illness. As Diana, a divorcee, says, 'I believe love is a mental disease; we should look for a medicine, similar to Prozac, to treat it properly'. The unstable mental condition of the lover may cause him to hurt, and even murder, the beloved.

Romantic Ideology appears to be especially dangerous in Western and individualist cultures, which demand a stricter adherence to romantic conceptions compared to the attitudes prevailing in Eastern collective cultures. In collective cultures, the individual's commitment, devotion and love are divided among many, and therefore dependence is defused into multiple close relationships, whereby romantic love occupies its place among other considerations; in individualist cultures, romantic love may overshadow everything else.[18] Thus, the greater importance assigned to love and the stubborn clinging to idealized love can be understood in light of the central role love plays in our culture.

In this section, we shall discuss four major dangerous aspects of love: love as the ultimate significance of life, love as sacrifice, the persistence of love, and love as an uncontrolled force.

The ultimate significance – 'I can't live, if living is without you'

I who have nothing,
I who have no one,
Adore you, and want you so.

Tom Jones

I love you, and you alone were meant to me

Nat King Cole

When she decided that she didn't want any part of me any more, I was left with nothing.... I used her as a source of existence, because I had nothing else.

A murderer

Popular media consistently remind us that love is all we need, but statistics concerning the rate of depression and suicides after divorce or break up of intimate relations, remind us what might happened if 'all that we need' is taken away.

We are brainwashed by declarations that are supposed to express great love, such as 'I can't live, if living is without you', since 'you are my heart and my soul'. This kind of description indicates love's risky nature. Numerous studies have suggested not only the emotional dependence that is inevitably related to the fusing of two individuals into a single entity, but also the association of such love with the physical survival of the lover ('I would die without you'). The impact of actual death or separation is usually compared to the pain of injury, a part of the body that has been torn out. Accordingly, the lover would be faced not merely with the loss of a beloved, but the meaning of life.[19] It is an extreme observation, yet it relates to what seems to be a common knowledge. The images of romantic love continue to resurface even among people who consciously disavow them, because the ideology is so all-encompassing that no one can envision an alternative. Although romantic love may sometimes seem like an infantile passion nurtured by conditions of immaturity, we continue to rely on love as an existential comfort and a buffer against anxiety.[20] However, when love is perceived to be the only thing that creates profound meaning in one's life, the partner becomes a hostage. Her importance in his life no longer relates to her merits but rather to her being, she becomes something to grab and hang on to.

An important factor that indicates a person's willingness to inhibit destructive urges is their readiness to compromise, which implies making concessions to actual circumstances in order to enjoy a smoother and more amenable alternative. The knowledge that one has access to desirable alternatives plays

THE ULTIMATE SIGNIFICANCE – 'I CAN'T LIVE, IF LIVING IS WITHOUT YOU'

an important role in one's willingness to accept rejection, to forgive, forget, move on, and leave the relationship behind.[21] However, at the basis of Romantic Ideology lies the disregard for actual reality; hence, compromise is incompatible with the very essence of idealized love.

To illustrate these points let us consider the story of Ron.

Ron was 26 years old when he killed his girlfriend, after an acquaintance that had lasted only a few months. Six years earlier, he had come from US to Israel to study and fulfill ambitions for a career in journalism. He never was absorbed here and never tried to become absorbed. He remained a stranger and isolated. However, he had a plan. He had goals. He was working to accomplish them. At the time of his relationship with his girlfriend he was experiencing a period when he felt that his life plan was about to collapse entirely. He felt that he was at a dead end, and at a total loss of control over what was happening in his life. That loss of control had a destructive effect on his feelings of self worth. As objective reality became more alienating and difficult to cope with, his girlfriend became more significant to him; she was the only thing left to cling to.

According to his interpretation of the circumstances of the murder, the significance that he attributed to the relationship with his girlfriend was the result – not the cause – of the collapse of his life plans and the related losses. His need for her was impersonal. It was not connected to her personality but to the function that she filled in his life. His love had no specific addressee, like the love of a drowning man for driftwood or a life buoy. She remains the only thing in his world, and therefore she becomes his entire world.

Throughout the interview, Ron struggles with the question that he himself raised: 'It sounds ridiculous, impossible to grasp. How could a young man of 26 murder a young woman after four months of acquaintance, because she left him?' The answer to this question is the central narrative of his story: he was an uprooted person in a strange country, in a reality of loss. In other words, his interpretation is that his estrangement and isolation, on the one hand, and the loss of his professional goals, on the other, were the matrix in which his relationship with her was planted. She was trapped in his lost and empty world and, sadly for her, became his savior and victim.

The first motif of his interpretation, which deals with his isolation and estrangement, is illustrated below in the following two quotations:

> In my case, what happened is connected to a great degree to my being here, to the isolation I was living in. I was isolated, but I also isolated myself to some degree. Maybe if I had made myself part of a group of people, part of the society, maybe I would have had better ways out of my frustration, and all this never would have happened. Because maybe things would have changed in connection to the university, to my financial problems.

> And I was also very lonely. I was a stranger, living in a strange state. I ought to have been used to the place to some degree after a number of years. It seems as if I was still estranged enough and isolated enough, so that she filled up a hollowness in me ... Maybe I wrong to define it as isolation. But from my point of view, it was isolation.

The strangeness and isolation that he reports were both imposed on him and chosen. As a result, they nourished one another. He was stranger by virtue of objective circumstances, which is why he found himself alone. However, because he did not try to escape his isolation, but rather sank into it, he continued to experience estrangement – in addition to isolation – even after a number of years. Thus, estrangement and isolation, which have a reciprocal causal relationship, became almost synonymous concepts presented together, as if each had the power to explain the other.

Ron's interpretation is that isolation created the hollowness, on the one hand, and blocked ways of escape, on the other. He did not try to acclimate himself socially and culturally in the country where he chose to live, and because all of his resources were concentrated on attaining his professional goals, he became particularly vulnerable. Furthermore, he had no external support systems that could help him either to solve his problems ('maybe things would have changed in connection to the university, to my financial problems') or to neutralize the negative emotions that he ultimately directed at her. The social void, along with estrangement and isolation, created an emptiness within him, which needed to be filled. Lacking any social resources, she became the sole filler of the void.

The second motif in his interpretation of the murder deals with his objective difficulties and his experience of loss, and again, his girlfriend filled this void too:

> I had problems at the university, I had severe financial difficulties ° and I was worried about money. I was worried about my studies, and also about my professional activity, that didn't exist. I didn't do anything for the press office. I didn't work. I was unemployed. The only good thing in my life – with two interpretations: the only thing that I felt I had control over or the only thing that I felt was stable in my life – was that relationship. She made me feel good. She gave me a feeling of self-confidence, a feeling of value. It's too bad I couldn't find that in other places; I had to find it in myself, in my work, in my goals. And for me that's the point – everything concentrated in her. I transferred everything to her. And when something didn't work, I got angry at her. I didn't get angry at myself.

From his point of view, she filled a space where there was nothing but her. He used her to fill the void that had opened up in his life. In a world that had been emptied of other goals, she was endowed with the role of savior. She was there to supply him with what he could not find in himself, in his work, in his studies. She was there against her will. He was the one who placed her there; he was the one who had given her control over his self-confidence and his feelings of self worth; and since he had allocated to her his sense of control over his self, his fate, and his confidence, he also focused his anger on her when 'something didn't work'. Clearly, in the role of savior, she was responsible for his unhappiness as much as for his happiness.

One formulates the meaning of 'good' in contrast to a background of characteristics of reality that one experienced as 'bad'. Similarly, the relationship with his girlfriend was imbued with a sense of good because of the contrast with the circumstances of his reality at the time. It became significant because of the function that it filled in his life at that time. The relationship was good, as it corrected or balanced his experience of reality. It was experienced as a fountain of stability and control within his dynamic context of disintegration and ruin. However, the concept of control here is laden with the meaning of being in control, yet it needn't be control of another person. When he speaks about control in the relationship, he is talking about the ability to foresee moves, to see the connection between behavior and result. Experiencing the good was the one thing that he believed was in his control, in the sense of being expected, predictable, and reliable. It would be there for him tomorrow too.

The difference between being in control and controlling is demonstrated in the following words:

> I don't think my problem was specifically one of control, because our relationship was the way I said, she was more independent than me. She had a car. She had money. She wasn't dependent either on her parents or on me. She managed in her studies. She was more together than me in every sense. I didn't try to control her.

When he analyzes this line of argument, i.e., that he attempted to control her (which was suggested to him by the police inspectors), he detaches himself from the subjective experience; his answer is no longer anchored in his personal experience but rather in the obvious logic of a reasonable person. Is it logical, he asks, examining all the data before him as though contemplating someone else, is there logic in the claim that he tried to control her? Could he have controlled her? His inferiority in comparison to her, he argued, renders the suggestion absurd, since logic states that the strong controls the weak, and not vice versa.

However, his response does not really allay the argument, for the issue is not whether he could control her, but whether he wanted to and actively tried to do so. From his point of view, the murder revolves around his lack of control over his life and not around his efforts to control her. However, the two issues cannot be separated; on the contrary, the fact that she was independent, stable, and strong, and he himself was weak and lacked control made her useful to him. She was his source of strength. She gave him a feeling of self worth; therefore, he needed her, and he was dependent on her: 'That was me, when I was dependent on her, that was me, when I enslaved myself to a situation like that ... that I believed that I couldn't function if I wasn't connected to her'.

Dependence of that kind necessarily gives rise to the need to control. Precisely because she was a source of existence for him ('I used her as a source of existence, because I didn't have anything else'), he *had* to control her. Control over the source of existence, like control over the supply of oxygen for a patient who needs it, assures existence.

The interviewee's remarks express the paradoxical need to control the person upon whom he is dependent. It is easy to control someone who is dependent on you. That person's weakness is the source of your strength. The ability to control someone upon whom you are dependent entails an inherent contradiction. Yet extreme dependence gives rise to *the need* to control. Thus, when the object of dependence is regarded as the supplier of life, control over that person is vital.

The severing of the cords that link a person with his daily reality – with work, studies, obligations, goals, and other people – is disastrous. With the collapse of the normative world that links one with other people, goals, schedules, and a daily routine, the possibility of separation from the partner and the relationship simply cannot be contemplated. Except for her, he is left with nothing.

The experience of 'nothingness' is disastrous not only because the woman becomes a hostage of the man's existence, but also because social detachment and loss of hope give rise to dangerous desperation. Here is Ron's testimony in this context:

> Maybe I would like to think that I have a certain kind of moral opposition to murder. That's the way things ought to be. I'm sure I had it, but at that point in time, the morality bound up in 'thou shalt not kill people', 'don't violate the law', don't do things that are forbidden, was always connected to society. And if you're not part of society, if you don't feel as if you're part of society, if you throw your whole world into the garbage – then you say, 'That's it! Everything's finished!' Do you understand? My whole life was over in that semester.

From the view emerging in this testimony, morality is a social construct that preserves itself by the continued existence of the social fabric. Morality is not defined by one's inner intentions; rather it is the feeling of belonging to a social construct that directs a person to behave morally. The condition of being alienated from one's context is related to the severance of social restraints. Therefore, it is not the ability to distinguish between good and evil that is impaired, but the willingness to obey the dictates that impose the distinction. According to this assumption, it is a thin line that separates the human from the savage. That line is hope. Where there is no hope, the feeling of belonging to that 'single human fabric' is gone. This gives rise to the understanding that 'throwing your whole world into the garbage' entails throwing away social constructs, which include moral values, for example.

The experience described here is limited in time. The murder, from this point of view, took place on the seam between two realities. One reality was finished, and the other, which included prison, began. Belonging to the human fabric requires hope. One can expect norms and moral values to be maintained as long as a person experiences himself as part of the social fabric. When he sees himself as someone who does not exist, as someone whose life is over, moral taboos, rules about what is permitted and forbidden – all of these become weakened and undone and they lose their restraining influence.

In conclusion, the meaning of separation from the woman cannot be understood in isolation from the context that produced it. The reduction of the world to a single person takes place in a reality of loss. It arises against the background of an escalating process of loss: resources of power, the components of identity – goals, functions, significant others, self-respect, and a feeling of self worth – are all beyond one's grasp. In these circumstances, an extreme dependence develops. Against her will, the woman is given power to dictate a person's fate.

The construction of one's psychological reality in terms of extreme dependence is to confine oneself to a position of weakness, which can also be used as a self-defense claim with which to 'explain' the murder. However, as previously mentioned, desperation bequeaths power. A person who has nothing left to lose is empowered to commit brash acts more than someone who has a hope to cling to. In this sense, the person who has lost everything has an advantage over the person who still has something to lose. Thus, the weakness becomes a source of power. The deeper the desperation is, the stronger the power it engenders. From this perspective, the ultimate exercise of force – murder – is merely an expression of complete weakness and loss.

Love as sacrifice – 'I would die for you'

It was love, love, love, love, love alone,
Caused King Edward to leave his throne.

Harry Belafonte

I'd slave for you, be a beggar or a knave for you.

Frank Sinatra

Yes. I loved her very strongly. I loved her a lot, really a lot…. I was even willing to sacrifice myself for her.

A murderer

An infinite number of poems, songs, children's stories, novels, films, myths, and fairy tales – all the threads from which culture is woven – portray love in terms of personal sacrifice and self-surrender. In fact, the view of 'Love as a new religion' is based on the fact that religious motifs, such as self-sacrifice, have become intertwined with the notion of love and serve as criteria for gauging whether one's love is 'true'. Personal sacrifice was found to be one of the most frequently generated characteristics of the experience of 'being in love'. In Sternberg's three-component view of romantic love, which refers to intimacy, passion and commitment, the commitment component includes devotion and willingness for self-sacrifice. Although the voluntarism ethic claims that only the self's free choices should determine action, self-sacrifice is encouraged as a product of 'free choice'.[22] If you love enough you are happy to make personal sacrifices. To love is to be willing to follow the loved one 'to unknown lands', even at a high personal price. The greater the personal sacrifice, the higher the ranking on the hierarchy of true love. Thus, it is no wonder that King Edward VIII of England's willingness to abandon the throne for his love, as he did for the sake of Wallis Simpson, has become the symbol of true love.

When love becomes one-sided, sacrifice becomes a license for emotional extortion ('after all I've done for you'), for whatever has been sacrificed on the altar of love becomes a debt that can never be repaid. Whatever has been done for the sake of love is now the basis for feeling deceived and vengeful. Studies have shown that in the face of rejection, the most extreme and vengeful behaviors are triggered by feelings of deception and humiliation.[23] The combination of anger and depression, which is frequently presented in the experience portrayed by wife killers, is the most dangerous one – the most common predictor for violent behavior. However, the most acute problem with personal sacrifice is the real and substantial damage that it can wield upon the very resources that are needed for coping with the termination of a love relationship. The danger lies in the very willingness to relinquish worthwhile resources such as one's aspirations, goals, values, identity, and dignity. Emptying out one's resources leaves one vulnerable, unprotected, and highly dependent. Nothing is there to lean on when love is gone. Once one's resources are depleted, and love is experienced solely in existential terms ('you are everything for me; without you I'm nothing'), then the end of the relationship is in fact experienced as the end of life.

As regards the dissolution of relationships, what is revealed is the problematic nature of social messages that encourage us to view love as an altar upon which to extol our personal scarifies. Whatever has been invested in the relationship becomes the partner's liability. Self-sacrificing behavior thus backfires.

The problem of contracting the world into a single person is that it creates enormous need and dependence that is liable to become a burden. When the beloved becomes the lover's 'whole world', he or she acquires impossible proportions. The lover has effectively erased his or her self, which can only lead to feelings of humiliation and deception, which in turn are likely to be translated into anger. Such thought and behavior patterns stem from the clichés of love that are rooted in Romantic Ideology. The problem with such clichés is that once in a while they are in fact an authentic expression of love

Let us now turn to the story of Nagib who was 20 when he tried to murder his former girlfriend and her new partner. The man died, and the woman was wounded. He was sentenced to life imprisonment plus ten years.

They had met during their (mandatory) military service. He is Druze, and she was Jewish. Their relationship encountered much opposition. The road to love was saturated with sacrifices and battles. Every battle took a toll in terms of personal identity. Every battle was a stage in the divestment of personal assets and resources that had constructed his whole prior life. He was willing to give up his family, his former fiancé, his friends, and even his religion. He was willing to let go of everything that had constituted his identity, including his values, his sense of honor, his goals, and his dignity. He had done it all willingly. It was a worthwhile price to pay for love:

> My friends left me. Everyone left me. I was left alone to fight against the entire world over a girl … I said to myself – the army? I will fight the army, I will fight the base, I will fight everyone, but she will be mine, no one will take her from me. And indeed this is what I did.

Every battle demanded an additional price to pay, and he was the heroic warrior who paid all and stopped at nothing. All of these losses, from his point of view, were sacrifices he made on the altar of love. At the end of the interview, he presented his defense speech, which he had composed but not presented at his trial:

> I said, people, look at what this is, what life is and what people are. Look: I gave her everything, I gave her my soul, I gave her money, I gave her everything. I was left [with nothing], she made a rag out of me and I took it. People step on me, I go again, I climb up. I do everything. I did worse than in the movies. In the movies people don't do things I did. I saved her from the hardest situations that there are. She was pregnant, I went with her. She wanted to commit suicide; I took the responsibility on myself. I got engaged to her. I promised her. What didn't I do? And all of that was for a girl. And the whole thing, I was just 20, remember.

He is a hero and a victim at the same time. He is a hero, whose heroic deed was to sacrifice himself. The more he got trampled, the more his heroism was emphasized. As a soldier, he was called upon to defend his country; he had to be willing agree to sacrifice what is dearest to him for its sake, and that was what he did. From there it was a small step to the role of a rescuer who makes self-sacrifices. The two roles combined to produce the heroic figure of one whose youth is offered on the pedestal of love and country.

In the real world, however, the role of the hero is played by a young man who has relinquished all internal resources of power and support. As his grip on other circles of life weakens, his grip on her becomes stronger. As his need for her increases, so does his willingness to sacrifice for her. The sacrifice of personal frameworks, goals, and identities – as son, friend, brother, soldier, and combatant – is complemented by values such as loyalty and honor. The losses feed into one another: the more he loses, the more he is dependent on her; as his dependence on her increases, so does his willingness to make sacrifices for her; and he continues to sacrifice, the greater his losses. Thus, she becomes the only thing left, and he must do whatever it takes to keep her in his life.

At the end of the 'war' he leaves behind him not only the world that he had known but also the person he had been. The emptying out is experienced as absolute. Once nothing remained of his earlier identity, she did not want him; she was afraid of the person he had become. Yet with nothing remaining of his earlier identity, separation from her became impossible. He could not allow her to leave. She was all that remained. The murderous vicious cycle was in action.

Here is his description of his reaction to the idea of separation:

> She said to me, 'How long is this going to last?' I told her, 'What are you trying to tell me?! Do you want to leave me now? You want to leave me in a situation like this? You're ready to leave me?' (Shouting) She said, 'I want to separate from you.' I – you know – I felt that she had ruined me. I felt that she had exploited me. I felt that she played with me. I told her, 'How dare you say that to me? In my life I never touched you to harm you, in my life I never shouted at you, in my life I never let you cry about anything. How can you say that to me? You took my blood, you took my soul', and now she says to me, 'Let's split up?!' She said to me, 'No, I can't, look where you are? How you've become?' I told her (shouting): 'But how was I?!' I told her, 'How was I? Remember what I was like. Why have I become this way? Because of who? Because of my dad and mom? Because of you I've become this way … and now, what? I have no parents, no house, no money. I don't have anything. Where have you thrown me? Where do you want me to go? Except for you, I have nowhere to go'.

His anger and indignation are based on what he perceives to be his undeserved and unjust fortune. He shouts his words, flooded with fury that is awakened anew, four years after the event. The anger, which is his first response to the idea of separation, is authentic, in that it reflects his genuine belief in the undeserved and unjust behavior toward him. However, his anger towards her serves also as a deterrent: he accuses her of being accountable for his sacrifices, and as such she is (equally) responsible for the person he has become. He implies that because she is guilty, she cannot simply walk away. Thus, to accuse her is also a way of clinging to her. On the one hand, she has no reason that he can accept as justified, since he can honestly state 'In my life I never touched you to harm you'. On the other hand, there is a reason why her leaving him cannot be justified, since in his mind, she bears responsibility for his being 'in a situation like this'. He lays out all his sacrifices before her. He emphasizes what she took from him and not what he gave to her. She is the one who '[took] my blood, [took] my soul'. She manipulated him. He was passive. Thus, his choice to do the things he did has vanished, and he denies his responsibility for his condition. The person he has become is placed at the doorstep of the one who made him that way: 'Why have I become this way? … because of you I've become this way'. The presentation of matters in these terms affords him a new source of power and increases his grip on her. Through his sacrifices he has accrued personal rights and deserts: 'look what I've done for you!' She, by contrast, has accumulated debts. His sacrifices become a bargaining chip, a means of emotional blackmail.

The catch is that the person he has become, a person who has lost everything, is not the person she wants. She fears the person he has turned into, that is, someone who has lost everything. The weapon of the weak is his weakness. Therefore, his anger becomes pleading, and it is replaced by the desperation of a person who has nothing. He tried to guilt-trip her by referring to his sacrifices. He used anger to weaken her and weakness to arouse her pity. He tried everything. He has thrashed in every direction and used all the ammunition he had: anger, indignation, emotional blackmail, pleading, and self-abasement. As an act of last resort, in an attempt to preserve his very existence, he was prepared to surrender his honor and be satisfied with the remnants of her love. He had tried everything, and in the end, he has also forfeited his self-respect.

This is what he tells about what happened to him after that event:

A. The story changed for me. Everything was downhill for me.

Q. Did you feel as if you suddenly started to hate her?

A. I felt … No, what does that mean, to hate? To hate someone because of jealousy for her. I started to see my own life … to see that I was taking the first step, the second step, I didn't know what would happen. I started to see life clean, in general, with one goal – just her! I forgot everything around me. I forget everything. Only she was on my mind. People might say, there's happiness, and I'd tell them, it's her. People might say there's enjoyment, and I'd tell them, it's her. People might say there's a world, and I'd tell them it's her. My life was a black curtain. Just her.

A black curtain came down on his life. That metaphor places him on a stage where the spotlight is on just one person – on her, but when the spotlight would move away from her, there would be nothing to light him up. Nothing was there except her. The experience of the world reduced to a single person, as reflected in his description, is not related to the prominence of this person within the fabric of life but rather making this person life itself. As it is emphasized in Romantic Ideology, his beloved and his life were identical. The whole world was not absorbed into the background; rather, it was handed over to her. She became the only goal that remained for him, and in her being were concentrated all the other goals that a person might seek: enjoyment, happiness, fulfillment, the entire world. Within the darkness that reigned, he describes himself as someone groping, step by step, to attain the one and only goal, the one that includes all others, without which he was left with nothing.

The persistence of love – 'Love can move mountains'

There is such a hungry yearning burning inside of me
And this torment won't be through
Until you let me spend my life making love to you.

Frank Sinatra

And gradually I started to think that way about her, too. That's it. I have to be with her. I started to relate to her that way, too. That's it. I insist on being with her.

A murderer

Love's ability to overcome all obstacles does not refer merely to external circumstances that impede the realization of the loving relationship, but also to internal obstacles and, in particular, to the beloved's rejection of the lover. The struggle over love is now taking the shape of persistence and pursuit, coercion and manipulation – whatever is needed to influence the partner's decision. The media and its heroes often portray persistent behavior as a successful strategy. Thus, the very behavior which may be perceived by the other side as stalking, that is, the unwanted attention, the pursuit of relationship despite rejection, is endlessly reaffirmed and reiterated in movies, books, poems and songs.[24]

Studies examining the experience of rejection have indicated how strong and prevalent is the belief that persistence is a worthwhile value, and that persistent efforts eventually pay off as they are rewarded by success. These studies, however, also reveal that Hollywood fantasies are misleading. In fact, in many cases people not only fail to reestablish the relationship, but also lose their self-esteem in the process, an outcome which then becomes a major problem afterwards. Persistence and indeed the whole cluster of stalking-like behaviors, not only victimizes the rejecter but also becomes a source of shame and humiliation for the rejected stalker. The lover's willingness to accept indignities in the attempt to regain the other person's love has been found to inflict the most profound distress during the disillusionment period. It is the willingness to be exploited, endure humiliation, and give up on self-pride that haunts him later on. The damage to self-esteem, initially caused by the rejection, is now intensified and aggravated.[25]

Humiliation and shame typically motivate one to either escape the situation or alternatively retaliate against whoever is perceived to have caused it. The strong links between humiliation, rejection and revenge indicate the dangers of humiliation perceived as inflicted by the partner. Humiliation and relative powerlessness are found to be important elicitors of hatred and potent motivators of revenge.[26]

While a substantial body of popular wisdom encourages persistence, and in fact portray it as an expression of real love, it should be noted that the end of the road is more typically characterized by bilateral victimization, rather than fulfillment and happiness.[27] Moreover, such persistence may in these days be considered in many circumstances as harassment. The unwillingness to give up on an unrequited love is anything but an expression of caring. The irony of the situation is that the self-preoccupation that characterizes the rejected lover who is focused on nursing his own needs, wants and feelings, makes him blind to what the other is experiencing.[28]

Even more troubling are the findings that show that it is not rare for such persistence to take the form of coercion, intimidation and stalking. Yet it is defined as love. Vocabularies of romance and love are used to account for these behaviors, and not only by the pursuers. It has been repeatedly found that abusive behavior in an attempt to reestablish a love relationship is treated with tolerance, even by the victims, whose feelings about the forced interactions are – perhaps surprisingly – markedly ambivalent. Declarations of love intermingled with stalking, threats, and abusive behavior are interpreted by both sides as meaning 'love'.[29]

The conflation of love, passion, and violence is partly due to vocabularies that convert romantic repertoires into effective strategies for maintaining unwanted interactions. As a result, 'not only do women perceive coercive and intrusive unwanted attempts as flattering and romantic but they are much less likely to consider them annoying or frightening'.[30]

Western thinking perhaps rejects the notion of external control over a love relationship; however, at the same time it does not tolerate the scenario in which one simply gives up and walks away. While historical love stories abound with the idea of relinquishing the loved one as an important part of the narrative, contemporary romantic narratives seldom include this possibility. What we now identify as individualism in love might well be described as entitlement.[31] To accept unwanted pursuit as an expression of love is to accept the contemporary social scripts and the ideological romantic vocabulary, available to the rejected lover who knows better than to give up. After all, the Ideology states, love will prevail, love can overcome any obstacle, love conquers all, and true love will find a way. Accordingly, 'the core dynamics in relational stalking – persistence in seeking a relationship in the face of continuing rejection – mirrors in extreme and dogged pursuit of 'true love' idealized in the culture and media'.[32]

Love as an uncontrolled force – 'I can't help it if I'm still in love with you'

> Maybe I'm addicted, I'm out of control, but you're the drug that keeps me from dying.
>
> Enrique Iglesias

> You're irresistible, you're natural, physical, it's indefinable, magical, illogical.
>
> The Corrs

> I loved her. What can I do? Love, how do people say: love is as strong as death.
>
> A murderer

Romantic love is most often constructed as irrational and uncontrolled. As Alexandra, a married woman in her early 30s, says about her married lover: "Reasonably thinking it would be better to forget him. I tried but that was impossible". According to Romantic Ideology, love is an overwhelming power and compelling force: one does not enter into love with deliberation; rather, one is 'gripped ... seized and overcome' by love, for love is beyond self control, beyond free choice.[33] The perception of love as a compelling force is presented as structure underlying Romantic Ideology. Thus, a textual analysis of popular feature films, as well as findings from a series of interviews with people getting married, indicated that love is explained by claims of irresistible force, suggesting that the emotional state indicative of 'true' romantic love must be one characterized by lack of resistance and control.[34] As Olivia Newton John says, 'I'm hopelessly devoted to you'.

The construction of love as irrational, irresistible, uncontrollable and as a compelling emotional force lays the foundation for explaining immoral behavior as an act that occurs independent of the self. Such a perception helps diminish and, in fact, eliminates free will, and hence responsibility. To be gripped by an overwhelming power no one can resist is to be controlled and yet to remain free, free from blame, free from liability. Love has driven me out of my mind. Consider what one interviewee said:

> She was everything to me. She was my soul. You don't always kill a woman or feel jealousy about a woman or shout at a woman because you hate her. No. Because you love her, that's love. My wife was the kind of woman you'd never murder in your life, unless it was for love, because of madness, at that moment, at that moment a person loses everything, he doesn't think, it's a moment of madness.... The only thing that I can say is that she was more honest than a Torah Scroll. So why murder someone like that? … At that moment, you don't remember. You don't remember anything. You don't know what you're doing. Love makes a person stupid. Or maybe, maybe it's not worthwhile loving a woman so much. Maybe you have to love less, less madly, that's the madness of love.... It's written this way in the bible, that woman – maybe they mean a woman stranger, but it's my wife, but I'll tell you: 'A good man before God will flee from her, the sinner will be trapped by her'. Did you understand that verse? Maybe I wasn't good before God. Maybe I was a sinner. I was trapped by her. What is that trap? It's love.

All but two of the interviewees construct a description of the murder in terms of temporary madness or loss of control. The meaning of loss of control is almost always portrayed as a scenario triggered by some provocation, which elicits such a powerful emotional response that it is grasped as a force outside the person. It is that force that caused him to act as he did. The presence of madness in the personal story almost never extends beyond the boundaries of the event. It is constrained in time, limited to the particular episode. The 'madman' is a guest. He is not the man himself, but rather a sudden, unfamiliar, and unexpected entity taking away the man's control over his actions, as if a demon had possessed him. Madness is an entity that dwells in the personal biography for a short time. As suddenly as it arrived, it passes.

The claim of madness and loss of control serves a number of purposes. One of these is to create a separation between the act and the person who performed it. Murder, an act of unparalleled gravity, one that cannot be justified, entails disgrace that cannot be effaced. This disgrace is based on the identification of the person with the deed: where there is a murder, there is also a murderer. Use of the claim of madness, like the use of an alien identity, separates the normative self from the murderer. By presenting the murderer as 'someone else, in fact', a person can claim continuity with his familiar, ordinary grasp of himself, the person before the act. The murder is attributed not to the person himself but to a strong force that deprived him, for a certain time, of the power of choice, decision, and thought.

Furthermore, the argument of madness and loss of control also implies lack of planning and premeditation. The established assumption (in conjunction with a social norm that receives legal backing) proposes an equation in which fierce emotions on one side equal reduced responsibility on the other, for the judgment of premeditated murder is not the same as that of murder motivated by a strong emotional force. The distinction suggests that planning and premeditation contradicts 'madness' or 'loss of control': as though premeditation means that the murder was committed in cold blood, whereas 'madness' indicates suddenness, an emotional outburst of a power strong enough to remove the social constraints of control over a person's actions. Therefore, in order to claim lack of premeditation and lack of intention, the murder itself must be characterized in terms of the flaring up of passions to the point of 'loss of control'. Finally, identification of the murder with powerful and overwhelming emotions also serves as a means of obtaining understanding and empathy. Cold-blooded murder, premeditated and planned, is an execution that turns a person into a monster. Powerful emotions do not deny the person's humanity; indeed, they do the opposite: they demonstrate it. Here is an example:

> Look at what I did. You can laugh at me. You can also not laugh. It's human. It shows humanity. What is a person? A person reacts. If he's not human, then he won't react the way he reacts. So, that comes from emotions, from inside, everything.

To react because of 'emotions, from inside' is the meaning of being human, says the interviewee. Therefore, the murder was motivated by emotions such as jealousy, humiliation, and anger, the kind of murder that might happen to anyone. We're all in the same boat, because emotional outbursts are a human phenomenon from which no one is immune. The murder is motivated by a flaring of passions that led to loss of control; thus, it is a murder that ostensibly can be understood, or at least it can be treated with forgiveness.

This madness or this 'explosion' was not created ex nihilo. In most cases, the madness erupted because it was ripe to be born. There was advance preparation. The continuum of emotions that preceded the murder created the psychological ripeness for its manifestation. The explosion took place only because the conditions had been set in place well in advance of the event itself. Nevertheless, love as a compelling force is useful for explaining the madness of murder.

Jealousy and romantic love: 'It hurts to be in love'

> It's hard to know another's lips will kiss you.
>
> Hank Williams

> Being mad by desperation I pierced him to the breast
> All this for lovely Flora, the lily of the west.
>
> Bob Dylan

At first I was happy, after that, no. When she turned on me – no. But I loved her more. Despite that behavior. I loved her more. I would be jealous and love her.

A murderer

The emotion of jealousy is often confused with that of envy, as both involve a negative evaluation of the good fortune of others. However, whereas at the basis of envy there is a negative evaluation of our undeserved inferiority (as compared with the good fortune of others), jealousy involves a negative evaluation of the possibility of losing something – typically, a favorable human relationship – to someone else. In envy, we wish for something that someone else has, while in jealousy, we fear that someone else will take something of ours away from us. Jealousy is typically associated with exclusive human relationships, whereas envy has no such restrictions. Jealousy is concerned with the most painful loss: that of an exclusive relationship in which our mate, or anyone who is closely associated with us, prefers someone else.[35]

Jealousy is likely to cause profound injury to our self-esteem, since it touches on significant aspects of our self-worth. The threat it carries is posed by a person with intimate and reliable information about us. The severity of that threat may explain why jealousy is so intense, despite the prevalence of sexual infidelity. The intense pain generated by jealousy is not because something extraordinary has happened, but because we may lose something of crucial importance to us. Similarly, although death is common and is expected, it nevertheless generates profound grief.

Jealousy is often interpreted as a sign of caring and love for the partner, and many instances show a positive correlation between jealousy and romantic love. Like love, jealousy typically presupposes some type of commitment underlying the relationship, and it cannot arise if our attitude is one of utter indifference. However, jealousy does not necessarily involve love. It may arise even in the absence of love and caring. A man who despises his wife may, nonetheless, become jealous when someone else looks covetously at her. Here the central feature is losing to a rival. In this case, jealousy is more germane to selfishness than to love. Jealousy, then, is not always indicative of love. Does romantic love always involve jealousy? Augustine claimed, 'He that is not jealous, is not in love'. It may be better to say that wherever there is romantic love, there is always the possibility of jealousy. This is because romantic love entails a favorable relationship which we value. The prospect of losing that relationship could provoke jealousy. The level of involvement in the relationship is often positively correlated with the level of jealousy.[36]

The focus of concern in jealousy is the threat to our exclusive position and, in particular, to some unique human relationship. We are afraid of losing our present favorable position to someone else and ending up in an inferior position. The cognitive element in jealousy is often imaginary, as the jealous person fears a future change. Jealousy often involves fantasy. Our jealousy does not usually die when we realize our error; any pretext whatsoever is sufficient to revive this emotion. Indeed, the most frequent event eliciting jealousy among married people is not actual infidelity, but involves the partner paying attention, or giving time and support to, a member of the opposite sex.[37]

The desert aspect is central in jealousy, which is associated with the belief that we are being treated unfairly. Although the norms violated also involve moral values, jealousy cannot be explained by merely referring to moral injustice. We can be jealous without believing our jealousy to be justified. For instance, a husband who has continual love affairs may recognize his wife's moral right to have affairs as well, but will still be jealous when she does.

Explaining the murder of one's wife as stemming from jealousy, that is, due to the fear of losing her, seems to be paradoxical. With his own hands, a man causes the destruction of someone else, because he does not wish to lose that person. The man who murders his wife is not motivated by the desire to rid himself of her: if his goal is to retain her, murdering her is even more counter-productive.[38]

In light of such difficulty, it has been claimed that such murders are the result not of any type of jealousy, but merely of extreme and pathological one.[39] In characterizing jealousy as extreme or morbid, one implies that it has pathological, abnormal traits. However, that claim reflects what appears as an unjustified effort to create distance between the familiar, daily emotion, which is experienced by all kinds of people in love, and the 'violent', alien, pathological emotion, that is experienced by murderers or violent men. Indeed, studies have demonstrated that the jealousy of violent men is not unique or more extreme than that of men who are not violent and are unhappily married.[40]

While most explanations usually emphasize the role of sexual jealousy and sexual possessiveness in triggering lethal attacks upon female partners, it should be noted that in most cases it is not the wife's infidelity alone that provokes the murder, but rather the threat of separation, whether or not it is accompanied by the woman's actual or perceived infidelity.

Hence, how central is jealousy in triggering the murder of a wife? In some cases, although in neither all nor even in most of them, jealousy indeed played a central role in the emotional experience during the period preceding the murder.

> What did I feel? I didn't see a thing before my eyes. I broke glasses. She said to me, 'What's the matter?' She said to me, 'Why?' I said, 'No, I remembered something'. I would feel burned up inside. I wouldn't say anything.... I would talk to myself, look what I'm doing for her, and how she relates. Why does she act that way? Maybe she loves him, her eyes ... God forbid, to get to a situation where we'd separate

from each other … From fear, so she wouldn't get mad, so she wouldn't say, 'Okay, bye-bye'. I couldn't sleep at night … In those six months, I don't know what was the matter with me. I got very thin. I used to weigh 67 kilos, I got down to 52. Pressure, pressure, completely pressure. But I loved her more. Despite that behavior. I loved her more. I would be jealous and love her. I didn't explain myself, and I used to take it to heart. I'd sit with her, and I'd be jealous, and I'd eat out my heart, and I'd laugh with her, but inside I wanted, really, to burn down the house. I paid attention to everything. Everything hurt me. I noticed everything, and I was hurt by everything.

Jealousy, as he describes it, has a dynamic of expansion. The first instance of the wound of jealousy sprung from the fertile soil of earlier suspicions, and was only a confirmation, marking the beginning of a new period. Henceforth, his jealousy became the prism through which the world received its meaning. Suspicion colored his picture of reality and supplied a permanent stratagem for interpreting her behavior. He was constantly testing her. Every movement was a sign. Thus, in an infinite vicious circle, the more reasons he found for jealousy, the more solid his suspicion became. As his suspicions became more dominant, the more reasons he had for being jealous. Jealousy became the framework through which he experienced the world. The violent energy of jealousy gathered up inside him and devoured him from within. The use of the image of burning inside, like in the expression 'eat your heart out', conveys the meaning of jealousy as a devouring force. This force, which was not channeled toward confrontation, either with his wife or with his rival, became a source of self-destruction. The expressions of pressure and distress became also physical. Another prominent motif in the interviewee's memory of jealousy is that of the joint presence, heightened simultaneously, of jealousy and love. As his jealousy increased, so did his loved. The two emotions, jealousy and love, fanned each other's flames. In the months before the murder, jealousy became the dominant emotional hue. It spread out and took control over his life.

The gap between the inner experience and the outer display of behavior is described also by another man:

A. It hurt me. Did it ever hurt me! It hurt me to see her with guys, hugging them. I used to stand at a distance, and her girlfriends came to me, swarming over me. They told me she has a boyfriend … but I wanted to see. I wanted to see what happened. A guy suffers. He wants to see … Is there mercy in people's hearts, or do people just like to exploit and take? I wanted to see. Leave me alone. I would see her walking with guys. Hugging them. Kissing them. Right in front of my eyes. And I would look and give a smile.

Q. You wouldn't say anything?

A. A smile, I swear to you, a smile. I held my eyes, so there wouldn't be any tears, held onto my heart so it wouldn't explode, held onto my hands, so that nothing would happen, with that smile on my face, calm.

The public nature of the event makes him, in his own eyes, someone subject to the gaze of others. When he watches her being friendly with other men, at the same time he watches other people as they are examining him and checking his responses to her behavior.

> The guy she used to go out with would sit in the house with me, the way you and I are sitting. I said, 'Watch over her, the way you watch over your eyes'. He said to me, 'Your word is holy'. He said to me, 'I'll watch over her like my own eyes'. And he took her away from me. I wasn't angry because he took her away from me. Believe me, I was angry because my girlfriend did something like that to me.

The story is told in a way that invites anger at the friend who betrayed him, but it is meant only to emphasize that at that time, there was no reason to expect any logical judgment from him. The interviewee wishes to emphasize: she is the one who did him wrong, and she is the one who will have to pay the price.

Does jealousy play a pivotal role in causing the murder of a wife? Although in some cases jealousy indeed played a central role in the emotional experience during the period preceding the murder, nothing indicates that it is a crucial component. Nor is there any indication that jealousy was a central motive for the murder. Typically, it was not the betrayal, or the suspected betrayal, that ignited the murderous emotions, but rather the woman's intention to leave. Despair, humiliation, anger, anxiety and jealousy – all were massively experienced at the time preceding the murder. Most of the men who reported incidents of sexual infidelity restrained themselves regarding the infidelity and continued to live with jealousy for many months. Thereby the focus on what appears to be 'extreme jealousy' is misleading. It neither reflects the emotional complexity, nor it comprehends the causal complexity of the act.

Jealousy, with all its ugliness and destructive potential, receives legitimacy because it is so predictable, human, natural, and inevitable, an emotion from which no one is immune. Jealousy is justified since it plays a role in preserving romantic love and in the preservation of intimate relations. It serves to estimate the degree of the spouse's commitment, and sometimes it is even used to increase commitment. It functions to preserve the safe paradise of exclusiveness, to cope with external threats against love, and, at the same time, to transmit a message of love. It is unlikely that love, with the enormous investment that it demands, could flourish without protection against threats and therefore jealousy is seen as an adaptive emotion which is formed in symbiosis with love. Therein it preserves and defends the fragile emotion that glues a couple together. Its absence – not its presence – is a harbinger of evil. Lack of jealousy is like emotional bankruptcy. Its absence will lead to the disappearance of the reciprocity of emotions, which is at the heart of intimate relations.[41]

Jealousy, thus receives legitimacy, yet it is difficult to accord similar justification to the concept of possessiveness. In fact, the very term of 'sexual possessiveness' is contaminated with a negative connotation connected with identifying the other as property.[42] The concept of possession and ownership, such as a person has over property, cannot be reconciled with the notion of individual autonomy and respect towards the other. Ownership over people is equated with slavery, and thus contradicts our right to freedom.

As noted, it is frequently claimed in the literature that the murder of wives is motivated by male possessiveness. The deed itself is perceived to reflect the motive behind it: 'The power of the male to control is demonstrated by the very act of destruction of his possession'.[43] But should we indeed consider possessiveness as an abnormal attitude in loving relationships?

At the very foundation of romantic jealousy lies the concept of entitlement: we fear the loss of something or someone that we feel entitled to have. Jealousy reflects our fear that someone else will unjustifiably take possession of something that belongs to us. Thereby romantic jealousy implies some kind of entitlement over another person; hence, the person's right to exert control. Asserting sexual exclusivity, for example, is in fact asserting the right to control the spouses' sex life. Indeed, the very perception of belonging ('we belong to one another') as it is reflected in popular culture ('she was my woman') bears a sense of ownership. Although ownership refers to property, it appears in Romantic Ideology as part of commitment and intimacy.

The manner in which the courts have related to what is usually regarded as crimes of passion further exposes the difficulty of delineating a border line between legitimate and illegitimate entitlement. When adultery is regarded to be a provocation severe enough to justify commuting a charge of murder to that of manslaughter, one must wonder about the message of ownership implied therein. The implicit entitlement to jealousy indicates an inherent ownership, which is perceived as violated. For what can explain the indulgent attitude towards crimes of passion if not an understanding of that passion? The sympathy demonstrated in regard to this passion can only be explained by an underlying perception of our right to fight for 'what is ours'. And, what reaction can we expect if not rage when what belongs to us is being taken away?

The nature and extent of the provocation generated by adultery depends on social and personal norms. Judge Holt expressed an extreme view in this regard. In 1707 he wrote that

> when a man is taken in adultery with another man's wife, if the husband shall stab the adulterer, or knock out his brains, this is bare manslaughter: for jealousy is the rage of the man, and adultery is the highest invasion of property.[44]

Holt even wondered why it should be lawful to kill a thief but not the man who comes to rob a man's posterity and family. Indeed, until 1974, it was legal in Texas for a husband to kill his wife and her lover if he did so while they were engaged in the act of intercourse. Social norms are also responsible for the different attitudes toward men and women and married and unmarried people. Thus, a husband's infidelity was not considered an extreme provocation justifying killing. Similarly, in many courts a married person who kills upon 'sight of adultery' can be charged with manslaughter, but an unmarried person killing under similar circumstances is charged with murder. Such differences are apparently connected with ownership and the significant role the person's self-perceived honor plays in jealousy.[45]

The role played by social norms in generating and justifying jealousy can also be deduced from the fact that an old man in a relationship with a younger woman, or an old woman with a younger man is unlikely to receive society's sympathy – let alone justification – if their jealousy is provoked by a young rival. Their 'right' to their partner seems to be in question, and hence the intensity of their jealousy is assumed to be weaker. Social norms also seem to dictate that men attach less importance to adultery when it concerns their own behavior. Hence, they are more likely to engage in such an activity. However, when it comes to the behavior of their partners, this is considered by them a greater insult than when they are engaged in adultery. In this respect, the popular view that 'Hell hath no fury like a woman scorned' seems to be wrong. Indeed, almost all of those who kill their lovers are men rather than women.[46]

The leniency toward crimes of passion is motivated by the court's willingness to regard jealousy as a state of mind under which losing one's self-control can be expected. However, to accept that jealousy over sexual infidelity is justification for 'uncontrollable' anger inevitably conveys a message of entitlement based on one's ownership rights. It is the right to exercise ownership over our spouses that entitles us not only to feel but also to express legitimate anger whenever the right of ownership is violated. The loss of control due to rage excuse tells us that our rage is sanctioned by society. This is precisely the message conveyed by the former President of the Israeli Supreme Court, Judge Aharon Barak, when he accepted the appeal of a man who had killed his wife and her lover, justifying it by the 'boiling blood' of the 'average Israelis' when they see their spouses betraying them. The implied endorsement of the betrayed husband's 'boiling blood' and its outward expression is a message about his right to ownership and the cost of the violating this right.[47]

It is especially important to note that not in all circumstances is the 'boiling blood' argument perceived to be an acceptable excuse for committing a crime of passion. Greater leniency is demonstrated when the perpetrators are married to their victims. This illustrates the tendency to distinguish between what is perceived to be a legitimate anger, which can be expected when we are robbed of what is legally ours, and illegitimate anger. Legitimate anger is based on ownership: just as ownership of land gives one the right to seize a trespasser, thus marriage, according to both ordinary and judicial thinking, gives one the right to experience and express justified jealousy and a boiling blood reaction, along with its consequences.

While we cannot argue that the judicial attitude actually conveys a message about the attenuating circumstances for a homicide; nevertheless, we cannot ignore the fact that it does convey a message regarding entitlement and ownership rights in the context of marriage. The sense of entitlement to possess what is legally mine is not a unique quality of men who killed their wives. The normative nature of possessiveness in romantic relationships and the perceived 'liability' of male possessiveness seem to undermine attempts to 'excuse' wife killing. Surprisingly enough, the reference to male possessiveness is simultaneously argued to be both normative – and therefore a non-deviant phenomenon, and, in complete contradiction of the former, the cause of a very deviant phenomenon such as murder. Clearly, if male possessiveness is recognized as well rooted in social conventions,[48] a normal mental state grounded in cultural messages, then it cannot be presented simultaneously as an aberrant mental state that leads to murder.

In the gray and deceptive area of the meaning of 'belonging' ('you belong to me baby'), it is difficult to mark clear boundaries that can distinguish between a normal conception of entitlement and one characterized as possessiveness or the conception of the woman as property. The judiciary attitude contributes to the blurring of these boundaries.

Understanding wife killing as an indication of extreme and deviant possessiveness is based on two unexamined premises: (1) men who murder their wives are more possessive than other men; (2) possessiveness is what motivated them to murder their wives. Such an explanation is not only tautological (male possessiveness is the cause of the murder, the murder is a clear evidence for the existence of male possessiveness; post hoc ergo propter hoc), but it also obviates the need to define criteria regarding the issue of possessiveness, possession, and the perception of the 'woman as property'.

The very use of the negatively charged term 'possessiveness' functions similarly in the attribution of adjectives such as extreme and morbid to male jealousy. The concept of male possessiveness is essentially pathological. Furthermore, the attempt to tie wife killing to the deviant personality of the killer has no empirical support. In fact, what seems to be so deviant in the phenomenon of wife killing is the non-deviant context in which most of the murders take place. In terms of motives, predictors, and the murderers' characteristics, wife killing is an exceptional kind of murder.[49] This argument is based not only on the impossibility to predict murder in non-intimate relations on the basis of sociocultural theories,[50] but also on findings that show that the sociodemographic profile of men who murder their wives is not similar to the typical profile of murderers in general. Wife killers are more heterogeneous in age, usually do not have criminal records, psychological problems, or a psychiatric history, and their representation among members of the middle class is much greater than that of other murderers.[51]

The phenomenon of wife killing does not grow in the same habitat that gives rise to delinquency and crime. In the case of wife killing, the environment that produces the potential for lethal violence is not pathological. The major difficulty in coping with the phenomenon may be the fact that the risk factors are related to prevalent deceptive images of love and masculinity. It is love's deceiving nature that makes danger so illusive, so hard to identify.

This is how one of the subjects responded to the question regarding the existence of 'the writing on the wall':

> There was writing on the wall ... but I think that even if it wasn't so prominent for the people around, for the family, for friends, the one for whom it was definitely prominent was the victim.... The victim ignored and believed that maybe it wasn't what she thought.

The writing on the wall deceives the victim, who 'believed that maybe it wasn't what she thought'. For pursuit, stalking and controlling behavior are most often perceived to be an expression of caring and love, and, if that is not enough, even physical violence does not destroy the image of love. On the contrary, sometimes it serves to defend the romantic illusion, since it represents what could be interpreted as concern.[52] The foreshadowing events are deceiving: instead of signaling danger, they signal love. The terms that are generally used to define love, masculinity, and the circumstances of life as a couple are also those used to produce the illusion of love. The deception is rooted in an enabling culture, one which perceives love as an ideal that justifies certain behaviors performed in its name; a culture in which masculinity implies power, control, and territoriality, expressed in a directive that calls for the man to retain what is his; a culture in which many women do not consider control as an impending bad sign. Therefore, the woman, who would appear to be in the best position to evaluate risk, may be confused by the duplicitous terms, and find it difficult to distinguish the risk factors.[53]

The murder of wives seems to be the consequence of various circumstances combined together. It emerges in a specific constellation, which creates conditions of risk. Perhaps the difficulty in identifying risk factors, in reading the writing on the wall in real time, before the murder, comes from the unique circumstances in which the terms of love and danger are the same. This strange amalgamation is culturally dictated and further reinforced through folklore. The prevalent beliefs about idealized love, about life as a couple, are the normative anchors of the murder. The narrow line that distinguishes the acceptable from the unacceptable is blurred in the arena known as love, where the normal is pathological.[54]

Hating the one you love – 'I hate you, but I love you'

Then Amnon hated her exceedingly; so that the hate wherewith he hated her [was] greater than the love wherewith he had loved her.

2 Samuel 13:15

If one judged love by most of its effects, it looks more like hatred than friendship.

La Rochefoucauld

You bring me misery, I hate you, but I love you.

Dead Milkmen

She was everything for me. She was my soul. You don't always kill a woman or feel jealousy about a woman or shout at a woman because you hate her. No, because you love her, that's love.

A murderer

Many testimonies, as well as fictional works, describe situations in which people find themselves hating the person that they love. This might initially appear to be contradiction, for how can one love and hate the same person at the same time? A discussion of this problem requires making a distinction between logical consistency and psychological compatibility. Hating the one you love may be a consistent experience, but it raises difficulties concerning its psychological compatibility.

Consistency and compatibility can be distinguished in the following manner: two states are compatible if it is possible for both to exist together; they are consistent if their content does not contradict each other.[55] Saying that I love you and I do not love you at the same time seems to involve a contradiction and hence it is inconsistent. Saying that I love you and hate you at the same time is not necessarily inconsistent if love and hate are not diametrically opposed. Nevertheless, even if love and hate are consistent, it is questionable whether they can be compatible for an extended period of time. To clarify these issues, we need to discuss whether love and hate are opposing attitudes.

Love is often described as opposed to hate. Indeed, the two emotions seem to be similar, except that one involves a general positive evaluation and the other a negative one. Likewise, whereas hate typically involves a profound wish to eliminate the object, love entails the opposite wish: a refusal to exist in a world from which the beloved is absent. Love usually (but not always) involves a pleasant feeling, whereas the feeling involved in hate is typically (but not always) disagreeable.

If indeed love and hate are diametrically opposed, then it is impossible to speak about hating the one we love without engaging in a logical contradiction. However, if we reject the claim that love and hate are diametrically opposed, we can argue that while hating the beloved does not involve a logical inconsistency, it does entail psychological incompatibility, which makes it difficult for the two emotions to coexist for a prolonged period. The next step, therefore, is to explain why love and hate are not diametrically opposed attitudes.

The claim that love and hate are diametrically opposed is problematic in light of various considerations. One such consideration refers to the fact that love is broader in scope than is hate, as it refers to more features of the object. While in hate the object is considered to be basically a *bad* agent, in romantic love the object is perceived to be both *good* and *attractive*. Accordingly, moral considerations play a crucial role – sometimes almost an exclusive one – in generating hate, or at least in its justification. Love, however, is motivated by much broader considerations, including aesthetic, economic, and physical aspects. In romantic love, attractiveness is often more important than moral concerns; in hate, the emphasis is on the harmful consequences of the object's character. The lesser weight of moral considerations in love is evidenced by the fact that we may love a vicious person. However, we usually suggest various excuses for the beloved's immoral behavior, such as a tough childhood or currently difficult circumstances. Such excuses indicate that unfortunate external circumstances have pushed the person – who is essentially decent, or at least not inherently vicious – to behave immorally.

Another consideration that casts doubt on the claim that love and hate are diametrically opposed arises from the fact that there are many varieties of each emotion, and each kind cannot be the exact opposite of all kinds of the other emotion. In addition, there are more kinds of love than of hate, and love and hate are perhaps the only pair of correlated emotions in whose case the positive emotion is more diverse than the negative one. This is due to the more essential role of the different kinds of love, all of which are important for maintaining the various types of attachments and relations in our social life. Love satisfies our need for human companionship, emotional support, and the survival of those related to us, especially our offspring. Hate is less important in this respect and is easier to avoid. Indeed, there are many people who report having never, or hardly ever, experienced intense hate, but very few, if any, claim to have never experienced intense love.[56]

Love and hate are therefore complex attitudes that do not form a unitary continuum at whose furthest edges are two diametrically opposed experiences. Love and hate are distinct rather than opposed experiences: they are similar in certain aspects and dissimilar in others. In light of the complex nature of love and hate, it is plausible that when people describe their relationship as a love–hate relationship, they may be referring to different features of each experience.

Emotional ambivalence entails our ability to refer to the same object from different perspectives, some of which may be conflicting, for instance, partial and global perspectives, short- and long-term perspectives, hedonist and moral perspectives, and perspectives focusing on the subject's value and the object's value. All these perspectives and their related conflicts are evident in romantic love. In sexual desire, which is more concerned with the immediate situation, ambivalence plays a less central function. The ambivalence here is not necessarily emotional; rather, it may reflect our attitude toward this urge or desire. The expression 'the morning-after effect' signals a significant change in attitude from the night to the morning.

At the basis of romantic love there is a profound positive evaluation of one or a few of the beloved's characteristics. This evaluation is typically associated with a comprehensive evaluation that extends the positive evaluation to other characteristics. By giving a significant weight to assorted characteristics of the beloved, lovers do not necessarily distort reality, nor are they completely blind to the beloved's faults; they simply do not consider such faults to be significant and sometimes they even perceive them to be charming. As Simon Blackburn nicely puts it, 'Perhaps we prefer Cupid to have dim sight rather than to be totally blind, but it is also just as well that he is not totally clearsighted'.[57] The psychological mechanism underlying love (and other emotions) does not merely evaluate the object's characteristics as good or bad, but also gives each characteristic a relative weight. This relative weight expresses the significance we attribute to each characteristic and accordingly establishes the nature of the emotional experience. Hence, a woman may say that she perceives her partner to be as handsome as she did when she first fell in love with him, but this no longer matters to her since the weight of his other (negative) characteristics has become so great that she no longer loves him and may even hate him.

There are psychological findings supporting the above conceptualization of love. Lisa Neff and Benjamin Karney proposed a model of global adoration and specific accuracy in love, whereby spouses demonstrate a positive bias in global perception of their partners, such as being 'wonderful', yet are able to display greater accuracy in their perception of their partners' specific attributes, such as being punctual.[58] In this model, spousal love may be conceived as hierarchically organized experience giving different relative weight to the global characteristic in comparison with the specific ones. Spouses appear to rate their positive perceptions as more important for the relationship than their negative perceptions. In this manner, an accurate perception of a partner's specific traits and abilities would not interfere with the global belief that one's partner is a wonderful person.[59] Since importance is a matter of degree, the impact of specific negative perceptions upon the positive global one depends upon many personal and contextual features.

As in love, the profoundness of the negative evaluation in hate is typically associated with an overall negative attitude; nevertheless, this attitude allows for a positive evaluation of some partial aspects of the hated person. Shame functions in a similar manner: it is concerned with an in-depth evaluation of one or a few characteristics or actions of ours; the emotion attached to these particular characteristics is broadened by association to encompass our whole character, rather than isolated to the case of these few – and perhaps negligible – characteristics. Accordingly, we may be proud and ashamed of ourselves simultaneously, as these two emotions are not related to the same characteristic.[60] We can be ashamed of crossing some normative boundaries, but proud of being independent enough to challenge those boundaries.

Returning to the love–hate relationship, we do not deny cases in which the revelation of negative characteristics in the beloved decreases the intensity of the love experienced. In such cases, there is some common ground upon which to compare the various evaluations and to form a single evaluation. This would be easy and obvious if love and hate were diametrically opposed characteristics existing on the same commensurable continuum. Our claim that this is not the case is compatible with the claim that positive and negative evaluations do not cancel each other out. Once it has been recognized that love and hate are not diametrically opposed attitudes and that love and hate are based upon a weighted – rather than a comprehensive – evaluation, explaining the phenomenon of hating the one we love becomes easier. In-depth evaluations can be directed at different aspects of the person and hence they are not contradictory.

The difficulty that arises as a result of feeling hatred and love toward the beloved, not merely at the same instance but also over an extended period, is not a problem of logic but rather a psychological problem: that is, the difficulty of coping with profound emotional dissonance (or incompatibility).

Although the presence of mixed emotions is not necessarily puzzling, the presence of different emotions that are both profound and all-encompassing, such as love and hate, toward the same person, seems to be psychologically incompatible. Although the problem is more severe when these emotions are present at the same time, it is also not easy to experience a fluctuation between such profound and comprehensive attitudes toward the same person recurring over an extended period of time. Such intermittent fluctuation is more familiar and easier to understand when it relates to more focused and time-constrained emotions such as sexual desire and anger; nevertheless, it also exists in more profound and comprehensive emotions such as love and hate.

By admitting the logical consistency of profound yet different emotions that occur simultaneously, we are not making an empirical claim concerning the question of whether the two attitudes can exist within the same second or whether they alternate during several fractions of a second. Since an emotional episode takes place over an extended period of time, the exact duration of the simultaneous presence of love and hate is less relevant to our discussion. The presence of profound emotional dissonance explains why deep hatred toward the beloved is infrequent. Coping with this dissonance is even more difficult if we remember that profound love tends to decrease the weight of the beloved's faults and increase the weight of the beloved's virtues in the beholder's eyes. In cases of love, it is more usual for the positive evaluation underlying love to be accompanied by negative emotions that are more moderate than hate, such as dislike, resentment, or anger.

In general, people describe their relationship as a love–hate relationship when the circumstances are such that the focus of attention changes under different conditions; hence the change in the emotional attitudes. When the lover focuses his attention on his partner's virtuous characteristics and the pleasure she has brought him, he loves her dearly. When he thinks about the humiliation and the suffering she brings upon him, he hates her guts. Thus people can say: 'I hate you, Then I love you ... Then I hate you, Then I love you more' (Celine Dion). 'Sometimes I love you, sometimes I hate you. But when I hate you, it's because I love you' (Nat King Cole). Such cases can be explained in light of the fact that emotional experiences are dynamic and different external and personal circumstances may often change our emotional attitude toward the same person.

A related common situation is that in which love becomes a fertile ground for the emergence of hate. When the intensity and intimacy of love turns sour, hate may be generated. In these circumstances, hate serves as a channel of communication when other paths are blocked, and it functions to preserve the powerful closeness of the relationship, in which both connection and separa-tion are impossible.

It is interesting to note that whereas love can easily turn into hate, hate less often turns into love. The reason is that whereas love requires closeness, hate involves the wish to avoid the other person. Following our close acquaintance with our partner, our attitude of love may change; in hate the change in the attitude is less likely to occur, as we tend to avoid any engagement with the other person and so we have scant opportunity in which to generate new information about them or alter our attitude toward them. There are, however, various cases in which initially negative attitudes such as hostility may turn into love, especially when one person sets out to win the heart of the other person. Another case in which this can occur is when one party is in deep distress or trauma, and their human need for love and identification becomes stronger than their initial hatred. This can be illustrated in the Stockholm Syndrome, where hostages begin to develop loyalty and even love toward the people who abducted them. There are other cases in which love is generated after people are forced to be together in a way that enables them to get to know each other better and they are able to reconsider their initial evaluations.

The claim that love and hate exist simultaneously is a more difficult case to explain; here we need to understand how two such divergent attitudes can be directed at the same person at the same time. A woman may say that she dearly loves her partner in general but hates him because of a certain vicious characteristic or action that profoundly hurt her – for example, his dishonesty or the fact that he deserted her after everything that she had done for him. Accordingly, people do say something like: 'I love and hate you at the same time'. In this kind of attitude the profound positive and negative evaluations are directed at different aspects of the person. In a similar vein, an unmarried person in an extramarital relationship might love the married person deeply, while also hating the beloved for preferring to maintain the bond with the spouse. Likewise, love is experienced when the focus is on immediate consid-erations, but hate reigns when the lover dwells on the fact that a long-term relationship with this person is most likely to be self-destructive. Another common case is that in which we hate someone *because* we love him and are unable to free ourselves of our love for him, or because this love is not recipro-cated. It seems that in these cases the beloved has a characteristic that affects the lover in such a way that she places a very low value on his negative charac-teristics, and yet she hates him for having this effect on her.

The above cases would be difficult to explain if we were to assume that love and hate are diametrically opposed and that both are necessarily simultaneous and comprehensive attitudes. As Aristotle indicates, you cannot at the same time have contradictory evaluations of the same aspect in the same sense. We have suggested that we can explain these cases if we reject such assumptions and accept the presence of emotional dissonance.

Assuming that romantic love is based upon assigning a significant weight to one or to very few characteristics raises several important implications for our understanding of love.

One such implication is that it becomes easier to understand why in some cases romantic love can last for an extended period of time. The lover, even if madly in love, cannot ignore the reality of the beloved's actual characteristics for a lengthy period of time. Assigning a specific weight to one particular attribute of the beloved is not a cognitive task that is true or false; rather, it is an evaluative task that refers, among other aspects, to the lover's wishes and needs; as such, this task is less sensitive to being repudiated by reality. If my beloved perceives, for example, my strength or my kindness as my most significant characteristic for her, then she will love me madly and her love will not be diminished when she discovers that I am not so smart.

The fact that love is based upon very few characteristics, many of which are accorded considerable and possibly inordinate weight, can also explain the opposite phenomenon behind the increase in romantic separation: love rests on very unstable pillars, which can be shaken when the lover begins to assign less weight to one of them. If more characteristics were evaluated in a positive manner, based upon their own merits, separation would probably occur only in cases of drastic changes in these characteristics or in their functional value.

The above account of love can also be used in explaining love at first sight, in which people supposedly fall madly in love with each other despite having very limited information about the other person. In order for such love to occur, you do not need information about the whole person – limited information about one or a few characteristics can be sufficient. Needless to say, such limited information may lead the lover to hold false beliefs about the beloved and once these are discovered as such, the whole relationship might collapse.

As we indicate in Chapter 7, the above account of love is also compatible with explaining the possibility of non-exclusive love (or multi-loving). If romantic love is based upon a few significant characteristics of the beloved, then it is easier to sustain an additional loving attitude toward another person, since that additional love can be based upon other characteristics that do not interfere or compete with the first love. As in cases of 'hating the beloved', non-exclusive love does not involve a logical contradiction (or inconsistency), but it may cause emotional dissonance (incompatibility) in light of the partial nature of emotions.

It is interesting to note that our desire for exclusivity arises in romantic love but not in hate. On the contrary, in hate we want to see our negative attitude shared by others. It seems natural that we want to share our negative fortune with others while wanting to keep the positive part merely to ourselves. In positive emotions, when we are happy, we are more open to being attentive to other people, but we guard the source of our happiness more.

To sum up: hating the one we love is possible from a logical point of view, as it does not necessarily involve a contradiction. This phenomenon, however, entails profound emotional dissonance, which in turn reduces the number of instances of such cases.

The love–hate relationships are dominant among the men who murdered their wives. The murder we are dealing with seems paradoxical: with his very hands, the man causes the loss of the person whose loss he fears. This paradox is embodied in the deed which appears to undermine the goals of its perpetrator: whereas a murderer's motives and emotions are ordinarily organized in a manner that advances his or her interests, the murder of a wife appears to undermine those interests.[61] Hence, it is tempting to regard the murder as an accident, the slip of a hand. However, the assumption that the murder embodies behavior that does not represent the perpetrator's interests ignores the persistent existence of negative emotions such as anger, jealousy, humiliation, and hate, which may result in murder.

The connection between violence and love is ambivalent. Injuring someone close to oneself both physically and emotionally naturally arouses the issue of mixed emotions. If violence in intimate relations bears the potential of mixed emotions, a fortiori, murder must do so. Love mingled with hate, or hate nourished by love, can provide some of the answers to the question posed here: how can one understand the most extreme expression of hate, the murder of another person, when it is planted in a context of intimacy, the closeness of love?

Owing to the profoundly negative evaluation of the object of hate, we wish to detach ourselves from the object, that is, to increase the subject–object distance as much as possible by avoiding or eliminating the object. In marital relationships hate is usually expressed by evading the situation and acting coldly as if the partner were not any more within the close relationship which is supposed to prevail in marriage. However, in circumstances typical of hate, the desired detachment is often impossible. Despite the profound negative evaluation of the object, and hence our wish to avoid or eliminate the object, we are compelled to cope and even communicate with this person. Hate is then directed at people whom we perceive to be too close to us.[62]

Indeed, mention of hate in the interviews of the murders was almost always in the context of denying its existence. Here is a representative example:

> Q. Was there a moment, were there moments, when you hated her?
>
> A. No.
>
> Q. Never?
>
> A. I never hated her. Never. Not even now. At this moment, I don't hate her. At this moment, I don't hate her. Even if I need to sit in prison for fifty years, I won't hate her.

Along with strenuous denial of the possibility of hating the woman, there is very often testimony to the strenuous denial of the possibility of hate at all. Thus, for example, another subject states:

> I have no hate for anyone. To this day ... I have no hate for anyone. Give me a slap, you may think that I'll hate you, but I won't hate you ... I don't hate anyone to this day, and I won't hate. Maybe I'll get angry. I'm human. You're also human, and you also have the right to get angry, but I don't hate anyone, and I don't take revenge against anyone. I leave revenge to Him, only the Holy One, blessed be. He will take revenge. He'll take revenge. He's responsible for everyone.

Anger, says this person, is legitimate. It's a human expression, 'permitted'. Hate, which in his view is connected to revenge, is not up to the individual. Revenge is the prerogative, perhaps even the obligation, placed on the general Master of responsibilities.

Unwillingness to admit hate is a common phenomenon. Perhaps this is because hate is regarded as an extreme and dangerous emotion which involves complete negation of the other, negation that is not limited just to his or her unjustified acts. Admitting hate may also entail a certain weakness, born of humiliation and bound up with the experience of lack of strength and lack of control over the situation.[63] In any event, whereas love was mentioned countless times in the interviews and was a central topic of discussion, hate was shunted aside, rejected as something disgusting. However, unwillingness to admit the presence of hate does not exclude its existence in the complex experience of love. And indeed we believe that a love–hate relation of the kinds mentioned above is often associated with the murderers' behavior.

The difficulties that arise in the romantic relationship can either engender negative emotional reactions, such as hate and anger, or they can be met with indifference. Accordingly, love is perceived as the opposite of both hate and indifference. In the former, there is still the wish to retain the relationship and hence the struggle for its survival. The struggle may be ugly or even violent, and accordingly should be severely condemned, but it may an expression of hope. In the latter case of indifference, there is an acceptance of the finality of the situation and no real attempt is made to change it. This assessment may be characterized by despair and probably depression as well. It is no wonder, then, that many lovers prefer the pain of struggle over the emptiness of indifference.

Chapter 4

Understanding wife killing
'See you at the bitter end'

I've been taking on a new direction, but I have to say … It scares me to feel this way.

Tina Turner

Let's say I committed this crime, even if I did, it would have to have been because I loved her very much, right?

O. J. Simpson

This chapter presents an explanation of wife killing in light of the previous discussions. It argues that contrary to the prevailing view, wife-killing is not a 'natural' continuation or the end of a path marked by male violence, and thus it should be understood as a separate phenomenon. In this chapter we examine the problematic notion of 'crimes of passion'. Following this, we discuss the background of such killing and consider the issue of whether we could identify any signs that might foreshadow the event of the murder. Then we analyze the nature of the phenomenon of murdering one's wife.

Crimes of passion – 'I just can't take any more'

She stood there laughing, I felt the knife in my hand and she laughed no more.

Tom Jones

Because of love I killed her … If I didn't love her, if I didn't love her, I don't think I would feel so much pain … It's like she took an arrow and stabbed me in the heart.

A murderer

Many have considered the 'heat of passion' as the single most important factor in determining the degree of culpability to attach to an act of homicide. A crime committed in the heat of passion is considered intentional, but it is recognized as committed at a moment of intense passion that was generated by a specific, recent and temporary provocation – before the system could cool off and resume its habitual control. Seeing a spouse in the act of adultery has been considered among the gravest of provocations, warranting a reduced charge, from murder to manslaughter.[1]

It seems that adultery provokes intense emotions. The question is whether this fact is relevant to our judgment of the person's behavior and the nature of the crime. The prevailing – albeit controversial – attitude claims that emotions are highly relevant in this regard and hence hot-blooded killings merit less severe conviction than do cold-blooded killings. This claim has been supported by two major assumptions: (a) the agent's self-control over his behavior is considerably reduced in the heat of passion; (b) the sudden emotional behavior is not a genuine expression of the perpetrator's true character. While generally accepting the first assumption, we question the validity of the second one.

In general, it is accepted that the correlation between emotional intensity and self-control is negative, as self-control indicates stability of a system, which is contrary to the circumstances typical of intense emotions. In the heat of passion, external factors have a great impact upon the agent's behavior, and in this sense the resulting behavior does not reflect what he believes ought to be done in such circumstances.

The second assumption states that emotional behavior is a less genuine expression of one's true character. Intense emotions are perceived to distort the person's 'real' character, thereby making him less culpable. In this view, cold-blooded murder might express a 'wickedness of the heart'. Acting in the heat of passion, when self-control is compromised, may indeed lead to acts which would not be carried out in normal circumstances. This, however, does not necessarily imply that such activities are not a genuine expression of our profound attitudes and values.

There is no doubt that emotions genuinely express our current attitude. An interesting question is whether they also express our more stable and profound attitudes. Take, for example, anger. Does anger express (a) a temporary outburst which involves losing control over our behavior and saying and doing things with which we do not really agree, or (b) what we really think about the other person? The first possibility is represented in the saying 'anger is a brief lunacy', and the second one by the claim: 'Never forget what people say to you when they are angry'.[2] The first possibility is explained by the fact that, like other emotions, anger expresses our current attitude toward a sudden change in our situation. In an intense emotional state, we are unstable, and since we focus on what is directly in front of us, we may overrate it in a manner which is incompatible with our long-term, stable attitudes. The second possibility is based on the assumption that emotions express our basic values and attitudes and hence are sincere. It seems that both options are adequate to a certain extent. It is true that emotions often express our temporary and partial attitudes, but these attitudes are based on more profound views and values that we hold. Therefore, we must analyze the specific context in order to determine the depth of conviction expressed in a given emotional attitude.

The question of the genuine nature of emotional behavior does not have to be settled in order to agree that the agent's self-control in emotional behavior is considerably reduced; accordingly, the agent is usually less responsible for it. Provocation, which causes the agent to be in a highly emotional state, is therefore relevant to legal considerations. Provocation is often used as an excuse, referring to circumstances that were beyond the agent's self-control. Thus, in the common law, adultery was considered an adequate provocation only if directly witnessed by the killer. However, it is worth noting that this interpretation suggests that it is the agent's unique personal view that constitutes the provocation, rather than the victim's behavior. Marcia Baron claims that the provocation defense also includes partial justification of the act, implying that it is a consequence of the provoker's faulty behavior; otherwise, it would not be termed 'provocation'. The underlying assumption is that the victim 'provoked' the murderer, and while it might not have been done intentionally, the agent is still culpable. Being justified in doing x implies that I did not act wrongly; by contrast, to excuse my doing x is not to say that what I did was not wrong but only that I am not, or at least I am less, culpable for it. Accordingly, the insanity defense offers an excuse while self-defense offers a justification.[3]

In order to understand whether the provocation defense includes a justification element in addition to the excuse element, let us draw a distinction between personal desert, moral right, and legal entitlement.[4]

Claims of personal desert, such as 'I deserve to win the lottery,' are based on individual merits; claims of moral right, such as 'she should receive better treatment from her husband', often refer to obligations constitutive of the relationships between agents. Claims of desert are not necessarily grounded in anyone's obligations, but rather in the way people perceive themselves in relation to their surroundings. Claims based on moral rights refer to some mode of *treatment* by other persons, whereas claims of desert also refer to the *fairness* of the situation. When we perceive our situation to be undeserved, we do not necessarily accuse someone else of immoral behavior; we assume, however, that for us to be in such a situation is in some sense unfair. In typical claims based on moral right, the agent is a person with some responsibility, whereas in claims of desert an impersonal cause can also be an agent. Heavy rain may be the cause of undeserved but not of immoral circumstances. Similarly, claims based on moral rights are directed at humans and sometimes at other living creatures, whereas claims of desert may also be directed at inanimate objects. One can say that 'Cleveland deserves better publicity, since it is an interesting city'.[5] It is not immoral for a rich person to win a big prize in the lottery or to marry another rich person; nevertheless, many poor people may consider it to be undeserved.

Claims of legal entitlement are part of our legal code and often express a profound moral right. Claims of legal entitlement, such as 'she is entitled to vote in the upcoming elections', refer to rights mentioned in the legal code. Some moral claims also involve legal entitlement. Thus, I am legally and morally entitled to be protected from those who want to murder me. Sometimes, however, claims of legal entitlement do not express a common, acceptable moral right. The right to remain silent in the face of possible self-incrimination may be a legal right which people are entitled to, but its moral grounds are disputable. Likewise, an informer who betrays his brother is legally entitled to the advertised reward, but not because of a profound moral right.

Returning to the issue of provocation, it seems that the provocation defense necessarily refers to a grave violation of one's perceived personal desert. The provocation defense may also refer to the moral, but typically not to the legal realm. When one uses adultery to explain provocation, adultery is perceived as violating the agent's personal desert and in most cases also moral norms; it does not necessarily violate the law. Violating personal desert generates intense emotional reactions enabling the inclusion of the excuse element in the provocation defense – the agent's deed is perceived as wrong but his level of culpability is reduced.

The justification element in the provocation defense seems to require more than just reference to desert claims, which are too personal for even partly justifying the killing of another person. This element cannot also refer to legal entitlement, as adultery and, of course, the mere intention to end a marital relationship, are not violations of the law. It seems then that if the justification element is part of the provocation defense, it should refer to moral rights. Indeed, some people identify moral rights to be a kind of justification component in the provocation defense. Take, for example, the claims made by Judge Robert Cahill upon sentencing in 1995 a man to 18 months imprisonment in a work-release program for intentionally killing his wife after discovering her adultery. Judge Cahill argued that nothing could provoke an uncontrollable rage more than adultery and added: 'I seriously wonder how many men married five [or] four years would have the strength to walk away without inflicting some corporal punishment'.[6] Cahill considered adultery to be an objective offense that partly justifies murdering the adulterer. Although this pronouncement was delivered by an official and high-ranking member of the judicial system, its extraordinary and appalling view serves to clarify the distinction: to imply that the murderer's behavior is not seriously wrong is morally unsettling. Even if a provocation defense does refer to an obvious violation of a moral right, it still cannot be regarded as moral justification. The justification should not be attributed to the murderer's deeds, but rather to his emotional perspective, and in particular to his perceptions of personal deservingness, which, when contradicted, are significant in generating intense emotions.[7]

Traces of a murder waiting to happen – 'Because it's something that is cooking up'

I'll die if I don't get a chance to make this just right, I'm sorry but I can't forget about the way I feel.

Daphne Loves Derby

There was handwriting on the wall ... but I think that even if the writing on the wall wasn't so prominent for the people around, for the family, for friends, the one for whom it was definitely prominent was the victim.... The victim ignored and believed that maybe it wasn't what she thought.

A murderer

Twenty years of research in the domain of intimate murder has consistently shown that the dynamics surrounding the phenomenon of wife killing often revolve around the woman threatening to or actually separating from her dating or marital partner. Most cases of wife killing (50–75 percent) take place after separation and are attributed by the murderers to the separation.[8] The woman's risk of being killed during this period is found to be two to four times higher than before the separation.[9]

While the linkage between the woman's initiative to separate and the subsequent lethal attack have been repeatedly confirmed throughout a long series of studies, the question of what makes the wife's intention to leave 'especially provoking' for some individuals has not been sufficiently addressed.[10] Most attempts to account for the phenomenon of wife killing have focused on the concept of male control. From such a point of view, wife killing is a response to what is perceived as an attempt to undermine the man's authority.[11] Whereas these explanations usually emphasize the role of sexual jealousy and sexual possessiveness in triggering lethal attacks upon female partners,[12] it should be noted that in most cases, it is neither a fear of – nor an actual – act of infidelity alone that provokes the murder, but rather the threat of separation, regardless of whether it is accompanied by infidelity.

Why is the perception of separation so threatening, and in what kind of relationships might the common act of separation become a motive for murder? It has been claimed that relationships that are at a particularly high risk of lethal violence are usually marked by previous incidents of male violence, sexual jealousy, controlling behavior, and attempts to separate. However, this information still does not help us understand why only a few cases of those with similar risk factors do result in murder. Leaving an intimate relationship is by no means a rare social phenomenon, therefore it is unclear 'why a few individuals should have such extreme reactions to experiences that are common to many'.[13]

According to one theory, violence against women reflects male sexual possessiveness, which unlike jealousy refers not only to a response to threats or suspicions of rivalry, but to a more pervasive mind set encompassing not just episodes of jealousy but also presumptions of entitlement and inclinations to exercise control over the woman. Violence against women is suggested to be a 'product of self-interested male motives directed at constraining wives' autonomy', and an expression 'of motives whose adaptive function is coercive control'.[14] The theory argues that although wife killing cannot be seen as an 'adaptive' act, it is rooted in this very same motive. Therefore, the wife's death is considered to be an unintended outcome of the use of violence intended to control and intimidate, but not to kill. Wife killing, from that point of view, is an act of violence that went too far. Death is the unintended outcome of asserting control through violence that slipped over the edge.[15]

An altogether different understanding emerges when analyzing the men's stories. The months preceding the murder could be best described as a time of sitting on a barrel of explosives. It was a period of time in which the notion of murder had been conceived and the explosive material was simmering, waiting for an opportunity to explode. One interviewee says

> Look, there are a few elements of the shooting here. A man who shoots his wife, that's abandonment, that's emotions, that's finances, that's ... everything. And there are some that what brings them to it is that she was unfaithful to him, but that's an excuse. Why is that an excuse? Because it's something that has been cooking up. I don't believe in a one-time act. I don't believe in that. That seems like excuses to me.

The intense affective states of despair, depression, anxiety, and anger that marked the weeks preceding the murder were shaping the way the world was experienced. However, precisely because the emotions were so intense, they were grasped as temporary. Their intensity and destructiveness limited their ability to persist. The breakdown of life, the loss of the ability to function, the psychological and physiological effects, all of these gave rise to awareness of impermanence. The emotional state that characterized this period of time was experienced as a corridor on a path that led toward something unknown, and sometimes toward something known and terrible. Out of belief that 'things could not continue that way' grew the realization that something was about to happen. The experience preceding the murder was bound up with a vague or certain realization of what was going to happen, with fear regarding the predictable end, with a feeling that the emotional tank was filled to the point of overflowing, and with the structuring of a threshold of explosion. Here are some examples, as reported by various men:

> I knew that it was going to happen. I told her there would be a disaster ... that I would take out myself or I'd take her out. Leave me alone. Go away. Leave me alone. Go away.
> Inside I felt ... all the time I had bad feelings, ... I had a feeling that something was going to happen. Believe me. All the time ... I swear to you. Something was going to happen. Either I would die in an accident, or I'd die by that girl's hand. Or that love would do something to me. All the time I had bad feelings. But I couldn't keep away from her. It was hard for me to keep away from her.

An emotional buildup of extreme tension is accompanied in some cases with an emerging insight that something terrible is going to happen:

> I got to a situation, no more ... if a little snafu happened, I would blow up ... I was afraid all the time, why, because I knew – only a little snafu, a little thing from the parents, from the girl, or if I heard that she betrayed me, I would explode. If the parents don't want me, I'd explode. I don't know what will happen, but everything was already about to ...

Whereas the event of the murder itself is almost always portrayed as composed of a provocation, followed by emotional reaction constructed in terms of temporary madness, momentary insanity, and loss of control, the interviews show that this madness or this 'explosion' was not created ex nihilo. In most cases, it was born because it was ripe to be born. A marginal event swelled to proportions of murderous rage, because the infrastructure was already there. The murder was anchored in foundations that had been laid long before. There was a building toward the explosion. On the day of the murder, the spark was supplied that ignited the powder keg.

The over-killing, which characterizes most of such murders, that is, an enormous number of stabbings, for instance, indeed points to rage, but neither the rage nor the immediate cause of this rage can explain the decision to kill. Indeed there was anger; but anger was useful in creating the physical arousal and the impulse toward murderous aggression. Even when the murder was predictable in advance, as it was in most of the cases, anger served as an auxiliary to it. It supplied the ammunition and the aggressive energy necessary for carrying out the act of murder.

Since the act of violence was intended to end in the woman's death, it is not 'loss of control' which best characterizes the murder's circumstances, but rather the choice to lose control. The transformation into a murderer does indeed take place in a moment, but it is usually not sudden. In most cases, the maturation of the murderer and of the act of murder took time, for the notion of murder is formed together with the maturation of psychological readiness. At a certain point, psychological readiness is produced, and then it awaits an opportunity.

Given that the psychological ripeness was already in place, the circumstances that surrounded the day of the murder along with the emotions that accompanied the event cannot, in themselves, provide insight into the reason for the murder or shed light on the place from which it emerged. The specific trigger that precedes the murder often makes no sense unless we examine the given context, as the seeds of the explosion were planted long before: the murder has been waiting to happen.

Wife killing: A crime of passion – indeed?

If you leave me now, you'll take away the very heart of me.

Chicago

My heart would break in two if I should lose you.

Elvis Presley

The various explanations offered for the phenomenon of the murder of wives share one common assumption, according to which the motivation for violence against wives in all its forms, including murder, is rooted in masculine possessiveness.[16] Although the existing explanations disagree about the acquired or inborn essence of male possessiveness, they share the view that an act of murder is the embodiment of the murderer's personality (as if to say: tell me who the man is, and I will tell you what the woman's chances of survival are). Sexual jealousy and anger are two emotions that, according to the common view, trigger wife killing.[17]

Another assumption that unites most of the explanations is that in terms of motives and emotional dynamics, murderous violence is not distinguishable from other manifestations of violence against women. The prevalent view considers murder the end of a path and the climax of a history of violence that preceded it, not a separate phenomenon.[18] However, unlike violence that is not connected to a specific behavioral stimulus on the woman's part, 20 years of research has pointed systematically to the fact that many cases of wife killing are connected to the threat of abandonment, and they take place in response to the woman's effort to end her relationship with the man.

Theories that refer to male possessiveness but overlook the context of potential abandonment cannot answer the question of why certain men murder their wives instead, they lead one to ask: 'how is it that so few men kill their wives?'

Our conclusions support the consistent pattern of findings that have demonstrated that the phenomenon of wife killing often revolves around the woman threatening to or actually separating from her dating or marital partner. However, they also led us to diverge from the assumption that the murder of female partners is a phenomenon that can be explained by a single, central variable such as male possessiveness. The findings point to the need to understand the murder of women partners as a phenomenon anchored in a certain constellation of factors that combine and create the 'conditions for murder'. From this point of view, the murder of the woman cannot be explained only as the embodiment of the murderer's possessive personality; rather, it must be seen as the result of an interaction between the specific person and the specific context. Conditions of murder may be created when a relationship characterized by deep emotional dependence of the man on his wife, when love is experienced in terms of paternalism and shared identity, when separation is seen as loss of personal continuity, when masculine identity is defined in terms of power and control, and when a rigid personal disposition accompanies the dangerous realization of Romantic Ideology's central theme – 'without you I am nothing'.

Deciphering the context in which the idea of murder ripens until it is carried out illustrates that understanding the motivation behind the act in terms of 'sexual jealousy' or 'masculine possessiveness' is extremely simplistic and partial. Although conceptions of ownership and paternalism, and emotions such as jealousy and anger all play a role in the full range of factors that produce a readiness to take the life of a conjugal partner, it is more accurate to consider the motive for murder in terms of conditions that are propitious for the development of murderous violence, rather than in terms of one central personality variable.

The basis of the potential for murder can be characterized in dimensions of space and time. In the spatial dimension, in terms of content, the murder of wives is, as noted, the result of a combination of factors. A certain infrastructure gives rise to the potential for murderous violence. There are conditions of risk, many of which are part and parcel of Romantic Ideology, that combine and act together: when the woman is the man's whole world; when separation from her is conceived of as loss of identity, of self; when reality is emptied of other sources of significance; when the conception of masculinity, which dictates power, honor, and control, turns one's dependence on the woman into an experience of weakness and impotence, grasped as a humiliating blow to masculine pride; when the feeling of need is joined to rigidity of personality; when rigidity is combined with aggression; when aggression is justified by Romantic Ideology; and when love legitimizes the worst sort of actions, in the guise of a desirable social ideal. When all of these combine, conditions of high risk are present.

In the temporal dimension, the murder must be seen as the climax of a dynamic process, during which a psychological readiness matures, specifically, the willingness to take the wife's life. Our findings point to a dynamics of progress toward the deed over a period of weeks and months. That period is marked by continued affective states such as jealousy, anger, fear, depression, and despair, which shape a very powerful emotional framework for grasping reality. In this emotional context, the idea of murder ripens, gathers a feeling of realism, and advances toward implementation. That advancement involves certain or vague knowledge about what is going to happen, anxiety about the anticipated end, a feeling of sitting on a barrel of explosives, predicting imminent danger. Something horrible is about to happen.

The day of the murder is the day on which a spark ignites the explosive mass. As mentioned, the psychological willingness was already in place, and therefore neither the circumstances surrounding the day of the murder, nor the emotions accompanying the act can offer insight into the reason for the murder or shed light on the place from which it emerged. The traces of anger, as well as the traces of the murder, lead backwards in time.

To further understand the phenomenon of wife killing as the climax of a dynamic process and as an act intended to cause the woman's death, we turn now to analyze both the nature of the murder and the underlying state of mind of the murderer.

The nature of the murder – 'I don't believe in a one-time act'

> Don't be cruel, can't you see, how does it feel, babe, to kill our destiny.
>
> Scorpions

> Inside I felt, all the time, that I had bad feelings. I had feelings that something was going to happen.
>
> A murderer

One common dichotomy used to distinguish between various kinds of murders is the dichotomy between expressive and instrumental murders. An expressive murder is considered to be an act of rage characteristic of highly intensive relationships, whereas an instrumental murder is characterized as a means for achieving a goal, as an act involving rational decision-making, intention, and planning.[19]

The intensive emotional context surrounding the wife killings naturally provides an opening for regarding the murder as an expressive murder, as a crime of passion, a deed motivated by the heat of 'uncontrolled' emotions and anger. However, this classification is also a source for reduced responsibility, following the prevalent view which claims that emotions 'overcome us'.[20] From this viewpoint, attributing the murder to a powerful emotional situation gives rise to lenience toward the man who commits murder and lessens his guilt and responsibility. Such a man is perceived to be overpowered by an enormous force and, therefore, 'he loses control of himself' and does not act freely. This common view is shared not only by the murderers, who describe the event in terms of 'loss of control', but also the judicial system, which tends to be lenient towards acts defined as crimes of passion.

This lenience, the partial exemption from responsibility, motivates not only the murderers, who seize upon emotional 'loss of control' as a life buoy, but also the scholars who use it for the opposite purpose: to avoid the labeling of wife killing as a crime of passion, and demonstrating instead the instrumental and therefore rational essence of the murder.[21] However, the effort to reduce the role of emotion in favor of a greater role of instrumental behavior raises another problem: since the goal of male violence, according to the prevailing literature, is control of the wife *and not* her absolute destruction, the act of killing seems to undermine the murderer's goal and therefore cannot be regarded as rational. Hence, the effort to grasp both ends of the stick gives rise to a paradoxical explanation. On the one hand, in an effort to prevent lenience toward murderous men, it is proposed to view the act as one motivated by rational considerations, as a means to obtain an end; on the other hand, the crime is irrational in the sense that it undermines the goal that it is meant to obtain. Underlying the emotional–rational dichotomy is the view of emotion as a blind power that blocks sober thought and ignores consequences. The crime of passion is regarded as inconsistent with the presence of rational and cold calculations attributed to planning, intention, and awareness of the consequences of the action.

We argue that in fact most cases of wife killing are neither purely expressive nor purely instrumental. Most of them can be traced along a continuum, rather than a dichotomy, as they are expressive and instrumental, motivated by intense emotions but also characterized by planning, choice, and rational, conscious decision. To clarify the meaning of this argument, the question of the intention behind the deed will now be examined.

One of the dominant theories in this area, the evolutionary theory, argues that the murder of wives is motivated by male possessiveness, which is intended to control and not to kill. Killing, therefore:

> presents a challenge to the evolutionary psychological premise that motives and emotions are organized in such a way as to promote the actor's interests. Killing is 'spiteful' … moreover, if the utility of the motivational processes underlying violence against wives raises in property control, killing seems all the more paradoxical.[22]

The paradox lies in the fact that the adaptive function of coercion and control is not obtained by means of killing one's wife. The researchers' conclusion is that murder is an unintentional and unplanned byproduct, an epiphenomenal product, of violence that went too far. It is an unintended outcome of the use of violence, which was used to control and intimidate, but not to kill. Violence, in this view, is a dangerous game, prone to slippage.

However, the possibility that the wife's death was the unintended result of violence that, 'by mistake' overstepped its boundaries seems to be inconsistent with the phenomenon of overkill, in terms of the weapons used and the manner in which the murder was committed (the large number of stab wounds, for example), and which is characteristic of most cases in which wives were murdered.[23] It also raises the question of how male violence manages to avoid overstepping its boundaries except in the specific cases related either to separation or to sexual infidelity. If a murder is an act of 'a hand that slipped', how does the hand manage to avoid slipping except in response to a specific threat?

An alternate approach to the distinction between expressive and instrumental violence emphasizes the component of choice: the instrumentality and rational choice of violence.[24] According to this approach, every act causing damage is to be viewed as a means toward a goal, and all violent behavior is to be seen as the result of a choice, an intention, or a decision. Use of violence in the service of punishment, the restoration of just deserts, and revenge, is indeed an 'expressive' violence because it is motivated by anger, but it is also violence in service of a goal. The decision as to whether or not to kill stands on a solid foundation that evaluates the degree of punishment appropriate to the severity of the infraction. It is the intention, the choice, and the decision behind the behavior that helps us to understand why wife killing is a rare phenomenon, whereas violence against women is far more frequent. Murder is rare because the damage entailed in the loss of freedom is a sufficiently effective deterrent to prevent the act of murder.[25]

In almost every instance of wife killing studied so far, the violence was *intended* to cause the woman's death; wife killing, in most cases, is a premeditated act. Nevertheless, understanding of the murder as the product of choice and decision and not as a result of 'uncontrollable' anger or an accident cannot obscure the fact that the decision was made in a certain emotional environment, which was prevalent before and during the murder, and thus guided the various rational considerations. An emotion, or more precisely stated, an emotional episode, is not an isolated experience, but an ongoing one. An emotional episode shapes or colors our present and future attitudes and behavior.

Wife killing then is not merely an impulsive act, nor solely an expressive one. The murder is the result of a decision made in a very volatile emotional environment and after due considerations, among them the personal cost that will be borne by the murderer himself. The murderer does not ignore the issue of the expected social punishment; rather, his assessment of the anticipated penalty is made in an emotional context. The significance of the personal price to be paid is colored by depression and despair and by his inability to cope with the impending separation. Therefore, the pros and cons are interpreted through the man's emotional prism. Thus, while the decision to commit murder included a consideration of all the outcomes, including his own destiny, it was also a choice made in an emotional environment that made it appear adequate and justified, or at the very least inevitable, despite the personal cost.

The feelings of anger related to the specific cause of the murder were not without function. The anger produces the courage, provides the physical strength and the physical arousal needed for violence, diminishes sensitivity to pain, and justifies the punishment and revenge that follow in its wake.[26] Precisely because anger has such an obviously recognizable function, it raises the question whether and to what degree the anger was ignited by choice and intentionally. Despite the fact that emotions are usually generated spontaneously, people have the power to elicit a certain emotional state as a means for achieving a goal. Thus, for example, a husband might purposely recall the insult in order to ignite the feeling of rage before a physical confrontation.[27] The phenomenon of emotional management, the ability to ignite and nurture certain emotions for certain purposes, as well as the ability to turn them off by behavioral or interpretive means, also includes the possibility of cultivating a negative emotion by making a choice intended to strengthen it.[28]

Indeed, some of the testimonies indicate a conscious effort to kindle anger in two main ways: (a) by giving a negative interpretation to the woman's words or behavior, and (b) by purposely entering situations which could have been avoided. Whereas the avoidance of situations that arouse negative emotions is one of the most useful means of reducing emotional intensity, purposely entering such situations is a useful instrumental means for increasing emotional intensity. For example, the man may initiate a 'chance' meeting with the woman on the day the divorce is issued, 'just to talk to her'. Or he may suddenly appear at the woman's residence after nursing the kind of thoughts that kindle enormous anger. Or he may go to meet his wife after fostering high and impossible hopes of reuniting. At that point, the writing was on the wall. The event was ripe and ready to occur, suspended only in anticipation of the opportune moment.

To sum up, wife killing is considered to be a classic example of a 'crime of passion'. We argue that its emotional nature does not contradict its deliberative and purposeful one. While the emotions preceding the act play a role in shaping the underlying dynamic, they should not be considered a blind force that eliminates the ability to think rationally and prevents understanding of the meaning of the act and its enormous costs. What may often seem to be loss of control is in fact the fruit of premeditation. The murderer had control over his 'loss of control'.

The murderer's state of mind – 'There's no me without you'

> You told me everything would be fine, why am I losing my mind, how come I feel like a fool.

Toni Braxton

> I was a man on the brink of madness, and I didn't get any help. I couldn't function, and I didn't function ... You feel dread, fear ... At a certain stage, you just want to die. You're ripe for death.

A murderer

The social punishment for taking another person's life almost always translates into an overwhelming loss for the perpetrator, the loss of everything except for life itself. Suggesting that wife killing is an intentional act, chosen *despite* its predictably high cost, raises the question of the mental state of a man prepared to carry out such an act. For the murderer, this choice entails two simultaneous losses. Not unlike Samson's last words as he annihilated the Philistines, 'May my soul die with the Philistines', a man who murders destroys not only another person, but also himself. Our study suggests that the emotions that play a central role in the murder of wives is not uncontrollable anger or sexual jealousy, as claimed in the literature, but rather profound despair, the loss of hope and, indeed, the loss of love.

The literature tends to draw a distinction between cases in which the wife is murdered and those cases in which it is accompanied by the husband's suicide. This differentiation is anchored in an implicit categorization: murder that is not accompanied by the husband's suicide is classified as violence, and the focus of the event is the motivation to cause harm *to another person*, whereas a murder accompanied by the perpetrator's suicide is classified as part of the suicide, and the focus of the event is an attack against *the self*.[29] Murder accompanied by suicide is claimed to have a different etiological pattern from that characterizing murder alone. However, we consider such a distinction problematic, as it is not based on the mental state of the perpetrator or an in-depth analysis of the motivation in both scenarios; rather it is grounded in interpretation of a manifest behavior – the murderer's act of suicide. Observations regarding the nature of the deed of murder, combined with insights offered in the literature regarding motives, context, and the mental state of murderers who commit suicide suggest that the mental state of the wife murderer as it emerges from our study is similar to that of the murderer/suicide victim. Thus, for example, the testimony indicates that most of the acts of combined murder and suicide took place at the time of separation from the wife and against the background of that separation. It also points to the deliberate nature of the act and the prolonged feelings of deep depression, despair, anxiety, and jealousy that preceded it.[30]

Likewise, the explanations offered for the phenomenon of murder–suicide, although they focus less on understanding the motivation of violence against the wife and more on understanding the psychological processes during the period prior to the murder, show a mental state like the one identified among murderers who did *not* commit suicide. It is argued that the principal emotional pattern in relationships that lead to murder–suicide is a vacillation between anger and love. The man experiences himself as dependent on the object of love, and at the same time, he is deeply enraged by that dependency and his resulting vulnerability. From his point of view, separation from the wife traps him in an impossible situation: he is unable to be with her and at the same time, he experiences in very strong terms his own incapability to live without her. Relinquishing this relationship and letting go of this partner is surrendering himself. With an understanding that this loss is final, the murder, which is the partner's answer to the severing of the bond, often appears together with suicide, which serves as the final 'closing' act. Loss of the object of love, which is experienced as unbearable, arouses both anger and depression. The depression is bound up with a strong feeling of impotence. The murder and suicide are perceived as the only way out of a situation with no escape: the man cannot maintain his love, nor can he conceive of living without it.[31]

Other explanations that focus on the motivation for self-destruction suggest that the central process underlying the phenomenon is collapse of the meaning of life, along with absence of resources for coping.[32] The act of murder and suicide, from this point of view, is understood as resulting from the inter-action between external crises and the collapse of the self. The man perceives himself as losing his anchor on what is meaningful in life – typically, significant relationships or career, an experience that is accompanied by painful self-awareness expressed as negative emotions directed at the self, as well as cognitive rigidity, and a crisis in the familiar conception of self.

The conclusion is an inability to conceive of continuity of the self beyond the loss. The assumption that links these various theories is that the motivation for both murderous acts is rooted in an identity crisis which, when nourished by certain personal and contextual characteristics, entails destruction of the self. There can be two possible scenarios for this self-destruction. One is the murder, an act that destroys the wife, a component of the self, and to a lesser extent the perpetrator, who pays the cost of a personal and social penalty. The second scenario combines murder and suicide, where there is equal emphasis on destruction of the self.

Not all the cases of wife killing studied here fit the proposed insights into murder–suicide. Nevertheless, with respect to the emotional experience underlying and leading to the murder, it is difficult to ignore the similarity between murder–suicide and the processes described by a significant number of men who murdered their wives. The emotional patterns and the conception of reality experienced before the murder suggest that there may be no reason to distinguish between murderers who committed suicide and those who did not. Significantly, some of the interviewees in the present study reported repeated suicide attempts after the murder. However, as noted, this is not the central point of similarity between murderers who committed suicide and those who did not. The similarity is rooted in the psychological processes that preceded the murder and created an emotional context that prompted a willingness to commit such an extreme act, in which the destruction of another person entails the destruction of oneself.

To summarize, we propose to understand the murder as (a) an act intended to cause the wife's death and (b) the climax of a dynamic and gradual process culminating in an emotional state in which one seeks to destroy another person even at the cost of self-destruction. This approach suggests that the dynamic underlying wife killing is different from that which characterizes other manifestations of violence.

Wife killing has been studied and conceptualized as part of the phenomenon of violence toward women. The murder is often presented as the climax of a history of violence, as the end of a path marked by coercion, threats, possessiveness, and physical violence of the man towards the woman.[33] Consequently, the murderous violence is located at the extreme of a continuum of various manifestations of violence and is not regarded as a separate phenomenon demanding a different understanding and approach. According to the continuum approach, murder and violence share a common explanation: violence against women, in all its forms, including the murderous form, is the result of the effort to curtail women's independence by those who regard themselves as entitled to rule over a woman's life.[34]

The claim that physical violence precedes murder is, at least in some cases, not groundless. Clinical studies based on more detailed data have documented a history of violence and threats made by some of the men who murdered their victims.[35] The findings of the present study also suggest that some of the murders were preceded by physical violence, and almost all of them were preceded by manifestations of control, coercion, threats, harassment, stalking, psychological aggression, and other kinds of bullying. However, even if there is no doubt that most instances of murder are preceded by manifestations of brute force, and it is clear that murder by the husband is only rarely an isolated act of violence, it is also true that most cases of violence *do not* end in murder. Moreover, a wife's intention to leave a violent man only rarely leads to her murder. Indeed, most beaten wives leave their marriages, and most of those who do leave are not murdered.[36]

Wife killing is undoubtedly the most extreme manifestation of violence along a continuum of possible manifestations of violence, and some of the cases examined in the literature and in the present study have indeed documented a history of violent relations. Nevertheless, one may doubt the claim that murder and violence reflect the same motivation, share the same dynamic, and are characterized by the same risk factors. There are many characteristics and behaviors that are common among men who are murderers and those who are violent. Among these are coercion and brute force, a masculine identity interpreted in terms of power and control, emotional dependence on the woman, fear of rejection, vacillation between love and anger, and a feeling of the loss of power in the relationship. These features of violence are all well known in the literature. They are presented in the present study as well. However, the existence of shared traits does not indicate identity of motive, mood, context, emotional dynamics, or purpose. There is a single significant difference between murder and violence: the difference between life and death. The difference in the outcome – for the victim and for the attacker – is also basic to understanding the phenomenon.

Murder and violence must be thought of as separate phenomena, because their basic motivation is not the same. Violence toward women, according to the accepted view, is a strategy of control. It is behavior intended to obtain obedience and to express authority and power.[37] Murder cannot achieve such a goal. Murder is aimed at a different goal: the destruction of the wife. The different goal also gives rise to different explanations to be proposed, which should rely less on the motivation of control and more on the motivation to eliminate the object of love.

A noticeable component in the context distinguishing the act of murder is the woman's intention to leave, an element which is not necessarily present in cases of violence, but is far from marginal in the cases of murder. This fact is significant for three reasons: (a) it reinforces the understanding that murder is not the same as violence that 'mistakenly' overstepped its boundaries; (b) it raises the question of the emotional dynamics that can lead to an act of destroying the self with the other. Understanding violence as behavior seeking to attain obedience and understanding murder as an act intended to cause the wife's destruction distinguishes between the phenomena and is sufficient to point to the need for separate research.

This chapter discusses the question of how to understand the murder of women by their husbands. The literature in the field maintains that wife killing is motivated by male possessiveness that is expressed in a form of violence toward women that is extreme but not distinct from other expressions of violence. The findings of the present study, however, show that the basis for understanding wife killing is in identifying and acknowledging the rarity of the phenomenon; therefore, our understanding of wife killing is necessarily different from the understanding of the phenomenon of violence towards women. The act of murder is (a) rooted in a unique constellation of factors and circumstances, which together create the infrastructure for the development of murderous violence; (b) the result of a process, the fruit of emotional maturation that creates the psychological resolve needed in order to be able to commit murder, rather than a temporary loss of control, which ostensibly makes the killer unable to understand the consequences and costs of his act; (c) motivated by a mood of deep despair, which creates the desire to destroy another person, even at the cost of self-destruction; (d) a phenomenon distinct from violence against women.

Finally, understanding the loving attitudes that underlie the murderer's experiences, as well as those of all other people, requires a distinction between the complex sentiment of love and the specific, acute emotion of love. The sentiment may be expressed through various acute emotions, different feelings and behaviors. The sentiment may give rise to negative emotions, such as jealousy and anger, as well as to positive ones, such as compassion and sexual desire. Thus, we may say that a man murders his wife out of the sentiment of love and the acute emotions of hate or anger. At the moment that crimes of passion are committed, the acute emotion of love may not be present, but rather the sentiment of love. Accordingly, the act of murdering a beloved can only spring from the complex sentiment of love, but not from the acute emotion of love. The immediate cause in this context is probably a negative emotion such as hate, anger, or resentment; however, these negative emotions are part of the more profound attitude of love – the sentiment. Love then is present in the background of the murderous behavior, but is not its specific focus. In a somewhat similar manner, in the Mafioso tradition people constantly violate expectations and ideals and then get murdered. However, those who ordered the murder often say: 'I love this person very much'. In many cases of wife killing, the act was premeditated and well-planned. The murderers set the stage to create the circumstances that can spontaneously trigger the negative emotions associated with love. In a sense, these are cases of cold-blooded – yet spontaneous – murders. The act may have been carried out at the spur of the moment, but it had already been envisioned beforehand.

In terms of the legal viewpoint, our suggested approach addresses the following two claims that are often put forth by the perpetrator: (a) the act of murder was somehow motivated by love, and (b) the murder was done in the heat of passion. Both claims could be raised in order to mitigate the punishment; however, it should be noted that they seem to contradict each other. The first statement refers to a larger set of circumstances associated with the relationship, which includes the weeks and months preceding the murder. In this context, the sentiment of love is part of the murderer's experience; however, if this prior history of love extends into the future and has a bearing on the murder, then surely the roots of the murder itself also reach back into the past. Yet the second claim refers to the moment of the murder, suggesting a seemingly spontaneous act committed in the heat of passion, out of rage rather than love. Clearly, the two claims cannot coincide. Therefore, an attempt may be made to use the heat of passion claim to mitigate the punishment, but if the act was also related to love, then it is also the outcome of a prior design that was feeding on negative emotions. In any case, the claim that the murder stemmed out of love does not, of course, justify the murder, nor should it imply a mitigated punishment.

Chapter 5

Boundaries of the possible

'Never give up on a good thing'

There never seems to be enough time, to do the things you want to do.

Jim Croce

I am in love with you, you set me free.

Beyonce

Human life concerns not only – or even mainly – the present, but rather, and to a significant extent, the realm of imagined possibilities. The fundamental human capacity of imagining the possible does not merely reveal reality, but often disregards it as well. The advantage of following the precepts of Romantic Ideology, which encourages us to overcome human limitations, is that it motivates us to do our best, and in this sense it compliments human nature. However, abiding by this ideology can be risky when preoccupation with imagined possibilities overcomes regard to reality: thus Romantic Ideology runs counter to the human characteristic of compromising with and accommodating oneself to reality.

The realm of potential possibilities is promising, but risky as well. To guide our walk through this unknown territory we have created boundaries that eliminate those options that seem immoral or risky. In many circumstances, these boundaries may be suitable as general guidelines, but they cannot cover all the various circumstances. Accordingly, overstepping the boundaries seems inevitable. This chapter deals with romantic possibilities and boundaries and our coping with the predicaments associated with them.

Fly, baby, fly – 'Knocking on heaven's door'

Fly on the wings of love, fly baby fly.

Olsen Brothers

I wish you'd hold me in your arms, like that Spanish guitar, all night long, all night long.

Tony Braxton

Our discussion of Romantic Ideology and the murderers' love has revealed a feature common to both: the belief in the totality of love and the refusal to take account of reality by making compromises. Love transcends reality and therefore it is reality that should change in accordance with such love. Indeed, people often say that love has shown them a new world that was previously closed to them. As Lisa said about her lover, 'My love for him is so huge; it has no boundaries whatsoever; it reaches the sky and beyond. He is my great, great eternal wonderful love. I love him beyond any words I can find to describe'. In idealized love there is no place for compromises, as love conquers all; there is no moderation in love, since love sets you on fire. And there can be no boundaries in idealized love, as there is 'no mountain high enough to stop my love for you, babe'. In this connection, Rosa, a single mother, says,

> I am a firm believer in moderation. Yet I don't think there is moderation in love (which is infinite) but there is moderation in the attachment to it, the desire for it, the cravings, the possessiveness, and addiction – which are all spin-offs but not love itself. In love, I don't want to have to feel careful. I want total abandon if that is what I feel. In many areas of my life, although it requires vigilance, I am able to stay quite balanced. But when it comes to my thinking about love, I cannot find moderation.

Lovers describe their experience as boundless love which makes them fly while knowing they will never fall. Such an unconditional and uncompromising attitude is common, as it stems from the human wish to overcome our basic limitations. Compromises, moderation, and boundaries are possible, and even necessary, when it comes to the implementation of pure love. The Western self-help culture is obsessed with the idea that there is a difference between the myth of love and its reality and that the implementation of true love must involve compromise and moderation. It has become one of the most common clichés about love, shared by psychologists and ordinary people.

The metaphor of touching the sky is common to many love songs. One song indicates: 'Got the wings of heaven on my shoes'. Another song states: 'I believe I can fly, I believe I can touch the sky'. And Frank Sinatra asks: 'Fly me to the moon, And let me play among the stars'. Lovers indeed describe their situation as if they touch the sky whenever they think about the beloved. In believing that we can fly and touch heaven's gates, we express the profound wish underlying Romantic Ideology – to overcome human limitations and live the way we want to. However, the attempt to overcome human limitations can turn into the wish to disregard human nature and reality. The flight to the moon is not merely unachievable for most people, but is also dangerous. It is one thing to ignore various unpleasant aspects of life and quite another to believe you can overcome fundamental human limitations. It is the latter belief that is assumed by Romantic Ideology and the murderers. Taking into account the impossibility of flying with the wings of heaven to the moon, and the danger in believing that we nevertheless can do it, raises the question of whether such a flight is actually the only desirable option open to lovers.

The risk in accepting the tenets of Romantic Ideology affects not only those men who may find the ideology supportive of their horrible murders, but also the vast majority of people who are disappointed when failing to fulfill this ideal and consider themselves and their relationships a failure. If indeed the total and uncompromising nature of Romantic Ideology has an increasingly negative impact, we should examine whether other options are available. Can a more realistic and comprising ideology of love, in which we cannot fly to the moon, be an attractive – yet plausible – option? This will be examined in the next two chapters, after analyzing, in this chapter, the nature of limitations, boundaries, ideals, and compromises associated with romantic relationships.

We begin this chapter by examining one of our greatest advantages over other animals: our capacity to imagine circumstances which are different from the present ones. Through imagination we can liberate ourselves from the captivity of the present and are able to fly to the moon. Imagination has its own risks – it unchains us from the limits of the present, but chains us to the prospect of the possible. Coping with such a risk is both a normative and a cognitive task: it requires us to establish a normative order of priority and to know the available alternatives. This task is expressed in establishing boundaries and ideals. Boundaries convey what we should not do; they provide us with a comfort zone in which our behavior is acceptable. Ideals are something we usually cannot entirely fulfill, but they are a beacon showing us where to go. Whereas boundaries limit and curb our desires and behavior, ideals nourish and encourage us to develop in certain manners. It is evident that we cannot entirely fulfill our ideals. Although less evident, it is also extremely difficult to always remain within the limited zone delineated by our boundaries, as only dead fish swim with the stream. Our attitude toward prevailing ideals and boundaries, and the way we manage their differences, are crucial features of our self-identity.

Enslaved by the possible – 'Ready for the times to get better'

Pretty women ought to be left to men without imagination.

Marcel Proust

Take my hand, I'm a stranger in paradise, all lost in a wonderland.

Tony Bennett

Imagination may be broadly characterized as a capacity to consider possibilities that are not actually present to the senses. In this broad characterization, which is epistemological in nature, memory and thought are types of imagination, since in both we consider such possibilities. A narrower characterization of imagination, which is useful in distinguishing imagination from other mental capacities, adds an ontological criterion to imagination: imagination refers to nonexistent events – or at least those believed to be such. Although this capacity may exist in a rudimentary form in animals – mainly in higher mammals and mostly concerning circumstances in the past and the present – the more complex form of this capacity is present only in humans.[1]

In the narrow sense then, imagination refers to an object that is not present to the senses and has never existed (or at least, on the basis of our current knowledge, has a very low probability of existing). This type of imagination can be further divided into two kinds: (a) the subject does not know about the falsity of the imagined content, and (b) the subject knows about the falsity of the imagined content. The first type includes cases of hallucinations, illusions, and simple mistakes. In the second type, which may be termed 'counterfactual imagination', the imaginary content is false and is known to be so. This type involves fantasies and reference to alternatives that could have occurred.[2] The significance in our life of the second type of imagination can be gauged from the impact of various forms of art upon our life. Art often describes events that do not actually exist, but are vividly presented.

Imagination has several major functions: (a) it helps us understand our environment and prepares us for future situations, (b) it helps us manage our affective attitudes, and (c) it encourages creativity. Although imagination may frequently be connected with illusion and self-deception, it is often advantageous in helping us understand and cope with the harsh reality around us. Imagination involves cognitive exercises, which can lead to a more reliable understanding of real situations and events. The advantage of being able to rehearse our response to imaginary events improves our chances of survival. For example, if a dangerous situation is first imagined and then experienced, we may be able to avoid the danger, instead of merely reacting to it. Imagination can also motivate us to pursue positive goals, rather than waiting passively for things to happen. Imagination has also the affective function of managing, and typically in improving, our emotional states. When daydreaming about the future, people tend to imagine themselves succeeding rather than failing. We further believe that we are more likely than the average person to live longer, stay married longer, have a gifted child, suffer less from a heart attack, and have a brighter future.[3] Occasionally, a harsh encounter with reality can be so painful as to prevent us from functioning properly; imagination can provide a necessary compensatory channel, making life more tolerable and less stressful. In such cases, the contents of our imaginings express our own nature more than that of the object.[4]

The imaginative capacity also underlies creativity and innovation, which involve crossing accepted boundaries. It is obvious then that higher forms of imagination involve more than merely perceptual capacities – they must involve a considerable amount of intellectual activity. Thus, if seduction entails a lot of imaginary activities, then you need to be smart to seduce. Indeed, intelligence is one of the most desired traits men look for in women.[5] This does not mean that in love we necessarily use the same logic or considerations used in scientific reasoning – on the contrary, people often say that when they are in love they feel like an idiot. It merely means that some kind of logic, as well as considerations of reality, is also present in love. Emotions have their own logic.[6]

We can overcome present difficulties by imagining possible desirable circumstances; in this manner we may also become aware of the shortcomings of certain possible imagined scenarios and the greater or lesser likelihood of their materializing. It is difficult to act without considering the infinite possibilities – what may be and what might have been. The imaginative capacity forces us to be concerned not only with the present circumstances, but also with past and future circumstances. Indeed, people think about the future more than about the past or the present. Many potential events are more pleasurable to imagine than to experience.[7] Imagination facilitates our flight from one such set of circumstances to another. The constant play between the actual and the potentially possible can generate profound emotional dissonances. A view in the Jewish tradition states that 'In the world to come, each person will have to account for anything that his eyes saw but he did not eat'.[8] In other words, the 'road not taken' is as significant as the one we ultimately choose. The more prevailing, conservative view, however, stresses the importance of not letting the imagination lead us beyond the limits of the normative. Both views express the problematic nature of the relationship between the potential and the actual situation.

The realm of potential possibilities considerably increases the importance of including a comparison in our quest to make a choice. When taking decisions in the present we constantly compare the present to possible alternatives. Thus, one employee may be satisfied and even genuinely happy with a 5 percent raise if he had expected a smaller salary increase, whereas his coworker may be disappointed with an 8 percent increase if he had expected more. Similarly, people assess their own lives more positively if a disabled person is present in the room.[9] The act of comparison that underlies the emotional significance attributed to an event encompasses a mental construction of an alternative situation.

The more available the alternative – or otherwise stated – the closer the imagined alternative is to being realized, the more intense the emotion.[10] The importance of the availability of an alternative is well illustrated in a study on singles bars: as closing time approached, men and women viewed the opposite sex as increasingly attractive. The looming possibility of going home alone increased the value of those that were present.[11] The Internet has considerably extended our notions of what we might consider possible. Cyberspace is the land of unlimited possibilities. You can be emotionally rich in no time, but you can also suffer many painful experiences and never reach the Promised Land.

The notion of the availability of alternatives may explain many seemingly puzzling situations, such as people who remain in unfulfilling marriages or jobs. Although their satisfaction from the present situation is low, these people perceive other possible alternatives to be even worse.[12] The other direction is found as well: people leave reasonable present situations for unknown risky ones; this is because in the comparison, the evaluation of possible alternatives often supersedes those of existing positions. We have become slaves to the possible and spoilers of the present. Since the realm of infinite possibilities so overwhelms us with tempting alternatives, we are not able to reasonably consider the present and existing alternatives. We tend to bow to the lure of immediate and ever-changing possibilities and neglect the more stable aspects of the present and the long-term future. An example of this phenomenon comes from a study in which two groups of men were asked to look at photographs: one group was shown highly attractive women, and the other, women of average attractiveness. Asked about their own partners afterwards, the men of the former group judged their own partners as less attractive than did the men from the latter group. Moreover, those who had viewed the more attractive women subsequently rated themselves as less committed, less satisfied, less serious, and less close to their partners compared to the self ratings of the men of the other group.[13]

The capacity to imagine different situations, either better or worse, enriches our mental life and makes it much more complex. In the movie *Adaptation*, John Laroche (Chris Cooper) says that he likes plants so much because they are so mutable; adaptation in his view is a profound process helping you to figure out how to thrive in the world. A married woman, Susan Orlean (Meryl Streep), responds that adaptation is easier for plants, as they have no memory, 'They just move on to whatever's next. With a person though, adapting is almost shameful. It's like running away'. Plants also do not have expectations for the future, and in general they lack the imaginative power; hence, they cannot consider values and possible alternatives. Referring to the potentially possible enables us not only to postulate moral ideals and rules, but also to undermine them by imagining ways to violate them. Our concern with comparison, which is generated from our ability to refer beyond the present, causes us to believe that the neighbor's grass is greener and deprives us of the possibility of being happy with our own lot. Sometimes, people overrate the weight of negative events in order to avoid them. Thus, healthy people imagine that 83 states of illness would be 'worse than death', and yet people who are actually in those states rarely take their own lives. Our psychological system tends to seek a balance that allows us to feel sufficiently satisfied about our situation, but bad enough to do something about its negative aspects.[14]

A common imaginary means for creating a better environment is that of positive illusions. Illusions refer to something that actually does not exist now; positive illusions are a kind of idealization of the present situation. Because our experiences are inherently ambiguous, finding the positive perspective is often simple.[15] The mechanism underlying positive illusions is often a kind of a filter for screening out negative information and thereby enabling us to perceive a better environment. Illusions, whether positive or negative, involve distorting reality and this can be harmful in certain circumstances. Moreover, imagination is usually effortless and works so quietly and effectively that we are insufficiently skeptical of its content. Although having an undistorted picture of reality is important for survival purposes, having an idealized picture may sometimes be advantageous as well. However, only a moderate and balanced dose of positive illusions can be beneficial.[16]

Two major types of illusions can be discerned: (a) an illusion whose content is factually false, and (b) an illusion whose content may materialize, but the probability of such a development is very slim. Concerning Romantic Ideology, we may say that beliefs such as 'you are everything to me', 'all you need is love', 'love can overcome all obstacles', 'we are fused into a single entity', 'you are irreplaceable', and 'love can do no evil' are, at least in their extreme forms, illusions of the first type. More moderate formulations can turn them into illusions of the second type, where the illusory aspect refers merely to the chances of fulfillment. Such is the belief that love can maintain the same intensity for as long as one lives, or that one will never love or desire another person.

Positive illusions are central to romantic love. Lovers are often blind to the beloved's negative traits and tend to create an idealized image of the beloved. We often love the idealized object rather than the real one. Indeed people say that they are living their dreams with their beloved. Idealization of the beloved is more typical of love at first sight and the initial stages of love, when spontaneous evaluations are based on little information. Sustaining a sense of security often requires weaving an elaborate, and often fictional, story that either embellishes a partner's virtues and overlooks, or at least minimizes various faults. Accordingly, some happily married couples avoid unpleasant topics, lie about their feelings, and deny their own or their spouse's statements. Enhancing a partner's qualities seems critical for maintaining the belief that this partner is the 'right one' and for protecting the relationship from doubt. This is not faking, but rather "making belief," or "as if" attitudes.[17]

The important role that positive illusions play in making romantic relationships more satisfying and less distressing does not imply that there is no place in such relationships for accurate understanding of the partners' real strengths and frailties. It is obvious that profound illusions can easily generate disappointments, which may ruin the entire relationship. A love based on the false premise that all of the partner's traits are perfect will inevitably prove to be fragile. In fact, spouses who entertain such a premise put their partners in the uncomfortable position of having to live up to an identity that by definition they can never uphold. There is evidence that the contrast between high expectations for intimacy and disappointing realities leads to suicides. The type of intimate relationship most commonly found among suicidal women involved male denial of affection, that is, the women expected normal levels of intimacy, but the male partners were uncaring and withdrawn. In the next most common pattern, the women had extreme and unrealistic expectations for intense intimacy, whereas the male partners offered only normal levels, which again fell short of the women's standards.[18] Romantic relationships require then a sort of combination between positive illusions and accurate knowledge.

A plausible combination, which is in accordance with some other claims presented here, has been proposed by Neff and Karney.[19] As explained previously, they propose a model that combine global adoration and specific accuracy, arguing that although spouses may demonstrate a positive bias in their global perceptions of their partners, which serves to protect their own sense of satisfaction, they nevertheless may have a more accurate perception of their partners' specific attributes. For instance, spouses who believe their partners to be wonderful people may be willing to perceive their partners as unorganized or as poor cooks. Given that there are fewer clear and objective standards for evaluating global attributes than for evaluating specific attributes, spouses have the latitude to place their partners in a more positive light. Whereas spouses may find it easy to support the claim that their partners are wonderful, they may find it more difficult to support the belief that their partners are well organized. Positive illusions or enhancement of certain qualities are not necessarily an outright denial of reality but rather are likely to expand on a kernel of truth. That is, spouses may enhance their overall description of their partners and yet be able to demonstrate a relatively accurate understanding of their partners' specific qualities. Trust in a spouse's love may be particularly high when global adoration is accompanied by specific accuracy, because spouses are thus communicating that they love their partners despite being able to recognize their faults. Findings indeed indicate that the latter individuals are those who provide their partners with a 'true' love that is likely to last longer. Love grounded in specific accuracy appears to be more resilient than love lacking in such accuracy.[20]

Eva Illouz argues that romantic love has such a long-lasting powerful grip on us because, among other things, 'love is a privileged site for the experience of utopia … love contains a utopian dimension that cannot easily reduced to "false consciousness" or to the presumed power of "ideology" to recruit people's desires'.[21] Imagination is also central in sexual desires, as it offers an effective way of coping with personal limitations, normative boundaries, and external constraints. One can always fantasize the most outrageous encounters done in exactly the way one wants and with precisely those who one most desires. Given the affective powers of imagination, it is no wonder that many women say they can achieve orgasm by fantasy alone, with no physical stimulation at all.[22] In Fisher's study of lovers, about 70 percent said that they fantasize while making love.[23]

Imagination and positive illusions can easily lead to self-deception. Many divorcees testify that they cannot understand how they overlooked their partner's characteristics.[24] This failure is not necessarily due to misperception of the beloved's traits; it may stem from attributing too little weight to these characteristics. Most married people are able to indicate their partner's character defects, physical defects, and bad habits. Moreover, we may love an evil person, an unintelligent person, an aesthetically unpleasant person, or an arrogant person while knowing this person to be so.[25] The epistemic change of gaining additional negative information about the other person does not necessarily lead to separation. However, if love is to be sustained, this epistemic change must be accompanied by an evaluative change compensating for the new negative information.

Although imagination can overcome various human limitations and boundaries, it is limited as well. We cannot imagine whatever we desire.[26] It is, of course, easier to imagine than to do, but even imagination requires certain conditions in order to take place; thus, the envisioned situation must be imagined in such a way that one can identify with it. Imagination does not completely ignore reality; rather it ignores certain aspects of it and improves other aspects. Imaginary sex, such as cybersex, overcomes the lack of physical touch by improving the activities involved in the act. It does this not by disassociating from regular sexual activities, but rather by imitating some of these performances in an improved manner. An exciting imagination places us in a certain environment and considerably improves it. We must remember, however, that because of the illusory aspect in the imaginary content, imagination can facilitate disappointment and despair.[27]

The play between imagination and reality is then complex. Consider, for example, the fact that while having sex many people fantasize about a different person than their current partner. This may be the case even when the person in their arms is the one they really want to be with. In these circumstances, people improve their affective state by imagining what they consider to be a better alternative. The woman who fantasizes about another man – even a faceless man – while having sex with her partner may love her partner, but still he is not the person she craves to have sex with. The wish to have the delightful feeling of sexual satisfaction often requires the help of the imagination, which transforms the current mundane circumstances into what is perceived to be a heavenly experience.

In light of the complexity typical of love and the fact that lovers are often unwilling to face reality, self-deception and mistakes are to be expected. We can be wrong in identifying the beloved's attitude, since the person can easily fake or hide true emotions. We can also be wrong in identifying our own attitude, one reason being that sexual desire can be confused with romantic love. This is especially true in the first stages of romantic love, when sexuality plays a dominant role. Imagination can be harmful, insofar as it may ignore or distort actual circumstances. Thus, constantly imagining positive situations may induce an unrealistic degree of optimism, which will generate frequent and profound frustration.

We can see that the use of imagination and idealization, which is so crucial to Romantic Ideology, is prevalent in other realms of life. The important issue in this regard is whether we maintain an awareness of our own limitations, not only in our life in general, but also specifically, in our implementation of Romantic Ideology. If one does not follow this caveat, then this ideology can be, as we have seen in the case of the murderers, quite dangerous.

Realizing our limitations – 'Nothing you confess could make me love you less'

I'd rather have a Paper Doll to call my own than have a fickle-minded real live girl.

The Mills Brothers

Don't go changing, to try and please me …
I could not love you any better,
I love you just the way you are.

Billy Joel

Imagination makes us aware of our limitations in relation to situations and norms we cannot achieve. Accordingly, the gap between our desires and our present circumstances constitutes a profound human predicament, and our attitude towards this predicament constitutes a significant component of our personal make-up.

The present is a kind of a confining shelter: it protects us from possible threatening events, but it also prevents us from enjoying possible favorable events. Leaving our narrow shelter forces us to cope not only with actual circumstances, but with possible ones as well. The existence of infinite possibilities emphasizes our deficiencies and limitations, since any number of these possibilities could be better than the situation at hand. Imagination can make us acutely aware of desirable situations that are beyond our reach: morally improper situations, as well as undesirable but inevitable situations. Knowledge of such possibilities and of our inability to either approach or avoid them entails awareness of our basic human limitations. Rosa, a single mother, is involved in an affair with a married man but nevertheless insists that because of moral reasons, she typically 'did not feel attracted to married men'. Rosa expresses her grasp of the limitation resulting from the gap between her desires and her circumstances thus:

> As long as I stay with the present gifts of our relationship (and there are so many), and I don't wander into fantasies about the future, I am much happier. I value our relationship and I would not try to terminate it just because of its built-in limitations. I am simply trying to navigate appropriately.

The disparity between our human desires and our actual experiences is expressed in several incongruities: (a) We are aware of desirable experiences that we want but may not have; (b) We are aware of undesirable experiences that we do not want but may eventually have; (c) We are aware of desirable experiences that we can have, but do not want to pursue. The first two incongruities clearly express human constraints; the third is related to our need to have a normative set of priorities. The first incongruity stems from the fact that we have limited capacities and resources but unlimited desires. The second one often relates to actual physical deficiencies, such as old age or our mortality, which inevitably involve extremely undesirable aspects. The third incongruity is due to the fact that there are inherent contradictions in our values and occasionally we must reject certain valued experiences in order to achieve others, which we value even more.

The first incongruity typical of human beings is that we desire much more than we actually have or may have. This incongruity is related to the fact that we have limited capacities and finite resources, but our desires are practically almost infinite and limitless. Given this incongruity, many human desires are doomed to remain unfulfilled and yet the mind tends to be on the road trying to materialize some of those unfulfilled desires. Human existence becomes a kind of unfinished business involving a never-ending, unsuccessful struggle to overcome our limitations. Schopenhauer claims that 'all happiness depends on the proportion between what we claim and what we receive ... all suffering really results from the want of proportion between what we demand and expect and what comes to us'.[28] Indeed, narrowing the gap between what we desire and what we have in reality is often done by compromising our desires, or more broadly stated, changing our view and expectations of reality, a relatively intelligent choice, since changing reality is much harder. The shift in attitude can be done either by assuming a better knowledge of reality and thereby eliminating unrealistic desires, or by detaching ourselves from reality, thereby eliminating the desires related to it. Various philosophers, such as the Stoics, Spinoza, and Schopenhauer, discussed the former approach, while Buddhism seems to recommend the latter.

Spinoza, who praises the value of accurate knowledge of reality, argues that the wise man

> who rightly knows that all things follow from the necessity of the divine nature, and happen according to the eternal laws and rules of nature, will surely find nothing worthy of hate, mockery or disdain, nor anyone whom he will pity.[29]

In accordance with the Stoics, Schopenhauer argued that only proper (intellectual) knowledge could abolish the difference between what we expect (in light of our desire) and what real life can provide. Such knowledge should also involve recognition of the temporary nature of the human experience. Hence, 'every keen pleasure is an error, an illusion, since no wish attained can permanently satisfy'. Overcoming the first incongruity can be done, according to this view, only by eliminating our desires and emotions: 'Therefore the wise man always holds himself aloof from jubilation and sorrow'.[30] Buddhism recommends facing the incongruity between what we desire and what we have by adopting the attitude of complete detachment from actual reality, which is expressed by even-mindedness and impartiality toward all conditional things. This approach does not propose ways to cope with reality, but rather suggests mentally abandoning it. However, this can also be viewed as trying to gain profound knowledge of reality by distancing oneself from its marginal aspects, which typically generate intense emotions. In this sense then, this approach also advocates proper knowledge of reality as a means for abolishing one's desires.

Both of these approaches may be effective, but they are highly costly and difficult to achieve. Thus, Schopenhauer suggests that it is hope that 'begets and nourishes the wish' – hence, it follows that all wishes would die and could 'beget no more pain, if no hope nourishe[d] them'.[31] Losing hope is a dear price to pay. A significant reduction in emotional sensitivity likewise may be harmful, as many of the emotions carry out a function that is important to our survival. Accordingly, rather than attempt to eradicate emotional sensitivity and hope, we should strive to moderate their intensity. Just as it is not advisable to cut off your head to get rid of headaches, it is not advisable to eliminate our hopes and desires to get rid of the predicament of their incongruity with reality. Coping with our inability to fulfill all our hopes and wishes while remaining sensitive to ourselves and our environment requires accepting our limited abilities. Since satisfaction is derived from, among other things, fulfilling our needs, it requires a distinction between the hopes and desires that we can fulfill and those we cannot.

The second incongruity, that is, recognizing that undesirable experiences that we do not want will eventually occur in our lives, is clearly expressed in our transient existence and bodily deterioration in old age. Our imaginative capacity enables us to refer not only to a prosperous future, but to a depressing one as well. We can, for instance, imagine ourselves living happily ever after, but we are aware that life is brief and death is imminent. People can imagine themselves young forever, and yet they are aware that they will get older. This incongruity is also expressed in believing in something which is highly unlikely, for instance, believing that the initial great intense romantic passion will remain the same forever. Imagining a dark future or terrifying events is part and parcel of human life.

The third incongruity, which refers to what we can attain but do not want to pursue, stems from our need to establish a normative set of priorities to govern our behavior. If the previous type of incongruity is characterized by wanting more than we can have, in this type, we reject something that we can have. As already noted, desires may remain unfulfilled due to limited capacities, scarce resources, and external barriers; however an additional reason is an inherent incongruity in our complex sets of values, when we value and desire things that are not compatible. Thus, people may enjoy smoking but do not pursue this enjoyable activity because of its health risk. A married person's decision not to have an affair is another example of a normative decision not to pursue something desirable. Moral dilemmas express a situation in which we have two incompatible values that cannot be simultaneously maintained. The issue of loyalty and justice is such an example. One may discover some criminal activity of a good friend, but out of loyalty decide not to report the case to the police. The decision to torture terrorists is another example of violating a certain value in order to maintain another.

Moral conflicts such as the above force us to establish a set of priorities, which implies choosing not to pursue things or activities that are valuable or desirable to us. We are able to choose to reject what we desire or to violate what we value only because we are capable of imagining its future negative effect on things that we value even more. To say that not all values are compatible is to say that they cannot all be realized simultaneously, not that they cannot all simultaneously be regarded as valuable. Hence, we may not pursue all of them together, but still believe in their adequacy.[32] Establishing an order of preference, which is an essential human activity, often implies violating normative boundaries. In this sense, we may speak about the pain of choice, which is so typical of human experience.

The above incongruities, which emphasize the limitations and deficiencies of human life, generate profound human predicaments along the axes of the actual and the potentially possible on the one hand and the desirable and undesirable on the other. The presence of such incongruities generates intense negative and positive emotions. Realizing the presence of unavailable desirable experiences or inevitable undesirable experiences is frustrating and distressing. However, the presence of imaginable desirable experiences can divert our attention from these harsh realities and make us feel better.

The perceived importance of love and its intoxicating feeling may cause people to overlook human limitations. For example, people may think that their love can be indiscriminate. However, as Frankfurt argues, only for an infinite being such as God, who has no limitations, can love be simultaneously intimate and indiscriminate; only God can love everyone. God can fulfill all his desires without fear of loving unwisely; God need not be cautious about his love. Unlike the safe, indiscriminate love of God, we are vulnerable creatures whose love must be limited. Hence, we must invest ourselves in love wisely. We must set boundaries, and 'maintain a defensive selectivity and restraint'.[33] It was said that God revenges human beings by letting them fulfill all their desires. Fulfilling all our desires places us in the position of God, but since we lack the resources of God, and since, unlike God, we are bound by limitations, fulfilling all our desires can be quite harmful for us.

Setting and violating boundaries – 'Promise me you'll try'

She smiled at me on the subway.
She was with another man.
But I won't lose no sleep on that, 'cause I've got a plan.

James Blunt

I'm in love with you baby, I'm gonna break every rule.

Tina Turner

It ain't no sin if you crack a few laws now and then. As long as you don't break any.

Mae West

In everyday life, the notions of 'limitations' and 'boundaries' may be used interchangeably; in this context, however, we usually use the first to refer to natural deficiencies, such as our inability to fly like a bird, and the second to refer to normative and social conventions, such as perceiving extramarital affairs to be forbidden. The notion of limitations generates less opposition, as there is nothing to do against such constraints. Other types of boundaries can generate heated disputes concerning their value and the possibility of violating them. When married people say 'Don't fence me in!', they refer to conventional boundaries rather than to natural limitations.

Drawing boundaries is essential for human society: living with other people requires some regulation of our activities. As Helen Keller said:

Keep in mind that you are always saying 'no' to something. If it isn't to the apparent, urgent things in your life, it is probably to the most fundamental, highly important things. Even when the urgent is good, the good can keep you from your best, keep you from your unique contribution, if you let it.

The issue of moral values is related to the distinction between ideals that we aspire to realize and those we should avoid despite the fact that we find them desirable. Boundaries express our set of normative priorities, but boundaries are also the source of the most frequent and fundamental acts of violence. Given that our personal and collective identities are informed and defined by the values and conventions we accept, it is clear that boundaries have a significant function in our lives, and when they are violated, the unity of our identity is threatened. The significance of boundaries is expressed also in the fierce reaction against those who violate them. To protect our identity we both suffer and commit the most horrific atrocities.[34] However, neither the setting of boundaries nor the effort of maintaining the values protected by them necessarily require acts of violence. Nevertheless, it is often the case that collective identities, such as religion, nationality, race, and marriage, draw on the option of violence for precisely these purposes.

Desires are broad in their scope (we want more than what we can have or believe we should have), not very organized (lacking a clear order of priority and frequently incompatible), and often unrelated to external constraints. As previously indicated, they reflect our wish to overcome basic human limitations and inadequacies. Boundaries have various degrees of depth and flexibility. The boundaries that prohibit murder are more profound and less flexible than those that prohibit lying. Boundaries are particularly important when existential threats are evident. In modern times, however, when existential concerns are less pronounced, normative boundaries become more flexible. The mounting sense of dissatisfaction with the current boundaries significantly challenges their content. While the critique weakens some of these boundaries, it does not necessarily eliminate them, since boundaries are essential for human existence. Accordingly, the interesting question is not whether we are heading towards a future world without boundaries, but rather what types of boundaries will prevail in the future, and what is the justification for keeping these and rejecting others.[35]

The normative boundaries that prevent us from engaging in desirable activities are typically contrary to the spontaneous inclinations that express our momentary desire; if the norms were in accordance with these, no boundaries would be necessary. In this sense, boundaries are highly inconvenient, but they also protect us and in this sense they generate pleasant feelings of comfort and security. Boundaries are necessary for leading normal everyday life. They clarify the zone in which we are supposed to be. Ideals are like positive beacons, signaling the direction in which we should head; boundaries indicate the lines we should not cross. While animals exhibit desires, only humans exhibit the desire to have certain kinds of desires but not others. This self-reflexive aspect of emotional life inevitably generates conflict among our various desires as well as between our desires and other values.

Boundaries are related also to another basic human feature, namely, ambition. We want more than we can get and more than we are morally entitled to have. The positive aspect of the wish to violate boundaries is expressed in the following saying from the Jewish tradition, 'If it were not for evil desire, would man build a house, marry a wife, or have children?'[36] This desire to transcend boundaries is inevitable, as moral rules often forbid that which people most desire. The natural desire for the forbidden is so great that in some societies the law permits something that can yield the same 'taste' of the forbidden sexual pleasure and in exceptional circumstances even the forbidden deed itself.[37] For others, however, it is the very postulation of boundaries that drives them to override them, as this framework threatens their autonomy. To prove their autonomy and self-worth, they defy social boundaries, by using drugs, shoplifting, or speeding. These people, who also disregard reality, challenge the very existence of boundaries and not a particular type of boundary.

As our normative boundaries are constitutive of our personality, ignoring them is tantamount to a failure to uphold our intrinsic dignity at a time when our central values are abused. The risk in such behavior is not limited to the possibility of being caught and punished, as the infringement of these boundaries often has not only moral but also legal implications, but also includes the risk of an internal crisis, which threatens to ruin the foundations of our self-identity. Accordingly, there is pride in the ability to maintain boundaries when confronting obvious temptations. Mahatma Gandhi demonstrated this point by routinely inviting to his bed beautiful young women with whom he would then sleep naked. In the morning, he reassured his wife (and himself) about his dignity, for he had withstood the temptation to make love.[38]

The relation between ideals and boundaries on the one hand and freedom on the other hand is complex. Ideals and boundaries imply that some things are more significant than others; in other words, ideals and boundaries determine meanings and thereby restrict freedom. Boundaries are often perceived as obstacles to an expression of what we really want, yet without such boundaries, no genuine identity or meaning can emerge. We may surmise that setting boundaries restricts our freedom in the sense of preventing us from doing what we really want. However, it can also be argued that neglecting to set boundaries actually means being enslaved to one's present desires and demonstrating an inability to direct life in light of our ideals. The dark side of being free from constraints such as ideals and boundaries is that it leaves people in chaos and paralysis, left to the tyranny of irrelevant factors.[39] The extent that we prize our fundamental values is exhibited in our readiness to sacrifice other values and needs, which we consider to be of lesser weight. Accordingly, we ought not to perceive self-control or the adherence to boundaries as the surrender to external pressures that are at odds with our desires. It follows that some of our deepest conflicts are not at the intersection of external boundaries and our desires; rather, they are situated between some of our most profound values.

People in love occasionally feel chained by external constraints preventing them from acting in accordance with their wilder passions, yet they are ready to let their beloved rob them of their liberty. They are ready to be chained to the beloved, to be magnetically attracted to the beloved and never leave. Lovers are happy to be in such a situation, as they consider acting in accordance with their loving heart as the greatest expression of freedom. Since our boundary setting is constructed of and yet constrained by our values, attitudes, and desires, our autonomy is both expressed and constrained in such an activity. We may speak here of a self-determining freedom: I am free when my decision is based upon my values and constraints rather than upon external factors.[40] People sometimes dream about a romantic union that will be the most natural and the only conceivable consequence of their loving circumstances. This union will not involve obligations and sacrifices, only voluntary care and desire for the other; and as such, it will express our most profound freedom.

Setting boundaries that serve to curb our emotional inclinations or solely to deter us from acting on these inclinations is tantamount to having little or no freedom at all. In either case, people become enslaved to either their desires or their ideals. In this sense we disagree with the verse from the unforgettable song by Kris Kristofferson, 'Me and Bobbie Magee': 'freedom's just another word for "nothing left to lose"'. When there is nothing left to lose, your actions are not determined by your own values, but rather by external forces that push you in various directions. Nevertheless, it is also true that things that are generally valuable to us limit our autonomy to do what we want at this very moment. Our autonomy is best expressed when there is no conflict between what we desire to do and what our values prescribe. In fact, it comes into play both when we behave according to our profound values, as well as when we follow transient desires that represent less entrenched values.

Ideals and boundaries are essential for human behavior. The need to prioritize implies both the establishment and the violation of boundaries. Prioritization is an expression of the rules we employ in deciding which values we should abide by and which we can ignore and even transgress. In this sense, we habitually cross boundaries that we perceive to be of lesser value. Each boundary is highlighted by a specific ideal. Although typically people have many such boundaries, they frequently fancy themselves free of any constraints and doing only what they really wish. And, where there is a will there is a way. In such cases, overstepping normative boundaries is as vital as establishing such boundaries. Along these lines, John Portmann shows the indispensable nature of sin.[41] The presence of God, which expresses our highest values and hopes, inevitably implies the existence of sin. Indeed, according to the Jewish tradition, everyone is actually a sinner: 'Surely there is no one on earth so righteous as to do good without ever sinning'.[42] Portmann argues that humans will always sin, though they may attempt to decrease the number and gravity of their sins. He further claims that 'the simple fact that you are bound to fail at some point in some way does not justify hedonism or utter lawlessness, does not justify refusing to try to play well with others'.[43]

The flexible nature of boundaries is particularly evident in love, whose significance in our lives makes the violation of boundaries 'in the name of love' acceptable. As Rosa, a single mother, claims, 'I have always been willing to take the kinds of risks involved in love; they don't really even feel like a choice. Love is always worth it'. Hence, in this view, violating boundaries is not necessarily an immoral deed. On the contrary, living by adhering strictly to such boundaries may be immoral, as it does not take into account unique, specific, personal and circumstantial features. In this regard, Stephen Toulmin argues that 'A morality based entirely on general rules and principles is tyrannical and disproportionate … only those who make equitable allowances for subtle individual differences have a proper feeling for the deeper demands of ethics'.[44]

Two major human capacities that are particularly relevant to the issue of violating boundaries are self-awareness and self-deception. We need a powerful capacity of self-awareness to recognize those moments or situations when we encounter the boundaries of our morality, but we also need the capacity of self-deception to allow us to occasionally cross these boundaries while believing that we do not. Both capacities are related to living in a realm delineated by transparent boundaries; these boundaries do not obscure from our view what lies beyond. On the contrary, by drawing a transparent line, they make the forbidden landscapes visible and known to us, allowing for various media, such as the arts and much of the entertainment industry, to work at seducing us to violate these boundaries – and often we do.

Yet many of our boundaries are outdated, unrealistic and even absurd. Thus, in England girls may legally have sex at 16 but cannot buy vibrators until they are 18. In various religions, sexual activities have been regarded to be taken from the 'lawful and given to sinners'; hence, the very experience of sexual pleasure entails the violation of normative boundaries.[45] As it is extremely difficult not to violate boundaries, the remaining hard issue concerns the manner in which this should be done.

Changes in behavior often precede changes in normative boundaries. It is no wonder that a common excuse for violating boundaries is 'everybody does it'. Accordingly, people do not merely violate more boundaries, but also feel less guilty about it. Hence, a culture of cheating has emerged in many realms of modern society.[46] The prevalence of cheating does not mean that people want to cheat, or that they do so with evil intent. On the contrary, people like to perceive of themselves as always being on the morally correct side of any issue, but when the boundaries they encounter are perceived as either inadequate or no longer pertinent to the current state of society, they do not consider crossing the boundaries to be immoral. As Iris, a divorcee in her mid-50s who maintained a sexual relationship with her husband and with her lover, with the full consent of both, says: 'I think I love honesty and clarity even more than sex!' People may say that love is more important than formal outdated rules, and giving freedom to their heart is more important than being loyal to an emotionally distorting framework such as marriage.

Eva, a married woman who is involved in a loving relationship with a married man said, 'When I am with him, I feel as light as a feather, and whatever we do together feels so natural and right'. To an external observer, the terms 'natural and right', may seem odd, as they violate what seems to be so natural and right – staying with their partner who loves them very much. The reference here is not to their current superficial circumstances but to their deep values and attitudes underlying their intense love. In a similar vein, if people perceive the current social and economic situation as basically unjust, they would not consider violating it as improper but rather as reshaping our values.[47] It seems that Romantic Ideology has presented such strict rules and ideals that people consider them to be irrelevant, and as they have been violated by many people, people can continue to feel that their own violation of the ideals underlying this ideology are also justified.

To decrease the violation of boundaries, we may want to make our normative boundaries more flexible, yet this in turn may weaken the safeguards against further violation. Take, for example, cyberspace where the romantic and sexual boundaries are much more flexible than in offline circumstances. This flexibility did not reduce the number of offline violations of boundaries but rather increased it. Romantic and sexual cheating increased with the expanded use of the Internet.[48] Rosa, a single mother who did not have sex for the last seven years, though she did pleasure herself from time to time, found an online married lover, who awakened her passionate romantic mood. A few weeks afterwards she began a romantic relationship with an old friend of hers who continued to pursue her company for a long time.

Another attempt for dealing with the deluge threatening to ruin our normative boundaries is the 'zero tolerance' policy, which strictly prohibits any type of boundary violation. This policy, which essentially disregards reality, is extremely harsh and hard to adopt.

It is easier to draw clear boundaries than to keep them. Normative boundaries are supposed to guide our behavior, but reality is more complex than what can be prescribed by simply marking dos and don'ts. There is no doubt that people who live in close proximity to each other need principles to guide their interactions, but the nature of such principles is unclear. Guiding principles should provide general directions, such as 'drive safely', rather than specific rules, like 'don't exceed 100 kilometers per hour'. What constitutes safe driving may vary considerably, depending on several factors, such as the competence of the driver, the conditions of the road, and how other people drive.[49] Similarly, normative behavior may vary considerably, depending on personal and contextual features. Guiding principles have no precise borderlines. They may be associated with some specific rules that are appropriate in most cases, but at the end of the day, personal and contextual features will play a crucial role in determining people's actual behavior in accordance with these principles. A virtuous person does not need specific boundaries, as they can determine the proper normative behavior by merely referring to the particular circumstances. Ordinarily, people use specific boundaries to help them form a model for their normative behavior. However, there is no golden rule telling them when to stay within those boundaries and when it is acceptable to go beyond.

Yoram Yovell refers to the issue of boundaries when training new students in psychotherapy. He says that new trainees are often reminded that they should maintain professional boundaries at all times in the therapy room. Yovell reasons that while this approach is perhaps useful in discouraging gross violations of professional ethics, such as entering into a sexual relationship with a patient, it instills in the beginning therapists' rigidity and fear of spontaneity that may stifle the therapeutic process. When Yovell teaches the subject to his students, he tells them that the border (or boundary) metaphor is indeed useful for their situation. He invites them to imagine themselves as soldiers stationed along a border and tells them that there are a few dangerous things about an unmarked border, for example, one may cross it without realizing that they are doing so. The purpose of a well-marked border is not that it should never be crossed under any circumstances, but rather that it should be clear to the person crossing it that he has indeed stepped over it. Then he tells them that in order to fulfill a mission, it might sometimes become necessary for a soldier to cross the border. Anyone considering the possibility of crossing the border should behave like a soldier who crossed the border: first, he should be aware exactly where the border lies. Second, he should behave cautiously, move swiftly and quietly, achieve the mission, and return to 'our side' as soon as possible. Third, and perhaps most important, he should remember that if he gets into trouble on the other side of the borderline, he cannot rely on any outside help; he is entirely on his own, and our professional protective shield does not cover him when he is across the border.

We often build fences around our boundaries in order to prevent ourselves from being merely one step away from crossing the boundaries. Thus, various religions demand that women adopt a modest appearance, in order to prevent temptation. Such fences, while intended to avert people from taking the last step before behaving in a forbidden manner, do more than just protect people from overstepping boundaries, they also prevent them from engaging in pleasant activities, which cross no normative lines. Sometimes the boundaries are also protected by formal obligatory contracts. In this case, crossing the boundaries is likely to involve punishment. A formal contract regulates cooperation between people by chaining them to formal boundaries. Here the earlier wish of those involved in the contract constrains any future wishes, upholding the cooperation. Catholic marriage constitutes a lifetime captivity with no possibility of regret, no matter what the quality of the marriage. Other marital arrangements regulate personal relationships while giving each person the right to withdraw at any time, without presenting a rational cause. Thus, divorce is now based on demand rather than on culpability: a love that has died out or the finding a new love constitutes a sufficient basis for divorce, and there is no liability attached to the withdrawal.[50] The lack of love is now an adequate justification for pursuing a divorce.

The Jewish tradition has the notion of *Batel Beshishim*, meaning, if the infringement is a case of one in 60, then the deed need not be considered a violation. As a practical religion, Judaism has various provisions intended to make sure that reasonable priorities be maintained and that minor violations do not ruin our evaluation of a basically good person. The Jewish sages knew that it is extremely difficult for people to comply with strict rules; they asked, therefore, that if such violations are unavoidable, they should at least be in discretion. Thus, Rabbi Illai the Elder taught in the Talmud that

> if one feels that his passion threatens to make itself master over him, he shall go to a place where he is not known, put on black clothes and do as he pleases, but he shall not profane the name of Heaven publicly.[51]

The consideration of minor breaches as acceptable recognizes our ability to take steps toward the forbidden zone without actually entering it. Contrary to the popular saying, 'once a cheater, always a cheater', human beings are able to moderate their activities as well as reform themselves.[52] In contrast to the zero-tolerance approach, a Scottish proverb says: 'better bend than break'. In other words, the only alternative to bending the ideal, i.e., fulfilling it only partially, is to break it altogether. Bending is the flexibility needed to keep the ideal for a long time. High-rise buildings also have this kind of flexibility, which enables them to move in strong winds without breaking. People who refuse to negotiate their borderlines are more likely to abandon them. Those who are more flexible are less likely to be furious with themselves and others, as they are better prepared to handle the occasional obstacles that prevent them from doing what they desire to do.

The type and degree of the violation are naturally relevant to its consideration as a significant or insignificant violation. Take, for example, romantic affairs. The 'oral sex doesn't count' rule refers to the nature of the violation. The assumption here is that only complete sexual activity counts as a significant violation of the rule that forbids extramarital sexual affairs. President Bill Clinton apparently held this assumption when he denied having sex with Monica Lewinsky. The 'one time rule' is a quantitative guideline referring to the frequency of the gap between what people want and what is allowed.

Other violations are considered so minor as to barely constitute a violation; instead, they are interpreted as simply requiring a mild degree of flexibility. A continuous love affair is likely to prevent a person from fulfilling the ideal of romantic exclusivity, which underlies Romantic Ideology. In this regard, if comparing divorce with extramarital affairs, we may say that people who regularly have affairs violate normative boundaries while maintaining the marital framework, whereas in divorce, people choose to abandon the marital framework, in order to maintain the socially normative boundary prohibiting extramarital affairs. Both approaches have their own rationalizations, and each may be considered to have a distinct value under different circumstances.

Crossing boundaries is a two-faced activity. In light of the importance of boundaries in our life of values, violating them is often risky, painful, and morally wrong. Such transgressions may rest on a sheer inability to read reality for what it is and to live happily. Crossing boundaries can be risky and frightening, as our environment becomes less stable making it increasingly difficult to find our way in it. However, crossing boundaries can be advantageous, in the sense that it enhances creativity and the ability to adopt new perspectives and insights. Globalization, which is quite beneficial from many aspects, is essentially an activity of crossing boundaries. Moreover, crossing normative boundaries can be an exhilarating experience.[53] This is in accordance with the saying: 'Stolen waters are sweet'. There is nothing in the ingredients of stolen water that is different from that of normal water; what is different is the experience associated with theft. In the same vein, your lover may not be so different from your spouse, but the very experience of being with someone different and crossing boundaries can sometimes be enjoyable.

Flirting illustrates the enjoyable nature of rocking the boat and teasing the boundary lines, as it adds spice to life and expresses a positive attitude towards other people. Flirting is subtle: it is typically not an explicit sexual activity, but rather an enjoyable, gentle prelude or substitute for it. Flirting is conducted within a tacit borderline; it is a kind of game, or rather a dance, in which participants move closer to the borderline – and sometimes even step across it – and then move back to a comfortable distance from it. Flirting is a type of (usually verbal) dance in which the boundaries of sexuality are not clearly drawn. Flirting is like an inactive volcano that can become active any moment. The line between innocent flirting and overt sexual innuendo is not clearly drawn; hence, crossing the line and activating the sexual volcano is a common – albeit not necessary – result of flirting. The playful dancing back and forth across the strict boundary lines is also expressed in the seemingly contradictory aspects of flirting: honesty together with an element of innocence, as well as a mild level of deception (expressed in flattery); caring for others – by listening to and showing interest in them – while not taking them too seriously; feeling confident and good about yourself while not attaching too much importance to it; intelligence flavored by emotional tone.

The magnitude of the effect of violating a given normative boundary is determined by various personal and contextual factors, according to the individual's specific circumstances. In addition to these factors, two other, more general, factors are relevant: the moral distance from the boundary and the temporal structure (mainly, duration and frequency) of the violation. Consider, for example, a transgression of the boundary prohibiting extramarital affairs. One general factor determining the magnitude of its effect would be the extent of the divergence from said boundary. Since sexual intercourse is considered a greater moral transgression than mere hugging, the effects of an affair consisting of the latter might be of lesser magnitude than an affair based on the former. The magnitude of the effect of violating a normative boundary is also determined by the temporal structure of the infringement, that is, its duration and frequency. Returning to the previous example of an extramarital affair, the duration would refer to the difference between a one-night stand and a relationship lasting several years; and the frequency would refer to the time lapse between each romantic meeting.

Determining the magnitude of violating a given boundary is quite complex, since the significance and relative weight attributed to each factor (distance and the temporal structure) is not evident but open to dispute. Is a brief sexual affair a more significant violation of the boundary than a prolonged non-sexual emotional affair? It would seem that the more frequent the violation, the greater its magnitude. Yet, how would one compare several brief and frequent affairs with a single long-lasting one? There is no common scale for all the different factors. Even if a common scale for all factors were to be found, we would still have to determine the relative weight of each factor, which is also far from obvious. This is because the weighted value of each factor would differ according to the characteristics of the aggressor, contextual features, and the type of violation. Thus, it may be that in some violations, the weighted value of the temporal structure would be considered greater than that of the distance, while for other violations the distance would be more significant. We may also expect personal, cultural and gender differences in this regard.

Our autonomy in love is expressed in both our wish to maintain certain boundaries and the desire to violate them. We desire to have open doors, but we do not necessarily want to go through these doors, once passage is permitted. There is here a dialectic process in which we approach the boundaries, perhaps even cross them occasionally, and then retreat to the safety they circumscribe. A love that hardly has any boundaries and tries to open all doors is very different from a love that is tamed by boundaries and surrounded only by closed doors. There is here a structural conflict, to which it is hard to find a satisfying solution. As Iris, a divorcee, says:

> I encourage clear agreements. However, often when it comes to the agreement to maintain one sexual or romantic partner, I notice wavering. So, I wondered: what is the 'drive' or 'passion', which seems so prevalent in marriage, to look outside of this primary commitment – to look elsewhere for something?

Crossing normative boundaries does not mean ignoring all boundaries. Portmann tells of a stripper who emphasized that the wall between watching and touching made a world of moral difference to her, and she did not allow men to touch her: 'It wasn't the act itself; it was a matter of setting up boundaries somewhere, so that one didn't feel like one's entire self was oozing away'.[54] Similarly, having an affair, which violates a prevailing rule, must have its own rules. We may speak here about an ethical code of adulterers (the function of which may somewhat resemble that of the ethical code among criminals). The basis of this code may be the wish to cause as little pain as possible within the primary relationship. This can be done, for instance, by diverting only a minimal amount of resources from the primary relationship to the affair or by protecting the privacy of the primary partner.

Recognizing boundaries does not imply only the avoidance of desirable relationships when they are considered improper, it also enables us to accept undesirable relationships. We can select, to a certain extent, those we are associated with, but we do so within certain boundaries. Typically, we cannot select our family members, bosses, neighbors and members of our sports club, yet getting along and having certain social ties with them is part of our boundaries.

Rigid boundaries are of greater value in relationships with strangers, whereas in close personal relationships boundaries are often of lesser value and tend to take the form of practical guidelines. Accordingly, good manners are of greater value in relations with strangers. Personal relationships involve the elimination of some boundaries typical between strangers, and at the same time keeping other types of boundaries (and sometimes even establishing new ones). Being part of a committed romantic relationship bestows privileges as well as commitments (or boundaries). We expect more from those who are close to us and we are more committed to these people. Part of our common-sense understanding of friendship is that we are often morally required to promote our friends' well-being to a greater extent than that of strangers. Toulmin argues that in dealing with our families, intimates, and immediate neighbors or associates, 'we both expect to – and are expected to – make allowances for their individual personalities and tastes, and we do our best to time our actions according to our perception of their current moods and plans'.[55] In dealing with complete strangers, our moral obligations are limited and chiefly negative – for example, to avoid acting violently, whereas with close intimates, our moral obligations are profound and chiefly positive – for example, to help them develop their capacities and fulfill their wishes.

In cyberspace, the effects of normative boundaries are considerably muted. One example relates to laws based on geographic borders: since online activities cut across territorial boundaries, their feasibility and legitimacy diminish considerably. Similarly, by changing one's name, gender, age or basic traits, identity boundaries can also be blurred. In the same vein, the efficacy of romantic frameworks and boundaries, such as marriage and romantic exclusivity, is also called into question. Does cyberspace transcend the need for boundaries? It may be argued that it does, as it has no actual boundaries, and accordingly, in cyberspace people display a propensity for disregarding what are otherwise considered profound human constraints, for example by overcoming the gap between their reality and their desires. In cyberspace, people feel that they can get almost anything they want and they do not have to take into account personal limitations and external constraints. Regarding her online affair, Rosa says, 'I do not have to restrict myself or adhere to important boundaries that exist when two people connect physically'. The reduced burden of boundaries within cyberspace stems from the unmarked boundaries of cyberspace itself. However, since the people having online affairs are real people with actual constraints in their offline environment, their online activity is necessarily affected – although by considerably reduced constraints. For instance, people involved in online affairs may choose self-imposed boundaries, such as limiting the affair to cyberspace or restricting the frequency of their affairs to virtual one-night stands (to avoid developing a more profound relationship). As in offline circumstances, adhering to these boundaries is difficult. As one woman remarked while telling her story on the Internet:

> I found myself truly surprised that mere characters on a keyboard could carry with them such an erotic and emotional charge. But the guy was married and although we did establish ground rules, I ended up 'coloring outside the lines' in a way I never thought I would.

Many married people testify that they set certain boundaries for their online activity, but then quickly violate them as they want to upgrade their online affair.

The absence in cyberspace of external constraints and the ability to overcome personal limitations by using the imagination make cyber love similar to infatuation, both of which approximate idealized love. It seems that in online relationships, people perceive only the smile; they deliberately overlook any constraints, which is what makes this affair so exciting. However, once they decide to upgrade their online romantic relationship into an offline one, they face the limitations that were previously ignored. Such an upgrade is, therefore, often doomed to fail.

Establishing ideals – 'Love of my life'

She doesn't need improvement, she's much too nice to rearrange.

Johnny Tillotson

Why does a woman spend ten years trying to change her husband and then complain, 'You're not the man I married!'

Barbra Streisand

Ideals have an important function in our life – they inspire us to improve and approach a standard that we esteem. Ideals constitute a standard of perfection – hence they are typically perceived as far beyond our capabilities; as such, they are often regarded as lacking practicality. Ideology is similar to ideals in that it poses desired goals, but it is more systematic and practical than mere ideals. Ideology may be characterized as a broad, systematic body of concepts and ideals – especially those that concern the quality of human life. The issue of implementation is central to ideology and, hence, ideologies are often associated with being imposed on people. This is one reason for the somewhat negative tone which is frequently implied in the term *ideology*. Another reason for the negative connotation is that the positive message of an ideology is frequently accompanied by numerous negative elements, which use the ideological framework for purposes that are not only irrelevant to, but also completely contrary to the ideology's main tenets. Thus, for example, the great communist ideals have become less valued, since we associate them with the brutal means used to enforce the communist ideology. Romantic Ideology is also loaded with sublime ideals, but the inability to fulfill them is frequently used for justifying, in the name of love, evil deeds. Although the core of love may not include evil aspects, it has certainly been used to generate much evil.[56]

Establishing ideals involves the activity of the imaginative capacity. Nevertheless, ideals do not merely describe a possible state, but establish norms according to which we should behave. Ideals stem from our inherent and constant striving to improve our situation; such ceaseless ambition enables us to face our present hardships.[57] Ideals typically express something we aspire to; we may approach an ideal, but to embody an ideal in its entirety is extremely difficult, if not impossible. Ideals can also be expressed in the form of certain people we adore: such as saints, celebrities, public figures, and, of course, our beloveds.

We all need ideals to guide our life. This is especially true concerning our meaningful and valued activities. Ideals provide hope and a reference point for a better situation. The loss of hope, which is the loss of the capacity to imagine that things can be better, is a most profound type of loss – perhaps, the most tragic kind.[58] Ideals are similar to positive illusions, in the sense that while neither refers to what is the current reality, both can have the beneficial function of motivating self-improvement. The terms differ in that *positive illusion* refers to a conceivable state of affairs, whereas *ideal* refers to an abstraction – not necessarily within reach. Both positive illusions and ideals play a major role in forming and implementing Romantic Ideology.

We may also distinguish moral rules from moral ideals. Moral rules, such as 'do not kill', 'do not deprive of freedom', and 'do not violate trust', prohibit actions that cause direct or indirect harm. Moral ideals are broader in scope: they encourage – rather than demand – the avoidance of the same actions that may cause harm. In light of the general and utopian nature of ideals, they can never be fully realized; they are merely a gold standard we are encouraged to approach. Accordingly, only the violation of moral rules needs justifying. Moral rules govern the very existence of human society, whereas moral ideals concern society's ability to flourish.[59]

In light of love's central role in our lives and our fundamental preoccupation with its meaning, it is only natural to have ideals concerning love. The ideals underlying Romantic Ideology express something we should aspire to. They serve as a beacon that guides and lights our love and its place in our lives. As a Buddhist proverb puts it: 'If we are facing in the right direction, all we have to do is keep on walking'.

As mentioned, ideals have an important function even when we cannot fully fulfill them; their very presence often has positive effects on our behavior. The optimal ideal is the one that is somewhat beyond most people's reach, but nevertheless they can approximate it and feel that they are improving themselves and fulfilling the ideal, at least partially. The realization that the ideals underlying Romantic Ideology cannot be fully implemented gives lovers the freedom to interpret and apply these ideals in various manners. An ideal that is not realized in its entirety can still function as a positive guide, as long as we believe that we have some flexibility in fulfilling it.

The definition of a reasonable approximation to a certain ideal is open to interpretation, which in fact makes the ideal more flexible. This kind of flexibility enables many people to consider themselves as fulfilling a given ideal. This is also the case regarding the ideal of love. Consider, for instance, the attitude toward romantic exclusivity, which is a central ideal in Romantic Ideology. One person may consider one single and brief extramarital affair a decade as maintaining the ideal of romantic monogamy, while a different perspective, iterated by Yves Montand states, 'A man can have two, maybe three love affairs while he's married; after that it's cheating'. There are many such attitudes expressing the flexible nature of fidelity, given the fact that achieving the ideal of total fidelity is difficult.

One's personal conception of the permissible gap between reality and ideals is an essential mechanism for coping with and maintaining these ideals. Contrary to the prevailing view that personal survival requires strict adherence to the ideal, in many cases, it is one's ability to be flexible in applying the ideals – including the acceptance of minor violations – that is both more beneficial and the key to personal survival.

We may compare the situation of the murderers to that of people on the verge of divorce. In both cases, the love that was supposed to last forever is ending: in the case of the murderers it is because of the spouse's wish and in the case of the divorcees it is either because of their own or the spouse's wish. In both types of circumstances, Romantic Ideology may not only serve as a justification for the termination of a relationship, it may in fact cultivate the ground that leads to love's withering decline, by propounding an unreachable ideal. Indeed, often people opt for a divorce because they consider their spouse to be too far removed from their image of an ideal lover and partner. Romantic Ideology thus becomes a factor that contributes to behavior that is dialectically opposed to the morals it supposedly upholds. Despite this apparent self-contradiction in Romantic Ideology, and its convoluted involvement in the pain and sadness that accompany separation and divorce (not to mention murder), surprisingly, many of the same people who suffered these inevitable consequences continue to believe in and uphold Romantic Ideology. Divorce is no longer associated with shame, as it used to be; nevertheless, one would think that divorced people would endeavor to learn an important lesson, namely that Romantic Ideology is, in a sense, an illusion. Yet divorced people continue to remarry in their attempt to grasp hold of this illusion.

Consider in this regard the case of Elena, a married woman in her early 40s who read many romantic novels and collections of love letters, and wished deeply to fulfill the ideal love described in these writings. She thought that her failure to achieve this ideal love stemmed from a personal fault, either in her or in her marital partner. Consequently, she engaged in numerous affairs while searching for the ideal beloved:

> What I have been doing is wandering around the world in search of a home for my heart, and every one of my efforts made clear only one thing, and that was that home was elsewhere. The most prominent feeling in my life was the feeling of loneliness, even when, or especially when I was with another person.

Elena violated the normative boundary of a monogamous relationship in order to try and implement her profound ideal regarding true love. It was clear to her at the beginning of most affairs that they were far from the love she was seeking; she felt that none of her lovers deserved her love-making, an activity which she felt was taking place 'outside of her' and which had nothing to do with her genuine self. Nevertheless, she continued having these affairs for a while, partly because of the excitement (which was in stark opposition to the boredom of her primary relationship) and partly because of her hope to turn one of them into a true love. These affairs were both a shield from her disappointment in her present primary relationship and a search engine for the future. However, these attempts failed dramatically in fulfilling any of these functions. She also felt profound personal failure. She left her first husband, not because he was unfaithful to her but because she was unfaithful to him; thus, she perceived what she considered to be her personal failure as indicative of the lack of love in her marriage. Her constant disappointment from herself and her lovers, most of whom she never loved in the least, rendered her an obvious victim of Romantic Ideology: she had neither past nor present to be proud of, and could retain only a dim hope for a better future. Being such an unwavering follower of Romantic Ideology constituted an enormous burden, as it both eliminated the option of improving the primary relationship and required her to choose the 'right' lover instead. Consequently, she was frequently depressed but never considered altering or compromising her ideal of true love.

Elena courageously distinguished between profound moral principles (which she maintains in a very extreme manner) and shallow rules (which she constantly violates). Most people follow one of these two paths: some violate the shallow rules, are consequently sliding on the slippery slope and end in violating profound principles as well. Many others maintain merely the shallow rules, as holding the profound principles is far too difficult for them. In both cases, the profound principles are violated, as in the case of the murderers. Elena was not completely mistaken in her search for ideal love. Maintaining the hope of having long-term passionate romantic love may be beneficial for coping with the current hardships, and perhaps may even be fulfilled or at least be better approached. Her deep conviction that things are not the way they should and could be helps to continue to function as usual – but the probability of finding her true love remains low. Hence, not fulfilling the ideal of true love, as not fulfilling many other ideals, should not make them disappointed and depressed.

The notion of beauty reflected in the idealized and glamorous images we see in movies and journals is another example where people work hard to maintain an ideal that cannot be fulfilled, at the cost of existential values and moral rules.[60] Seeing these ideals of beauty embodied by supposedly 'real' people creates feelings of inadequacy, which often lead to costly investments that may prove both useless and risky. Indeed, while plastic surgery soars, feminine self-esteem sinks (about 80 percent of women report disliking their looks).[61] Such is also the case of anorexia, which begins as an effort to approximate an ideal and ends up as a life-threatening situation. Similarly, the ideals put forth by Romantic Ideology makes people feel that their own relationship is inadequate, and encourages them to take steps which may be found, at the end of the day, useless.

The remedy for having an ideal that cannot be fulfilled is not necessarily to abandon the ideal but rather to accept one's own limitations, and in particular the inherent inability to fully embody one's ideals. Being equally aware of the gap between Romantic Ideology and reality and of our inability to overcome it may lead to less frustration, a greater readiness to accept the ideology as a guiding principle, and to a moderate form of ideology, which has a limited impact upon us. Upholding the ideology in its strictest sense not only generates disappointment for those who are in a committed relationship, but can also deter people from entering such a relationship. Sadly, there are many people who are waiting for the perfect lover, finding it impossible to compromise with someone who they consider to be less than the ideal.

Some claim that upholding a certain ideology without actually materializing it is better than not having any ideology whatsoever. In this sense, a certain degree of hypocrisy, that is, when people do not behave in the way they publicly endorse, may be preferable, in certain circumstances, to an ideology of cynicism, that is, the relinquishing any desire for ideals. A leader's public endorsement of ideals may have a certain positive and motivating impact not only on the intended audience, but also on the endorser himself. Moreover, politicians' behavior may also be associated with their objective inability to materialize their professed ideology. By contrast, a cynic rejects the very notion that there are values worth upholding. It seems that hypocrisy is often considered more justified when used by leaders than when used by private individuals. Whereas in the former case, there are usually some profound objective obstacles preventing the ideology's implementation, in the latter case, hypocrisy is typically limited to that person's personal gain.[62]

To summarize, to determine whether a certain deviation from Romantic Ideology is insignificant and hence justified – or at least excusable – is a complex task and often depends on specific personal and contextual considerations; as such, it is open to various interpretations. The nature, size, and perceived cause of the gap between the actual and the ideal are important factors in this regard. If the gap can be explained by referring to structural or environmental factors beyond one's control, it is possible to uphold Romantic Ideology. It is also acceptable if one assumes that perfection is unattainable and thus ideologies cannot be entirely accomplished. However, when the gap is interpreted by the individual as due to one's own flaws, while perceiving that others manage to embody the very same ideals, this person may experience extreme disappointment and depression. The prevalence of Romantic Ideology in modern culture causes many people to attribute the deviation of their own intimate relationship from the ideology to some flaw in themselves or in their own relationship and not to a structural problem inherent in long-term intimate relationships, nor to the nature of ideals. In this case, Romantic Ideology has a considerable negative impact upon many people.

When the deviation from Romantic Ideology can be attributed to external circumstances beyond the control of the individual, the person can continue to consider herself as fulfilling the ideology. Take, for example, the following case. Tiffany, a woman in her mid 20s who has been living with a boyfriend for several years, has an affair with Mark, a single man of her age, whom she dearly loves. Tiffany does not want to leave her boyfriend as she dreads the devastating impact upon him. Mark loves her and is ready to marry her. Tiffany considers herself as behaving in accordance with the ideals underlying Romantic Ideology, since her reason for not leaving the boyfriend is not a self-ish one, but rather stems from profound care for him. Accordingly, she becomes extremely upset and hurt upon hearing that Mark, after waiting for about two years, is now having an affair with another woman. Tiffany perceives his behav-ior as a betrayal of the romantic ideals she holds. The difference between them, Tiffany surmises, is that she has a profound problem which cannot be over-come; whereas Mark's affair merely stems from his superficial sexual desires. His excuse is not profound enough to justify a deviation from the ideals they both hold. Mark, on the other hand, considers himself to be as entitled as Tiffany to have an additional romantic relationship. In this example, both Tiffany and Mark believe that their own deviation from Romantic Ideology is justified, whereas the deviation of the other is not. Each sees him- or herself as continuing to uphold and even fulfill the ideals of Romantic Ideology.

It seems that some kind of idealization is always present in profound romantic love. When asked whether true love remains for ever, one woman answered in the affirmative, citing her first love as an example, despite the fact that she terminated this relationship six years ago. In this case, the situation that prevails is an idealization of the past. This idealized love, which could not contend with certain features of reality, was eventually terminated, thus enabling the continuation of the ideal. It is commonly recognized that love involves a positive construction of the beloved, which to a certain extent distorts reality. To persist in an idealized loving relationship requires then a moderate but constantly distorted perception of reality; its moderate nature enables the lovers to believe in it despite its known inaccuracies. Stable and satisfying relationships reflect the intimate partners' ability to see their imperfect partners in an idealized light. People who are in love for a prolonged period of time maintain the idealized notion of their beloved for the whole period.[63] As Solomon, who has been happily married to his wife Ziva for the last forty years, says, 'When I look at my wife now, I still see the young and beautiful Ziva I first met'.

The absence of illusions is indeed evident in loveless marriages. Karen Kayser characterizes what she terms as 'marital disaffection' as 'the gradual loss of an emotional attachment, including a decline in caring about the partner, an emotional estrangement, and an increasing sense of apathy and indifference toward one's spouse'.[64] Unique to the beginning of the whole process of disaffection is the feeling of disillusionment, which involved the reduction of both idealism and high expectations for the marriage. Spouses stated that they were disillusioned with their partner; the reality of their marriage and partner was not living up to the dreams, fantasies, and expectations they had prior to their marriage. Accordingly, spouses felt disappointed and deceived. When describing their feelings of disillusionment, spouses refer to radical changes in the partner's behavior after the wedding; however, what had actually changed, for the most part, was not the partner but the spouses' perception of their partner.[65] As Ouida (pseudonym of Marie Louise de la Ramee) already said, 'The loss of our illusions is the only loss from which we never recover'.

Second Life – 'You only live twice'

> There is no one in sight
> And we're still making love
> In my Secret Life
>
> Leonard Cohen

> You only live twice …
> One life for yourself and one for your dreams.
>
> Nancy Sinatra

The wish to overcome human limitations is clearly expressed in the recent growing popular invention of the Second Life. Second Life is a 3-D Internet-based virtual world built and owned by its residents. A downloadable client program enables its users, called 'residents', to interact with each other through motional avatars, and provides an advanced level of social network services. Residents can explore the world, meet other residents, socialize, participate in individual and group activities, and create and trade items and services from one another. Upon joining, residents fashion their own 'avatar' – a virtual self – in any shape they like. Not surprisingly, it appears that most residents chose 'young and sexy' as their signature look. Much like in real life, residents can enter into sexual relationships with others in the thriving mature community of Second Life.[66]

The virtual environment of Second Life allows you to choose how you want to look and what you want to be called, and leaves you free to do anything you want, on the way to making your every fantasy come true. As in online relationships, the interactions that take place in Second Life are between actual flesh-and-blood people and they tend to reflect, often in a more authentic manner, people's genuine desires. Taking flight into Second Life is not a denial of reality as much as a form of exploring and playing with it. Unlike previous imaginary forms, which were typically passive, as in art for example, Second Life provides a forum in which imaginary forms interact, more so than in other forms of cyberspace. Although Second Life is framed within its own distinct world, it blurs, like other virtual reality frameworks, the boundaries between actual and virtual reality; indeed, for many people, such virtual realities are more real than the actual one. In fact, there can be no doubt that there is spillover from Second Life into the actual one: for example, some people may become addicted to the Second Life thereby neglecting their commitments in the first life, while others may consider Second Life to be so meaningful that they become less frustrated with their failures in the 'first' life.

Turning to the romantic realm, Second Life offers greater and more vivid activities that resemble actual sexual and romantic activities more than do other types of virtual realities. Sex in Second Life happens through a combination of poses, animations, scripts, and typing. The main activating component is known as Poseballs: objects with scripts in them that trigger a user's avatar to play certain animations or poses.[67] When people make love in Second Life, they can actually see the activities conducted by them and their lovers. Second life is an endless virtual world with many romantic and sexual experiences to explore. You can meet new people, you can conduct a relationship with people you know and have virtual sex with them, in any variation imaginable. Indeed, sex is everywhere in Second Life. As one woman says, 'I joined Second Life to admire the architecture, but I started cybering within 20 minutes of arriving. That was months ago, and I still haven't seen more than a handful of the buildings'.[68]

The most fascinating aspect of Second Life is that it enables people to re-live or re-do experiences. If they fail or are displeased with the outcome of an action, they can do things again in a different way, in situations in which in actual life they may not have such a possibility. Moreover, they can do things that they would never try in actual life. Thus, people can in fact experience more in Second Life than they do in actual life. Second Life, at least in its future and more sophisticated form, may provide a more comprehensive environment, where more desires will be perceived as fulfilled, and relationships will be considered perfect and complete. Accordingly, it is not unlikely that Second Life will come to substitute, in some aspects, for the 'first' life to such an extent that the wish to transform Second Life into an actual environment will become unnecessary and diminish. The fact that people build their own avatar, often disregarding certain aspects of reality, makes them more acutely aware of the impossibility of having identical circumstances in actual reality. It is possible that the perfection attained in Second Life would make romantic affairs in it seem less exciting (compared to unfinished business, which is more exciting); nevertheless, its vivid and complex nature renders such affairs still more exciting than regular online ones. Consequently, people engaged in Second Life devote a greater deal of time to *it* than they would to other online affair alternatives. In addition, performing the activities in Second Life requires more time; and furthermore, Second Life in general may provide more opportunities for exciting developments. Accordingly, addiction is a major problem in Second Life.

There are two major risks to take into account regarding virtual, or Second Life extramarital affairs: the affair may transform into a real, offline affair, and the participant will most likely devote a more considerable amount of time to the virtual affair than to the primary relationship. The first risk pertains to regular online affairs more than to Second Life affairs, since the former are of a more incomplete nature and thus there is a yearning for their completion in the form of offline affairs, whereas Second Life affairs can be continued and consummated within the realm of the virtual. Therefore, it is the regular online affair that constitutes a greater threat to the real and primary relationship. However, as relates to the second risk, spouses may consider the lengthy time that their partner spends in Second Life a form of dedication to this kind of hobby or game, behavior which is often gauged as acceptable (provided that spouses are not expected to spend their entire time together).

An environment somewhat similar to that of Second Life can be readily found in actual extramarital relationships where participants often see themselves as forming a second world (or life) that remains untouched by the 'first' world of the primary relationship.

As Eva says about her relationship with her married lover, 'Just like in the movies and fairy-tales, he stepped into my life when I least expected it, and turned my life into something new, exciting, and ever so different'. The second world cannot be touched by the first world of the primary relationship. It is like a bubble unseen by residents of the first world and therefore it is protected, to a certain extent, from the corroding processes present in that world. Robin, a married woman in her 40s, who has had several affairs, says she never let her lovers speak about transforming their relationship into a formal, public one: 'I know very well that such exciting relationships can exist only in an emotional euphoria that can only be found within our bubble'. Despite its imaginative nature, residents of the second world often describe relationships there as fulfilling compared with the emptiness of their first world. The second world, which has its own ideals and boundaries, is private to the two lovers, but is not entirely illusory; it disregards some constraints of reality, but genuinely reflects the lovers' profound attitudes. Consequently, this second world relationship is often very open and sincere. As Eva further says,

> I am so much like a baby, I always must share with him whatever is on my mind, and even when I want to hide it, as there is no answer to a certain thought, I still must share it, and only then I can be calm again. I always try and hide from him my sadness, because I do not want to make him sad as well, but then I cannot do it. I feel so much that my real life is happening in my heart, where my lover is.

Iris, who is having an online affair with a married man, refers to the imaginary aspect of this second world: 'I like the Placebo Effect of this love. I am having such a wonderful experience being in love that I do not care whether I have the real thing or the placebo'. Bernard, who has been married for 15 years, says he considered the time his married lover spends with her husband as an exile from her genuine home where her heart really wants to be. Indeed, she constantly asked him to help her hold out in the desert. In many cases the two worlds may conflict, but in some cases, where separation is carefully maintained, the second world may hold certain advantages to some people. Accepting the very existence of the two worlds, without trying to abolish one of them, is central to the feasibility of such an arrangement.

In this chapter we have described the nature of boundaries and ideals and their implications concerning the inherent need to compromise and accommodate, a need that is absent from both Romantic Ideology and the murderers' perspective. In the following chapters, we shall present further evidence for this need and then examine what can be done in this regard.

Chapter 6

Structural difficulties in romantic love
'Hard times for lovers'

Love lives and stirs within me, and I must give it a path and an outlet. To me, love's rush seems too powerful, dangerous and destructive to remain constantly present between a man and his wife. The wife that a man marries keeps his home, she is the right-hand staff upon which he perpetually leans; she is too distinguished and significant to be the object of intense love. A man's wife is his home, with her he cultivates life; she is the air he breathes. In her he plants the seeds that form in him and from her come the fruits of his life's creation. The wife is the ally who blends into life's activities until we cease to dream of her, no longer is she the focus of our passionate illusions, the object of our imaginings. She exists next to us, presupposed; the soil of our lives; the source and agent of our endeavors; the material that embodies our ever-changing and evolving spirit. The wife, the partner, becomes so deeply embedded in our own being that the din of love and its passions cannot remain permanently anchored in her. And so, our love wanders to find foreign objects outside ourselves, to women we have not known, who harbor the enchantment of unconquered mystery that awakens the scream from within, the supreme drive that yearns for the unknown.

Yehuda Ben-Ze'ev

When somebody loves you, it's no good unless she loves you – all the way.

Frank Sinatra

In the previous chapter we examined the capacity of imagination, which makes it extremely difficult to implement an uncompromising ideology. Analyzing imagination, and the ideals and boundaries established by it, has indicated their flexible nature. Ideals can rarely be entirely fulfilled and boundaries are often violated. Morality accepts this state of affairs, and one of its major tasks is to recommend optimal behavior when such extenuating circumstances arise. Moral norms associated with romantic behavior have continuously been revised throughout human history, and there is no reason to assume that this process will end now. A more perplexing question refers to whether our emotional attitudes can follow suit. This is the major issue of the three concluding chapters.

We begin this chapter by presenting a short description of some characteristics of emotions in general and of the emotion of love in particular.[1] This will help us understand the psychological difficulties in Romantic Ideology and the nature of our proposed approach. We then examine the role of change and exclusivity in our emotional behavior. These features indicate structural difficulties in maintaining long-term passionate romantic love. After discussing these issues, we shall describe some changes in modern society, which make these structural emotional difficulties even harder to cope with and facilitate the collapse of long-established romantic frameworks and practices.

Attractiveness and praiseworthiness – 'You're beautiful and you're mine'

You have made my life complete

Elvis Presley

Jewish women do not believe in sex after marriage.

From the movie *Suzie Gold*

The emotional system has its own logic – or structural mode of operation – which determines the nature and intensity of emotions, as well as their basic limitations.[2] We shall show that some of the difficulties of Romantic Ideology stem from such structural emotional features. Before doing this, we briefly describe some characteristics of emotions and love.

The affective realm includes emotions (such as envy, anger, romantic love, and sexual desire), sentiments (such as enduring love and enduring grief), moods (such as being cheerful, satisfied, 'blue', and gloomy), affective traits (such as shyness and enviousness), and affective disorders (such as depression and anxiety). Emotions and sentiments have a specific intentional object, whereas the intentional object of moods, affective disorders, and affective traits is general and diffuse. Emotions and moods are essentially occurrent states; sentiments and affective traits are dispositional in nature. These differences are expressed in temporal differences. Emotions and moods, which are occurrent states, are relatively short, whereas sentiments and affective traits, which are essentially dispositional, last for a longer period. Emotions typically last between a few minutes and a few hours, although in some cases they can also be described as lasting seconds or days. Moods usually last for hours, days, weeks, and sometimes even months. Sentiments last for weeks, months, or even many years. Affective disorders last for a very long time, and affective traits can last even a lifetime.[3]

We consider emotions to have four basic components: cognition, evaluation, motivation, and feeling. The cognitive component consists of information about the given circumstances; the evaluative component assesses the personal significance of this information; the motivational component addresses our desires, or readiness to act in these circumstances; the feeling component is a mode of consciousness expressing our own state. When Brian loves Mary, Brian has some information about Mary, evaluates her in a very positive manner, desires to be with her all the time, and has various types of pleasant feelings while being with her.[4]

The complex emotional experience of romantic love involves two basic evaluative patterns referring to (a) attractiveness – that is, an attraction to external appearance, and (b) praiseworthiness – that is, positive appraisal of personal characteristics.[5] Romantic love requires the presence of both patterns. An attractive woman may want to be loved not merely for her beauty but also for her actions and personal traits. An unattractive woman may wish the contrary: that her beloved would value her external appearance as much as he values her kindness or wisdom. People realize that genuine romantic love requires the presence of both evaluative patterns and they want to satisfy both, even if they consider themselves at an apparent disadvantage insofar as one of the patterns is concerned. One would be offended if one's partner said: 'You are rather ugly and I am not sexually attracted to you, but your brilliant brain compensates for everything'. One would also be offended if one's partner declared: 'You are rather stupid, but your attractive body compensates for everything'.

Some people would like to change the relative weight of one of these patterns – not in terms of the beloved's attitude toward them, but regarding their own attitude. Thus, some people wish that they could attach less significance to attraction, which may carry less value in the long run. Others might wish the opposite: that their love were more spontaneous and less calculated; they wish they could attach more weight to attraction. The familiar unsuccessful experience of trying to love the 'right' person indicates the importance of attraction in love. The familiar experience of being attracted to a handsome person, up until the moment he opens his mouth, indicates the importance of praiseworthiness in love.

The relative importance of the two evaluative patterns depends, to a certain extent, on personal and social factors. For example, with age, people typically accord less weight to the issue of attraction. We can also expect to find that a given society influences the determination of the relative weight of the patterns. Factors related to the relationship itself are also important in this regard. Thus, the impact of physical attraction decreases as people move toward a long-term relationship; it is particularly high at the beginning of the relationship.[6]

The two kinds of evaluative patterns involved in romantic love are not independent: a positive appraisal of your partner's characteristics is greatly influenced by their attractiveness. There is much evidence suggesting that attractiveness significantly influences ratings of intelligence, sociality, and morality. A common phenomenon in (romantic) relationships is the 'attractiveness halo', in which a person who is perceived as beautiful is assumed to have other good qualities as well.[7]

In contrast to romantic love, where both evaluative patterns are essential, in sexual desire attraction is far more dominant. Sexual desire is a simpler attitude, based largely on spontaneous and non-deliberative evaluations, whereas romantic love often requires both spontaneous and deliberative evaluations. Sexual desire is largely based upon perception (and imagination), whereas love encompasses in a more significant manner capacities such as thinking and memory, which are important for appraising personal characteristics. Sexual desire is typically focused on limited aspects of external appearance; romantic love is more comprehensive in this sense.

No precise borderline between romantic love and sexual desire exists. The latter is usually an essential component of the former. Hence, elements that are typical of the one are often found in the other. The close relation between romantic love and sexual desire indicates that we cannot be as unromantic about sex as we are about eating, but it does not deny cases in which sexual desire has nothing to do with romantic love. Many people think that love and sex can be separated, but would prefer to have them combined. Moreover, most people consider sexual involvement between their partner and a rival as a threat to their romantic relationship.[8]

The evaluative pattern of attractiveness is related to the emotional characteristic of change (as Mae West said, 'Between two evils, I always pick the one I never tried before'), while the pattern of praiseworthiness is closer to familiarity ('To know you is to love you'). It is often the case that in long-term relationships, praiseworthiness may increase where attractiveness typically decreases. The difficulties of these phenomena regarding long-term romantic relationships will be discussed in the next section.

Change and stability – 'You've been around too long'

You're window shopping ... you're just trying to find the best deal in town.

Hank Williams

The experts bray love fades so fast, then tell me why is my heart still beating?

Joe DiPietro

Intense emotions are essentially transient and unstable states. Emotions are typically experienced when we perceive a significant change in our situation – or in that of those related to us. Like burglar alarms going off when an intruder appears, emotions signal that something needs attention; when no attention is needed, the signaling system can be switched off. We respond to the unusual by paying attention to it. It is the change, rather than the level of a given stimulation, that is of emotional significance, and hence, the presence of instability. However, instability and the resulting mobilization of all emotional resources cannot last for long: given that a system cannot function normally over a long period under such circumstances, and that the newness of the situation cannot be prolonged, the emotional intensity associated with change will also decrease, enabling the system to return within a relatively short period to normal functioning.[9] On successive occasions we adapt to the event and the experience yields less pleasure; Daniel Gilbert ironically notes that psychologists 'call this *habituation*, economists call it *declining marginal utility*, and the rest of us call it marriage'.[10] Most primitive animals habituate to various stimuli and in doing so stop responding to them or respond less than they used to. One way to counter habituation is to change the stimulus, and, in fact, we try to do this in many aspects of our life. Another way is to extend the time between two similar events. Thus, even if salmon is our favorite food, we cannot eat 12 identical servings of it at the same meal.[11] Modern society, with the encouragement of the advertisement industry, promotes changes to an extreme. Thus, it is told of the mythological editor of *Vogue* magazine, Anna Wintour, that she never wears an item of last year's fashion, nor does she wear the same item twice. One needn't be a devoted follower of the fashion world to easily translate such transitory values into the romantic realm and continually look for a constant change in this realm as well.

We posit that the alliance between passionate romantic love and a committed relationship is problematic – at least in part – due to the crucial role of change in generating emotions: change intensifies emotions, whereas commitment is based on stability. For many married people, change is not an option. The delight experienced initially as the change of falling in love is difficult to sustain in long-term relationships, as the impact of reality and routines is often devastating. Additionally, the easy availability of seductive alternatives poses a real threat to the continuation of the relationship. Referring to Maistre's view, Isaiah Berlin indicates that it is irrational to believe that two people should be together with each other for the rest of their lives merely because they happened to love each other at a certain stage of their lives, which belongs to the past. However, it is also destructive and irrational to let the regime of short-term free love govern us.[12] Both change and stability are important for our loving relationships.

Stephen Mitchell argues that although romance can often give meaning to our lives, its impact is typically transitory, as it tends to be short-lived and then fades.

He further indicates that a major reason why romance fades is because it is inspired by idealization, and idealization is, by definition, illusory; whereas idealization posits a stable situation, nothing stays the same, especially not people. Moreover, romance thrives on novelty and it is dispersed by familiarity. Enduring romance, Mitchell concludes, seems to be a contradiction in terms.[13] Violating a stable arrangement and boundaries is usually exciting, as it brings people to a novel, dynamic situation. Accordingly, the refusal to conform to prevailing norms excites us; it is no wonder that an important element in romantic seduction is ambiguity, a state in which prevailing norms can be perceived as fluid.[14]

The importance of change for emotions, and hence their instable nature, is also expressed in the fact that infatuation and intense romantic love often have the characteristic of 'unfinished business', as 'A lover's dream … has no end' (Bee Gees), or 'Love remains like an endless flame' (Alabama). We are typically excited by anything that is incomplete, unsettled, unexplained, or uncertain, since we perceive it to be unusual and so it demands our attention and thoughts.[15] When the situation becomes stable and normal, there is no reason for the mental system to be on the alert and invest further resources. As Betsy Prioleau argues: 'Love goes brackish in still waters. It needs to be stirred up with obstruction and difficulty and spiked with surprise'. Hence, 'What's granted is not wanted.'[16] Ambiguous states have this kind of incomplete nature and hence have a certain lure. Resolving ambiguity often eliminates positive illusion, leading to less satisfying situations. In this sense, the resolution of uncertainty constitutes a negative outcome, which psychologically outweighs a potential positive outcome, and therefore may lead on average to worse emotional states.[17]

The above considerations partly explain why courtship, flirting, and extramarital affairs are exciting. The period of courtship obviously has the nature of unfinished business, as we yearn for a future situation in which we might upgrade the current stage of our relationship. Flirting does not have such an obvious yearning, yet it may have its own intrinsic value. The seemingly contradictory aspects encompassed in flirting, e.g., consent and refusal, honesty and a mild level of deception, etc., are characteristics of dynamic and unsettled situations associated with unfinished business.[18]

Also extramarital affairs usually have the nature of unfinished business, as they are not complete and comprehensive the way normal primary relationships tend to be. In such affairs, lovers may feel profound satisfaction but they still desire more profound fulfillment of their yearning. Numerous novels and movies deal with romantic relationships that are not complete, and therefore maintain a high level of intensity for a long time. In the play, *Same Time,*

Next Year, a man and a woman, who are married to others, meet by chance at a romantic inn and spend the night together. They then meet on the same weekend each year and stay in the same room. The tagline of the play is: 'They couldn't have celebrated happier anniversaries if they were married to each other'. Robin, a married woman, says that she and her current married lover never set up a fixed schedule for their weekly meetings. When their meeting ends, no one knows when and where their next meeting will take place; this, she said, increases uncertainty and hence excitement. Although each extramarital affair is by nature a kind of unfinished business, this couple has enhanced this aspect by leaving their schedule unsettled. (It should be noted that sometimes fixing the date generates a lot of excitement as well, since people expect the date and constantly think about it, thereby increasing its significance.) Another type of an incomplete romantic relationship that entails unfinished business involves close emotional ties, but no sexual intercourse. In this case, the intensity of the romantic relationship is due, among other things, to its incomplete nature – to the implicit desire to include another aspect in the relationship. Unfinished business does not imply merely thrill, but suffering too, since the element of frustration for not achieving what we really desire is central here as well.

The incomplete nature of many intense romantic relationships is particularly evident in courtly love, espoused by the twelfth-century troubadours, and in cyber love. The troubadours talked about 'a new kind of tender, extramarital flirtation which (ideally) was unconsummated sexually and which, therefore, made the chaste lovers more noble and virtuous'.[19] Thus, the two nonsexual lovers were supposed to sleep naked beside each other for the whole night without engaging in any sexual activity. This was supposed to test whether their love was strong enough to sustain the introduction of this new element into their relationship. It has been claimed that courtly love was perpetually unsatisfied as it did not allow the full possession of the (married) lady. Such unending love is more intense and hence was preferred to the love that achieved 'fulfillment' and 'satisfaction'.[20]

Like courtly love, cyber love also consists of passionate and enjoyable attitudes that are basically incomplete, as they lack actual physical interaction. This further increases the passionate desire to maintain the relationship at least until such interaction is achieved. Cyber love is also similar to courtly love in the sense that in many cases it involves at least one married person who does not want to leave the primary partner. This prevents the two lovers from sharing their daily, public life with each other, which further exacerbates the incomplete nature of the relationship. Cyber love can indeed become extremely intense. People often testify that their online love has been the most intense love of their life and their cybersex the wildest sex they have experienced. People even claim that before their online love, they did not know what love is.[21] One major difference between courtly love and cyber love is that only the former espouses the ideal of fidelity to a single partner; in cyber love, the object of one's desire changes frequently and one's desire may be directed at several people concurrently.

Somewhat surprising findings indicate that the free availability of pornography, mainly on the Internet, may have led to a significant reduction in the number of rape and sexual assault cases.[22] It seems that the great availability of free sexual materials has de-mystified sex, and provided an easy avenue for the sexually desirous to 'get it out of their system'. Other findings suggest that young adults who are sexually more active tend to be more anxious and depressed.[23] Novel opportunities increase both excitement for fulfilling these opportunities, and frustration for failing to do so.

In characterizing the perfect seducer, Robert Greene indicates the importance of maintaining elements that emphasize the incomplete nature of the romantic interaction. Those include increasing ambiguity, sending mixed signals, mastering the art of insinuation, confusing desire and reality, mixing pleasure and pain, stirring desire and confusion, toning down the sexual element without getting rid of it, refusing to conform to any standard, being able to delay satisfaction and not to offer total satisfaction.[24]

Two features that are closely associated with the impact of novelty upon emotional experiences are those of complexity and relevancy. Complex objects give rise to many experiences of novelty, since the object has various aspects to be revealed in the process of becoming familiar. Relevant events are generally more significant, and hence increase emotional intensity. A situation of complete familiarity is not complex, since there are no novel aspects to be revealed; accordingly, such a situation involves low emotional intensity. Partial or contextual novelty is usually of greater emotional intensity, as it involves both complexity and relevancy.

The relation between familiarity and liking is complex. In a recent study, Michael Norton and his associates argue that although we tend to prefer the company of individuals we know, often learning more about a specific individual leads, on the average, to like him or her less. There is a positive correlation between liking and information across individuals but the opposite correlation regarding any given individual. We may speak here about the lure of ambiguity: reducing ambiguity, by having more information about each other, usually leads to less liking. The study shows that additional information about the other reduces the initially thought shared similarities and hence reduces liking. There are, of course, cases in which the above correlations do not hold, and the more we know a person the more we like her.[25] When further acquaintance deepens our initial impressions, the intensity of liking will increase.

The relation between complexity and emotional intensity is nicely exemplified in a study on the role of familiarity in liking music.[26] There is evidence indicating that frequency of listening to a certain kind of music may increase the preference for this kind. We like what is closest to a relevant evaluative schema. We tend to like music that is typical of its kind. A continuous activation of an evaluative pattern increases the familiarity and hence the liking. However, too much familiarity produces boredom. Accordingly, we may not like a particular music style any more, due to the fact that we hear it more. To explain the different effects of familiarity, the factor of complexity needs to be taken into account: with increased exposure, simple music is liked less while a complex piece is liked more. The interaction of familiarity and complexity causes listeners to dislike the incomprehensible, enjoy the newly understood, and be bored by music that is well known.[27] The importance of complexity is further increased as novelty is equated with the unfamiliar, hence, a simple object will be quickly evaluated as not novel.

Romantic love can be explained along similar lines. Indeed, Nina, a married woman, described the time she spends with her lover in the following manner:

> I truly believe that even if we would spend together every minute of the day and the night for the rest of our lives we would tell each other new things – also about each other – all the time. I think that even if the familiar part becomes bigger, which is inevitable, the new part will always be endless and hence even greater than the familiar one.

Concerning the classical question of whether 'birds of a feather flock together' or 'opposites attract', there is consistent evidence for similarity, but very little evidence for opposites. Romantic partners show strong similarity in age, political, and religious attitudes; moderate similarity in education, general intelligence, and values; and little or no similarity in personality characteristics.[28] For instance, Ryan, a divorcee in her late 40s who holds conservative views, said: 'I would not be able to marry a man who was a leftist, even if I found him very attractive – although most of the men I have slept with are leftists'. Thus, while strong attitudinal similarity clearly plays a part in mate selection, it is the similarity of personality-related domains that ought to be considered when selecting a mate. Findings suggest a positive correlation between similarity and marital quality via personality-related domains but not via attitude-related domains.[29] It seems that, in fact, people are attracted to – and end up marrying partners with – similar attitudes and values, but the partners often differ in personality traits. However, once in a committed relationship, it is primarily the similarity in personality that influences marital happiness. The attitudinal similarity, which is easier to detect, seems to be more important for the initial stages of the relationship, but personality similarity becomes more important as the relationship increases in commitment.[30]

We tend to fall in love and stay with people who share with us profound similarities, which can be expressed differently in various stages of the relationship; the presence of such essential similarities need not preclude – and may even encourage – differences related to surface manifestations within the basic similarity. Following Chomsky's distinction between deep structures underlying a linguistic expression and its surface forms, which manifest the same meaning in a different manner, we may note that profound love involves deep common structures and different surface manifestations. Differences attract, but only within a shared general framework which leaves ample space for complementary differences. Nina compares herself to her lover thus:

> There are so many deep things I find in him that are like me, and this attracts me so much. And on the surface I find so many exciting things that are new to me, and this attracts me to him so much, too.

Whereas romantic love is directed towards a complex psychological personality with numerous aspects, sexual desire takes into account only a few, mainly external, aspects. Accordingly, sexual desire can be increased by replacing the object, since too much familiarity produces boredom. In contrast, increasing the intensity of love often involves increasing familiarity with the object. Enhancing novelty and excitement in romantic love does not necessarily mean replacing the object; we can speak about contextual novelty, which reveals the object in a new light and can make for heightened excitement.

A combination of novelty, familiarity, and relevance can increase emotional intensity considerably. The more familiar and relevant the object is to our self-image and goals, the greater its emotional significance. Familiar objects are typically more relevant for us, as they are more often associated with us. However, since such objects have a low degree of novelty, their emotional impact is limited. Complex events are more novel as they involve unknown features. Empirical findings indicate that the appraisal of novelty (and then the feeling of pleasantness) is followed by the appraisal of relevance.[31] This makes a lot of sense: first we should be aware of the presence of novelty, then we should examine whether, and to what extent, the given event is relevant to us.

The tension between stable boundaries, which secure our comfort zones and within which events are familiar and predictable, and the wish to experience novelty, which is typically generated by stepping beyond these boundaries, is an essential feature of human life and the experience of love; this is also the tension between the ideals of freedom and commitment.[32] Although 'looking elsewhere' is typically perceived as a response to dissatisfaction, it may also exist in a generally satisfying relationship. Pursuing a limited type of change can be compatible with satisfaction from a current stable framework, and may prevent its deterioration. Mitchell argues that romantic love does not entail devotion in a static state but rather in a dynamic one that includes uncertainty. Romantic commitment should 'not be so rigid as to override spontaneity and spontaneity not be so rigid as to preclude commitment'.[33]

Emotional meaning is generated by the interplay between stability and change. Although emotions typically arise when we perceive significant changes in our situation, an event can be perceived as a significant change only when compared with a stable background or framework. Not only change, but also stability, and in particular familiarity, increase emotional intensity: the familiar person is emotionally closer than the stranger. The unique combination of change, which is related to excitement and risk, and stability, which is related to commitment and security, is crucial for emotional excitement. Romantic relationships consist of both change, which increases excitement, and familiarity, which enhances commitment and liking. The positive role of familiarity may lead love to grow and become deeper over time.[34] However, the lack of novelty may make the element of passion less intense. As David Barash and Judith Lipton put it, 'we don't normally speak of a passionate marriage. A good marriage, a happy marriage, a comfortable and compatible marriage, yes, but only rarely a passionate one'. They further argue that a passionate marriage would be exhausting, as to 'live in a state of perpetual passion would be to forgo much of the rest of life, and, in truth, there *are* other things. Love can deepen and broaden ... but it rarely becomes more passionate'.[35] Likewise, although sex in a long-term relationship may be less passionate, it may prove more satisfying, because familiarity and knowledge of each other over time is likely to lead to a more relaxed and intimate familiarity, and in such a situation it is easier to acquire better techniques as well as to learn how to please one's partner. Moreover, stability in marriage and well-being are not one and the same: a stable marriage does not necessarily mean that marriage is particularly gratifying or vital.[36] There is no general solution to the problem of the 'right' amount and type of change required for more profound and enduring romantic love.

In analyzing our emotional attitudes regarding a familiar versus a novel person, two types of overestimations prevail: (a) a novel person is more exciting than the familiar person we are with ('the neighbor's grass is greener'); (b) the loss of a loving relationship is more painful than not gaining another loving relationship ('A man in the house is worth two in the street' – May West). Assuming that the objective worth of the two people is similar, the first attitude includes overestimation of the novel person as compared to that of the familiar one; the second attitude involves an opposite type of overestimation: the familiar person is overestimated as compared with the novel one. These two common attitudes emerge in different circumstances. It would seem that the more profound the relationship is perceived to be, the greater is the worth of the familiar relationship, where many resources have been invested.

Maturity seems to act in counter to novelty and excitement. No wonder young people are considered to be more emotional than mature people. The term 'mature' has several dictionary definitions; the more relevant ones are: 'based on slow careful considerations'; 'having attained a final or desired state'; 'of or relating to a condition of full development'.[37] These definitions refer to a state different from that of emotional experiences: emotions are an urgent and fast response which is typically not based upon careful considerations, and emotions are of the nature of unfinished business rather than the arrival at a final stage or achieving full development. Emotions are generated by change, while maturity involves getting used to changes and perceiving them as less significant. In maturity, we enjoy familiarity rather than novelty.

Emotional maturity is related to the ability to be satisfied with one's lot, which is crucial to our long-term happiness. Maturity means accommodating and accepting compromises. Mature people assign less weight to the uncompromising emotional attitudes while allocating greater weight to their limitations and to long term considerations. As Naomi, a widow in her late 50s says, 'I must accept that there always will be a woman who is younger, smarter and more beautiful than I am. Losing a boyfriend or not getting the one I want is inevitable'. Adulterers are often charged as being immature, that is, failing to demonstrate the requisite degree of self-control and civilized repression. Like habituation, maturation often kills desire and as such may be lethal to romantic relationships. Maturation reduces both positive and negative emotional experiences. In maturity, expectations are reduced, though not eliminated, and the desired object is often replaced by the feasible and the reasonable.[38] Accordingly, it has been suggested that natural seducers are people who retain some of their childish traits; they retain the spirit of children and remain as powerfully seductive as any child. As people become mature, they protect themselves against painful experiences by closing themselves off.[39] Their concern is not with having more, but with losing less.

Some people make their failure to maintain passionate love within marriage an ideology claiming that they actually do not want to be in love because of the risks associated with it. Consider also the case of Nancy, a married woman in her early forties, who candidly describes her attitude toward love: 'It is good for me not to be in love. I love but am not in love. I don't want to be carried away and lose myself. I feel good when I'm in control'. Nadia, a married woman in her late thirties holds the same attitude: 'I prefer loving over being-in-love and so, I am rather relieved to be out and away of the initial excitement and into the more mature and settled phase'. People often use the distinction between being-in-love and love to refer to the infatuation stage and the subsequent stages of compassionate love. Nadia further explains her attitude: 'I think that very many people are willing to bear up with unsatisfactory romantic relationships not because they don't crave satisfaction in love, but because they prefer the good of their children, and family life over passionate love'. Nadia makes clear that she gives up passionate romantic love for the good of her children— so actually she is not even in the stage of romantically loving her spouse.

We suggest, therefore, that the disinction between being in love and romantic love be used to designate different degrees of romantic love rather than an emotion totally lacking the passionate aspect.

Partiality and exclusivity – 'I think of you day and night'

My heart is too big for just one guy.

Edith Piaf

It's incredible that someone so unforgettable thinks that I am unforgettable too.

Nat King Cole

The emotional element characteristic of change is incompatible with Romantic Ideology, which states that love is eternal. The basic emotional characteristic of partiality is more compatible with this ideology, as it emphasizes the exclusive nature of love. As change and partiality are essential in emotional experiences, romantic love cannot ignore them.

The exclusivity of the beloved stems from the partial nature of emotions. Emotions are partial in that they focus on a narrow target, such as one person or very few people, and express a personal and interested perspective. Emotions direct and color our experience by selecting what attracts and holds our attention; they make us preoccupied with some things and oblivious to others. Not everyone and not everything is of emotional significance to us. We cannot assume an emotional state toward everyone. The intensity of emotions is possible due to their focus upon a limited group of objects. Emotions express our values and preferences; hence, they cannot be indiscriminate. Being indiscriminate is tantamount to having no preferences or values; in other words, it is a non-emotional state.[40]

Love is partial in that it focuses on the beloved.

A long-term romantic relationship is clearly incompatible with the unstable nature of emotions; however, it is somewhat more compatible with their partial nature.[41] Since an emotion necessitates limiting parameters, such as time, attention, and other types of 'mental energy', the number of its objects must be limited as well. We have greater resources to offer when we limit the number of emotional objects to which we are committed. The intensity of emotions is achieved by their focus upon a limited group of objects, just as a laser beam focuses upon a very narrow area and consequently achieves high intensity at that point. The exclusivity of emotions acts in the opposite direction of the impact of change, as it enhances our attachment to those who are unique and familiar to us in the sense of sharing common history.

Together with its partiality love has also the aspect of being able to compassionately attend to other people. As Kierkaegaard asked. 'Is not loving you to love the world?' In love, when 'the world is shining brighter' and 'I want to tell the world how happy I am', we can be more attentive to other people's needs. As Lynn, a divorcee, says about her new lover, 'I know that I have been very present for others during this intense time of thinking about him. It's as if I have two extremes, my attention for him—which I crave—but when I am away from it my attention with others is enhanced'.

Exclusivity appears to be more pronounced in romantic love than in other emotions. Romantic love must be exclusive and limited in scope, as it requires much of our resources. The depth of love can be achieved because of its more discriminative nature. Ortega y Gasset argued that whereas sexual desire involves superficial knowledge and evaluation of many objects, love involves a more profound knowledge and evaluation of very few objects. Like other instincts, sexuality tends 'to amplify indefinitely the number of objects which satisfy it, whereas love tends toward exclusivism'. In love, there is 'a progressive elimination of the things which formerly absorbed us. Consciousness contracts and is occupied by only one object'.[42] The partiality of romantic love is mostly evident in infatuation. However, an intense partial attitude cannot last for a long time, as the system needs the resources for its other needs. If this attitude is to be prolonged, it would typically become less partial and less intense.

People may be satisfied with a somewhat adjusted degree of romantic or sexual exclusivity, but the need for some type of exclusivity is profound, since it is considered to express the partial nature of emotions and one's romantic commitment.[43] Thus, a woman who was divorced for a long time told a reporter: 'For six years, I had an affair with a married person. I loved him very much and we had wonderful sex. Once I found out that he had affairs with other women, I terminated our relationship'. In a similar vein, Rosa says about her online married partner: 'Yes, he has a wife, to whom he is faithful. I accept this. But I could feel the place in me that didn't want him to have other online affairs'. It is clear that these women did not have an exclusive relationship with their married partner, but they did expect some kind of limited exclusivity. Once this limited exclusivity was abrogated as well, they could not continue the relationship. Even the presence of a limited exclusivity enables Andrea, who has been having an affair with a married man for the last three years, to say 'The thing I like most about him is his loyalty to me – he will never cheat on me'. Violating the (more flexible) boundaries will result in negative emotions.

People can cope with flexible love as long as the terms of flexibility are clear and respected. Thus, Rosa says:

> I am surprised, but I get a very warm and loving feeling inside of me thinking about him with his wife. I believe this is because I have framed my relationship with him in a particular way … and his being with someone who nurtures him and loves him is thrilling to me and touches me in a loving way.

Rosa is not merely able to live with this framework but can also see various advantages to it. People can cope with flexible love as long as the terms of flexibility are clear and kept. Similarly, before her marriage, Sandra, a woman in her 30s, had on two separate occasions a lover in addition to her stable relationship with a boyfriend. She said that in both cases she loved the boyfriend and the lover and felt good about it. The first case happened when Sandra's relationship with her boyfriend was quite fresh, in the infatuation stage. Paradoxically, the additional affair showed Sandra's boyfriend, who demanded its immediate termination, that indeed he did want to be with her at that time and its occurrence had the effect of strengthening the relationship (they moved in together). In the second case, the affair erupted when Sandra was involved in a relationship of three years, and in that case, Sandra and her boyfriend agreed that an additional affair 'is not the end of the world'. Nevertheless, a month after the affair was revealed, the primary relationship was terminated – though both of them still love each other. Asked to respond to the possibility that her boyfriend, rather than she, would have a secondary affair, Sandra claimed that she might accept this as long as everything would be out in the open and she would participate in choosing this woman, who might become an important part of her life as well.

Modern life makes it very difficult to maintain a significant measure of partiality, one reason being that it takes increasingly more people to satisfy a person's needs. It has also become significantly easier to form personal relationships, since we meet many people at work and in other circumstances. Unlike the era before the Industrial Revolution, when almost everyone worked at home, in modern society many work outside home. Furthermore, since people spend increasing amounts of time at work, they often spend more time with their colleagues than they do with their spouse at home, and thus much of their needs is satisfied by people other than their spouses. A married women who is conducting an online and offline affair with a married man notes: 'I have spent more time with him than with anyone else'. People may find that they have more in common with their colleagues and feel closer to them than to their spouse, about whom the colleagues may know nothing.

The introduction of the Internet has indeed notably increased the possibility of establishing personal relationships with many people. The Internet enables more married people to have an online affair without leaving their marriage. Consider the following message posted by a 50-year-old man:

> I'm married and intend to stay that way. I'm not looking for a soul mate, the love of my life, or someone to grow old with. I'm just looking for someone like me who is a little bored with the same ol' same ol'. If you would like to forget who you are for a little while, break the boredom, and a little no-strings-attached fun, get in touch. I don't care what you look like.[44]

It is worth noting that Casanova, who is the symbol of a lover seducing so many women, had 'merely' 124 women; an average user of the Internet today may have more online lovers in a matter of a few months.[45] The significant implications of online dating are far from being realized. It is plausible, however, that if adultery becomes too easy and commonplace, it could endanger the whole institution of marriage.

The assumption that one person can and should satisfy all the needs of another person is obviously problematic especially concerning some types of needs, for example, intellectual stimulation, psychological support, and social connections. Nevertheless, many people still believe that it is better, from a normative point of view, to have most of the beloved's needs satisfied by one person, or at least by very few. It is obvious that a person's intellectual needs can and should be satisfied by various people. It would be hard to defend the claim that a person should satisfy their intellectual needs by talking with only one single person or reading the writings of a single author. Exclusivity is of no relevance to intellectual needs. On the contrary, underlying the intellectual needs is the curiosity to enlarge our knowledge and be aware of novel perspectives and phenomena. Unlike emotions, which are quite focused, curiosity is expansive.

In the realm of social needs, the issue of exclusivity is of some relevance, but not to a very significant extent. A man may be jealous of the time his wife spends with her associates, but, typically, the objection is related to the issue of the quantity and the quality of these relationships, not to the idea of having social relationships with others. It is clear that one cannot have social relationships with everyone, as these relations require limited resources, such as time. Moreover, social relations may also require some preferential treatment, which cannot be given to everyone. Thus, we really should care more for those with whom we are having social relationships (especially those who are near and dear to us) than we do for strangers, yet this should not be an exclusive concern that violates the rights of strangers. Having close social relationships with several people should not preclude having a more profound relationship with one person. The type of attitude exhibited toward each person may be different. As Iris, a divorcee who had two lovers at the same time says:

> My attention is split – but the attention each of them gets is very different. I am not sure that true love exists with each of them, but I want to explore it. I am actually wondering if I want a 'constant companion'. I don't know if I want marriage or exclusivity. I may only want a part-time lover. At least I am starting to be creative in my preferences ... and starting to look at my life and recognize that I may not want to have someone in my life 24/7.

The difficulty in believing that a single person can satisfy each and every one of our needs better than anyone else is illustrated by way of analogy: the efficiency of a tool intended to fulfill one task is superior to that of a tool used for multiple purposes. Thus, using a multipurpose knife to cut both meat and vegetables produces slices that are less clean and precise than those produced using two separate knives for each task. Likewise, a race car may function well for racing, but would be highly inconvenient for family trips and many other purposes. In the same vein, Laura Kipnis claims that the female clitoris, which is devoted exclusively to pleasure, is far superior to the multitasking penis in producing constant sexual pleasure. This may be associated with the fact that 'women are the ones capable of multi-orgasm, like a sexual 24–7 ... multiple-orgasm store'. Clitoral orgasms are also 'far more powerful and thrilling'.[46] The downside of a very specific tool is that it requires greater proficiency for its use and can be valuable only in the very specific circumstances for which it was designed. Accordingly, the one-purpose clitoris is more efficient in generating ongoing intense sexual pleasure, but its use requires higher proficiency and is limited to more specific circumstances. Thus, although women are more capable of multi-orgasm, it is more difficult for them to have an orgasm. One survey found that whereas 75 percent of men report always having orgasms, only 29 percent of women say the same.[47] The operation of the multipurpose penis is easier and is less discriminating; it is, however, limited to a single orgasm and, hence, to a one-time show. (In some cases, after much hard work and begging, an encore may be provided as well.) These differences may partly explain why women tend to enjoy superficial casual sex less than do men, and they frequently seek the special circumstances associated with romantic love. The discriminatory aspect associated with the optimal function of the clitoris may be related to the woman's need for the absence of mental distractions. The complexity involved in preventing such distractions is one reason for the difficulty women face in reaching orgasms. In this sense, becoming familiar with each other and engaging in romantic exclusivity may make women more comfortable and reduce the amount of distraction. It seems that cyberspace provides better circumstances for being undistracted, as it enables lovers to enjoy their own private enclosed environment. Hence, women testify that it is often easier for them to achieve multiple orgasms while being on the Internet.

A 'multipurpose relationship', as well as the more 'specific relationship', has its advantages and disadvantages in everyday life. Determining the specific type and extent of the combination between these alternatives in our personal, intimate life depends on context and personality, but it is highly unlikely that a single person in an exclusive relationship can satisfy all our personal needs. Nevertheless, some degree of exclusivity is essential in personal relationships.

In the romantic realm, the fact that love demands the use of a substantial amount of a person's resources has been translated into the normative requirement that one should have only one romantic partner at any given time, who will fulfill most of one's needs. It is easier to fulfill this requirement during the infatuation stage of a romantic relationship; in later stages of the relationship, it is much harder. Romantic exclusivity may refer to various aspects: some types of attention (for example, fantasizing about or spending qualitative time with other people, looking at pornographic pictures), verbal activity (such as flirting), activity which may have romantic connotations (like going to a movie or a restaurant with other people), and sexual physical activity. Although in our society attention constitutes the least serious violation of romantic exclusivity and sexual physical activity the gravest, various societies ascribe different weights to such violations.

From a psychological point of view, the gravest violation is that involving profound emotional involvement with another person. Sexual activities are often perceived to entail such an involvement, and this may be one reason why such activities are usually considered the greatest violation of romantic exclusivity. However, this does not have to be the case – sex with a sex worker may generate less emotional involvement than an enduring romance lacking physical sexual activity. The issue of sexual and emotional exclusivity is of particular significance in committed relationships. Nevertheless, the practice of proclaimed monogamy with clandestine adultery is quite prevalent.[48] In the graphic words of Kipnis, 'taking an occasional walk on the wild side while still wholeheartedly pledged to a monogamous relationship isn't an earthshaking contradiction'.[49]

Not long ago the sexual realm was normatively limited (mainly for women) to marriage, whereas now it is acceptable in most parts of modern society to be part of casual relationships before and after marriage. The only stronghold that the sexual revolution has failed to destroy is the prohibition of married people to have sex with people other than their spouses. One can have various types of close emotional and social relationships without violating the prevailing norms of romantic exclusivity – going to a movie with one who is not your spouse or describing your profound wishes to this person are no longer considered activities that violate romantic exclusivity. From a normative point of view, married people seem to be allowed to do almost anything – except engage in sexual activity – with other people. Will married people be normatively able to join the party some time in the near future and satisfy their sexual needs outside of their committed framework? Do the boundaries of marriage reflect the boundaries of morality, or rather, as George Bernard Shaw said, 'the Trade Unionism of the married'? Not unlike other trade unions, that of the married couple attempts to keep its own existence by postulating rigid rules and boundaries. Do such rules and boundaries make people happy at the end of the day? Returning again to Shaw's ironic formulation, 'If the prisoner is happy, why lock him in? If he is not, why pretend that he is?'[50] Although there is no indication that the course of the sexual revolution has ended, the answers to the questions above are not obvious, as sexual relationships are associated with the core of close emotional ties.

It seems that caring, which involves profound friendship and helping the partner realize their full potential, is no less significant to romantic love than is exclusive sex. For one thing, sex is not as personal as caring. Indeed in the Aristotelian view, the essence of love is acting for the good of someone else for its own sake; such acting is closer to caring than to sex. Hence, in defining love, Aristotle does not mention the pleasure and pain associated with it, indicating perhaps their ancillary status.[51] George Bernard Shaw claims that the sexual drive which throws people into one another's arms at the exchange of a glance

> over-rides and sweeps away all personal considerations, and dispenses with all personal relations. The pair may be utter strangers to one another, speaking different languages, differing in race and color, in age and disposition, with no bond between them.[52]

Given that a unique personal attitude is crucial for profound romantic relationships, sex does not appear to be the best choice for defining the essence of romantic love. Unlike friendship, which may consist only of caring, romantic love involves also the aspect of attractiveness; hence, sexual desire plays a significant role in it. In romantic love, caring and sex do not compete with, but rather complement, one another. Caring and sex are of a different nature. The requirement for caring is a kind of guiding principle, whereas the demand for exclusive sex is a type of rigid rule. Unlike guiding principles, rigid rules have no degrees and are often less appropriate, as they cannot account for the complexity of contextual and personal circumstances. It is true that it is easier to detect violations of rigid rules, such as the prohibition of extramarital sex, than violations of guiding principles, such as the promotion of care in romantic relationships, but this is not a profound reason for postulating sex as the essence of love.

Caring should be of greater importance in genuine romantic relationships than exclusive sex. Any type of love involves caring, but many kinds of love, including the romantic one, may be devoid of sex. Indeed, a loveless marriage is characterized by the absence of caring, not of sex.[53] It also seems that caring is more closely associated with trustworthiness, which is apparently the characteristic that people desire most in others, who are supposed to be dear to them.[54] Unlike sexual activities, which involve reciprocity and the active participation of all parties, caring can be unidirectional without even the explicit knowledge of the other person. Since caring does not entail strict exclusivity in the sense attributed to sex, strict exclusivity may not be so essential to romantic love as it is assumed in Romantic Ideology.

The central place attributed to sex in profound romantic love can be challenged from the fact that some people are having sexless romantic love. Moreover, situations in which sex stands by its own have been criticized as degrading a human being into a commodity. It is surprising that those people – many of whom are religious or conservative – now consider sexual exclusivity as the hallmark of romantic love. Yet another, somewhat unusual, challenge to sexual exclusivity comes from couples who have sex with other people but only in the presence of each other. Joanne, who has been married to Paul for three years, says that she lets Paul have sex with her friends while she watches; she also organizes sex parties in her house and often has sex with up to six men in one session. She claims, however:

> It sounds mad, but Paul and I have very clear boundaries. He's not allowed to text any of the girls we sleep with or meet them alone. I'm not allowed to contact the guys either. That would be an affair in our eyes. Sleeping with friends is like fantasy, nothing more – and I've never been tempted to take it further … Paul and I are totally committed to each other – we're just honest about not wanting one sexual partner for the rest of our lives … Ultimately, love will always come before sex – and that's what counts.[55]

Determining the types of violation of strict exclusivity that may be tolerated is a complex task, highly sensitive to personality and contextual factors. Intense extramarital sexual relationships extending over a long period seem now to be the most blatant violation. Emotional ties are usually perceived to be of lesser weight and so are one-night stands. However, when emotional ties with the lover are profound and the extramarital affair consists of infrequent sexual encounters, it becomes more difficult to weigh the degree of hurt that can be caused to the partner. The severity of the violation may also be related to whether the new relationship has some added value compared to the primary one. Thus, going to an opera with a friend may be seen as a lesser violation if your partner dislikes opera. Similarly, in many circumstances a purely online extramarital affair may be regarded as a lesser violation than an offline affair. We can see that determining the degree of violating romantic exclusivity should take into account many factors and its results are not clear.

The pain experienced when finding out that a partner is engaged in another romantic relationship is often described as involving a loss of resources, such as love, time, attention, sexual energy, and financial resources. Rosa, a single mother, based her initial opposition to extramarital affairs on this reason: 'I believed that I only have a certain amount of time and energy for romance. So it is best spent with someone that is open to all the various possibilities of its development'. After a while, however, Rosa did find the time and energy for such affairs and twice was involved in affairs with married men, claiming that:

> I love who I love. Marriage may put restrictions on how I can be with married men, but it doesn't seem to impact how I perceive them and how I experience the fit with me. I still believe I wouldn't pursue a married man … wouldn't let myself open to him knowing he was married. Both these two just snuck in.

It seems that in principle she is opposed to having an affair with a married man, but yet appears quite flexible when circumstances prevail.

The unfaithful person is described as transferring such resources from the spouse to the lover. In accordance with this description, it has been claimed that infidelity consists of taking sexual energy of any sort – thoughts, feelings, and behaviors – outside of a committed sexual relationship, in such a way that it ruins the relationship.[56] There are two empirical assumptions here: (a) we have a given amount of sexual energy, and (b) having an affair decreases the sexual energy directed toward the spouse. It is not evident that these assumptions are always correct.

In many extramarital affairs loss of resources occurs, but its extent is unclear. Robin said that after 20 years with her husband she hardly thinks about him when they are not together, and therefore when she is with her lover she does not take away any emotional resources from her husband, as such resources are hardly devoted to him anyway. She argues that her current three-year extramarital affair even strengthens her primary relationship, by giving her more vitality to be in such a routine relationship. There are situations in which the partner involved in the extramarital adventure, for reasons of guilt, personal considerations, or a better emotional state in general, lavishes extra attention on the spouse. Along this view, it has been claimed that people should share their sexuality 'the way a philanthropist shares her money – because they have a lot of it to share, because it makes them happy to share it, because sharing makes the world a better place'.[57] It is obvious, however, that in many other cases, an extramarital affair reduces sexual desire and activity within the primary relationship, as resources and attention are directed away from the primary partner.

Analyzing the postulated exclusivity of the beloved from an economic point of view, we may speak of two seemingly opposed effects. One is the consumer effect, in light of which a product becomes more desirable when perceived as desired by others. The second is the rarity effect, in light of which the rarer the product is the more desirable it becomes. The price of a flawed coin is often much higher than that of otherwise identical coins which were minted in large quantities. The two effects are compatible in the sense that we do desire more what is desired by others, but for exactly this comparative issue, we value it more if it is ours alone. Thus, a man may desire a woman more if other men desire her as well (and accordingly, demonstrating that others are interested is a good way of increasing the interest of your partner), but this man will value her more if she will remain exclusively his romantic partner. She is a kind of trophy he won while the others did not.[58]

Even if loss of resources does exist in extramarital affairs, it is unclear whether this loss, rather than the loss of exclusivity, is the focus of concern here. In these cases, too, the spouse may develop negative emotional attitudes, such as jealousy and hostility. In light of the exclusive nature of emotions, romantic intimacy with someone is likely to impair such intimacy with another. This suggests that the value of certain activities is enhanced if people engage in them only with each other, despite the fact that they may reap some benefit in violating such exclusivity. Certain rewards may lose much of their value if they are not exclusive. This is true even when the violation of exclusivity is only imaginary. Jealousy exists also when the spouse is merely sexually interested in someone else, even when this interest is restricted to the level of fantasy.[59]

Despite the various challenges to the requirement of exclusivity in love, the requirement is not baseless, as it expresses a genuine psychological concern. Moral norms have changed and will change in the future – so we can expect to have such changes affect romantic and sexual exclusivity as well. Indeed, many people gossip about extramarital affairs of others without any negative moral connotation. It seems that in light of its greater presence, a growing number of people do not consider such behavior to be morally wrong. Consider, for example the following attitude of Rosa, a single mother who initially opposed to have an affair with a married person:

> I could never go ahead and make love to a married man unless I knew it would enhance his marriage. And the only way I could be sure of this is if there was no deception and no entering into it without prior consent from his wife.

Even this somewhat conservative woman does not see anything morally wrong with having an affair with a married man, when it is in the open and with the consent of the wife. Esther, a widow, terminated one of her many affairs with a married man, when she found out that he lied when he told her that he was divorced:

> Having such affairs is fine with me, as long as both of us choose to do it. I can be involved with a person who deceived his wife concerning his affair with me, but I cannot live with a liar who deceived me about his marital status. The only hard part of such a relationship is that it may hurt other people.

It appears then that a more pressing problem in this regard concerns the psychological aspect of the partners of those involved in extramarital affairs. Non-exclusive love may be accepted on a moral level, yet be quite painful on the emotional one. Married people having an extramarital affair may still feel intense jealousy when suspecting their lovers might be having an additional affair. Thus, Eva says that it so difficult for her to imagine her married lover being in the arms of another woman – the fact that he may be in the arms of his wife did not disturb her as much. She also promised her lover not to let anyone else beside him ever touch her – not referring, of course, to her husband, although indicating that she does not like making love to him.

The presence of intense romantic jealousy in so many people, even those who reject monogamy, is another indication of the profound psychological basis of romantic exclusivity. Two striking examples of such people are the psychiatrist Wilhelm Reich and the philosopher Bertrand Russell, both of whom rejected monogamy and promoted free and open love. Reich's wife reported that he was often insanely jealous:

> He would always emphatically deny that he was jealous, but there is no getting away from the fact that he would accuse me of infidelity with any man who came to his mind as a possible rival, whether colleague, friend, local shopkeeper, or casual acquaintance.

It is told of Russell, who had a long love affair with Lady Ottoline Morrell, that he was quite jealous of her and demanded she cease allowing her husband, Philip, access to her bed. Russell was also jealous of Ottoline Morrell's intimate, but nonsexual, relationship with Lytton Strachey, who was a homosexual.[61] Although sexual exclusivity may become in the near future less rigid, it is still of considerable psychological weight. Consider also the case of David, a married person in his late 40s, who can bear the fact that his married lover is having sex with her husband but is hurt upon hearing her stories about previous affairs she had while being married. As her marital framework is a given, sex within it can be tolerated; however, outside this unalterable framework, he would have liked his married lover to be exclusively his – even if this refers to past events. Although he is very confident in her immense love for him, his being one among other lovers diminishes the uniqueness of their relationship; it may also testify to the tentative nature of his lover's attitude. Concerning his own wife, David used to enjoy the stories about her affairs before they were married, since this gave him the feeling that he had won a real trophy. In all such examples, intellectual persuasion cannot overcome profound psychological attitudes, which seem to be a major force against non-exclusive love.

The current crisis of romantic love – 'Almost doesn't count'

Tonight you're mine completely …
Will you still love me tomorrow?

Carole King

One has my name, and the other has my heart …
To one I am tied, to the other I am true

Jerry Lee Lewis

Marriage is one of the chief causes of divorce.

Anonymous

No doubt, these are 'hard times for lovers', times in which we witness a high rate of romantic crises and marital dissolutions. Lovers have always had hard times, as romantic love is fragile and can end any moment, either because of external factors, such as death, or because of human factors, like finding a new love or experiencing declining intensity in a current relationship.

This problem is particularly evident in the case of sexual desire. There is a considerable amount of evidence indicating that sexual response to a familiar partner is less intense than to a novel partner. Consequently, the frequency of sexual activity with one's partner tends to decline steadily as the relationship lengthens, reaching roughly half the frequency after one year of marriage compared to the first month of marriage, and declining more gradually thereafter. A similar pattern of decline has been found also among cohabiting heterosexual couples and among gay and lesbian couples.[61] This decline is especially difficult to handle as the present dull situation is compared with the passionate past or the ideal postulated by Romantic Ideology.

Modern times are difficult for lovers – perhaps more so than in most previous eras. There are two major reasons for this: on the negative side, there are hardly any constraints preventing leaving the current romantic framework; on the positive side, there are many tempting accessible alternatives to the current romantic relationship. The romantic realm of reduced constraints and greater options lasts longer today. Compared with the past, people today live longer and have a greater capacity to materialize these alternatives at an older age. The invention of Viagra enables men to extend the period of their lives when they are sexually active and it has been claimed that older women reach orgasm more often than do younger ones.[62] The introduction of the Internet enables young people to be aware and involved from a much younger age in this romantic realm of reduced constraints and greater options. In light of the absence of clear romantic boundaries and the abundance of accessible romantic alternatives and their long duration, love in modern times becomes a more fluid concept and, accordingly, romantic bonds tend to be frailer than in the past.[63] This casts further doubt on the importance of rigid exclusivity, which is typical of the economy of scarcity employed in Romantic Ideology.[64]

Nowadays, there is greater freedom of choice. More than at any other time in human history, we can choose where we wish to live, what we want to do, and with whom we want to do it.[65] Moreover, our freedom to choose our beloved has now become potentially not just a one-off choice, but rather an ongoing experience. Lovers do not simply choose a beloved and then rest passively for the rest of their lives; they are in a fluid state, which requires constant effort and deliberation. Freedom, thus, has its own cost, and excessive freedom can increase people's uncertainty, insecurity, dissatisfaction, and depression. Therefore, having a greater choice can be a mixed blessing.[66] Indeed, sometimes adding options makes the task of choosing less attractive and more cumbersome; consequently, there are people who (occasionally) prefer others to make choices for them.[67] As Barry Schwartz persuasively shows, too much freedom from constraints is a bad thing, as unconstrained freedom leads to paralysis and becomes a kind of self-defeating tyranny. He further argues that due to the multiplicity of choices available at all times and on all fronts, people no longer know how to be satisfied with 'just good enough'. They always seek perfection. Such freedom also undermines the notion of deep commitment and social belonging to groups and institutions, bonds which are vital to our mental health.[68] Freedom constrained by ideals and boundaries may in fact be easier to bear and less dangerous than unconstrained freedom.

The decreased significance of normative boundaries in modern society has made people more indifferent and, hence, less emotional toward issues that in the past used to be considered emotion-provoking. If something is of lesser value, it is less meaningful, and hence less exciting. If, for example, the value of marriage is reduced, people become less emotional about the violation of its boundaries. Accordingly, people in modern society are more indifferent than people in previous societies concerning many issues, which were once emotionally loaded. This, however, does not imply that people in modern society are less affected by emotions than before. On the contrary, the vast amount of accessible, tempting, and risky alternatives can evoke high frequency emotions concerning issues that previously were out of reach.

Through much of human history, people hardly had an alternative and had to get used to their unsatisfactory romantic situation within the family. When no alternative is available, the current situation is accepted and its value is likely to increase. When many alternatives are available, settling for one's lot is extremely difficult. In addition to the fact that about 50 percent of all marriages end in divorce, the majority of the remaining 50 percent have at some point seriously considered divorce. In a study interviewing hundreds of couples, 80 percent said they had seriously considered divorce; the primary factors that kept them from divorce were economic considerations and concern for their children. In another large survey, 56 percent of people said that in the past five years they had considered breaking up but did not.[69] In light of such difficulties, Arlene Skolnick argues that 'The death of marriage has been proclaimed countless times in American history; and yet no matter how many times it fails to die, the threat never seems to lose its power.'[70]

Divorce may not indicate the rejection of the framework of marriage, but rather the rejection of a particular person. Similarly, the absence of divorce does not indicate the quality of the marriage. Some people decide not to divorce legally and to remain with a partner from whom they are divorced emotionally. In such cases, the pursued alternative is intended to supplement the marriage and to cope with the emotional emptiness within the marital relationship.[71] It is obvious, however, that the increased number of both divorced and virtually divorced people considerably increases the pool of tempting alternatives. It seems that the high rate of divorce is partly a result of people's exaggeratedly high expectations from marriage, rather than an indication that the ideal of a loving marriage is being abandoned; indeed, most people still expect to have a loved-centered marriage.[72]

Today, when external constraints on marital romantic relationships hardly exist, and so many tempting alternatives are available, being outside the romantic arena is harder and more frustrating. This is true both for those who are in a decaying romantic relationship and for those who are not in any intimate relationship. When the romantic environment offers people attractive alternatives, which are constantly available right at their fingertips, it becomes harder to avoid them. It is so hard now for those with no love to be happy with their lot.

A crucial element in emotions is, indeed, the imagined condition of 'it could have been otherwise'. Accordingly, 'almost' situations or 'near misses' come to have intense emotional effects, as it is so easy to imagine the alternative. These days, people are living in constant 'almost romantic' situations; their environment is so enticing – many people are perceived as romantically attractive and, what is more important, as being available and wanting to be so. Ignoring potential alternatives generates the feeling of a missed opportunity, which is associated with regret. Regret is basically a sorrow over a past alternative which was available to us, but we missed; regret concerns missed opportunities that we could have had if we had taken a different road. The more available the opportunity was, the more intense is the regret. Since our lives are full of missed opportunities, regret is inevitable. Failed actions and roads not taken are part and parcel of human existence. We are condemned to feel regret, a feeling which will be enhanced in the future as modern life is characterized by a significant increase in possible alternatives.[73]

The hard times that modern lovers face consist not only of constant doubts about which road to take, but also of constant regret of the many roads not taken. The abundance of alternatives and the perpetual possibility of getting something 'better' undermine commitment. The gap between the present and the potentially possible can never be bridged, although it seems to be so easy to do so. In this manner, the realm of infinite possibilities becomes a tyrannical force, keeping one from enjoying the present.

Searching for an alternative makes a lot of evolutionary sense, as alternative circumstances may worsen or improve our present situation. However, in many intimate relationships, the alternative will not make a drastic difference. An alternative is often more tempting from a distance, as the negative aspects are less discernable. Hence, when the brave modern lovers go on the road and make the tempting alternative real, the probability that they will eventually be disappointed is high, since the alternative may not be essentially different from what one already had at home. The constant search for change often prevents people from finding love. Several love songs refer to this issue: 'You can't be happy, while your heart's on the roam, you can't be happy until you bring it home' (The Brothers Four). And, 'My lonely heart wonders if there'll ever come a day, when I can be happy, but I can't see no way, because I let my mind wonder … (Willie Nelson).

George Levinger speaks about the cohesiveness of a personal relationship, which results from the total field of forces acting on the two partners to remain in the relationship. Levinger indicates three major categories of such forces: (a) the attractiveness of the relationship itself to each partner; (b) attractiveness of (actual and potential) alternatives; (c) external barriers that prevent the partners from leaving the relationship. Categories (a) and (c) increase cohesiveness, while (b) decreases it. Hence, reduction in attractiveness of the partner and fewer barriers tend to increase the vulnerability of relation-ships, while reduction in the attractiveness of the alternative increases the relationship's cohesiveness.[74]

The first category maintains its validity throughout the periods of the relationship: as time goes by, it is highly probable, although not inevitable, that the spouse will be perceived as less attractive, consequently reducing the attractiveness of the relationship. Do young, marrying couples fully realize the likelihood that they will lose their beauty and e.g., gain weight, or could it be that they think this only happens to others? It may be the case that the couple will find other points of attraction in each other or will evaluate the whole relationship as better when referring to features other than the spouse's external attractiveness. Nevertheless, since getting old does not, on the whole, make us more physically attractive, it should be assumed that the relationship as a whole ought to improve in order to offset the reduction in personal attractiveness.

The second category, the attractiveness of the alternatives, is more pronounced in modern society which is much more flexible in its structure and in the prevailing romantic relationships. Accordingly, in addition to having more available alternatives in modern society, there are also more attractive ones.

The most significant change that modern society introduced regarding the above categories concerns the reduction of barriers (or boundaries); this reduc-tion indirectly influences the attractiveness of both the partner and the alterna-tive. Among the boundaries whose significance has been reduced – although not completely eliminated – are women's economic dependence, legal obstacles to divorce, religious opposition to separation and divorce, harmful consequences for the children, and the social stigma of separation and divorce.[75] The main constraints remaining, although in a weaker form, are emotional ones, stem-ming from common history and types of attachment, which are not necessarily romantic. Among the emotional constraints, the one referring to possible harm to the children is particularly significant. It is no wonder that the two major factors that positively influence the stability of a marriage are the length of the marriage and the number of children the couple has: as duration and number of children increase, so does the stability of the marriage.[76]

In light of the above changes, the framework of marriage has been trans-formed from a formal contractual bond with hardly any possibility of future regret into an agreement that can be dissolved without the need to find cause, fault, or justification. The agreement is based on the desires of the heart, rather than on obligatory commitment. Hence, there is scarcely any reason to be ashamed of following one's heart and terminating the marriage, or even in having an affair of the heart.[77] The fact that often marital agreements now include most of the rights of the parties in case of separation (and otherwise) indicates that despite the couple's current intense love, they are seriously taking into account the possibility of separation. Such an agreement is inconceivable to those who uphold Romantic Ideology, which assumes that love lasts forever.

Ellen Berscheid and Bruce Campbell indicate that the aforementioned reduction in barriers does not only influence the marriage dissolution directly but also indirectly, as its influence permeates the relationship, casting a pallor over the partners' perceived satisfaction. Such varied and significant reductions in barriers make romantic dissatisfaction a real threat to marriages and increases the weight of justifying a particular marital framework through the examination of its specific qualities; thus, the 'sweetness' of a marriage, and in particular love itself, become the focus of intense scrutiny. Since both partners now have perpetual choice, they must invest more and more resources in maintaining the romantic relationship and in calculating the probability of its demise by the partner's withdrawal. The greater burden of maintaining the relationship may in some cases decrease its attractiveness and make it more ambiguous, and often more distressing to the partners, as they are constantly vulnerable to anxieties, distrust, and insecurity.[78]

It could be argued that not having what some consider the false security of a wedding ring may make people work harder to maintain their committed relationship. In this regard, the modern transition to a love-centered marriage demonstrates a similar trend, in which a more voluntary commitment also implies working harder to maintain it. While we would have expected the presence of a voluntary framework to have increased the quality of marriages, the high rate of marriage dissolution seems to counter this assumption.[79] As Iris, a divorcee, says:

> I know that after my divorce, while being with my lover of seven years, I never had a moment where I desired to stray in my fantasies or with my body; my fantasies and actions were always with him. It took no learning or willpower; I only desired him. However, I was not virtuous in my marriage – because I desired to be, and indeed was, with others.

The claim that it is people's fault inspires the prevailing belief that there is nothing wrong with the institution of marriage, it's just that you happened to get the wrong person with the wrong ideas. Accordingly, people who are disappointed by a certain romantic relationship try to build a similar type of relationship, but hopefully more successful, with another person. This kind of serial monogamy recognizes no structural problem in the alliance between a committed framework and passionate love. Adultery as well does not entirely undermine the institution of marriage: it is often conceived by some people as a practice that enables people to overcome the structural problem in marriage, and by others as a practice stemming from the specific person they are with and not from a problem generally inherent in marriage.

Blaming individuals for the difficulties in their romantic relationships is the basis of the tremendous boom of the counseling industry and the emphasis upon the need 'to work on your relationship'. This belief, which is associated with the belief that love can last forever, puts us in a perpetual search for prescriptions, interventions, and aids which are supposed to help love survive.[80] Bauman argues that the prevailing assumption is that the complexity in romantic relationships is 'too dense, too stubborn and too difficult to unpack or unravel for individuals to do the job unassisted'. People hope to hear from the counselors 'how to square the circle: to eat the cake and have it, to cream off the sweet delights of relationship while omitting its bitter and tougher bit'. This is, of course, an impossible task; consequently, the demand for counseling will never run dry, since no amount of counseling 'could ever make a circle non-circular and thus amenable to being squared'.[81]

The increasing demand for therapy and relationship advice is understandable in light of the dramatic decrease in external barriers preventing partners from leaving the relationship. It seems that although this kind of help is of some benefit, in many cases it is not sufficient. Accurate understanding of the inherent difficulties in maintaining romantic love within a committed framework may make the situation easier – but not easy.[82] The prevailing dissatisfaction with romantic relationships is due then not merely to personal flaws of certain individuals, but also to features relating to the nature of emotions and romantic love, and to rapid changes in modern society. Romantic Ideology is hardly suitable for romantic coping – on the contrary, it makes such coping next to impossible. It appears that a more profound solution is that in which Romantic Ideology is significantly revised.

Facing the challenge – 'I will survive'

> People say that love's a game,
> A game you just can't win.
> If there's a way, I'll find it some day.

Paul Anka

> The chains of marriage are so heavy that it takes two to bear them, and sometimes three.

Alexandre Dumas

Falling in love is easier than staying in love, and the process of falling out of love is a more gradual one than that of falling in love; hence, we may speak about the gradual deterioration of love as 'stumbling out of love'.[83] As Mitchell indicates, 'Love and marriage may go together like a horse and carriage, but it is crucial that the horse of passion quickly be tethered by the weight of the carriage of respectability to prevent runaways'.[84] Coping with the romantic challenge to maintain long-term romantic love requires the distinction between the loving attitudes that become routinized and those that are hopelessly stale. Whereas it seems that the latter must be dissolved, the former may be saved with much effort and work.

In its infatuation stage, romantic love hardly requires any work or effort. The wish to turn this stage into a lasting romantic relationship is a challenge entailing the investment of blood, sweat, and tears. Kipnis sharply criticizes the demand 'to work on your relationships' claiming that when it comes to love, trying is always trying too hard: work doesn't work. Working on our relationship means we are now both working a double-shift. When you are 'working at it', you know it has gone wrong. Kipnis further argues that domestic life has become such a chore that staying at the office is more relaxing; hence, love has become a form of alienated labor. And in any case, she asks, 'why should we work so hard? Why work when you can play?' Kipnis also mentions that no one works at adultery and adultery hardly needs endorsements; it's doing quite well on its own.[85]

In response to this view, we should distinguish between long-term personal relationships and acute emotions, such as romantic love and sexual desire. There are various experiences and situations in life that require constant work. Keeping in good physical shape requires constant hard-working activities. Given that we live in a dynamic environment, maintaining our current situation constant – not to mention improving it – requires various activities that involve investing in resources and sacrificing other needs. However, the generation of spontaneous short-term emotional experiences, such as anger, sexual desire, and romantic love, may not need prior work. Getting angry typically does not require work; by contrast, effort is undoubtedly required in order to decrease the number of hostile or anger generating experiences within a long-term ongoing relationship. Even maintaining good sex does not just happen; it also requires investing effort and preparatory activities (which may be enjoyable in and of themselves). Maintaining emotions at a certain desired level of intensity and frequency within a long-term relationship requires work. Sometimes the work is easy and pleasurable; sometimes it requires much more effort and other types of investment. Enduring personal relationships require work for maintaining their high quality. Love does not suddenly float into our life, and maintaining it is not an effortless experience: we do search for love and we do work for its continuation.[86]

The work underlying an enduring personal relationship is neither a sufficient condition nor a necessary one for the emergence of love. Nevertheless, work can in many circumstances enhance love. This is evident not only in the case of maintaining the intensity of love but also in obtaining new love. In both cases effort is of considerable weight. We invest more effort in something which is significant for us; at the same time it is also true that something we invest more effort in becomes more significant. The saying 'easy come, easy go' reflects situations in which something we have gained without much invested effort is of lesser significance to us and, hence, we don't mind losing it. In this regard, Georg Simmel argues that:

> It is not only the attractiveness of a commodity that determines the price we are willing to pay for it. There are, rather, countless occasions on which the item is attractive and desirable to us only because it costs something.[87]

It is interesting to note that online love has considerably reduced the effort required for its emergence; consequently, ending this kind of relationship is easier as well. Mitchell rightly points out that passionate desire may not be contrived, but nevertheless we can do a lot in constructing the contexts in which such a desire typically occurs.[88] Working on our romantic relationship should do just that. It may not only be conducive for coping with some of its difficulties, but may augment love as well. We should not then think that 'in love things just fall into place' as if they were meant to be there all along. Leaving things to chance is not taking love seriously.[89] Keeping a long-term love requires patient cultivation. Finding the right person is not the end of the story, it is the beginning of a long journey demanding a lot of work and which may be seen later on as not worth the effort.[90] The idealization of love may be a natural need or dream most people share. However, fulfilling such love, or even approaching it, is neither natural nor easy, as it requires much personal sacrifice and effort.

Many people are intellectually aware of the fact that ideal love is almost impossible to achieve and even harder to keep. Many are even emotionally persuaded in the impossibility of such love. As Patsy Cline sings, 'True love has no chance to win. I've loved and lost again'. Nevertheless many people endlessly continue their search for such an endless love. As Lynn, a divorcee who could not find yet her true love, says, 'I know love is there … just as the sun is always there behind the clouds – regardless of how thick they might be … and how great the obstruction to accessing the love/light/warmth'. Even those who criticize Romantic Ideology may want to experience such love. They have an unfulfilled need for being in such a loving relationship. It is interesting to note that an overwhelming majority of people (over 85 percent of Americans) said that they would not marry someone they were not in love with and about

50 percent of Americans believe that they have the right to divorce when romantic love fades. These attitudes express the profound wish to combine romantic love with marriage.[91] Moreover, a 2007 ACNielsen's survey indicates that 70 percent of people surveyed said that marriage is for life and 60 percent said that marriage is one of their lifetime goals. Although the attitudes toward marriage are largely dominated by a country's cultural and religious beliefs – with very opposing views among people in the developed West and the emerging East – the wish for a stable, long-term relationship is still a desired goal.[92] Little wonder that most romantic movies end in marriage or very close to it.

Skolnick argues that most family researchers 'see the combination of high marriage rates and high divorce rates as the paradoxical outcome of the high expectations Americans bring to marriage'.[93] Facing the challenge of the modern framework of marriage has to do with, among other things, changing the expectations and values associated with this framework. One way of facing the problematic connection between romantic love and marriage is to accept that marriage should essentially involve a companionable love rather than a romantic one; if romantic love and passionate sex do occur in a marriage, it should be seen as a fortunate bonus. Many people adopt this view. However, as indicated above, most people still seek to combine romantic love with marriage or attempt to find some other long-term romantic relationship.

Infatuation makes its subjects highly attractive to each other, hence providing favorable circumstances for the personal relationships to endure. If indeed the emotional intensity of romantic love is bound to decrease as time goes by (as is the case of all other types of emotions), it is beneficial to have a very high level of emotional intensity at the beginning of the relationship, which may involve positive overestimation of the partner, in order to still have some intensity left once the expected decrease will occur. If people are skeptical about their beloved at the very beginning of the relationship, they will not invest the efforts needed for the flourishing of their relationship.

Romantic Ideology wants to enjoy the best of all worlds: having intense excitement together with stability, security, and long duration. This combination is rare, if at all possible. As indicated, a mental system cannot be unstable for a long period and still function normally; it may explode due to continuous increase in intensity. If emotions were to endure for a long time regardless of what was occurring in our environment, as is required in ideal love, they would not have an adaptive value. Infatuation is the closest we can get to ideal love. Infatuation, however, lacks a broad range of emotional perspectives which are so critical for an enduring emotional attitude. Accordingly, infatuation does not last for ever; its emotions are essentially tentative.

Idealized love can be found also in cyber love, but this love has its own limitations: it lacks physical touch and it typically involves a profound wish to be upgraded into an offline love. Also cyber love does not last forever. It is interesting to note that people who know the limitations of cyber love may not want to upgrade it into an offline relationship fearing it will end at this point. Rosa, who conducts a romantic relationship online, is an example in this regard: 'Ironically, the closer I feel to him, the less I want to imagine being lovers in actual reality. I don't want to take the chance of doing something that would jeopardize our increasing closeness'.

Facing the romantic challenge requires paying attention to reality and to ourselves. It is time now to examine a possible alternative to Romantic Ideology.

Chapter 7

Novel romantic reality
'You've got to take the bitter with the sweet'

You've got to give a little,
Take a little,
And let your poor heart break a little,
That's the glory of love.

Bette Midler

You don't know anything about love if you don't accept compromise.

Clive Owen, in the movie Closer

In Chapter 5, we showed that our imaginative capacity underlies our formation of ideals and boundaries; consequently, we are incapable of fulfilling these ideals in their entirety. As ideologies are comprised of ideals and boundaries, it is natural that they cannot be sustained in their entirety. However, since ideologies are not merely theoretical frameworks, but have also significant practical implications, their implementation is of great concern to their advocates. In Chapter 6, we showed that in addition to the general difficulties of implementing ideologies, Romantic Ideology presents even more difficulties, which are related to the structure of the emotional system as well as to changes in modern society. In light of these increasing challenges, it is highly probable that in implementing Romantic Ideology, significant revisions will have to be made – even to the extent of proposing a different approach.

In this regard, we suggest distinguishing between compromise and accommodation: a compromise consists of making concessions to something that is perceived as negative, whereas an accommodation is introducing change so as to eliminate the negative element. Major compromises and accommodations prevailing in the romantic realm are postponement of romantic gratification, accepting declining romantic intensity, modifying the exclusive nature of the romantic relationship, choosing serial monogamy, and loving a number of people simultaneously. In this sense, the future is now. In the next chapter, we shall present an alternative to Romantic Ideology – the Nurturing Approach.

Compromises and accommodations – 'Love me less but longer'

I'm no angel, but does that mean that I can't live my life?

Dido

Blow me a kiss from across the room ...
Touch my hair as you pass my chair,
Little things mean a lot.

Kallen Kitty

In this chapter, we indicate that contrary to Romantic Ideology's extreme uncompromising nature – for example, in terms of temporal duration, intensity, and exclusivity – the reality of romantic relationships in fact includes many compromises and accommodations. Paradoxically, both the extreme form and the compromising behavior exist simultaneously within modern society.

Many people suffer because of the gap between their ideal notion of a lover and their real-life partner. One way of coping with this gap is to alter the ideal notion; this will be discussed in the following chapter. Another way of to cope is to change the partner – either by subjectively changing the lover's perception of the partner or by objectively regulating the partner's behavior. The subjective manner uses various cognitive tactics such as positive illusions, and looking on the bright side of the relationship by focusing more on the partner's virtues. As this manner has been discussed throughout the book, we would like now to say a few words about the potential value of the objective manner in regulating the partner's actual behavior.

The discrepancy between the ideal lover and the actual partner is not easy to accept and may motivate a desire to replace the partner. Before doing this, people often try to regulate the partner's behavior in order to change that behavior and bringing it closer to the ideal. Although partner regulation seeks to improve the relationship, the considerable difficulties in actually changing another person's behavior – particularly when that person is one's partner and one is trying to adjust that behavior to an ideal that may be unrealistically perfect – generally produce negative outcomes in the relationship. This is because such attempts are likely to increase awareness of the discrepancy between the idealized lover and the partner and they are also likely to communicate lack of acceptance of the partner.[1] In concluding their extensive study on this issue, Nickola Overall and his colleagues argue that the greater the attempt to change the partner, the greater the gap becomes between the perception of the partner and the ideal standards, and the more negative perceptions of the discrepancy are produced. This may seem counterintuitive, particularly given that the aim of the regulatory attempts is presumably the exact opposite. However, attempts to change the partner are powerful signals that he or she is failing to meet expectations, so that the greater the amount of attempted regulation to which people are subjected, the less they believe that they match their partner's ideal standards. Accordingly, regulatory efforts tend to backfire, and people become even unhappier with their relationship.[2] The limitations and even negative value of attempts at partner regulation further underline the importance of compromises.

At the beginning of any revolution, when a new order is established, the prevailing attitude of the revolutionary leaders is typically extreme: there is an idealization of the novel, to the extent that most previous values are perceived to be inadequate. As time goes by, the need to find a new middle ground becomes urgent. In the process of finding this golden mean, we give up some of the revolutionary ideals, but since the new attitude is more sensitive to the dictates of reality, the ideology's vitality and longevity is secured. In such circumstances, both the extreme form and the compromising behavior exist together within the same society. Does this mean that we must compromise the ideals themselves and not merely their implementation? Can we speak about compromising love and still leave room for intense romantic experiences?

Concerning most emotional experiences, particularly negative ones, we usually appraise compromises that people make in a positive manner; thus, we praise the person who has not behaved angrily despite being provoked to do so. In love, such compromises typically carry negative connotations, as they are compared to the tenets of Romantic Ideology, which assumes that 'love can conquer all' and therefore needs no compromises. Also the ideology that purports that 'love can do no evil' encourages people to reject such compromises on the part of the lovers. Accordingly, the great romantic heroes do not make compromises – and in this sense are not mature.[3] Indeed, when people speak about mature love they do not refer to a stormy, exciting experience, but rather to something akin to companionable love. Mature love is typically morally good, but it is not what passionate romantic love is about. Hence many people may say that they never want to become mature, because settling for what is feasible while ignoring the desirable is an obvious sign of decay.

Situations, which are perceived as ideal and are supposed to be ageless, cannot continue to exist unaltered within a shifting reality. The unique structure and constraints of reality can never be fully compatible with the inalterable and eternal characteristics of the perfect ideal. Accordingly, perfect or ideal love is easier to achieve in an imaginary environment, for instance, that of cyberspace or long-distance relationships, where many constraints are absent. In reality, moderation and compromise, which come in various degrees, are much more common. Can we apply them to romantic love?

At first, moderation and compromise seem to be in diametric contradiction to emotions in general, and romantic love in particular. People do not say to their partners that they love them moderately; such a statement would be an insult. Loving at a moderate intensity is perceived in this case as an expression of deficient love. Indeed, lovers tend to emphasize their extreme attitude. As Flora says about her married lover, 'I adore, love and desire this man to the extreme. The universe has never seen a greater love'. However, in fact, unlike the total and uncompromising nature of ideal love, in reality, love comes in degrees and entails various behaviors and various degrees of intensity, moderation and compromise.[4] The value of moderation is emphasized in the Jewish tradition, for example, in which sexual intercourse is said to be one of eight things that are beneficial in small quantities but harmful in large quantities.[5] Similarly, Erich Fromm believed that satisfaction in love involves true humility, courage, faith, and discipline.[6] Whereas the initial stages of love often involve disregarding reality, long-term satisfaction cannot be maintained in such a manner. Hence, it may even be argued that maintaining long-term romantic love can only be done by being moderate, by knowing your limitations and not thinking that you can have it all. Only moderate people can eat their cake and have it too, since they do not eat the whole cake. It is indeed difficult to take moderate bites of a delicious cake and not desire to eat it all of it. An easier approach is not to eat the cake at all, to avoid it completely; but in this case the cake is of no value. Thus, moderation need not be perceived solely as the elimination of pleasure contrived to reduce one's vulnerability to the desirable; rather, it can be understood as a means for securing long-term pleasure.

Moderation and compromise raise one of the major difficulties of Romantic Ideology: its disregard for reality. George Bernard Shaw, in his *Don Juan in Hell*, argues that earth is the home of the reality's slaves, heaven the home of its masters, and hell is home to the unreal and to the seekers of happiness. On earth you must take account of reality, in heaven reality is of no concern as you can master it, and in hell you overcome reality by disregarding it. In hell you escape the tyranny of the flesh and 'you are a ghost, an appearance, an illusion, a convention, deathless, ageless: in a word, bodiless'. In hell there are no social, political, or religious constraints, and no hard facts to contradict you – 'nothing but a perpetual romance'.[7] It is questionable whether on earth we must be the slaves of reality: unlike animals, human capacities give us some degree of freedom, thereby enabling us to play with reality to our benefit. It is evident, however, that on earth we must take account of reality. This can be done by revising our ideals or at least their implementation in a way which is more compatible with reality.

From the standpoint of the individual upholding the ideal, there are two main methods to achieve this: compromise and accommodation. In compromising, we agree to make the required revision without actually making a suitable personal change in our attitudes and preferences; accommodation implies making such a personal change. To compromise is 'to make a concession to something derogatory or prejudicial'; to accommodate is 'to make fit, suitable, or congruous'.[8] A person may be regarded as a compromise partner only within a certain framework. He may be a compromise in comparison to the fairytale prince on the white horse, but not in comparison to most, or even all, other men. Speaking about compromising love seems odd. Thus, one would not say to his beloved, 'I love you darling, though this love is a compromise for me'. However, one could say, 'I love you darling, and I am ready to accommodate myself in order to make our relationship successful'. In compromises, which may involve concessions that are considered depressing, one does not change one's attitudes but rather, unwillingly, agrees to something that is essentially negative but nonetheless can be tolerated when a more valuable end is achieved. In accommodation, the lover changes his or her own attitudes in order to perceive the other in a positive manner; this person is perceived now by the lover as a suitable partner rather than a problem.

Accommodation may be characterized as positive growth, expansion of capacity, adaptability, and flexibility. The process of accommodation involves learning and adaptability, whereby accepting the change is accompanied by some modification in the creature. In this sense, accommodation sustains a more profound and durable process. Not all compromises can be accommodated, since this process may require a change in constant character traits and attitudes. In such a situation, we are required to adopt the compromise while being aware of its problematic nature. There is no doubt that we must make compromises in our life; the question is how many of those can be turned into accommodations and how many will remain derogatory concessions. One measure of the profoundness of a romantic relationship is the ability to turn what seems to be a compromise into an accommodation.

As in other important areas of life, love requires both compromises and accommodations. The challenge is to maintain romantic love despite them. However, sometimes we compromise when we do not need to (and should not) do so. Sometimes, we compromise to the wish of others and thus relinquish our love in return for temporary comfort. This may be what is meant in the lines of a Patsy Cline song: 'I cried all the way to the altar, a smile was on my face, but tears were in my heart … I've thrown away my chance of happiness with you.' Compromises are often made too early and too easily. Many people are aware of their compromises, and even see themselves as getting a raw deal, already at the wedding ceremony or soon after. Other people may be in a situation that hardly requires any compromise and accommodation; yet, as the current crisis in romantic relationships clearly indicates, these are a very few. Needless to say, compromises and accommodations do not guarantee the continuity of passionate romantic love, but they are often necessary.

The following are major types of prevailing compromises and accommodations made in romantic relationships.

- *Postponing romantic gratification* – waiting for example, a few years for the beloved to be available.
- *Declining romantic intensity* – measured, for instance, by the frequency of sexual activities or the time spent together.
- *Flexible exclusivity* – enlarging the scope of activities which are not restricted to the beloved.
- *Serial monogamy* – keeping the ideal alive, but maintaining it only for a limited period of time.
- *Polyamory* – loving more than one person at the same time.

The above types of compromises and accommodations are not mutually exclusive; people may engage in several of these compromises and accommodations at the same time. In the next sections, we discuss these types in more detail.

Postponing gratification: – 'Never giving up all this love'

One day I know I'll be back again, please wait till then.

The Mills Brothers

Lonely rivers cry, wait for me, wait for me,
To the open arms, wait for me.

Elvis Presley

This kind of compromise, in which people postpone their romantic gratification by waiting for appropriate circumstances, does not undermine the foundations of Romantic Ideology and is even encouraged by it. Unlike online love, where love promises to 'take the waiting out of wanting', true love involves a lot of waiting and effort.[9] Thus, we are told in the Bible that 'Jacob served seven years for Rachel; and they seemed unto him but a few days, for the love he had for her'.[10] True love can wait and prevail even when the accompanying suitable circumstances are not present. However, such waiting is not due to maturation or accommodation, but rather to the great value of the beloved and the refusal to compromise for less than the perfect person. Lines such as: 'I'll be waiting for you till the sun don't shine'; 'waited in the darkness patiently', 'I will patently wait for you till the end of time', and 'save your love for me' are common among lovers and appear in many popular songs and other cultural works. A similar type of compromise is expressed by a woman who, on her 50th wedding anniversary, says, 'The first 30 years were difficult, but after that it became easier'. In this kind of accommodation, people compromise over the less significant temporal aspect in order to avoid compromising over the more significant aspect: the identity of the beloved. This delay implies a profound rejection of significant compromises in love. As Barbra Streisand puts it, 'I am a woman in love, and I'd do anything, to get you into my world'. In Romantic Ideology, compromises function as a necessary means to an end; they have no value of their own.

Lovers are prepared to be patient and to make compromises necessitated by their unique situation (and that of their beloved) when this is the only way to fulfill their desired love. As Lisa, a married woman who is waiting for her own and her lover's divorce to come through, says about her married lover, 'since all my life I have been waiting for a love like this, I am ready to further wait for him to be mine'. In such cases, love is present and the desired end that justifies the delay is its complete and actual materialization. Due to the immense intensity of their love, lovers are ready to wait, in the hope of implementing such a precious love. Thus, lovers express willingness to compromise over the accompanying circumstances associated with true love, such as the freedom to be together whenever they want, but not over love itself. At the end of the day, these lovers believe that genuine love should make no compromises, but that the road to this paradise is full of unavoidable obstacles. Moreover, the highly valuable nature of the end makes the long and treacherous path a worthwhile experience, through which the lovers demonstrate their morally strength in overcoming the obstacles. As one troubadour said, 'Each day I grow better and am purified, for I serve and revere the most suave lady in the world'.[11] Waiting also reveals additional qualities of the beloved. Lisa says:

> Every day I am seeing more wonderful attributes in him, and although I think I would love him without finding them, because there are enough of them already, it is so wonderful to see that there are more and more of them and that they never end.

There are cases in which the perfect lover is even ready to sacrifice his love for deeds which may benefit more people. Rhet Butler in *Gone with the Wind* restrains his desire to be with Scarlet when he decides to go to the battle 'for his country', from which he knows he might not return.

Such compromises are in accordance with the purity of love assumed in Romantic Ideology.

It appears that the only way of fulfilling the ideal love in its entirety is by disregarding reality. Reality requires compromises, which Romantic Ideology despises; words such as 'convenient', 'comfortable', 'feasible', and 'compromise' are not part of the vocabulary of idealistic lovers. Romantic Ideology describes love as involving a boundless desire, which is compatible with the belief that love can conquer all. On the one hand, compromises are fundamentally inappropriate in such love, yet on the other hand, due to this very quality, lovers are constantly obsessed with the need to seek beyond their normative boundaries, as they cannot accept anything less than an embodiment of the ideal.

Declining intensity – 'Shouldn't I be less in love with you?'

And it's too late baby, though we really did try to make it, something inside has died, and I can't hide [it].

Carole King

Give it all, give it all to me.

Carly Simon

The kind of compromise referring to the decline in romantic intensity could easily turn into an accommodation; this compromise entails altering some of love's typical activities, rendering it more compatible with the absence of novelty. This could be done by narrowing one's expectations in terms of the features associated with love; however, most likely this would also diminish the relationship. There is also the possibility of attributing less importance to certain types of feelings and behaviors involved in romantic love, so as to maintain the love overall without jeopardizing the entire relationship. For instance, in a loving relationship, sexual desire and activity may decrease as time goes by, while caring and the desire to spend time together may increase. Accepting that the frequency of sexual intercourse is not the only measure of romantic love – nor even the most important one – means attributing less significance to it within the entire romantic framework. Thus, recognizing that each feature of love may be weighted differently and that the significance of a single feature may shift over time can even help flame the romantic fire. This approach is different from the one that advises us to 'expect less from marriage'. Lowering our level of expectation may reduce the risk of disappointment and temper our excitement, yet it does not offer a solution to the issues that arise in long-term romantic relationships; it merely indicates one way of escaping them. By analogy, cutting off one's head to prevent headaches is not a recommendable course of behavior.

The coping method suggested here is to expect less in one domain but to expect more in others; in such a way, people are still able to experience all aspects of love. Nevertheless, there are certain features which are necessary for romantic love: relationships from which passionate desires are completely absent cannot be considered romantic love.

In Chapter 4 we suggested the distinction between the sentiment of love, i.e., the dispositional, attitudinal complex of love, and the specific, acute emotion of love. The sentiment may be realized by various eruptions of the acute passionate emotion. When love is at its initial stages, the intervals between each eruption may be brief; as time goes by, the hiatus between each eruption will become longer. Accommodating the growing interval, while filling it with committed care or other types of valued togetherness, is typical of long-term romantic love. A relationship can be officially declared dead when no eruption happens, or if the intervals are not filled with valued togetherness. Accepting the existence of longer intervals between each passionate eruption implies that the person does not have to apologize for not wishing to be romantic at a certain time. The obligation to feel romantic whenever the other person requests it actually undermines this type of accommodation and prevents people from enjoying their togetherness. One can try occasionally to kindle romantic love and thereby decrease the length of the intervals between each eruption, but the very existence of relatively lengthy intervals is something that ought to be accepted.

The above claims can be illustrated by reference to happiness. There are various determinants of human happiness, such as income, work, age, and genetic structure. A particular relevant factor for our present discussion is the frequency of the occurrence of the acute emotion of joy. This factor has been found to be the single best predictor of enduring happiness.[12] In a sense, long-term enduring happiness, which may also be described as the sentiment of happiness, consists of acute brief emotions of joy; thus, a succession of positive experiences will increase our long-term happiness. Accordingly, the psychologist David Lykken provided the following practical advice:

> A steady diet of simple pleasures will keep you above your set point. Find the small things that you know give you a little high – a good meal, working in the garden, time with friends – and sprinkle your life with them. In the long run, that will leave you happier than some grand achievement that gives you a big lift for a while.[13]

As in happiness, also in love 'little things mean a lot'. When love comes in small but frequent doses, it may be even more profound.

A relationship in which intensity has declined is by no means the same as a disaffected relationship. Disaffection refers to the absence of loving feeling and not merely to declining intensity.[14] In a loving romantic relationship, sexual desire, which is an important component of romantic love, can decline in intensity, but still remain alive.

Reducing exclusivity – 'Till you opened my eyes'

To be true to one alone, don't seem to matter any more.

Patsy Cline

Never marry a railroad man, he loves you every now and then.

Shocking Blue

The compromise of reducing exclusivity challenges the rigidity of various romantic boundaries and makes them more flexible. As the major stronghold of romantic exclusivity is sex, the process of reducing exclusivity will largely be concerned with this realm. Reducing romantic exclusivity conflicts with a basic emotional characteristic – that of partiality – while maintaining another important characteristic – that of change and novelty. Reducing exclusivity goes to the heart of ideal love, i.e., the perception that the beloved is the one and only person suitable for the lover's profound love.

Historically, the social framework of marriage has been considered advantageous, since it offered benefits in areas such as overall life satisfaction, sex, children, living arrangements, social companionship, and financial security. Not all of these factors have had a constant weight through history. Thus, in some sectors of certain societies, personal fulfillment and sex were not significant to marriage. Currently, society provides alternative forms of relationships that can offer these benefits, too. There are plenty of sexual opportunities outside of wedlock, some of which are considered to be more exciting than others. There are fewer children in each family: single-child families have become quite widespread, and it is now possible to raise children outside of the marital framework. There are no significant problems in finding proper living arrangements for single people, and these people can have rich social lives and financial security (though sometimes divorce increases the financial burden). It seems that marriage has lost many of its traditional advantages over other forms of relationships.

In light of these changes, there has been a significant increase, over the last few decades, in the percentage of single households in modern society.[15] Such an increase by no means suggests that marriage is dead, but that a growing number of adults are spending more of their lives single or living unmarried with partners. Nevertheless, it seems that the desire for marriage remains strong and constant.[16] The new circumstances have significantly increased the autonomy of individuals and in particular that of women. The greater independence of individuals weakens the expectation for romantic exclusivity of the kind that involves significant dependence upon the partner. Lovers who do not live together see each other for limited times, do not depend upon each other for their major needs, and thus they need not abide by any formal dictates or constraints.

As we acknowledge that love and happiness depend upon a variety of enjoyable experiences, it becomes clear that one single person is unlikely to be the source of all such experiences. Focusing all of our emotional investment on one person may be as risky as investing all our money in one stock. Diversifying our emotional investment may be as beneficial as diversifying our financial investments. With this approach we should not expect to have a one-time significant windfall profit, but our investments may benefit us in the long run, or, in other words, we may have constant enjoyable experiences. Needless to say, the above comparison between stock market and relationship diversification is quite limited, for many features are dissimilar and incomparable. Thus, while stockholders are constantly searching for a better stock than the one they hold, lovers want their beloved to stay forever and will replace them only if they cannot be together any more. Although investment in a relationship indeed may be risky, the main goal is to maintain its value for the long run, whereas the goal of having a stock is to sell it at the most opportune moment. Moreover, unlike stocks, the beloved can decide single-handedly to leave the relationship.

Given that Romantic Ideology rejects the possibility of being devoted to more than one person, it must also deny the possibility that it takes more than a single person to satisfy one's needs. The contention of this ideology is 'all you need is love'; it is not surprising, therefore, that it expects the beloved to fulfill all of the lover's needs. Susan, a married woman in her 50s, loves her husband dearly and is aware of his profound devotion and love to her; nevertheless, she finds herself profoundly dissatisfied with his intellectual and cultural shallowness. As Susan upholds Romantic Ideology, she expects her husband to fulfill all her needs, including her intellectual and cultural ones: in this sense, Susan is yet another victim of Romantic Ideology. The fact that one dislikes opera does not imply that he is an unfit parent or an unloving husband. It is told of Albert Einstein that he liked boating very much, whereas his wife hated it; so, he went boating with other women, a fact which his wife found difficult to accept. Although such non-exclusive activities are more acceptable these days, people may still be uncomfortable with them, especially (in the case of heterosexual people) when the chosen companion is of the opposite sex.

The problematic of romantic exclusivity is also reflected in the particular ways in which people choose their mates nowadays. Modern technology, and especially the Internet, enables people to choose their future partner according to very specific features. When one writes, for example, that he wants to find a vegetarian Jewish woman who is interested in wild animals in Africa, he does not necessarily assume that this woman will be the most suitable sexual partner, his most intimate friend, or the one best suited to help him develop his intellectual capacities. The same tendency to focus in on specific features can be seen in the search for the best sexual partner, which is sometimes conducted by describing the precise length of his sexual organ. It is obvious, then, that the desired person being described is not meant to assume the roles of friendly and intellectual companionship. Limiting the search to such specific details is yet another indication of the practical bankruptcy of the concept of romantic exclusivity.

The only realm in which exclusivity is still abided as the norm is sex. Our partner may not be considered to be the best person to satisfy our sexual needs, but he or she is the only one who is allowed to do so. From a psychological point of view, such privileged access can be understood in light of the very intimate nature of sexual relationships. Nevertheless, this status can be challenged. Indeed, as society's perception of sex shifts, we find ourselves in the process of redefining its constraints and its relation to marriage. One such change is illustrated in Havelock Ellis' statement that a man who:

> never once, during 30 years of married life, is sorely tempted to engage in adultery for purposes of sexual variety is to be suspected as … abnormal; and he who frequently has such desires and who occasionally and unobtrusively carries them into practice is well within the normal health range.[17]

There is little doubt that in the process of redefining sex, its connections to marriage will be weakened. In addition to the difficulties inherent in long-term romantic relationships, modern society, with its emphasis on personal freedom and sexual openness, makes the crisis of marriage even more profound.

The reduced significance of strict exclusivity is expressed in various relationship rules that put forth a more flexible notion of fidelity, albeit within certain boundaries. Included in the revised framework are rules such as the 'doesn't count' rule (which allows for oral sex), one time sex, out-of-town sex, phone sex, and even mental infidelity; the 'must-confess-all' rule; the 'don't know don't care' rule; as well as 'anything goes – except love', 'sex and nothing more', 'no couple-like behavior outside the bedroom', and 'anything above the waist isn't cheating'.[18] In such attitudes, 'coloring outside the lines' is not always a grave violation of normative behaviors. Consider, for example, the following attitude of Lynn, a divorcee:

> If I was with someone who really wanted to have other sexual relationships, I might now be more accepting of this. It isn't what I would want (necessarily) but I don't

think I would make it out to be as big as it seemed to me ten years ago; it doesn't have to be. If I loved someone and wanted to be with him, and he wanted to be sexual with others, since I couldn't change his desire then I think I could simply allow it and see what it truly means. I don't have now the same need to protect myself from jealousy (like I did back then).

The notion that one person cannot meet all one's needs does not contradict the idea that there are, however, needs that are best fulfilled by one or a few particular people. Emotional meaning acquires its significance by exclusivity. Some activities, like some merchandise, are cherished for being exclusive. Our wish to spread the fulfillment of our needs among various people does not imply that all people are of equal emotional significance to us. On the contrary, emotional significance is by its very nature partial and discriminative. We should expect, therefore, some boundaries in the sexual and romantic realms to continue to exist. Sex is an emotional experience and, as such, has its own structure and boundaries. A love and sex policy of 'no strings attached' is unlikely to prevail, as boundaries are intrinsic for meaningful human inter-actions. It is also likely that despite the greater flexibility of normative bound-aries, the old time habit of proclaimed monogamy combined with clandestine adultery, as well as other boundary violations, will also continue to prevail.

The gradual process of disassociating marriage from its past relative advan-tages in areas such as sex, child-raising, living arrangements, and financial security, will probably continue. Accordingly, the survival of marriage depends upon (i) its ability to fulfill its intrinsic emotional function, that is, by offering a more satisfactory form of life, and (ii) its ability to be at least as beneficial as other alternatives. It seems that marriage can be quite beneficial in matters of raising children, living arrangements, and financial security; the emotional function is more difficult – although not impossible – to fulfill.[19]

Serial monogamy – 'Just in time'

Kiss me quick while we still have this feeling,
Because tomorrows can be so uncertain,
Love can fly and leave just hurting.

Patsy Cline

You win a while, and then it's done –
Your little winning streak.

Leonard Cohen

In this type of compromised commitment or exclusivity, the ideal of monogamy in romantic relationships is maintained within a limited period. In the increasingly popular romantic pattern, people still believe in some moderate form of ideal love, but give up their basic pretense that it should last forever. The beloved is still regarded to be unique, but in many cases it is so for a limited time.

There is amounting empirical evidence indicating that monogamy has been prevalent only among a minority of human societies (less than 20%) and an even smaller minority among mammals (about 3%). Most of the world's peoples, throughout history and around the globe, have arranged things so that marriage and sex do not necessarily coincide. Moreover, in many otherwise monogamous societies, extramarital sex has been permitted under special conditions (e.g., certain holidays) or with particular partners (such as the husband's brothers).[20] On the basis of a comprehensive study, David Barash and Judith Lipton concluded that there is no evidence that monogamy is somehow 'natural' or 'normal' for humans; on the contrary, there is abundant evidence that people have long been prone to having multiple sexual partners. However, they also reject the claim that monogamy is unnatural or abnormal, especially since it is the way most people have been living in recent times. Human beings are enormously flexible creatures and exhibit adaptability in dealing with the issue of monogamy and romantic exclusivity.[21]

The accommodation required in serial monogamy is not merely in giving up the dream of eternal romantic love, but also in relinquishing certainty and living in some sort of make-believe environment. People behave as if their current romantic relationship will last forever, and they really hope it will be so, but they will not be devastated if it does not turn out that way. In this case most people will look for another ideal love and some may even find someone whom they perceive to be closer to the ideal lover; however, this again may be for a limited time. People are taking their monogamous relationship seriously, but they do not necessarily believe that it must also be eternal.

Let us illustrate this point by referring to a few real examples. Barbra had four husbands, all of whom died while married to her. She says that she dearly loved each of them and never thought of having an affair with another person. She can think of no difference in the immense intensity of her love to each of them. Later on she admitted that once when her husband was already quite ill, she did love at the same time another man, but did not manifest this love till his death. She further says, 'Although I am 85 and had four great loves, I am still hoping to meet the fifth love of my life'. The movie producer Arnon Milchen said, 'I was first married for ten years and had three children; then I lived together with my girlfriend for 12 years, and now I am with Amanda for three and a half years. I am a one-woman man'. Milchen is indicating here that while he is in a relationship with a woman, he is indeed a one-woman man – but that his association with each woman may be limited in time.

Unlike serial killers, who may have multiple personalities, serial lovers often express their own unique personality. Lori, a divorcee who at the age of 30 has engaged in four serious consecutive romantic relationships (two of them were in the form of marriage), has considered all four men to be ideal lovers to whom she has been totally devoted. Although she considers herself to be a victim of Romantic Ideology, she still believes, though in a somewhat moderate version, in most elements of this ideology. She is just tired of the constant search for the ideal lover: 'if one more time I have to tell another man how many brothers and sisters I have and what they are doing, I will seriously consider jumping off the roof'. A similar attitude is expressed by a gay woman: 'Sometimes I get tired of going through the life negotiating relationships and working it out. Like, will I ever arrive at some kind of plateau where I finally get the results of my labours?'[22] People may admit to being the victims of the Romantic Ideology but still believe that their painful search was worthwhile, once they found their true loving home. The problem is that such people may not be the majority.

Monogamist societies prevail because they give people some kind of certainty and security that enable them to devote their resources to other issues. Serial monogamy gives such a sense of certainty and security for only a limited time, but this is the kind of accommodation people make for having greater novelty and romantic excitement in their life. Indeed the number of people having several marriages is increasing; however, the success rate of second marriages is lower than that of first marriages.[23]

Serial monogamy does not involve profound emotional difficulties; on the contrary, it is in accordance with the brief nature of emotions and the significant role that the notion of change plays for this generation. Furthermore, despite its limited duration, this pattern also provides some sense of stability and exclusivity. Accordingly, serial monogamy has been the most prevailing form of romantic relationship and is likely to continue to be popular.

Polyamory – 'Me and Mrs Jones'

Torn between two lovers
Feeling like a fool,
Loving both of you
Is breaking all the rules.

Mary MacGregor

I've got two lovers and I ain't ashamed
Two lovers, and I love them both the same.

Mary Wells

A little bit of Monica in my life, A little bit of Erica by my side,
A little bit of Rita is all I need, A little bit of Tina is what I see.

Lou Bega

As described in these songs, romantic love can be directed at more than one person at a time. Although this seems to be the most radical type of romantic compromise, the phenomenon of loving several people prevails in parental love and is also possible in romantic love.

Polyamory concerns stable intimate personal relationships rather than casual sex; people involved in polyamory are different from swingers, whose main concern is casual sex. The classic group of polyamory is sexually exclusive and do not engage in sexual relations outside the group. One version of polyamory is that in which a group of three of more lovers consider themselves married to each other and allow romantic relationships within the group. In another version of polyamory, there is no group; rather, only one person carries on an intimate relationship with more than one partner. People in polyamory sometimes differentiate their relationships as primary, secondary, or tertiary, to describe the varying levels of commitment involved. The presence of polyamory relationships is expressed in the fact that people who engage in such relationships have their own organization and magazines. The huge success of the American television drama *Big Love* also serves to illustrate that this type of relationship has become mainstream. This hit series is based on the romantic ups and downs of a suburban man and his three wives.[24]

Empirical evidence clearly suggests that humans are capable of having sex with more than one person and also of loving more than one person at the same time.[25] Indeed, most people we talked with said that they can romantically love, and actually have loved, a few people at the same time. Let us consider now a few examples of such love.

Esther, a widow who was a great advocate of Romantic Ideology, confesses: 'In the seven-plus years that I have been dating since the death of my husband, I have never been seeing just one person'. Also Iris, when she was married to the father of her children for 15 years, loved two men at the same time:

> I got involved with another man while I was still living with my husband. We did it openly. My husband even supported it for a while and the three of us lived together – to see if we could make it work. During that brief period, I had sex with both of them – one upstairs and one downstairs. There was a time when I slept with both of them – even on the same night at different times – but I still wouldn't want this situation. I did it because I was torn – I loved them both and wanted to reassure and comfort them both. It wasn't for my sexual needs that I was physical with both of them. I truly wanted to be present for them in whatever way was best for them.

My lover was very clear that he did not want to break up my marriage. This overlap was confusing and strange – but always out in the open. We never made love the three of us together. We wanted to co-habituate, but my husband got very jealous and angry and we were not able to continue with this living situation.

To summarize, it was possible for a while – albeit confusing – for Iris to love and have sex with two men at the same time; the person who experienced the greatest difficulty was her husband, who could not accommodate to the new terms.

Although both Esther and Iris have loved two people at the same time, each really craved the old-fashioned romantic love. Thus, later on in her life, when she had three potential lovers, Iris admits that 'I don't like having three men from which to choose. I liked the simplicity of one'.

And Esther admits:

I subscribe to Romantic Ideology. I want the Perfect Guy … or one slightly imperfect guy. But my experience has been just the opposite. There isn't just one who has been able to satisfy me. And I haven't even seen that as a negative. Even when I went out with Elliott for four years, there was always a secondary (minor) relationship. In the past seven years, I have not found anyone … and I mean no one person who embodies it all … who can satisfy me intellectually and emotionally and sexually and culturally. And while I more or less try to find that One Person with my left hand, with my right hand I am reasonably happy having a couple of very dear, very meaningful, very important relationships.

The story of Hazel and Ralph is unique in this regard. They met when they were in their 30s, when Hazel was engaged to Dylan; Ralph wanted them to be together but despite her affection for him she decided to proceed with her plans to marry Dylan. A few years later, Ralph married another woman. Hazel and Ralph worked together and continued to love each other very much. Ralph asked Hazel to divorce and marry him, but she refused. After over 30 years, when Hazel was 70 years old and both their spouses died, they began to live together and finally got married. Hazel said that although Ralph was the love of her life, she also loved Dylan very much. Her love for each was different as they were different people. At age 85, she still does not see any difficulty in loving two men, but she said that she suffered a lot from this situation, since she could not be with Ralph the way she so wanted to be. In any case, she says, 'I never compromised my great love for him; I have only compromised some of its behavioral manifestations'.

The story of Yadin also illustrates the possibility of polyamory. Yadin, a divorced businessman who travels a lot, actually lives in both England and Israel. He has had for a long time a romantic relationship with Kathy, a divorcee who lives in England. Then, in Israel, he met Helen, another divorcee of his age, with whom he was involved for a period of three years, except for half a year in which he had a romantic relationship with Sigal, a single woman in her early 30s. Yadin insisted that there were times in which he loved them all. Kathy knew about Helen and Sigal, and Sigal knew about Kathy and both were ready to accept it – Sigal even suggested making it a permanent living arrangement. Only Helen knew nothing about Yadin's other lovers, and in any case she would not have allowed it, as she is an extremely jealous person. All of the relationships involved sex, but it was the most central in the relationship with Helen; Kathy gave Yadin feminine caring and tenderness, while intellectual stimulating conversations were the hallmark of the relationship with Sigal. Natalie, a single woman in her 50s, also simultaneously had romantic relationships with two men, who were good friends. She explains that while the first relationship was going downhill, the new one was full of excitement. Early on, when she was only in her 20s, she had already decided that she would not marry, as she recognized that she would need more than one man to satisfy all her needs.

It is somewhat easier to have two (or more) romantic relationships simultaneously when the two relationships are at different stages: one may be at the initial stage while the other is more grounded; hence, the relationships will be at different levels of intensity. The relationships may also focus on different aspects: the two beloveds may be significantly different and satisfy different needs. In a similar vein, it has been shown that jealousy increases when the rival's qualities pertain to a domain relevant to one's self-esteem. Thus, individuals who attribute great importance to physical attractiveness are more likely to demonstrate a jealous reaction if their rival is unusually attractive.[26]

Some cases of polyamory may exhibit wholehearted devotion, despite the absence of monogamy, that is, without total exclusivity. This could be described as a local, total devotion, a devotion that is exercised within a restricted environment. Thus, both the man and the woman in a polygamous marriage may adopt Romantic Ideology: he is honestly committed to whichever partner while he is with her, and she is not (dangerously) jealous of his other women partners, but only of women outside the marriage. A similar attitude toward a flexible Romantic Ideology is found in the following case of Robin, a married woman who has had a married lover for three years. In an informal conversation she indicated her surprise when asked whether she had other sexual relationships (which are easily available to her at work). She said that though she does not consider such sexual relationships to be immoral, she cannot engage in any, as she is loyal to her heart and cannot sleep with someone else beside her lover, except, of course, her husband. Robin tries to separate the two relationships; she does not let the affair enter into what she considers to be her real life, i.e., the relationship with her husband. The affair is perceived to be a kind of fantasy which is not intended to cross its boundaries. Robin even argued that the two relationships she has are compatible with each other, as each fulfills different needs, and that there is a positive correlation between the qualities of the two relationships. Right now, the relationship with her husband is flourishing and so is the relationship with her lover. It is indeed the case that when you feel sad – for any reason, and especially, one stemming from a relationship, you lack the energy and the mood to be active, especially in another relationship. The opposite is also true: when you are happy in one relationship, that happiness tends to affect other relationships as well.

As suggested, polyamory may entail some type of limited exclusivity. A woman who loves two men may be wholeheartedly devoted to each of them within the given general framework of having two lovers. Consider also the case of Sarah, a married woman in her mid-40s, who believes that it is not immoral for a person to 'choose what she does with her body'. Nonetheless, Sarah also wants to pursue her notion of the totality of love, which she believes in. She would like her married lover (as well as her husband) to be wholeheartedly and completely devoted to her. Such a wish would appear impossible, even from a purely technical point of view: her lover cannot devote himself to her entirely while being engaged in his own primary relationship. However, Sarah expects a more limited sense of devotion, which excludes his primary commitments: with the exception of his primary relationship, he should behave in a manner befitting that of a devoted lover. Thus, he should think about her and talk to her as often as he can. After having sex with her, he mustn't go without talking to or meeting her for more than a few days, since in genuine love, the lovers want to be with each other as much as possible. Sarah expects her lover to demonstrate localized total devotion. This attitude is not as implausible as it may seem: also when regular romantic exclusivity prevails, devotion cannot be all-encompassing, since one has other (non-romantic) obligations that preclude the bestowing of constant and total attention on the romantic partner.

Sarah's expectations are conventional, in the sense that she tries to combine the essence of love – a certain devotion to the beloved – with the given practical constraints of her situation. Her approach is unique in two senses: (a) she includes romantic exclusivity among the constraints of the secondary relationship, although she has allowed herself to violate it in her primary relationship; and (b) she demands a variant form of total devotion, which is not entirely exclusive. The assumption underlying the first observation seems straightforward: love cannot be entirely total and uncompromising, as it must take account of various personal and contextual constraints. Romantic exclusivity is one demand that, as she demonstrates, cannot be absolute, since she – as well as many others – may have more than one person in her heart. The second aspect particular to her approach provides a way for her to maintain – to some extent and within the given constraints – the notion of romantic exclusivity, which apparently is, after all, an essential element of love. Sarah is able to consider her lover's marital status as a given, in the same way that a spouse accepts the partner's professional obligations. However, once these obligations are completed, Sarah expects her lover to be totally devoted to her. Hence, she would find it intolerable if her married lover chose to have a romantic relationship with another woman besides herself and his spouse. Even though Sarah exhibits a flexible approach to romantic exclusivity, she would not agree to concede to a completely non-exclusive romantic relationship. Hers is a more accommodating type of exclusivity.

Along these lines, Robert Green suggests that Don Juan may have conquered so many women because the moment he crossed a woman's path, he made her think that she was his whole world. Of the hundreds of women Picasso seduced over the years, most had had the feeling that they were the only one he truly loved. Casanova and Madame de Pompadour did not merely seduce their targets into a sexual affair; they made them fall in love with them. An ideal love gives the sense of total devotion.[27] Although it is feasible that Don Juan, Picasso, Casanova, and Madame de Pompadour did not actually love all of their partners, and in some cases they merely let them feel as if they did, the fact that this behavior was rewarded and reciprocated illustrates the need for and viability of localized yet total devotion. Sexual surrogates, trained in the psychology and physiology of sex so as to help people resolve serious sexual difficulties, often exhibit this attitude. A woman who runs a sex clinic reports that while providing treatment, some surrogates may feel or behave as if they are indeed in love with their patients; in such cases, the treatment is more likely to be successful.

The above examples of attempts to maintain a localized and ideal romantic relationship that includes exclusivity, despite the relationship's polygamous nature, indicate the significance of exclusivity – albeit in its redefined formulation – in romantic relationships. Indeed, Barash and Lipton claimed that 'what makes human beings unusual among other mammals is not our penchant for polygamy, but the fact that most people practice at least some form of monogamy'.[28]

Romantic Ideology endorses strict monogamy as it requires total devotion to the beloved – it limits the whole world of the lover to that of the beloved. Consider the following popular song: 'I want give you all I have, I would do anything to be with you, but one thing I won't do, is share you'. Thus, according to such an ideology, any non-exclusive romantic relationship – including serial monogamy which implies that love is replaceable, is rejected. Although this ideology encourages lovers to compromise on various aspects of life in the name of love, it rarely – if at all – sees any need to compromise any aspect of love in order to promote life. Indeed, people will often say that for the sake of love they are ready to sacrifice their well-being in other realms; they are less explicit about their willingness to compromise love for other realms of life. This is the attitude demonstrated by the wife-murderers, who cannot accept their wives' wish to separate from them. This may be due to the central role that Romantic ideology has in our cultural norms.

Polyamory expresses a revolt against human limitations; it involves the belief that we can have it all. It is similar to Romantic Ideology in its refusal to accommodate human limitations; however, each version of love is concerned with a different set of limitations. Polyamory rebels against the notion of humans as temporally constrained beings incapable of committing their love to more than one person at a time; Romantic Ideology revolts against the idea that humans are imperfect beings who must accommodate love to the constraints of their reality. Both approaches are problematic.

In cyberspace, where human resources are enhanced and human limitations are fewer, the belief that we need not be restricted by our limitations is somewhat more realistic (within this basically unrealistic environment). Cyberspace provides an idealized, imaginary environment that transcends everyday limitations and personal flaws. People can be excellent lovers, since in cyberspace this accomplishment requires fewer resources and talents than needed in a non-cyber environment. Accordingly, both ideal love and polyamory can be carried out with greater ease in cyberspace. Cyberspace seems to enable a form of non-exclusive – yet ideal – love. Despite the infinite attraction of cyberspace, neither polyamorous nor conventional lovers can spend their entire time in cyberspace; hence, it is highly probable that their actual everyday relationships will be influenced by their additional online relationship.

If, as we postulated earlier, romantic love is indeed based upon a few significant characteristics of the beloved, loving more than one person at a time may not be entirely unfeasible, as the additional love would be based upon a different set of characteristics, and thus the two loves could be considered complementary rather than contradictory. Another context for polyamorous love is having two lovers who may be somewhat similar; however, the relationship with each is at a different stage: one could be at the infatuation stage and the other at a later stage. Just as there is no logical contradiction in simultaneously loving and hating the same person, there is no logical contradiction in romantically loving two people at the same time. In both cases the issue is psychological, as it generates profound emotional dissonance. In the case of loving and hating the same person, the dissonance stems from the simultaneous presence of two essentially different attitudes, whereas in the case of loving two people at the same time, the dissonance stems from the fact that by definition, emotions demand partiality, that is, the preference of one over another, which (by extension) entails exclusivity. Emotionally, it is extremely painful to imagine your lover in the arms of another person. Indeed, most of those who told of being romantically in love with two people at the same time and pleased with the experience also claimed that they would not like to be at the other end of the relationship; that is, they would find it enormously difficult – if not impossible – to share their beloved with someone else.

How can human society cope with such emotional dissonances? One approach may be to adapt our accepted norms concerning romantic and sexual exclusivity to reflect the occasional dissonances of our reality, a change which has indeed begun to take place in modern society. People now allow their spouses to have more freedom in their personal relationships with others, and attitudes are more flexible concerning sex. In many societies, for example, extramarital sex is disapproved of socially; nevertheless, the transgressor is only mildly penalized for such activity. Similarly, many people consider extramarital sex 'closer to a misdemeanor than a felony', and in many such cases, the reaction to it is a moderate and not a violent one.[29]

Indeed, extramarital affairs have begun to be described in more neutral terms. Instead of the highly negative terms of 'adultery' and 'betrayal', some people have begun to use the more neutral term of 'parallel relationship'. Many are joining online communities of men and women who seek affairs without any intention of leaving their partners. They even see such affairs as aiding and as helping to preserve their marriage. Thus, Sophie says that her affair with another man saved her marriage by providing what is missing in it. She adds, 'I believe I've found my soulmate, and in another time and place I would have chosen Jerry [her parallel partner] as my life partner. We have to face up to the fact we can't be together—it would hurt too many people and I feel it would blight our relationship'. And Felicity argues: 'The spark is alive and well in my marriage, but I think that's because being an adulterer makes me a more fulfilled partner'.[30] Although a married person's lover may appear, physically at least, to occupy back stage in the daily activities of the beloved, not letting the world realize the extent of their love, emotionally lovers are at the center stage of their beloved's hearts. Being together physically, occupying centre stage together, certainly has its own glory and pleasures, but many lovers may not mind forgoing these advantages if they know that they are center stage in their beloved's heart.

The deeper problem, however, does not concern normative values, but rather emotional ones. Even if this process of relaxing of norms continues – and there is no reason why it shouldn't – a major problem remains: the partiality that colors our emotional system. Changes in societal norms may somewhat revise and moderate our emotional reactions, but they cannot completely change the partial nature of our emotional system. A more promising manner of coping with this problem is to bypass it by ignoring the information which may generate it. This can be done by taking advantage of our imagination and positive illusions. Indeed, studies indicate the importance of positive illusions in intimate relationships and even suggest that positive bias in partner judgments can be a normative and consciously accessible feature of intimate relationships.[31] This is in accordance with the findings indicating that people who are depressed are more realistic than those who are optimistic, and those who are perceptive are more likely to be pessimistic and depressed because they have a more accurate picture of life and its troubles. Nevertheless, most people appreciate optimism more than pessimism.[32]

Some implications – 'Feel so right'

If you need … me to be with you, I will follow where you lead.

Carole King

Thanks for the times
That you've given me
The memories are all in my mind

Lionel Richie

The previous discussion describes various types of compromises and accommodations that can be made in romantic relationships. The first type, that of postponing the realization of love accommodates reality merely in regard to its temporal aspect – love can wait, but once it takes place, it must be in the idealized form promoted by Romantic Ideology. The next two types of compromises and accommodations take place within a given romantic relationship: People in a committed relationship accept that their romantic intensity may decrease over time and that the likelihood of exclusivity may be reduced. Finally, serial monogamy and polyamory propose to maintain the tenets promoted by Romantic Ideology, but do so in multiple (sequential or simultaneous) relationships.

These compromises and accommodations may be perceived as attempts to uphold the ideology. Thus, the suggestion that implementing the behavior associated with love can wait implies that there is nothing wrong in principle with the ideology, but there is merely a temporary impediment which soon will be over. Similarly, the claim that oral sex does not count as a betrayal (since it is not 'real' sex) may express one's desire to circumvent a violation of romantic exclusivity. While serial monogamy and polyamory may be motivated by a similar desire to maintain the perfection required by the ideology, they nevertheless imply a novel approach to love, one which includes more than a single object of love.

The need for accommodations is universal, and is furthermore compatible with the need to grasp the perspectives of others. Understanding the perspectives of others involves at least an appreciation, and to a certain extent an acceptance, of some of their aspects. One does not have to adopt all types of compromise and accommodation in order to maintain a viable romantic relationship: personality and specific circumstances are relevant in determining the most befitting types and the extent of their implementation. It is obvious, nonetheless, that in principle, some types of accommodation are urgently needed. Those fortunate enough to maintain passionate romantic love by investing no effort or making no significant accommodations are few in number. More commonly, love is maintained only with the investing of much effort and the acceptance of significant accommodations. Still there are those who have not been able to find or to maintain passionate romantic love, either because they were not ready to invest and accommodate or because their investment and accommodations were to no avail. Thus, the investment of effort and readiness to compromise is not enough to maintain love.

The type of accommodation one ought to adopt depends on various complex contextual and personal variables. Thus, it matters whether one's main concern is with the passionate aspect of love, which is of shorter duration, or the caring aspect, which is of longer duration. In other words, the weight attributed to the various aspects of love will help determine what accommodations are chosen. Different people need different types of accommodation. Similarly, how you invest your money will depend on when you want to enjoy its fruits. If it is needed in the long run, you may want to invest in the more stable bonds, but for short-term goals, stocks may be of greater interest despite their risky nature. No doubt, there is no one size fits all accommodation for maintaining love; there may be, however, general patterns which are evident in many cases.

Herbert Simon's notion of 'bounded rationality' refers to the claim that most people are rational only in certain aspects of their lives, while in other aspects their behavior is irrational (which in his view is emotional).[33] In a similar vein, we propose the term 'bounded love,' which acknowledges the fact that most people allow considerations of love to determine their actions only up to a certain point, while their intellectual calculations play a larger role. Love is essentially bounded by aspects related to the environment in which we live, such as moral norms, scarce resources, and the amount of effort involved; and to our own psychological structure, such as the partiality of emotions, the role of change in emotions, the search for happiness, the fear of loss, and the comfort of convenience. But love has its own vitality, enabling it to be flexible in coping with such aspects. In this sense, love is both bounded and flexible; it fluctuates within a bounded framework. Bounded love is contrary to both Romantic Ideology and the notion of totally fluid love, both of which overlook (from different perspectives) the crucial role of such limitations in love. The significant increase in modern society of romantic opportunities has not abolished all normative boundaries, although it has reduced their weight. The real predicament does not refer to whether love should be bounded, but to what extent it should be so. Although the general direction of modern society is toward a significant increase in the extent to which we allow love to influence our decision making, the optimal extent is heavily dependent on personal and contextual circumstances.

In light of the considerable need for accommodation in maintaining romantic love, it becomes clear that the relaxation of normative boundaries, as well as the individual's capacity for accommodation, should be significantly promoted. Unlike Romantic Ideology, which generally rejects the notion of romantic compromises, accommodations are in fact worthwhile, in love, as in many other realms. Accommodations are not the least of all evils; they are part and parcel of valued and satisfactory life. Lovers want very much and are happiest when they find a common ground where they can share with their beloved and settle their differences. Yet, as long as they uphold Romantic Ideology, which rejects compromises and accommodation, they can rarely settle down at all; they are always restless, rejecting middle ground and searching for the ideal. Given the greater flexibility demonstrated in the prevailing romantic trends that characterize relationships nowadays, future generations may be more willing to accept the kinds of compromises and accommodations suggested here.

These compromises and accommodations, which make love less bounded, entail difficulties and hence may not be suitable for everyone in every circumstances. One such difficulty, a considerable one in modern society, is a lowering of the level of commitment, which is due both to the reduction in constraints for dissolving relationships and to the presence of so many tempting alternatives. Since successful long-term relationships involve being relatively immune to mild relationship threats, the uncertainty associated with the continuation of romantic relationships in modern society has an impact upon people's commitments. Indeed, it has been found that members of a less committed couple are more vulnerable to negative partner characteristics than are highly committed members. Less committed individuals lack the motivation to ignore negative partner information.[34] Thus to some extent, commitment is a self-fulfilling prophecy. One related difficulty is that of paying greater attention to one's own personal needs. In this regard, it has been found that people who score high in social absorption tend to be supportive and understanding in their relationships, whereas people who score high in social individuation tend to maintain greater distance from their partners. Marital satisfaction was significantly lower in dyads in which there were two members who were low in social absorption and high in social individuation.[35]

The above are examples of genuine difficulties lovers face in our dynamic modern society. Coping with such difficulties is challenging and complicated. However, as we cannot stop the sands of time, we have no choice other than to find ways of dealing creatively with the new contexts surrounding our love lives; moreover, these new difficulties bring with them many significant gains. In the next chapter, an alternative approach will be presented that offers valuable ways of coping with the above difficulties and of taking advantage of their potential.

Chapter 8

The nurturing approach to love
'We walk in the dream,
but dream no more'

And I looked and looked at her, and knew as clearly as I know I am to die, that I loved her more than anything I had ever seen or imagined on earth, or hoped for anywhere else.

Vladimir Nabokov, *Lolita*

I've been waiting for a girl like you to come into my life.

Foreigner

Previous chapters have indicated that love needs compromises and accommodations, which people do in fact make even while they maintain, deep down, some of the basic assumptions of Romantic Ideology, which in essence is an uncompromising ideology. This incongruity is not without cost – it underlies the current romantic crisis experienced by so many people in modern society. In this chapter, we present the alternative Nurturing Approach approach to love, which emphasizes the agent's self-worth and autonomy. We do not argue that this approach is feasible or appropriate for everybody; there are many paths leading to romantic love, including that of Romantic Ideology. Our claim is more modest – we present one kind of romantic love that seems to us to have a greater chance of survival at this time. We do not recommend practical manners by which people can arrive at this love, partly because this is an individualistic task and partly because it would require a complete book on its own. Here, we limit ourselves to just describing the foundations of this kind of romantic love. In such love, the difficulties and risks involved in the idealized love promoted by Romantic Ideology are avoided; this is particularly true concerning the great dependency and extremism associated with this ideology. In the approach outlined below, love does not mean a total dependency on the other, but rather the individual's autonomy and development.

The Nurturing Approach is presented by making various distinctions concerning commonly held assumptions about love. In the suggested approach, we adopt a self-validated model of romantic relationship over the prevailing other-validated model. In this approach, intrinsically valuable activities, in which the value of the activity lies in the activity itself, become more important than extrinsically valuable activities, which aim at achieving a certain goal. The emphasis upon self-worth is also expressed in the Nurturing Approach in the central role played by promoting, rather than preventing, types of behavior. Accordingly, caring is more significant in love than prohibiting various types of sexual practices. We further argue that in romantic love, uniqueness is more significant than exclusivity. Uniqueness focuses on nurturing ourselves and others, while exclusiveness entails preventing others from certain actions or forms of behavior. In the proposed approach, the lovers' attitude toward each other is that of functional harmony rather than mechanical fusion. In the last section of this chapter, we offer a few concluding remarks concerning the possible termination of love, and the value of love in modern society.

Nurturing romantic love – 'Listen to your heart, there is nothing else you can do'

> You've got to get up every morning with a smile on your face and show the world all the love in your heart.
>
> Carole King

> You are just too good to be true, can't take my eyes off you.
>
> Frankie Valli

One meaning of 'to nurture' is to promote and sustain the growth and development of someone. Nurturing often refers to the way we help someone else, usually a child, to grow and develop. In raising our children, for example, we place emphasis on their nurturing capacities, talents, tolerance, and friendships. However, we can also nurture ourselves and our own intimate relationship. As Portmann rightly argues, 'To the extent that we prize the self, we naturally nurture it'.[1] It is this feature – which is almost absent from, and at best not emphasized sufficiently, in Romantic Ideology – that is crucial for enduring romantic relationships.

At the basis of our Nurturing Approach to romantic love is the conviction that satisfied people, who are able to further develop and flourish within a romantic relationship, are those who are most likely to stay in love. Although romantic love has to do with giving to others, such giving can be done best by a person who is growing and flourishing within this relationship. Unlike Romantic Ideology, which involves total dependence on the beloved (as the two are one and the same), in the suggested Nurturing Approach the starting point is one's own position; only when the lover feels at home in the relationship can the beloved promote their lover's well-being (and vice versa). The shift in emphasis from the other to the self is crucial for the longevity of a romantic relationship as it enables the lover to flourish; this puts them in a position in which they can be more giving and more tolerant toward the beloved. Nurturing oneself may be as important in love as nurturing the beloved and investing in the relationship with the beloved.

It is important to distinguish our approach from the following assertions, presented by Martin, who has been married for 38 years: 'The only true love is love of the self – it lasts for ever. All other loves are byproducts that can disappear. Even when you love your kids or wife, it is only because it favorably affects you'. Our approach, in contrast, is not formulated in terms of 'love of the self', but rather in terms of awareness of self-worth. In this approach, loving others for their own sake is essential to love. Every individual lives in a society and our connections with others are of great value to our well-being. The Nurturing Approach is much closer to Iris, who is keenly aware of the importance in her life of both self-worth and concerns for others:

> Ironically, self includes awareness of the others to whom it must relate as part of its system. I am not totally separate and autonomous, as much as I would like to think I am. Even among simple cells, there is an unerring recognition that they are in a system, so there is a profound relationship between individual activity and the whole.

In certain periods of social history, romantic love was not connected to marriage; both were held to have different purposes. When, a few centuries ago, the two became part of the same relationship, the need to provide certain constraints and incentives dictated the emerging framework of relations. The constraints took the form of various types of penalties for dissolving the marital framework and the incentives took the form of various benefits that were granted only to those within this framework. Indeed, impressive empirical evidence indicates not only that a happy marriage is one of our most important objectives, but further, that married people live longer, experience better health, earn more money, accumulate more wealth, feel happier, enjoy more satisfying sexual relationships, and produce happier and more successful children than those who remain single, cohabit, or are divorced.[2]

In modern society most of the penalties for dissolving a marriage have been removed and many of the incentives can be obtained in other social frameworks. The choice of staying within a marriage depends, therefore, more on the issue of whether it facilitates personal development and satisfaction, including that of love. If a person feels that their present marital relationship prevents them from developing or does not provide the depth of love that they seek, there is little incentive for them to stay in the marriage (religious injunctions against divorce or separation have little impact in many Western societies nowadays).

Paying attention to our own personal needs does not mean loving ourselves above all else; our love for others is in no way diminished, and is probably increased, by our interest in our own activities and our desire to adequately and satisfactorily fulfill our other commitments – to ourselves, our family, our friends, and our work.

In presenting the Nurturing Approach to romantic love, we draw the following related distinctions:

- *Self-validated versus other-validated model of romantic relationship* – the other-validated model is based on the anticipation of one's partner's acceptance, while the self-validating model relies on one maintaining one's own autonomy and self-worth. We argue that while romantic love involves both types of attitudes, the self-validated model is by far more significant.

- *Intrinsically versus extrinsically valuable activities*: An extrinsically valuable activity is a means to an external goal and its value lies in achieving that goal, whereas in an intrinsically valuable activity, our interest is focused upon the activity itself, not its results. We argue that while romantic love involves both types of activities, intrinsically valuable activities are of much greater significance.

- *Promoting versus preventing behavior*: Promoting behavior is behavior that focuses on nurturing, whereas preventing behavior is behavior that focuses on protecting and securing the relationship. We argue that while romantic love involves both types of behavior, promoting behavior is of much greater significance.

- *Uniqueness versus exclusivity*: Exclusiveness is characterized in negative terms that establish rigid boundaries, whereas uniqueness is characterized in positive terms that celebrate an ideal. We argue that while romantic love involves both features, uniqueness is of much greater significance.

- *Functional harmony versus mechanical fusion*: The closeness between lovers does not depend upon a mechanical amalgamation that involves the loss of each person's personal identity: rather it arises from the experience of growing and developing together. We argue that the connection in love can be considered as a functional harmony.

The Nurturing Approach holds different assumptions to those implicit in Romantic Ideology. Whereas Romantic Ideology claims that love gives our life meaning, the Nurturing Approach claims that life and love give meaning to each other. Instead of assuming that love can overcome all obstacles, it is assumed that love can overcome some obstacles in life and that a certain kind of life can overcome some obstacles in love. Instead of arguing that the two lovers are fused into a self-enclosed, exclusive entity, the claim is that the two lovers form a functional harmony. Romantic Ideology considers the beloved to be exclusive and irreplaceable, whereas in the Nurturing Approach the beloved is held to be unique and may be replaceable. Unlike Romantic Ideology's precept that love is always morally good, the Nurturing Approach holds that love may or may not be morally good.

Self-validated versus other-validated model of romantic relationship – 'You're so vain'

Please don't ever change ... I kind of like you just the way you are.

Beatles

You can dance every dance with the guy who gives you the eye ... But don't forget who's taking you home ... So darling save the last dance for me.

The Drifters

The encounter with the other is central to both emotions and ethics—this expresses the importance of the evaluative aspect in both of them. In both emotions and ethics, the other consists of wishes and values that may have a profound impact upon us. In addition to moral evaluations, emotions involve other types of evaluations, such as aesthetic, commercial, and egoistic. Whereas in morality, the other is the focus of concern, in emotions the self constitutes this focus. Although the scope of emotional evaluations is larger than that of moral evaluations, their focus of concern is more limited. In romantic love, the other is typically one person or a very few people. However, our sense of morality extends far beyond one or a very few people, although even here there is a gradation of moral obligations—we feel more obligated toward those who are close to us than toward other people. We do not criticize a woman for not loving someone beside her spouse, but we would criticize her if she failed to care morally for anyone other than her spouse. Conversely, we would criticize someone for failing to help a single refugee from Darfur, but we would never criticize her for loving her spouse exclusively, nor would we condemn her for not having sex with at least one refugee from Darfur.

The other-validated model is expressed in its extreme in Emmanuel Levinas' view, which considers the other to constitute the center and the ultimate preoccupation of a person's meaningful world. Hence, 'the relationship with the other is not symmetrical ... at the outset I hardly care what the other is with respect to me, that is his own business; for me, he is above all the one I am responsible for'. Love 'is originally without reciprocity, which would risk compromising its gratuitousness or grace or unconditional charity. According to this view, one should even be prepared to sacrifice one's life for the beloved.[3]

The issue of reciprocity is of less concern in all the other-validated models of romantic relationships. Such a stance may also be held by people who do not follow the Romantic Ideology. Shirley, a successful and attractive woman at her mid-forties, admits that there is no passion in her marriage of 20 years and that there never was. Her husband now wants a divorce, yet she says she still loves him in a way—after having decided years ago to do so. She does not mind the absence of reciprocity in their relationship and does not intend to search for a new love, since she does not believe in long-term passionate romantic love. This reduction in the importance of romantic reciprocity, as is implicit in the desperate attitude of Shirley, is compatible with the other-validated model of romantic relationships.

In this regard a distinction should be made between superficial and profound reciprocity. The former involves mechanical calculations about what I give and what I get out of the relationship. In the case of profound reciprocity, each person seeks the profound happiness and well-being of the other, without focusing unduly on superficial calculations. When I do something for my beloved, I do not do it because I expect to get something in return, but because I care so much for her that I want to do it. Genuine romantic love should involve first of all profound reciprocity, which is indicative of the crucial caring aspect. Of course, even in such love, we would find it difficult if only one partner gave the other birthday presents, remembered anniversaries, or offered cups of tea—while the other offered none of these symbolic acts of giving. Here it is not the mechanical giving that matters as much as the symbolic act of gift giving or remembrance, acts that indicate the other's significance. The issue of both profound and superficial reciprocity is of lesser weight in parental love. A mother can love her son even if at this point in his life the son is extremely ungrateful.

In accordance with Romantic Ideology, a most prevailing model of the romantic relationship involves the expectation of acceptance, empathy, validation, or reciprocal disclosure from one's partner. Such other-validated intimacy is inherently limiting and manipulative because it focuses upon the self-presentation of the lover to her beloved, rather than upon genuine self-disclosure. Such dependency on the other can be seen in the following claim by Nina, a married woman, about her lover: 'I can be so professional and cool, but as soon as it comes to him I feel so vulnerable, and my heart feels so naked, and I also feel so helpless, as if nothing except him can save me'. She adds that she is afraid her lover will end their relationship and leave her alone again. Nina is already alone in her loveless marriage, but has nevertheless decided to remain in that marriage and validate her self-worth through another man – her lover. The hardship involved in adopting the other-validated model makes people dislike the experience of being in love. Consider the case of Nancy, a married woman, who prefers not to be in love because it involves dependency on another person:

> When I was once in love, I lost control of my happiness; my happiness belonged to someone else. It is important for me that I experience my happiness not through someone else whose moods and sanity I do not control.

Indeed, in Kayser's study of disaffected marriages, the major events responsible for the deterioration of love involve the partner's controlling behavior, in particular behavior that consists of unilateral decision-making that disregards the respondent's opinion.[4] This study indicates that spouses tried, with little success, to stop the process of disaffection by seeking to please their partners even more. Here are a few examples. A 42-year-old woman, married for 24 years, says:

> I tried to be more the perfect wife. To go home from work and bake a pie so that I could put a piece in his lunch. Basically providing him with the same home he had when he lived with his parents ... I never blamed him. I felt the only problem was that I couldn't adjust. I was creating the problem.

A 26-year-old woman, married for four years, expresses a similar attitude, 'I would always agree with his suggestions – whether I thought they were wrong or not, I would always agree'. Another instance of the attitude implicit in the other-validated model is voiced by a 29-year-old woman, married for four years, 'I changed my interests so that they were more acceptable to my husband'. The other-validated model accords with various religious teachings. Consider the following statement by a 30-year-old woman, married for four years:

> I was raised by Christian missionaries. And we were always taught J-O-Y. Jesus first, then Others, Yourself always come last ... I'm sure that was part of the problem in the marriage. He always had to come first.[5]

Kayser points out the obvious dangers of such an attitude, since 'continual self-denial over time can rob a person of fulfillment of his or her own needs and ultimately change one's feelings about the marital relationship'.[6]

As an alternative to the other-validated model, David Schnarch proposes the model of self-validated intimacy, which relies on each person maintaining their own autonomy and self-worth. In this model, the foundation of long-term marital intimacy is differentiation, which is the ability to maintain our sense of self while in close contact with other people who may pressure us to conform to their perceptions or needs.[7] This model does not attempt to maintain the exciting period of infatuation forever, but rather encourages the self-development and fulfillment of each partner and thus requires greater autonomy, sensitivity, and flexibility in the process of differentiation. Each must keep pace with the other's development in order to keep the relationship alive; similarly, each must exhibit self-control and not try to control the other. The self-validated model of love requires commitment, but this commitment is to one's basic values, not to another person. Hard work does not have to be driven by feeling of inadequacy or emptiness (as is the case in extrinsically valuable activities), but can be done by feeling adequate and fulfilled (as in the case of intrinsically valuable activities).[8]

The desire for a self-validated model is clearly illustrated in the following assertions made by Grace, a married woman who has maintained a long romantic relationship with a married man:

> I thought so much about this relationship and I think that I know very well myself what I want to do, what I need to do, and also what I should not do, and nobody can ever tell me this. Even in my situation – I mean, while being married – I am still an individual in her own right who, after all and everything, is alone in the universe, responsible towards myself (which includes my care and commitments toward other people), with every right (and responsibility) to listen my own heart and mind. And this is what I will always do.

The importance of a self-validated model of romantic relationships is further enhanced by the fact that a sense of satisfaction with the self has been found to be the strongest predictor of life satisfaction.[9] Satisfaction with the self consists of three major aspects: Self-esteem – a sense of worth or self-value; control – a sense that one can adjust the environment to one's wishes; and optimism – a positive outlook on the future. Accordingly, any romantic relationship – indeed, any relationship at all – would benefit if it enhanced the other's self-esteem, sense of control, and optimism. The self-validation model better sustains a deeper form of intimacy, which is based upon the lover's significant characteristics rather than upon the characteristics of the beloved, or those of anyone else. Thus, instead of asking, 'Am I the best lover you've ever had?' we should ask 'What do you like best about my love-making?'[10] Although this model emphasizes the agent's freedom and autonomy, it does not assume total freedom, but rather a restricted form of freedom, one that takes account of existing ideals and boundaries. As Schwartz rightly argues, an attempt to extend self-determination to everything would prevent people from functioning in an optimal manner.[11]

The shift in emphasis from the other to the self should be distinguished from egocentrism or self-centeredness. Attempting to nurture your capacities and genuine needs, while at the same time developing a loving equal relationship with another person, is not necessarily egocentric. The Nurturing Approach also refers to nurturing the other. The burden of the other imposing upon one's self-identity may lead some people to prefer solitude over intimacy. It is impossible to satisfy both the longing for intimate connection and solitude simultaneously while holding the other-validated model of intimacy. It is possible in the self-validated model, where a personal space is maintained within the intimate unit.

In contrast to the romantic ideal of unity, marriage counselors warn that spending too much time with the beloved can decrease love.[12] Indeed, it seems that some kind of distance, providing a greater personal space, is important for a personal relationship. Significant and temporally extended physical distance may harm it, but a more limited distance may be beneficial. As the saying goes, 'Absence makes the heart grow fonder'. Several studies indicate that long-distance couples are more satisfied with their relationships and with their communication and are more in love than are geographically close couples; accordingly, the former relationships enjoy a higher rate of survival.[13] It seems that the distance may focus the partners' attention on the profound aspects of their relationships and help them to disregard the superficial ones. These people are likely to value their relationships even more, while the distance increases the likelihood that they will idealize their partners. In and of itself, distance is not necessarily harmful to romantic relationships. As more and more contemporary couples enter into 'commuting relationships' as a result of work, the time apart may save as many marriages as it destroys. Finding the right measure and nature of physical and emotional distance is crucial for a satisfactory romantic relationship. Distance may have its own costs, but an appropriate distance can minimize the impact of those costs. While many married couples are busy thinking how to reduce the distance, others would like to enlarge it in order to provide more room for the individual's desires while keeping the common framework intact. Determining the appropriate distance is not an easy task, but it is crucial for easing the enormous burden put upon lovers who are supposed to form a perfect unity. Alas, there is no formula for love.

Consider the case of Ariel, a married woman in her 50s, who at the age of 27 was confronted with the possibility of marrying a young man who she passionately loved and a divorced 50-year-old who she loved, but not passionately. She chose the older person as she thought that he would be better able to bring out the best in her and help her to realize her potential. When she looks back on her life, she has no regrets whatsoever – time has only deepened her love for her husband. Ariel says that she has never believed in Romantic Ideology, as she has never liked illusions or fantasies. She places particular importance on her personal space and freedom. In all the places they have lived, she has had a separate bedroom and an office of her own. They have mostly lived apart, but they speak on the phone several times a day and when they meet on weekends, they take great pleasure in their time together. Despite Ariel's enjoyment of her private space, she never uses it for sexual affairs; she explains this by saying, 'I am too puritan'. Although Ariel is an extreme example of the self-validated model, she cares for her husband deeply and feels very committed to him.

In a flourishing relationship, the importance of a significant personal space cannot be exaggerated. The existence of such a space enables each lover to have a fuller and thus more meaningful life. This space does not necessarily involve sexual freedom (as we have just seen in the case of Ariel), but even if it does, it remains valuable as in relationships where there is no personal space available, sexual affairs may prosper. Indeed, attempts to prevent or significantly limit personal space may give rise to sexual affairs, as a partner who feels trapped without that space is likely to begin to view the relationship itself as negative and so may be encouraged to seek that space in an affair. Thus, Laura, a divorcee in her early forties, said that when she and her former husband lived in a commuting marriage:

> I felt good about having my own personal space so I did not have extramarital affairs. After eleven years of marriage, when we moved with our three girls to a house of our own and stayed in the house every day, I felt that my personal space and freedom were being violated by my husband and as if I was in captivity; at that time I began to have affairs.

In the song cited above, the man allows his partner to have her personal space by dancing 'with the guy who gives you the eye' providing she remembers who will be taking her home and for whom she should save the last dance.

As we shall see in the following sections, the self-validated model has various implications for romantic relationships. Here, we want to illustrate the value of this model by referring to two issues: Behavioral consistency and the relative status of lovers.

An important issue in personal relationships is that of consistency. There is a basic survival value to consistent behavior – without it, we could not understand and control our environment. Consistency is needed in personal relationships in order to predict, and hence control, the other's behavior. This need is obvious, but its presence in emotional behavior is often illusory. Consistency is an intellectual demand that has a doubtful connection with emotional attitudes. In emotional attitudes, which are generated by change and are more sensitive to contextual factors, the demand for consistency is of lesser value. The behavior of extreme people, who have a diminished awareness of or response to reality, is rigid and consistent, but those who consider the changes around them must be more flexible and accordingly less consistent – unless consistency in the given circumstance is defined by highly specific details, in which case its explanatory value would be considerably reduced.

The charge of inconsistent behavior in a romantic relationship often implies a denial of the other's complexity. Concerning ourselves, the need for consistency is weaker, as in our internal imagined world we know that we are so complex and that our circumstances vary so much; consequently, it would seem strange, or at least inflexible, to require consistency of ourselves. Thus, most people who told us about their own experiences of loving two people at the same time did not criticize either the experience or their subsequent behavior; rather, they sought to explain the complexity of the situation and focused on their claim to love different aspects of their beloveds. However, most of them refused to recognize the complexity of their partner's situation and said that they refused to tolerate such behavior from their partners. It is easier to be simplistic in our view of the other's internal world because we know so little about it, and what we do know is only what the other person is willing to share with us. If the strong demand for consistency could be abandoned, relationships would become not only more genuine, but also more complex because each person's personality and environment is astonishingly complex. Under such conditions, attitudes that are absolute, uncompromising, and unconditional, such as those espoused in Romantic Ideology, are less likely to be useful; more complex and flexible attitudes are more beneficial. The strong need for consistency is compatible with the other-validated model where your whole identity is based upon the other; when people cannot predict the behavior of their beloved, they cannot validate, in this model, their own identity. If a person's validation is based more upon herself, inconsistency in her lover's behavior is less likely to destabilize or threaten her.

The issue of the relative status of lovers is also of concern to enduring happiness. The equity theory postulates that those involved in an inequitable relationship consider themselves to be undeserving.[14] This is the case both for the 'over-compensated', who feel guilty for receiving more from the relationship than they feel their partner does, as well as for the 'under-compensated', who feel indignant at being unappreciated or inadequately treated by their partner. Involvement in extramarital relationships can sometimes serve as a way of compensating for such inequity. The under-compensated may perceive extramarital relationships as something they deserve because their spouse gets more from the marriage than they do, while the over-compensated tend to be involved in extramarital relationships (a) to escape the unpleasant state of inequity and (b) to prove to themselves and to their partner that they actually are deserving and attractive to the opposite sex.[15] In a similar vein, it was found that the person who stands to lose the most is apt to be the least likely to risk ending the relationship by having another sexual partner. Accordingly, if the woman has a higher level of education than her partner, she is more likely to risk the relationship by having a secondary sexual partner than if both members of the couple have equal levels of education.[16] These considerations are more likely to be dominant in the other-validated model of romantic relationships. In the self-validated model, the precise comparative measurement of individual standing and contributions are less relevant. In this model, affirmation, which is the degree to which spouses appreciate each other and bring out the best quality in each of them, is more important. Indeed, affirmation has been found to be the most important type of support for emotional well-being – particularly for wives.[17] Following these lines, research has demonstrated that when a close romantic partner views you and behaves twoard you in a manner that is congruent with your ideal self, you experience movement toward your ideal self—this has been termed the 'Michelangelo phenomenon'. Just as Michelangelo released the ideal form hidden in the marble, our romantic partners serve to 'sculpt' us in light of our ideal self. Close partners sculpt one another in a manner that brings each individual closer to his or her ideal self, so bringing out the best in each partner. In such relationships, personal growth and flourishing is evident and is typically demonstrated in claims such as: 'I'm a better person when I am with her'.

Some of the basic assumptions underlying the Nurturing Approach are similar to those underlying democracy. Anthony Giddens characterizes democracy as:

> The creation of circumstances in which people can develop their potentialities and express their diverse qualities. A key objective here is that each individual should respect others' capabilities as well as their ability to learn and enhance their aptitudes… Autonomy means the capacity of individuals to be self-reflective and self-determining.[18]

Giddens further argues that democracy does not imply a 'leveling down', but an elaboration of individuality. Democracy does not necessitate sameness, nor is it the enemy of pluralism. However, 'Democracy is an enemy of privilege, where privilege is defined as the holding of rights or possessions to which access is not fair and equal for all members of the community'.[19] In the case of romantic relationships, also, no member of the relationship should be privileged above the other; however, those involved in the relationship enjoy an essential privilege or partiality that is not conferred on those outside it.

Intrinsically versus extrinsically valuable activities – 'Heaven can't be far from where we lie'

You make me feel like a natural woman.

Carole King

Loving you is easy because you are beautiful.

Minnie Ripeton

Aristotle distinguishes between extrinsically and intrinsically valuable activities.[20] An extrinsically valuable activity is a means to an external goal; its value lies in achieving that goal. This goal-oriented activity is always incomplete: As long as the external goal has not been achieved, the activity is incomplete, and the moment the goal has been achieved, the activity is over. The major criterion for evaluating such activities is efficiency – that is, the ratio of benefits to costs. Time is one of the resources we try to save when engaging in extrinsically valuable activities. Examples of such activities are building a house, paying bills, cleaning the house, and attending job interviews. We do not value these activities in themselves – in fact, we may even resent performing them, as they are painful and costly. We still engage in such activities when the external goal is perceived to be beneficial. In an intrinsically valuable activity, our interest is focused upon the activity itself, not its results. Although such an activity entails results, it is not performed in order to achieve them; rather, its value lies in the activity itself. Accordingly, we do not try to finish this activity as quickly as possible. Listening to music is an example of an intrinsically valuable activity: we listen to music because we value doing so and not because of a certain external goal. Another example may be intellectual thinking, when the basic motivation is creativity or intellectual curiosity, not the ensuing money or academic publications.

Most human activities have both intrinsic and extrinsic value. The factors underlying each type of value often conflict (specifically, with regard to how long activities should continue or how many resources should be invested in them). Many human activities can also become either intrinsically or extrinsically valuable activities. Take, for example, dancing. Dancing can be an intrinsically valuable activity, in which case our focus is upon the experience itself. Dancing, however, can also be an extrinsically valuable activity whose goal is to find a romantic partner. In this case, our attention is not focused on dancing but on the people who are in the dance hall – here, dancing is a means to achieve an external goal. In many cases, dancing involves both types of activities: You may value dancing for its own sake, but also use dancing as a good opportunity to meet attractive people. Reading is another example for an activity that can be both intrinsically and extrinsically valuable: It can be done for its own sake, as well as for practical purposes.

In the proposed approach, which emphasizes the lover's self-worth and autonomy, the lover's intrinsically, rather than extrinsically, valuable activities are crucial. Intrinsically valuable activities involve optimal functioning, using and developing an agent's essential capacities and potential in a systematic manner; the activities are essential for the agent to flourish – they cannot be done by someone else or for someone else. In the Nurturing Approach, the value of love is not determined by its practical value as a means to achieve ends that are external to the relationship. 'Loving', as a means to satisfy one's sexual desire or to become rich, is a partial and transient activity: The moment the end is achieved, or a better means is found, this 'love' disappears. In the Nurturing Approach, romantic love is an intrinsically valuable activity done for its own sake and not for the sake of external ends. In this sense, loving activities are not like the process of consuming food, which can fill us to the point that we cannot think about eating for a while; they are more like a continuous journey within an exciting landscape in which we encounter a never-ending series of pleasant and interesting experiences.

A sexual activity can be an extrinsically or an intrinsically valuable activity. Sex is an extrinsically valuable activity when the other is used as a means to satisfy one's sexual desire or to gain wealth, status, or attention; in such cases, it is usually efficient and brief and the moment the end is achieved, the partner is no longer of any value. This is the mind-set behind the enormously popular American television show *Sex and the City*; this time, however, the women do the seducing, not the men. The female protagonists routinely find themselves longing for the next sexual thrill. When sex is an intrinsically valuable activity, it does not have to be efficient and save time. In this sense, Mae West is right in claiming that 'Anything worth doing is worth doing slowly'.

In addition to profound intrinsically valuable activities, there are also superficial intrinsically valuable activities, such as watching television, sex, going to a movie, or having dinner, in which for a brief period of time people enjoy the activity for its own sake, even though such activities may not contribute much to the development and flourishing of the agent's capacities. Superficial pleasure is an immediately rewarding, relatively short-lived experience requiring few or no profound human capacities; such pleasure merely sustains the individual's interest and joy, but does not satisfy it profoundly in the long run.[21] This is the difference between a fleeting pleasure and a lasting treasure.

Feeling good may be good enough in the short term (at least *For Me and Bobby MacGee*), but it is certainly not enough for enduring happiness. In some cases, superficial intrinsically valuable activities may even have a negative functional value, since we may pursue them instead of engaging in more beneficial activities. Kierkegaard's *Diary of a Seducer* long ago set out what happens to people who cherish the immediate thrill of infatuation but who do not value the long, sometimes monotonous, trajectory of a romantic partnership. A sexual activity can be intrinsically valuable in the superficial sense of providing pleasure to the participants. It can be intrinsically valuable in the profound sense only when it is part of a more profound attitude, such as love.

In light of the above considerations, we may say that if intense love is to continue over a considerable length of time, it should involve profound intrinsically valuable activities that are available for each person and some that are common to both. Such activities require normative boundaries expressing the valued way a particular person wants to live in order to flourish over a long time. The satisfaction here is not transient, as it involves the optimal development and function of the individual. When activities are perceived as intrinsically valuable, they entail seeking the good of the beloved for her own sake, while at the same time being profoundly satisfying for the lover. Profound love does not stem from subordinating one's activities to those of the beloved, but from considering the activities for and with the beloved as compatible with one's own intrinsically valuable activities. In this case there is much less need 'to work' on the loving relationship, as such 'work' will no longer be considered work, but will rather constitute a profound pleasurable and satisfying activity. The choice of such activities cannot be arbitrary, as it must be of benefit to and compatible with the agent's flourishing.

Increasing the ratio of intrinsically valuable activities to externally valuable activities is of crucial importance in establishing and maintaining profoundly satisfying loving relationships. As with other intrinsically valuable experiences, romantic love also involves goal-oriented activities that have an extrinsic value. Since love is frequently expressed within a certain social framework, such as marriage or cohabitation, it often requires performing extrinsically valuable chores for maintaining this framework – for example, cleaning the house, ironing clothes, or buying food. Love involves doing things for the beloved that are not profoundly satisfying for the lover. Performing these goal-oriented chores without being resentful is one sign of the profoundness of love. Another important measure of such profoundness is the extent to which lovers share intrinsically valuable activities, such as walking together, dancing together, speaking with each other, or doing other activities together. The enjoyable and valuable nature of such activities provides the circumstances that are suitable for generating profound happiness.

The importance of intrinsically valuable activities in romantic relationships is further clarified by studies that investigate our attitude toward communal behavior, such as doing a favor for our partner and doing tedious chores.[22] These activities, which typically do not have an intrinsic value, can be regarded as the cost of maintaining the relationship. However, when these activities were positively appreciated by the partner, they were positively associated with relationship satisfaction; when relatively unappreciated, the association with relationship satisfaction is negative. When appreciation was felt, people were more likely to regard these activities as 'wants' rather than 'shoulds', thus imbuing them with intrinsic value. It appears that satisfaction in romantic relationships depends in part on the way lovers frame their attitude toward the most routine, menial tasks that arise within the daily life of the relationship. Satisfaction here is not necessarily associated with doing less of these tasks, but with embedding them into an appreciative framework within the valued relationship.

Another related significant measure of the depth of love is the scope of activities that become intrinsically valuable only in relation to the beloved. In such circumstances, the beloved becomes an intrinsic element of the lover's own identity. Take, for example, the common enough scenario in which two lovers go to a movie that proves to be not very good, yet the lovers nevertheless greatly enjoy being together at the movie. This kind of common, intrinsically valuable activity is clearly illustrated in the way Lynn, a divorcee, describes the change she experienced after being with her new lover:

> For a long time my attitude toward foreplay (including oral sex) was that 'this is a good thing to do' or 'he likes this so I want to do it' or 'how long do I have to do this for?' etc., etc. At that time, it felt like a chore. Now, after meeting this wonderful man I can hardly wait to do it; it has become such a turn-on for me. So it is actually part of 'my own' foreplay. I want to do it for me! Yet the 'me' can't be totally separate from the other. The foreplay now doesn't belong to him or to me – it belongs to the space between us – as it brings both of us pleasure simultaneously.

In judging the value of a certain activity, we are not completely dismissing the nature of the activity and assuming that all that matters is the person with whom you engage in this activity, but neither should we take the other extreme and entirely dismiss the importance of the person with whom you share the pastime.

Profound love and profound happiness cannot be achieved by doing nothing or by merely engaging in extrinsically valuable activities. Love and happiness cannot be achieved by only repeating pleasant experiences. An enjoyable event is often progressively less enjoyable with repetition (as is the case with repeated viewings of a good movie). A new acquisition, highly valued at first, comes to seem ordinary. Hence, acquisitions alone cannot provide profound, enduring satisfaction. Love and happiness are not isolated achievements; rather they are an ongoing, dynamic process. Attaining a specific goal may make us feel momentarily pleased, but it is insufficient for profound long-term love and happiness.[23] The distinction between the two types of intrinsically valuable activities is related to the distinction between the transitory emotion of joy and the more profound sentiment of happiness. An experience consisting of transitory joy includes immediately rewarding, relatively short-lived pleasure. Profound happiness is typically associated with optimal functioning, using and developing the agent's essential capacities and attitudes in a systematic manner over a sustained period of time. Profound happiness is to be found in complex activities that we value for their own sake.

In accordance with the Nurturing Approach, the Self-Determination Theory in psychology has posited three basic psychological needs: Autonomy (feeling uncoerced in one's actions), competence (feeling capable), and related-ness (feeling connected to others). Optimal well-being results when these three psychological needs, which are also at heart of the Nurturing Approach, are satis-fied. Indeed, empirical findings suggest that those who are more fulfilled in these three needs tend to enjoy a better quality of relationship after disagreements have occurred, primarily because they have more intrinsic or autonomous reasons for being in their relationship. Need fulfillment is associated with greater indi-vidual well-being (i.e., higher self-esteem, more positive emotions, less negative emotions, and more vitality), more secure attachments (i.e., less tendency toward avoidance or anxiety, better relationship quality (i.e., higher satisfaction and commitment), less perceived conflict, and more adaptive responses to conflict (i.e., showing greater understanding and less defensiveness).[24]

The need for autonomy refers to the extent to which people feel self-directed in their actions. We find it gratifying to exercise control, to feel successful in our ability to do things that we like.[25] Intrinsically valuable activities are highly necessary and appropriate for facilitating this experience. However, autonomy does not involve independence or detachment from others. Rather, it involves a sense of volition, agency, and initiative. Thus, fulfillment of one's need for autonomy does not preclude feeling related to and connected with others. Indeed, autonomy is positively associated with relatedness and well-being, and research shows that those who function more autonomously have more posi-tive social experiences.[26] Optimal human functioning arises out of social contexts that provide nutriments consistent with need fulfillment. The auton-omy can be conceptualized by distinguishing between psychological 'origins' and 'pawns'. In contrast to origins, pawns do not feel as if they are the origins or instigators of their behavior, and so they do not feel a sense of being fully engaged in their actions.[27] A wide literature has demonstrated the importance of ongoing feelings of competence for optimal functioning and well-being. For example, feeling competent is an integral contributor to self-confidence, believ-ing that one can bring about desired outcomes is an important determinant of psychological health, and believing that one is effectively making progress toward one's goals is psychologically beneficial. Individuals who generally experience greater fulfillment of their autonomy and competence needs tend to have better days on average, as indicated by their tendency to experience more positive effects and vitality and less negative effects or physical symptoms (headaches, stomach discomfort, difficulty in sleeping, etc.). Relatedness is the strongest unique predictor of relationship functioning and well-being. Empirical findings suggest, for example, that among married couples, the feeling that one's partner knows one accurately is associated with experiencing greater intimacy, and feeling cared for by one's partner is associated with feelings of greater relationship security. The more opportunities participants had to interact with their significant others within a given day, the more positive effect they experienced.[28]

The fulfillment of these three psychological needs underlies the Nurturing Approach, which emphasizes the importance in romantic relationships of people's autonomy, their ability to fulfill their goals and perform their intrinsically valuable activities, and their profound connectedness to others. Unlike the other-validated model, where the relationship with the partner impedes self-growth based upon intrinsic motives, in the proposed self-validated model relatedness is closely connected with autonomy and competence. Indeed, it has been shown that being in a relationship for intrinsic or more self-determined reasons is associated with more adaptive couple behaviors, which is in turn associated with greater couple happiness. It has been further found that the benefits of need fulfillment, specifically as they pertain to relationship functioning and well-being, are not limited to one's own need fulfillment but carry over to one's partner as well. Hence, people are more securely attached to those who meet their needs for autonomy, competence, and relatedness. When both partners experience greater need fulfillment from their partner, individuals experience better relationships in terms of greater satisfaction, less perceived conflict, and less defensive responses to conflict.[29]

The postulation of intrinsically valuable activities, which involve developing the agent's essential capacities and enabling the agent's flourishing, is connected to another central psychological notion – the meaning of life. The place of meaning in life is central for survival, health, and well being. Thus, perceiving life to be meaningful positively relates to well-being at virtually every age in the life span. The experience of meaning in life happens when an individual feels that their life is coherent and fulfilled in terms of both personal accomplishments and significant encounters with others. Lives are experienced as meaningful when they are felt to have significance beyond the trivial or momentary.[30] Being able to consider much of our activity as intrinsically valuable is central to our experience of life as meaningful, and hence life acquires the positive implications of such activities.

Promoting versus preventing behavior – 'The best is yet to come'

> You give me hope and consolation, you give me strength to carry on.
>
> Elvis Presley

> Love is more than just a game for two.
>
> Nat King Cole

The notion of intrinsically valuable activities and the self-validated model of romantic relationships emphasize the importance of promoting individual growth in romantic love (and in happiness in general). It is useful to refer here to Tory Higgins' distinction between promotion-focused behavior, which is concerned with strong ideals related to attaining accomplishments or fulfilling hopes, and prevention-focused behavior, which is concerned with strong 'oughts' related to protection, safety, and responsibility. This distinction highlights the difference between nurture-related and security-related behavior. In the prevention mode, interactions between people occur only when something is going wrong – when some oughts are violated. The promotion mode is characterized by ongoing activities related to the creation of optimal conditions for fulfilling strong ideals. In the prevention mode, there is no sense of progress; in the promotion mode, there is a sense of progress toward fulfilling shared ideals.[31] In a somewhat similar manner, Isaiah Berlin distinguishes between negative and positive notions of freedom. Negative freedom refers to the limits within which the individual can act unobstructed by others; positive freedom is the state in which the individual can be his own master. Whereas the negative freedom is a freedom from certain negative obstructions, positive freedom enables the individual to develop and flourish, to lead his or her chosen lifestyle.[32]

The promotion mode focuses on nurturing ongoing, positive behavior, which develops one's potential, whereas the preventing mode focuses on obviating one's potential negative behavior, such as adultery. Fostering learning and encouraging caring are examples of a promoting mode of behavior; controlling the places to which someone can go and prohibiting extramarital sex are examples of the preventing mode. Promoting activities are a matter of degree, and they are therefore more difficult to characterize; there are various degrees and forms of caring in different circumstances and there is no one activity that embodies the essence of caring. Preventing behavior, such as the prohibition against sex with a minor, is easier to define and detect, as it typically has clear boundaries – in this case, the age of the partner. Romantic relationships involve both ideals and boundaries, and so they require both types of activities. We need to promote various aspects of our loving experiences, and at the same time we need to preclude other aspects. The exercise of affective bonds always involves a fine balancing act between nurturing and controlling. It is more evident in parenting, where there is an obvious (though overstated) need for control, but it is present in all relationships.[33] It would seem that Romantic Ideology results in an inappropriate emphasis on the preventing mode, whereas the Nurturing Approach involves greater emphasis on promoting behavior, leading to a more appropriate balance between the two types of behavior.

Uniqueness versus exclusivity – 'Let it be me'

Till I waltz again with you
Let no other hold your charms

Teresa Brewer

I'm gonna make you see,
There's nobody else here,
No one like me,
I'm special, so special.

Pretenders

The combination of the notion of intrinsically valuable actions that promote the flourishing of the self with the self-validated model of romantic relationships implies that in such relationships, uniqueness outranks exclusiveness.

Exclusive is characterized in negative terms that establish rigid boundaries: It entails 'not permitting', 'restricting', 'not dividing or sharing with others', 'excluding some or most, as from membership or participation'. Unique is characterized in positive terms that establish distinctiveness: 'being one of a kind', 'different from others in a way that makes somebody or something special and worthy of note'.

The difference between uniqueness and exclusiveness is expressed in the attitude articulated by Iris, who, after her divorce, had another long-term relationship with a man to whom she was highly attracted. Although she knew that this man had several affairs while he was her lover, she never thought of having such an affair herself. Iris was ready to allow this behavior as long as she felt that she was still special to him. In this manner she maintained some kind of exclusivity, which eased her pain:

> I always maintained the belief that we each have something special with one another – in that, it is unique. When I held this belief I did not need to control others in order to sustain this place of inner security. And based on this, we can be sure that we also have a unique relationship with everyone. That would mean that I could still feel special even if my lover had other lovers. It still is not what I want – but I can see the potential in me to be able to live with it … and still feel special to him. But in this case, I felt that I was replicable, that I was not indispensable; I saw how this contradicted my belief that I was special to him.

What bothered Iris was not that her lover was having sex with other women, but that she no longer felt that she was special to him. Iris expresses an important point – the essence of romantic relationships for her is being positively unique to the beloved. At the basis of her loving attitude is not the need to forbid the beloved from acting in a certain manner (though this need may also be present in a mild form), but the wish to be valued differently than others.

If my beloved considers me unique, it is plausible that certain activities, but not all, remain exclusive to us. It is also possible that I am unique to my beloved in the sense that there is no other person with whom they are involved in so many intimate activities, but this does not mean that there are activities that are restricted to me alone.

The preference for uniqueness over exclusivity is clear in Internet dating sites where people are asked to give a detailed description of their own uniqueness as well as what sort of people they like to date. Moreover, the technology enables choice in a way that was previously unknown. This requires a deep look inward at the uniqueness of one's self. On the other hand, in online love affairs, the methods of finding a partner and the lack of some types of information show how human beings can be treated as standardized merchandise and sex partners as public commodities.[34]

The need for uniqueness is indeed a basic emotional need; we need to consider ourselves as very special: 'We don't always see ourselves as *superior*, but we almost always see ourselves as *unique*'.[35] No wonder we want to see our beloved, who in a sense is part of our enlarged self, as unique as well. Being unique is being different and it expresses a kind of change that, like other changes, excites our emotional system. Consequently, emphasizing our uniqueness, which is an essential element in the Nurturing Approach, is compatible with greater emotional satisfaction. We need to see ourselves as unique, just as we need to see our beloved as unique: and to a certain extent, this is a true perception. Although each of us should remember that everyone else is also unique, just as we are, the feeling that we ourselves are unique is of great value for our happiness.

People often identify 'exclusive' with 'unique' and the uniqueness of the beloved is perceived to imply her exclusive position. Such implication may be found in Levinas' view, which assumes that to love 'is to exist as if the lover and the loved one were alone in the world'.[36] In this view, love is based upon the uniqueness of the other which stems from chosenness, and not from the other's characteristics. Basing love upon being chosen—which is the reason for the other's uniqueness—is the opposite of basing it on the sweetness of the relationship. One may say that the sweetness is never enough, as a greater sweetness may be found in others. This kind of a desperate position indicates that there is nothing in the content of the relationship that can prolong it: hence the need for an arbitrary external framework based on a postulated moral obligation rather than on the psychological aspects related to the sweetness of the relationship. Such a sense of obligation is more suitable for parental love than for romantic love. Indeed, you cannot replace your own children with other kids who may seem to be more talented or sweet, but you can replace your lover with another one who seems to provide you with a more profound sense of satisfaction.

Functional harmony versus mechanical fusion – 'Got my heart set on you'

> i carry your heart with me (i carry it in
> my heart) i am never without it (anywhere
> i go you go, my dear; and whatever is done
> by only me is your doing, my darling).

e.e. cummings

The distinctions proposed above entail a different characterization of the affinity between lovers – a functional harmony instead of a mechanical fusion. The aspiration for romantic unification is often associated with the sacrifice of personal independence and the idea of shared identity: The self becomes 'we' and the other is seen as a part of one's self-identity.[37] The proposed affinity between the lovers does not mean that the two lovers fuse into each other or have identical values, but rather that they enjoy functional harmony. In his very first encyclical letter as the new Pope, Benedict XVI, who considers romantic unity to be similar to the one between Man and God, distinguishes between union and fusion: 'Union is no mere fusion, a sinking in the nameless ocean of the Divine; it is a unity which creates love, a unity in which both God and Man remain themselves and yet become one spirit with Him'.[38] Functional harmony does not involve melting the lovers into a unified whole; rather, it suggests a mutual development of the lovers' capacities. Unlike the situation in fusion, where once the mix occurs, we can longer distinguish the constituent parts from one another, romantic love in the Nurturing Approach does not aspire to a loss of identity, but rather to partnership between autonomous, equal agents. The two lovers are different and will remain so; however, their intrinsically valuable activities are not incompatible. A considerable obstacle to romantic harmony is the lover's free will, but if each person's will is based upon compatible values that enhance the flourishing of both lovers, each of them will actively seek such functional harmony.

This type of harmony decreases the importance of universal normative laws and increases the significance of a person's individuality and sensitivity to the partner. The compulsory ties to the general social framework are less tight, but the connection to the partner is in many senses greater. On the one hand, it is easier to accommodate to a partner than to the general social framework, which is less specific and can be subject to different interpretations. On the other hand, compatibility with a partner is a more subtle matter, requiring greater sensitivity, awareness, and skill; hence, it is harder to achieve.

The basic attitude in the approach to functionally harmonious romantic relationships is not one of controlling, but rather of coordinating. If you really love someone, you typically accept their needs apart from considerations of what you are giving or receiving. Being in a romantic relationship should not mean controlling or being controlled; nor should it involve balancing the books to see who is giving or receiving more. Functional harmony does not abolish the need to invest efforts in the relationship, but those are mainly, though not merely, enjoyable efforts associated with intrinsically valuable activities and invested for the flourishing of both the lover and the beloved.

The psychological environment of each person involves interactions with various people who have different significance and roles. The two lovers should neither be diminished by nor merge into the other's ocean of needs; they should let each other flourish independently as well. Such flourishing requires a lot of coordinated individual work, which involves accommodating and taking account of – but not necessarily strictly adhering to – ideals and boundaries. It requires being sensitive to the partner, but at the same time respecting the partner's and one's own autonomy. The two lovers are very important to each other, but they should not make one another their entire world or reason for existing, as is suggested by Romantic Ideology.

We may compare the implementation of the Nurturing Approach in the romantic realm to that in education. Hara Estroff Marano argues that in the Industrial Age (now officially over, although many of its institutions live on, especially in education), the average schoolchild attended school as a young child and then was finished with education for life. The schoolchild packed everything into whatever number of years were deemed necessary or appropriate to their social class or work prospects, after which education was limited to apprenticeship or reading the daily newspaper. Schoolchildren were given a standardized, one size fits all education, and the curriculum was set down in stone, decided in advance for all children, irrespective of their talents, difficulties, or interests. Just as this industrial model of education is no longer appropriate, the model of love that prevailed then is similarly outdated. In the world in which we now live, we are subjected to movement, change and development and we know that whatever our children learn at school, and even at university, may be superseded by new information within a few years. The increasing awareness of different forms of learning disabilities is a clear reminder to us that a single model of education cannot serve everyone – if indeed it ever could. Applying to love Marano's criticism of the high cost of invasive parenting, we may speak about the high cost of invasive partnership. Just as in education, in love too it is typically counterproductive to attempt to exercise control. Whatever comfort and certainty such attempts give the controller, they undermine the love object's affection. Efforts to control a lover almost always breed resentment. Research is indeed proving that many things that were once (and in many educational establishments, still are) strictly outlawed in the classroom, including talking, gesturing, moving about, and working collaboratively, are actually good for learning. The advent of Google has shown that when you make information freely available, people will often delight in seeking it out on their own. They can devise their own education. Learning is now a constant activity, not a one-off burden.[39]

Similarly, we are currently witnessing the emergence of a new model of love. The prevailing model of Romantic Ideology that provides a one size fits all type of love is of limited use to most people. Love is not a one-off activity so that once you have entered its magic garden, you no longer have to be concerned with pursuing it any further. Romantic love is an ongoing project, not a one-time achievement. In this sense, love can be essentially a nurturing, rather than preventing or controlling activity. Like information in the Google age, love is also more freely available and people can choose to seek it at any time. In such circumstances, nurturing our love, rather than controlling it, becomes a complex, but nevertheless rewarding task.

Realizing the value of the Nurturing Approach for promoting long-term romantic relationships can be further enhanced by distinguishing two major means for maintaining anything for a long time: (a) extrinsic means preventing outside destructive factors from ruining the object we want to retain, and (b) intrinsic means promoting the object to preserve its optimal situation. The first approach is simpler and easier to take as it is typically concerned with one-time acts that protect the object from external dynamic changes in reality and personal differences. The second approach is more complex and harder to maintain as it involves an ongoing activity that is sensitive to dynamic changes in reality and to personal differences. Accordingly, we can speak about two major metaphors for memory: (a) a storage place for mental entities, and (b) a capacity to arrive at similar mental states. A storage place is a kind of passive container for holding something: we keep an item 'on ice' as it were, so that it will remain unchanged until we want to use it again. In the other approach, memory consists of various activities that are continuously performed in order to maintain the ability to preserve the given information.[40]

In the romantic realm, we can speak about a preventative approach that tries to maintain the relationship by introducing significant constraints on meeting other people or dissolving the relationship, and an approach, like the Nurturing Approach, in which intrinsically valuable activities are the major means for promoting and preserving the loving relationship. Although both types of activities are valuable in different circumstances, the preventative approach is more prevalent in the romantic realm. It is easier and simpler to build a fence, which is a one-time activity, than to nurture flowers, which is an ongoing activity. Once you build a fence, you need to do hardly anything else. But sometimes fences are so high that they block the sun and hence cause the demise of the flowers by their very presence.

The comeback of love – 'The best of times, the worst of times'

When other nights and other days
May find us gone our separate ways
We will have these moments to remember

The Four Lads

The book of life is brief
And once a page is read,
All but love is dead.

Don McLean

Life without love is one dead end street.

Carole King

Our proposed alternative to Romantic Ideology is more compromising and less demanding – it pays greater attention to individual differences and to personal development. The Nurturing Approach upholds the importance of personal flourishing, autonomy, and the uniqueness of a romantic relationship and of each lover. It assumes that the two lovers' development, rather than the restriction of their partner, has a unique role, but not an exclusive one, in each one's process of growth. In such circumstances, a romantic relationship is not a mechanical fusion of two people, but a functional harmony in which the two grow and flourish together while developing their individual capacities and increasingly engaging in intrinsically valuable activities. We should acknowledge various ways of growing together   monogamy may be a prominent one, but it is not the only one. The presence in romantic love of profound intrinsically valuable activities augments the intrinsic value of the relationship and is thus a significant means for coping with the vast number of tempting alternatives.

At the heart of the Nurturing Approach is the assumption that we can achieve profound romantic love. When divorce was not a real option, and people had to remain in their given relationship, romantic love was not accessible to many people. Now that the external constraints on romantic changes are considerably reduced and positive alternatives are abundantly available, love is making an impressive comeback. Romantic love is all around and its mere existence enhances its presence. Love breeds love, and the taste of love keeps inviting us back.[41] Rosa speaks about her online lover, whom she has never met:

> He has awakened a longing in me. Until he came into my life, I had remained attached to the last man I was with, and I just hadn't strayed in six years! By knowing him and imagining him, I have opened myself to the possibility of being with someone else again, as he makes me horny so very often.

This kind of romantic and sexual awakening can be found also among those who believe they love their partner but may nevertheless discover that there is love that is more exciting around the corner.

We would like to illustrate the prevalence and value in modern society of basic features of the Nurturing Approach by referring to the real case of Wally and to the popular movies *Something's Gotta Give* and *Waitress*.

Wally, a divorced woman in her mid-fifties, who for the last few years has lived with her boyfriend, speaks about four major stages in her romantic life. She regards stage A as the first nine years of her marriage. In this stage, she believed firmly in the Romantic Ideology: She loved her husband dearly and found life enjoyable. Wally's main roles during this stage were to be a wife to her husband, a mother to her three young children, and a daughter to her father. Although Wally did not feel profound happiness during this period, she nevertheless felt optimistic and most of the time she enjoyed her relationship and engagement with these people. From time to time however, she asked herself why she did not feel deeply happy and why she did not feel utterly at peace with herself. She believed these feelings to be due to some fault within herself. This period was a kind of illusionary bubble for Wally, a bubble that eventually exploded when her beloved husband left her for another woman. This was the beginning of Stage B where Wally was devastated and began to perceive reality in a more realistic manner. During this period, which was relatively brief, Wally seldom dated other men as she felt too depressed to engage in a relationship with a man. After a while, she embarked on stage C, a hedonistic stage in which she attempted to behave according to her short-term desires, following the spirit of 'Eat, drink, and be merry, for tomorrow we shall die'. However, fulfilling her immediate sexual desires did not make her happy. Stage D, the stage in which Wally is now, is similar in many respects to the circumstances described by the Nurturing Approach. Wally loves and cares for her boyfriend, but this is not the extreme passionate love she once knew. Wally finds a type of security, enjoyment, and calmness with this kind man, who she knows will take good care of her if she were sick.

During stage A, Wally hated the word 'compromise'; now that she is in stage D, she accepts it as normal. In this stage, Wally is doing much more of what she deeply wishes to do. She enjoys her work and her other activities. She may have brief affairs with other men but these are not superficial one-night stands, but rather involve a deeper engagement and satisfaction. She says that she is happier than ever before. Wally realizes now both the limitations and the value of long-term romantic love. She is happy with her current romantic relationship, but would not be devastated if it ended. She has not given up love, but recognizes its limitations and fragility. Wally is satisfied with her current lot, which is not as strictly defined as it once was. She has greater personal space, but it is not a chaotic or limitless space. She still dreams from time to time about her prince from the realm of romantic ideology, but she is also satisfied with her own domain. During her stage C, Wally dated men who she hoped would help her cope with the situation in which she found herself— a situation she abhorred. But since these men could not change her situation, they did not last long, and Wally repeatedly suffered 'the morning-after' effect once her assignation with them was over. Now, in stage D, Wally dates men because she feels good about herself and her personal space. She enjoys these relationships and wishes they would last longer. Wally believes that a very few, carefully selected and enjoyable affairs that she can remember with happiness for the rest of her life may in fact improve the quality of her life and even her romantic relationship with her partner. In any case, Wally considers that one man cannot fulfill all her needs; she believes that in a way she is even reducing the burden on her partner by enabling him to focus on only a few of her needs, while the rest are fulfilled by others.

These stages that Wally describes are quite typical, although not all of us will experience them all. Many people are not able to overcome a stage in which they do not enjoy themselves, even one in which they suffer. Not everyone can be happy with the fourth stage; some may enjoy the first or the third one more. Accepting the fourth stage—or the Nurturing Approach in general—requires maturity and a significant revision of our conventional norms, and as such it will not be appropriate for everyone. But its existence in some cases demonstrates that it does offer a feasible and satisfactory approach to relationships.

The comeback of love in modern society, expressed by the ability to look for and find love in all circumstances, enables people to fall in love for the first time in their life at any age. In the wonderful movie, *Something's Gotta Give*, Harry (Jack Nicholson), who has a reputation for dating girls a third his age, falls in love with Erica (Diane Keaton), the mother of his current young girlfriend. When they both confess that their affair has turned their life upside down, Harry tells Erica, 'Then let's just each get our bearings', to which Erica replies: 'I don't want my bearings. I've had my bearings my whole goddamn life. I feel something with you I never really knew existed. Do you know what that's like, after a 20-year marriage, to feel something for another person that is so … right?' Erica tells her daughter that she knew how to handle the life she had before, but now 'I'm in love. Ain't it great? Seems like I gotta learn how to … that love-them-and-leave-them stuff, you know?' She concludes: 'You can't hide from love for the rest of your life because maybe it won't work out … maybe you'll become unglued. It's just not a way to live'. Despite his many affairs, Harry declares: 'I'm 63 years old … and I'm in love for the first time in my life', while Erica notes: 'I let someone in, and I had the time of my life'. Her daughter, however, confesses: 'I've never had the time of my life'.

The very successful recent movie, *Waitress* (Adrienne Shelly was the writer and director), expresses messages and values that are compatible with the basic assumptions of the Nurturing Approach. In this movie, Jenna is trapped in an unhappy marriage with a controlling, jealous husband and the last thing she wants is a baby, so when she discovers she is pregnant, she is terrified. Matters seem hopeless for Jenna until she begins an affair with her handsome, married gynecologist who treats her with love, generosity, and simple kindness. Their affair expresses genuine love at its best. Her fellow waitress Becky has a sexual affair, while another waitress, Dawn, gets married and has a wonderful relationship with an unattractive, even ridiculous, man who is a firm adherent to Romantic Ideology. Some of the messages and values emerging from the movie and criticizing Romantic Ideology are:

1. Affairs may be valuable, but usually for a limited time only; affairs may provide profound happiness (when involving genuine love) or superficial pleasure (when merely consisting of a sexual affair)—in both cases people have a smile on their face when they wake up the next morning.

2. We all search for love but the probability of finding it and maintaining it for a long time is not high.

3. Love does not conquer all, and it is untrue that all you need is love—self-satisfaction is more important. There is a great value in starting fresh and being independent.

4. The attitude that leads to a desire to control the beloved is clearly problematic and belongs to those who should be relegated to the past.

5. Single parenthood is a perfectly valid alternative to the nuclear family.

Some of the messages and values of the movie are consistent with Romantic Ideology. These indicate, for example, that romantic love has a great value in life; the value of affairs is limited in that they are brief and satisfy only a limited number of needs; happy marriages can still be found and they can be wonderful (although they are rare and are found in those less attractive people who, it is implied, have little alternative); and children can bring a lot of happiness (though there are some normal people who may doubt that).

The availability of love outside marriage has forced people to give love a more significant place in marriage. Alas, the duration of each instance of this love is often limited. It is probably the case that marriages involving institutional commitment lasts longer than romantic relationships based upon voluntary commitment. There are indeed indications that spouses who believe in marriage as a lifelong commitment are less likely to experience marital disaffection. These people may not be seeking personal fulfillment and happiness in their marital relationship and may be more satisfied with a relationship that offers them security and stability.[42]

The Nurturing Approach does not aim at prolonging romantic relationships but at improving them, which at the end of the day may also prolong many of them. The issue of the possible end of such relationships will remain challenging, as we live in a constantly changing environment. In this concluding section, we return to the issue of the possible demise of love, which has occupied our discussion throughout the book.

The attitudes toward the possible death of love may be compared to those toward literal death. Indeed, the echo of death is associated with personal relationships that lack sufficient emotional resonance; we speak about 'dead marriages', 'mechanical sex', 'cold husbands', and 'frigid wives'.[43] And after romantic separation, 'Love seems dead and so unreal, all that's left is loneliness, there's nothing left to feel' (Dusty Springfield). The close affinity between love and death is also expressed in the fact that people are ready to sacrifice their life or to kill others for love. (The French famously refer to orgasm as 'la petite morte', or 'the little death'.)

The three main strategies for coping with our looming death can be described as: (a) denying the value of life, (b) denying death, and (c) 'business as usual'. The first strategy takes death seriously and draws immediate implications concerning insignificance of life. The second denies death altogether, while the third puts death in brackets and recommends getting on with life as if there were no such thing as death. All strategies may become, to a certain extent, self-fulfilling prophecies—the first by facilitating death, and the other two by prolonging life.

The first strategy assumes the relatively insignificant nature of life because of its brief and temporary nature. This strategy may involve indifference, expressed by withdrawal from all types of activity, or wild behavior, expressed by disregarding long-term considerations and behaving in the spirit of 'Eat, drink, and be merry, for tomorrow we shall die'. Many people who are seriously ill and have lost hope do become indifferent to their surroundings. Others, who internalize the temporary nature of life, focus upon presently enjoyable activities; if indeed life is so short and there is nothing after life, then we had better enjoy the brief time left to us by focusing upon superficial pleasurable activities.[44] However, filling our days and thoughts with such activities alone may in fact shorten our life and reduce our pleasure. The duration of life and pleasure is likely to increase when they involve profoundly satisfying activities.

The duration of life and pleasure is likely to increase when they can be regarded as involving profoundly satisfactory activities. This can be done by either denying death or behaving as if death does not exist. Taking the former option seems to solve all difficulties associated with death, since death appears not to exist. In this case, one can attach profound value to one's activities as they have a long duration and provide meaning to one's existence. This option offers benefits to those who can believe in it. However, since there is no empirical evidence to support such a belief, and relevant data indicate the presence of a significance change after death, this is not a viable option for many people. The more feasible strategy is a kind of agnostic attitude in which one just merely behaves as if death does not exist. The emotional system tends to use this strategy and despite our imminent death, behaves along the lines of 'business as usual'. A major function of the human emotional system is that of bracketing or essentially ignoring disturbing issues such as death or the limitations of bracketing or essentially ignoring disturbing issues such as death or the limitations of humans; it does this by bestowing profound personal meaning on transient and insignificant events, such as, for example, treating sexual conquests an aim in life.

The 90-year-old woman who is enthusiastically studying for her graduate degree in history is enriching her life by putting her imminent death in brackets and behaving in the manner of business as usual. Indeed, the fact that all of us will someday die does not mean that we should not attach any significance to present events. This is in accordance with Spinoza's claim that 'a free man thinks of nothing less than of death, and his wisdom is a meditation on life, not on death'.[45]

As death is always in the background of life, taking it too seriously, as the first strategy suggests, may damage the process of bestowing significant value on everyday events, nearly all of which may appear insignificant in comparison with death. Why should I feel happy about improving my performance at work when I know that in the not too distant future I will be dead? When people concentrate overly on the profound meaning of life and death, they often retreat from everyday activities, thus becoming emotionless, for instance, or losing hope, and indeed begin to share attributes similar to those who are dying. However, it is not always feasible to divert our attention away from undesirable events. Thus, sometimes people cannot avoid imagining the last hours of their dying friend. Moreover, it is a bad strategy to ignore death completely, as death has various implications upon our life. While we should embrace life and living, we should also pay some attention to death.

Our strategies concerning the end (death) of love are often similar to those toward literal death. We may speak here then about the strategies of denying the value of love, denying the possible death of love, and behaving as if love will not end. As in the case of literal death, the two first strategies are highly problematic. In light of the crucial role of love in our life, denying its value seems to be counterproductive. Giving up on love has a similar self-fulfilling nature as giving up on life. If you do not believe in the chances that your romantic relationship will last, its chances of surviving are virtually nil. Indeed, the partner's optimism is associated with a better and longer-lasting relationship.[46] As in the case of literal death, also concerning the end of love, putting the end in brackets and exercising the strategy of 'business as usual' is in most cases the optimal strategy. Not believing in the eternity of love does not mean, of course, that we cease to value love or to invest effort in the romantic relationship; contrary to Kitty's objections to buying flowers in *The Painted Veil*, it is not at all ridiculous to put significant effort into something that is soon to die. Unlike God, we all exist for a limited duration, and therefore to invest merely in the eternal would be to repudiate the conditions of human life. Recognizing the tentative nature of love does not mean repudiating love. It may, however, involve a certain degree of positive illusions and contentment with what we have, in the spirit of 'Let's share the good times while we can'. It avoids both the nihilism that senses death to be just around the corner and the illusion that everything will last forever.

In love, as in life, a measure of positive illusions, accompanied by some awareness of reality as well as compromises and accommodations, is of great survival value. We can put in brackets the limited duration of love, as we do with life, and behave as if it will endure forever; however, we should also be aware that in the case of love, there is a possibility of its end. It is easier to behave in this manner in love since some loving relationships may indeed never die; they may even show no signs of decay. In the same way that we must invest a lot of effort in order to prolong and improve our quality of life, we should make similar investments in love. The sad realization that love may end is associated with a more encouraging perspective – that such an end is not inevitable and that in any case, another love can come after it, which may even be better. First love is not the only enjoyable love, and not even necessarily the most enjoyable. Lovers do not have to lose their identity in order to flourish together with the beloved. Love can foster, rather than hinder self-development; hence, the end of love does not entail the end of the lovers. We should not sacrifice ourselves at the altar of love, but rather let love increase our well-being.

Compromises, like serial monogamy or reduced exclusivity, may make people more vulnerable, as their current romantic relationship may feel less secure. The expectation of possible frustrations and painful ends does not imply that we should devote less effort to our current relationship, or that we should prepare a reservoir of additional relationships for rainy days. Worrying too much about the future can ruin our present. We should trust our ability to cope in due time with painful experiences, at which point there will be time then to build other relationships. President Harry Truman was once frustrated by his council of economic advisors' recommendations, which were always equivocal: On the one hand you should do this and on the other hand, you should not do it. In exasperation, Truman announced, 'I'm tired of this one hand, other hand business. What I want is a good one-armed economist'. Recommending romantic practices is even less precise than predicting the economy, and lovers cannot expect to find a good one-armed counselor, a role that is sometimes accorded to Romantic Ideology. Romantic love is complex and full of compromises and accommodations that require different attitudes and patterns of behavior in different circumstances. The acceptance of romantic diversity increases the complexity of the relationships and in many cases also enhances their quality.

Ludwig Wittgenstein has argued that the task of philosophy is to point out the obvious; this should be done after critically examining the alternatives and the nature of the obvious.[47] At the end of our critical journey through Romantic Ideology, we seem to be returning to praising love, and even adopting some elements of this ideology; however, we are doing so from a different perspective. It is no longer a total and uncompromising love, but a more sober and accommodating one. Nevertheless, love continues to involve various illusory aspects – in particular, the belief in the idealized nature of the beloved and in the everlasting duration of love.

Taking Charles Dickens' saying about the French Revolution into the romantic realm, we may say that these are 'The best of times, the worst of times'.[48] These are indeed hard times for lovers: Many romantic relationships do not last for long and many others are crumbling; lovers are constantly perplexed about their current relationship and possible tempting alternatives. But these are also flourishing times for love, even its renaissance. Love is on the mind of a great number of people and its presence is a major criterion for more relationships. Love cannot be dismissed anymore as silly fantasy; it is perceived as realistic and feasible for many more people. Love has made an impressive comeback. And rightly so.

Endnotes

Introduction

1 Fisher, 2004: 176.

Chapter 1

1 We should distinguish the Romantic Ideology discussed here from romanticism which refers to the approach, especially in literature and the arts, prevailing from the late eighteenth to the mid-nineteenth century, and discussing various ideas, such as those about truth, good, and beauty.

2 http://www.harrisinteractive.com/news/newsletters/k12news/HI_TrendsTudes_2003_v02_i02.pdf.

3 Jones and Cunningham 1996; Murray and Holmes 1997; Murray *et al.* 1996a, b; Sharp and Ganong, 2000; Sprecher and Metts 1999; Weaver and Ganong 2004.

4 Berscheid and Campbell 1981; Freedman 1978.

5 Rougemont 1956.

6 See also Fisher 2004: Chapter 1; Holland and Eisenhart 1990.

7 Fisher 2004: 17–18.

8 Lerner and Miller 1978.

9 Wilding 2003.

10 Swidler 2001.

11 Finkel and Campbell 2001.

12 Berscheid and Campbell 1981.

13 Fromm 1956: 52–53.

14 Nozick 1991: 418.

15 Bauman 2003: 17.

16 Schnarch 1997: 108.

17 Aron and Aron 1996; Aron *et al.* 1992; Djikic and Oatley 2004; Duck 1994; Evans 2004; Landis and O'Shea 2000; Wilding 2003.

18 Genesis 2: 24.

19 Merino 2004.

20 Armstrong 2002: Chapter 5.

21 Nozick 1991; see also Ben-Ze'ev 2000: 422–425.

22 Fisher 2004: 21.

23 Frankfurt 2004.

24 Sokolon 2006: 69–75.

25 Frankfurt 2004: 42, 60–61.

26 Sokolon 2006: 72–73.

27 Brown 1987: 24–30; Frankfurt 1988: 155; Pitcher 1965.

28 Fromm 1956: 26.

29 Galeano 1992: 91; see also Hendrick and Hendrick 1989.

30 Blackburn 2004: 23.

31 Armstrong 2002: Chapter 12; Mitchell 2002: 55.

32 Fisher 2004: 8.

33 Benedict 2005.

34 A poem from the tradition of courtly love; cited in Rougemont 1956: 89.

35 Keats 1958.

36 Barash and Lipton 2001: 202–203.

37 Jeremiah 3: 19–20; Ezekiel 16.

38 Benedict 2005: 11.

39 Schwartz 1997: 3, 68–69.

40 Schwartz 1997: 3–4.

41 Djikic and Oatley 2004; Illouz 1997.

42 Wilding 2003.

43 *Guardian* 2006; see also Gert 2004: 4.

44 De Sousa 1991: 477.

Chapter 2

1 Buss 1994: 44.

2 Ortega y Gassis 1941: 12.

3 *Nicomachean Ethics*, Book 8.

4 Armstrong 2002: Chapter 16.

5 Baumeister *et al.* 1993.

6 See also Frankfurt 2004: 62.

7 Mitchell 2002: 55.

8 Kipnis 2003: 65.

9 Baumeiter and Dhavale 2001; Sinclair and Frieze 2000.

10 Sinclair and Frieze 2000.

11 Schaum and Parrish 1995; de Backer 1997.

12 Mullen *et al.* 1999; Sinclair and Frieze 2000.

13 Baumeiter and Dhavale 2001.

14 Baumeiter and Dhavale 2001: 68.

15 Hatfield and Rapson 1993; cited in Fisher 2004: 169.

16 Fitness 2001; Leary *et al.* 2001; Sinclair and Frieze 2000.

17 Spinoza 1677: IVp50s; see also Ben-Ze'ev 2000: Chapter 5.

Chapter 3

1 Tversky and Kahneman 1982: 86.

2 Tversky and Kahneman 1983.

3 Polk 1994; Wilson and Daly 1998; Browne, Williams and Dutton 1999.

4 Fehr 1988; Regan *et al.* 1998; Shaver *et al.* 1987.

5 Sternberg 1988.

6 Regan *et al.* 1998.

7 Dunn 1999.

8 Emerson *et al.* 1998: 292.

9 Aron and Aron 1996.

10 Holmberg and Mackenzie 2002; Averill and Boothroyd 1977.

11 Murray and Holmes 1997; Sprecher and Metts 1999.

12 Dunn 1999; Henton *et al.* 1983: 474; Sprecher and Metts 1999.

13 Djikic and Oatley 2004.

14 Swidler 2001.

15 Hui and Yriandis 1986.

16 Illouz 1997: 30

17 Fisher 2004: 182–183.

18 Medora *et al.* 2002; Rothbaum and Tsang 1998.

19 Aron and Aron 1996; Djikic and Oatley 2004.

20 Djikic and Oatley 2004; Swindler 2001.

21 Fitness 2001; Rusbult *et al.* 1991.

22 Regan *et al.* 1998; Sternberg 1988; Swindler 2001.

23 Sinclair and Frieze 2000.

24 Baumeiter and Dhavale 2001; Baumeister *et al.* 1993; Sinclair and Frieze 2000.

25 Baumeiter and Dhavale 2001.

26 Baumiester 1997; Kim and Smith 1993; Fitness 2001; Fitness and Fletcher 1993.

27 Baumeister *et al.* 1993.

28 Sinclair and Frieze 2000.

29 Cate and Lloyd 1992; Henton *et al.* 1983.

30 Dunn 1999: 440.

31 Evans 2004.

32 Emerson *et al.* 1998: 292.

33 Averill and Boothroyd 1977.

34 Wilding 2003.

35 Ben-Ze'ev 2000; it should be noted that in various languages the meaning of the terms 'envy' and 'jealousy' often overlap.

36 Neu 1980; Bringle 1991: 124–5.

37 Fitness and Fletcher 1993.

38 Wilson and Daly 1993.

39 Polk 1994; Wilson and Daly 1998; Browne, Williams and Dutton 1999.

40 Barnett, Martinez and Bluestein 1995; Holtworth *et al.* 1997; Murphy *et al.* 1994.

41 Ben-Ze'ev 2000; Buss 2000; Lazarus and Lazarus 1994.

42 Wilson and Daly 1998.

43 Polk 1994: 44.

44 Cited in Horder 1992: 39.

45 Buss 1994: 129; Dressler 1982: 440; Salovey and Rodin 1989.

46 Baron 2004: 355.

47 Moriss AzualusAagainst the State of Israel, Criminal Appeal, 3071/92.

48 Dobash and Dobash 1998; Koss *et al.* 1994; Wilson and Daly 1998; Stark and Flitcraft 1996.

49 Avakame 1998; Parker 1989; Parker and Toth 1990; Gauthier and Bankston 1997; Stack 1997.

50 Frye and Wilt 2001.

51 Easteal 1993; Bean 1992.

52 Gelles 1997.

53 Bean 1992.

54 Neu 1996.

55 De Sousa, forthcoming.

56 Ben-Ze'ev 2000: 414, 426–427; Ellsworth and Smith 1988; Fredrickson 1998.

57 Blackburn 2004: 101.

58 Neff and Karney 2002, 2003, 2005.

59 Neff and Karney 2003, 2005.

60 For a different view, see Neu 2000.

61 Goetting 1995; Wilson and Daly 1993.

62 Ben-Ze'ev 2000.

63 Ben-Ze'ev 2000; Fitness and Fletcher 1993.

Chapter 4

1 Dressler 2002; Baron 2004.

2 Henry Beecher, ttp://www.brainyquote.com/quotes/quotes/h/henrywardb150003.html.

3 Baron 2004.

4 Ben-Ze'ev 2000: 146–150; Sher 1987.

5 Sher 1987.

6 Baron 2004: 359–360.

7 Dressler 2002.

8 Barnard *et al.* 1982; Crawford and Gartner 1992; Campbell 1992; Stout 1993; Wilson and Daly 1993.

9 Wilson, Daly and Wright 1993.

10 Barnard *et al.* 1982.

11 Baker, Gregware and Cassidy 1999.

12 Polk 1994; Wilson and Daly 1998.

13 Browne, Williams and Dutton 1999: 72.

14 Wilson and Daly 1993, 1998: 200, 228.

15 Wilson, Daly and Daniele 1995, pp. 287.

16 Baker, Gregware and Cassidy 1999; Polk 1994; Wilson and Daly 1998.

17 Dutto 1995; Polk 1994; Browne and Williams 1993.

18 Wilson and Daly 1993; Stark and Flitcraft 1996.

19 Decker 1996.

20 Posner 2001: 1980.

21 Stark and Flitcraft 1996: 143.

22 Wilson and Daly 1998: 206–207.

23 Crawford and Gartner 1992; Browne *et al.* 1999.

24 Felson and Messner 1996.

25 Posner 2001.

26 Lazarus and Lazarus 1994; Oatley and Jenkins 1996.

27 Posner 2001.

28 Ben-Ze'ev 2000.

29 Palermo 1994; Milroy 1998.

30 Rosenbaum 1990; Cooper and Eaves 1996; Starzomski and Nussbaum 2000.

31 Stack 1997.

32 Palermo 1994; Starzomski and Nussbaum 2000.

33 Koss *et al.* 1994; Stark and Flitcraft 1996; Wilson and Daly 1998.

34 Baker *et al.* 1999; Polk 1994; Wilson and Daly 1998; Wilson *et al.* 1993: 286.

35 Campbell 1992; Crawford and Gartner 1992.

36 Holtzworth-Munroe *et al.* 1997; Stout 1993.

37 Dobash and Dobash 1998; Stark and Flitcraft 1996; Polk 1994.

Chapter 5

1 For a detailed discussion of imagination in the emotional realm, see Ben-Ze'ev 2000, Chapter 7.

2 Roese and Olson 1995.

3 Gilbert 2007: 18–19.

4 Spinoza 1677: Vp9d.

5 Prioleau 2003: 121 153.

6 Ben-Ze'ev 2003.

7 Gilbert 2007: 17–18; Roese and Olson 1995.

8 The Palestinian Talmud, y. Kiddushin 4.12 (66d); cited in Biale 1992: 41.

9 Strack *et al.* 1990; cited in Frank 1999:132; for a discussion of the role of the comparative concern in emotions, see Ben-Ze'ev 2000: 17–29.

10 Kahneman and Miller 1986; Lazarus and Lazarus 1994: Chapter 8; see also Ben-Ze'ev 2000: 21–23.

11 Gladue and Delaney 1990.

12 Baron *et al.* 1992: 3.

13 Buss 1994:64–5; Kenrick *et al.* 1989.

14 Dolan 1997; Gilbert 2007: 168 177–178.

15 Gilbert 2007: 175.

16 Gilbert 2007: 26, 98; Taylor 1989; see also Djikic and Oatley 2004; Srivastava *et al.* 2006.

17 Murray and Holmes 1997; Murray *et al.* 1996a, b; Neff and Karney 2005; Rusbult *et al.* 1991.

18 Baumeister 1990.

19 Neff and Karney 2002, 2003, 2005.

20 Neff and Karney 2005.

21 Illouz 1997: 7.

22 St. Claire 1996.

23 Fisher 2004: 83.

24 Baker and Emery 1993.

25 Tennov 1979: 31; Thomas 1991: 471–2.

26 Seelau *et al.* 1995.

27 Illouz 2007: 95–107.

28 Schopenhauer 1969: 87–88.

29 Spinoza 1677: IVp50s.

30 Schopenhauer 1969: 88.

31 Schopenhauer 1969: 87.

32 De Sousa, forthcoming.

33 Frankfurt 2004: 62–63.

34 Schwartz 1997: 5.

35 See also Portmann 2007.

36 Genesis Rabbah 9.9; cited in Biale 1992: 43.

37 Biale 1992: 47–48; Westheimer and Mark 1996: 29.

38 Portmann 2004: 103.

39 Schwartz 2000.

40 Taylor 1991.

41 Portmann 2007.

42 Ecclesiastes 7: 20; cited in Portmann 2007.

43 Portmann 2007.

44 Toulmin 1981.

45 Blackburn 2004: 5; Westheimer and Mark 1996: 44.

46 Callahan 2004.

47 Callahan 2004: 96–97.

48 Orr 2004.

49 Averill *et al.* 1990: 34.

50 Cohen 2006.

51 Cited in Westheimer and Mark 1996: 29.

52 Portmann 2004: 107, 173–174.

53 Portmann 2004.

54 Portmann 2004: 39–40.

55 Toulmin 1981.

56 Illouz 1997.

57 This is a basic principle in Adler's individual psychology; see e.g., Adler 1956.

58 Bloch 1988; see Kipnis 2003: 45.

59 Gert 2004: 22–26.

60 Etcoff 1999.

61 Prioleau 2003: 81.

62 See also Portmann 2007.

63 Zentner 2005.

64 Kayser 1993: 6.

65 Kayser 1993: 32–35.

66 http://en.eikipedia.org/wike/Second_Life

67 http://www.mmorgy.com/2005/10/state_of_sex_second_life_1.php

68 http://www.theregister.co.uk/2007/01/09/good_sex_in_second_life/

Chapter 6

1 The description is based on the conceptual framework suggested in Ben-Ze'ev 2000.

2 Ben-Ze'ev 2003.

3 Ben-Ze'ev 2000: Chapter 4; Rosenberg 1998.

4 Ben-Ze'ev 2000: Chapter 3.

5 Ben-Ze'ev 2000: Chapter 14; Ortony *et al.* 1988; the discussion here is based on Ben-Ze'ev 2004: 160–165.

6 Buss 1994.

7 Etcoff 1999: Chapter 1.

8 Freedman 1978: Chapter 4; Hunter 1983: 17; Tennov 1979: 73–79.

9 Frijda 1988; Illouz 1997; Lazarus 1991; Oatley 1992; for a detailed discussion on the role of change in generating emotions, see Ben-Ze'ev 2000: 13–17.

10 Gilbert 2007: 144.

11 Barash and Lipton 2001: 206; Gilbert 2007: 144–147.

12 Berlin 2002: 145.

13 Mitchell 2002: 27.

14 Greene 2001: 41, 51.

15 Gilbert 2007: 207–208.

16 Prioleau 2003: 14.

17 Norton *et al.* 2007.

18 Ben-Ze'ev 2004: 149; Simmel 1987: 134–138.

19 Clanton 1984: 15.

20 Barash and Lipton 2001.

21 Ben-Ze'ev 2004.

22 James McConvill, 'Pornography has its benefits', *On Line Opinion, Australia's e-journal of social and political debate* 29/9/06. http://www.onlineopinion.com.au/view.asp?article=4845.

23 Twenge 2006.

24 Greene 2001.

25 Norton *et al.* 2007.

26 Gaver and Mandler 1987.

27 Gaver and Mandler 1987.

28 See e.g., Berscheid, and Reis 1998; Klohnen and Mendelsohn 1998; Lou and Klohnen 2005; Watson *et al.* 2004.

29 Luo and Klohnen 2005.

30 Luo and Klohnen 2005.

31 Grandjean 2005.

32 Mitchell 2002: 39, 41.

33 Mitchell 2002: 199.

34 Armstrong 2002: Chapter 21.

35 Barash and Lipton 2001: 206.

36 Veroff *et al.* 1995: 3.

37 *Webster's New Collegiate Dictionary* 1980.

38 Armstrong 2002: 152–157; Kipnis 2003: 46; Mitchell 2002: 45.

39 Greene 2001: 55–57.

40 Ben-Ze'ev 2000: 35–40.

41 Ben-Ze'ev 2000: 33–40.

42 Ortega y Gasset 1941: 76, 43.

43 Forste and Tanfer 1996.

44 Orr 2004: 134.

45 Illouz 2007.

46 Kipnis 2006: 47, 61.

47 Kipnis 2006: 47; Michael *et al.* 1994.

48 Ben-Ze'ev 2004: 230–232.

49 Kipnis 2003: 12.

50 Shaw 1952.

51 Sokolon 2006: 71.

52 Shaw 1952.

53 Kayser 1993.

54 Cottrell *et al.* 2007.

55 *New Woman*, May 2007: 64.

56 Shaw 1997: 29.

57 Easton and Liszt 1997.

58 Ben-Ze'ev 2000: 410; Buss 1994: 59–60 112.

59 Ben-Ze'ev 2000: 294.

60 Barash and Lipton 2001: 154; Van Sommers 1988.

61 Buss 1994; Metts *et al.* 1998.

62 Prioleau 2003: 85.

63 Bauman 2003; Kayser 1993.

64 Illouz 2007: 90.

65 Gilbert 2007: 259.

66 Schwartz 2000.

67 Beattie *et al.* 1994.

68 Schwartz 2000: 81.

69 Lederer and Jackson 1968; Pines 1996: 53; http://personals.yahoo.com/us/static/singles-life_breakup-survey.

70 Skolnick 2006.

71 Kayser 1993.

72 Kayser 1993.

73 Ben-Ze'ev 2000: 514–519.

74 Levinger 1976; see also Berscheid and Campbell 1981.

75 Berscheid and Campbell 1981; Berscheid and Lopes 1997.

76 Kayser 1993: 12; Wallerstein and Lewis 2004.

77 Cohen 2006.

78 Berscheid and Campbell 1981; Berscheid and Lopes 1997.

79 Kayser 1993.

80 Kipnis 2003: 66.

81 Bauman 2003: ix; see also Kipnis 2003.

82 Schnarch 1997: 46.

83 Kayser 1993: 1, 5.

84 Mitchell 2002: 41.

85 Kipnis 2003: 20–23; 45–46.

86 Orr 2004: 143; Schnarch 1997.

87 Simmel 1987: 134.

88 Mitchell 2002: 199.

89 Greene 2001: xxii.

90 Armstrong 2002: 159.

91 Fisher 2004: 212–213.

92 http://www2.acnielsen.com/news/20070214.shtml.

93 Skolnick 2006.

Chapter 7

1 Overall *et al.* 2006.

2 Overall *et al.* 2006.

3 Armstrong 2002: 153.

4 Frankfurt 2004: 46.

5 Gittin 70a; cited in Biale 1992: 45.

6 Fromm 1956.

7 Shaw 1952.

8 *Webster's New Collegiate Dictionary* 1980.

9 Bauman 2003: 7.

10 Genesis 29: 20.

11 Arnaut Daniel, cited in Rougemout 1956: 118.

12 Diener *et al.* 1991.

13 Cited in Goleman 1996.

14 Kayser 1993.

15 Now for the first time in the history of the USA, married households are in the minority among all households: 49.7 percent of American households in 2005 were made up of married couples down more than 52 percent from five years earlier and down 84 percent from 1930 (*New York Times* 15 October 2006).

16 http://www2.acnielsen.com/news/20070214.shtml.

17 Cited in Barash and Lipton 2001: 204.

18 See, e.g., Kipnis 2003: 12.

19 Ben-Ze'ev 2004: 229–230.

20 Barash and Lipton 2001.

21 Barash and Lipton 2001: 153.

22 Hite 1988; cited in Giddens 1992: 136–137.

23 Finkel and Campbell 2001.

24 Fisher 2004: 217; http://www.openweave.org/NCPoly/PolyPrimer.html.

25 Barash and Lipton 2001.

26 Salovey and Rodin 1989:229; see also DeSteno and Salovey 1996; Salovey and Rothman 1991.

27 Green 2001: 25–37.

28 Barash and Lipton 2001: 154.

29 Barash and Lipton 2001: 150–151.

30 *Cosmopolitan*, UK edition, September, 2007: 113–116

31 Boyes and Fletcher 2007; Srivastava *et al.* 2006; Taylor 1989.

32 Alloy *et al.* 1990; Kinder 1995: 143; Snyder 1994: 16–18.

33 Simon 1957.

34 Arriga *et al.* 2007.

35 Charania and Ickes 2007.

Chapter 8

1 Portmann 2004: 9.

2 Kayser 1993: 120; Perlman 2007; Waite and Gallagher 2001; see also, Ben-Ze'ev 2004: 227–230; Freedman 1978: Chapter 5; Michael *et al.* 1994.

3 Levinas 1998: 105, 228–229.

4 Kayser 1993: 30–31.

5 Kayser 1993: 112, 36–37.

6 Kayser 1993: 112.

7 Schnarch 1997: 106–110.

8 Schnarch 1997.

9 Cummins and Nistico 2002.

10 Gilbert 2007: 182.

11 Schwartz 2000.

12 Kipnis 2003: 60.

13 Rohlfing 1995; Stafford and Reske 1990; Stephen 1986; see also Ben-Ze'ev 2004: 51–55.

14 Prins, Buunk and Van Yperen 1993.

15 Prins, Buunk and Van Yperen 1993.

16 Forste and Tanfer 1996.

17 Kayser 1993: 121.

18 Giddens 1992: 185.

19 Giddens 1992: 188.

20 See, e.g., Aristotle, *Metaphysics* 1048b18ff 1050a23ff; *Nicomachean Ethics* 1174a14ff. For further discussion and some relevant literature, see, e.g., Nussbaum 1986, Chapter 11. This discussion is based on Ben-Ze'ev 2004: Chapter 6.

21 Ben-Ze'ev 2004: Chapter 6; Csikszentmihalyi 1990; Persson 2005: 40–42.

22 Berger-Janoff-Bulman 2006; Clark and Grots 1998.

23 Ben-Ze'ev 2000: 456–458; Ben-Ze'ev 2004: 126–129; Csikszentmihalyi 1990.

24 Our discussion of the Self-Determination Theory is based on Patrick *et al.* 2007.

25 Gilbert 2007: 22–25.

26 Patrick *et al.* 2007.

27 De Charms 1968; Patrick *et al.* 2007.

28 Patrick *et al.* 2007.

29 Patrick *et al.* 2007.

30 King *et al.* 2006.

31 Higgins 1997.

32 Berlin 2002.

33 Marano 2008.

34 Illouz 2007: Chapter 3.

35 Gilbert 2007: 252.

36 Levinas 1998: 20.

37 Oatley and Jenkins 1996.

38 Benedict 2005: 10.

39 Marano 2008.

40 Ben-Ze'ev, 1993, Chapter 6.

41 Portmann (2007) says the same about sin.

42 Kayser 1993: 122–126.

43 Kipnis 2003: 22.

44 See Portmann's (2004) discussion of 'raving'.

45 Spinoza 1677: IV, 67.

46 Srivastava *et al.* 2006.

47 Wittgenstein 2001: 89; see also, 109, 127, 129.

48 Perlman 2007.

References

Adler, A. (1956). *The individual psychology of Alfred Adler.* New York: Basic Books.

Alloy, L. B., Albright, J. S., Abramson, L. Y. and Dykman, B. M. (1990). Depressive realism and nondepressive optimistic illusions: The role of the self. In R. E. Ingram (ed.), *Contemporary psychological approaches to depression.* New York: Plenum.

Aristotle, *The complete works of Aristotle: The revised Oxford translation.* (J. Barnes, Ed.). Princeton: Princeton University Press, 1984.

Armstrong, J. (2002). *Conditions of love: The philosophy of intimacy.* London: Penguin.

Aron, E. N. and Aron, A. (1996). Love and expansion of the self: The state of the model. *Personal Relationships, 13,* 45–58.

Aron, A., Aron. E. N., and Smollan, D. (1992). Inclusion of other in the self scale and the structure of interpersonal closeness. *Journal of Personality and Social Psychology, 63,* 596–612.

Arriaga, X. B., Slaugeterbeck, E. S. Capezza, N. and Hmurovic, J. L. (2007). From bad to worse: Relationship commitment and vulnerability to partner imperfections. *Personal Relationships, 14,* 389–409.

Avakame, E. F. (1998). How different is violence in the home? An examination of some correlates of stranger and intimate homicide. *Criminology, 36,* 601–632.

Averill, J. R. and Boothroyd, P. (1977). On falling in love in conformance with the romantic ideal. *Motivation and Emotion, 1,* 235–247.

Averill, J. R., Catlin, G. and Chon, K. K. (1990). *Rules of hope.* New York: Springer-Verlag.

Baker, L. A. and Emery, R. E. (1993). When every relationship is above average: Perceptions and expectations of divorce at the time of marriage. *Law and Human Behavior, 17,* 439–450.

Baker, N., Gregware, P. and Cassidy, M. (1999). Family killing field: honor rationales in the murder of women. *Violence Against Women, 5,* 164–184.

Barash, D. P. and Lipton, J. E. (2001). *The myth of monogamy: Fidelity and infidelity in animals and people.* New York: Freeman.

Barnett, O., Martinez, T. E. and Bluestein, B. W. (1995). Jealousy and romantic attachment in maritally violent and nonviolent men. *Journal of Interpersonal Violence, 10,* 473–486.

Baron, M. (2004). Killing in the heat of passion. In C. Calhoun (ed.), *Setting the moral compass: Essays by women philosophers.* Oxford: Oxford University Press.

Baron, R. S., Kerr, N. L. and Miller, N. (1992). *Group process, group decision, group action.* Buckingham: Open University Press.

Bauman, Z. (2003). *Liquid love: On the frailty of human bonds.* Cambridge: Polity Press.

Baumeister, R. F. (1990). Suicide as escape from self. *Psychological Review, 97,* 90–113.

Baumeister, R. F. (1997). *Evil: Inside human violence and cruelty.* New York: W. H. Freeman.

Baumeister, R. F., Wotman, S. R. and Stillwell, A. M. (1993). Unrequited love: On heartbreak, anger, guilt, scriptlessness and humiliation. *Journal of Personality and Social Psychology, 64,* 377–394.

Baumeiter, R, F. and Dhavale, D. (2001). Two sides of romantic rejection. In M. R. Leary (ed.), *Interpersonal rejection*. Oxford: Oxford University Press.

Bean, C. (1992). *Women murdered by the men they loved*. New York: Harrington Park Press.

Beattie, J., Baron, J., Hershey, J. C. and Spranca, M. D. (1994). Psychological determinants of decision attitudes. *Journal of Behavioral Decision Making, 7*, 129–144.

Benedict, XVI, Pope (2005). *Encyclical letter*. Libreria Editrice Vaticana.

Ben-Ze'ev, A. (1993). *The perceptual system: A philosphical and psychological perspective.* New York: Peter Lang.

Ben-Ze'ev, A. (2000). *The subtlety of emotions*. Cambridge, MA: MIT Press.

Ben-Ze'ev, A. (2003). The logic of emotions. In A. Hatzimoysis (ed.), *Philosophy and the emotions*. Cambridge: Cambridge University Press.

Ben-Ze'ev, A. (2004). *Love online: Emotions on the Internet*. Cambridge: Cambridge University Press.

Berger, A. R. and Janoff-Bulman (2006). Costs and satisfaction in close relationships: The role of loss-gain framing. *Personal Relationships, 13*, 53-68.

Berlin, I. (2002). Two concepts of liberty. In *Liberty*, pp. 166–217. Oxford: Oxford University Press.

Berscheid, E. and Campbell, B. (1981). The changing longevity of heterosexual close relationships. In M. J. Lerner and S. C. Lerner (eds), *The justice motive in social behavior: Adapting to times of scarcity and change*. New York: Plenum Press.

Berscheid, E. and Lopes, J. (1997). A temporal model of relationship satisfaction and stability. In R. J. Sternberg and M. Hojjat (eds), *Satisfaction in close relationships*. New York: Guilford Press.

Berscheid, E. and Reis, H. T. (1998). Attraction and close relationships. In D. T. Gilbert and S. T. Fiske (eds), *The handbook of social psychology*. New York: McGraw-Hill.

Biale, D. (1992). *Eros and the Jews*. New York: Basic Books.

Blackburn, S. (2004). *Lust*. Oxford: Oxford University Press.

Bloch, E. (1988). *The utopian function of art and literature*. Cambridge, MA: MIT Press.

Boyes, A. D. and Fletcher, G. (2007). Metaperceptions of bias in intimate relationships. *Journal of Personality and Social Psychology, 92*: 286–306.

Brown, R. (1987). *Analyzing love*. Cambridge: Cambridge University Press.

Browne, A. and Williams, K. R. (1993). Gender, intimacy and lethal violence: Trends. *Gender and Society, 7*, 78–98.

Browne, A., Williams, K. and Dutton, D. (1999). Homicide between intimate partners. In M. D. Smith and M. A. Zahn (eds). *Studying and preventing homicide.* Thousand Oaks, CA and London: Sage.

Buss, D. (1994). *The evolution of desire: Strategies of human mating*. New York: Basic Books.

Buss, D. (2000). Prescription for passion. *Psychology Today, 33* (3), 54–61.

Callahan, D. (2004). *The cheating culture: Why more Americans are doing wrong to get ahead.* Orlando, FL: Harcourt.

Campbell, J. C. (1992). If I can't have you, no one can: Issues of power and control of homicide of female partners. In J. Radford and D. E. H. Russell (eds), *Femicide: The politics of woman killing*. New York: Twayne.

Cate, R. M. and Lloyd, S. (1992). *Courtship*. Newbury Park, CA: Sage.

Charania, M. R. and Ickes, W. (2007). Predicting marital satisfaction: Social absorption and individuation versus attachment anxiety and avoidance. *Personal Relationships, 14,* 187–208.

Clanton, G. (1984). Social forces and the changing family. In L. A. Kirkendall and A. E. Gravatt (eds), *Marriage and the family in the year 2020.* Buffalo, NY: Prometheus Books.

Clark, M. S. and Grote, N. K. (1998). Why aren't indices of relationship costs always negatively related to indices of relationship quality? *Personality and Social Psychology Review, 2,* 2-17.

Cohen, N. (2006). The decline and rise of a promise of marriage, *Hamishpat,* 21, 10–22.

Cooper, M. and Eaves, D. (1996). Suicide following homicide in the family. *Violence and Victims, 11,* 99–112.

Cottrell, C. A., Neuberg, S. L. and Li, N. P. (2007). What do people desire in others? A sociofunctional perspective on the importance of different valued characteristics. *Journal of Personality and Social Psychology, 92,* 208–231.

Crawford, M. and Gartner, R. (1992). *Woman killing: Intimate femicide in Ontario 1974–1990.* Toronto: Ministry of Social Services.

Csikszentmihalyi, M. (1990). *Flow: The psychology of optimal experience.* New York: Harper Perennial.

Cummins, R. A. and Nistico, H. (2002). Maintaining life satisfaction: The role of positive cognitive bias. *Journal of Happiness Studies, 3,* 37–69.

de Becker, G. (1997). *The gift of fear.* Boston: Little, Brown and Company.

de Charms, R. (1968). *Personal causation.* New York: Academic Press.

de Sousa, R. (2007). Truth, authenticity, and rationality of emotions. *Dialectica,* 61, *32,* 3–345.

de Sousa, R. (1991). Love as theater. In R. C. Solomon and K. M. Higgins (eds), *The philosophy of (erotic) love.* Lawrence: University Press of Kansas.

Decker, S. H. (1996). Deviant homicide: A new look at the role of motives and victim–offender relationships. *Journal of Research in Crime and Delinquency, 33,* 427–449.

Delgado, A. R., Prieto, G. and Bond, R. A. (1997). The cultural factor in lay perception of jealousy as a motive for wife battery. *Journal of Applied Social Psychology, 27,* 1824–1841.

DeSteno, D. A. and Salovey, P. (1996). Jealousy and the characteristics of one's rival: A self-evaluation maintenance perspective. *Personality and Social Psychology Bulletin, 22,* 920–932.

Diener, E., Sandvik, E. and Pavot, W. (1991). Happiness is the frequency, not the intensity of positive versus negative affect. In F. Strack, M. Argyle and N. Schwarz (eds.), *Subjective well-being.* New York: Pergamon.

Djikic, M. and Oatley, K. (2004). Love and personal relationships: Navigating on the border between the ideal and the real. *Journal for the Theory of Social Behavior, 34,* 199–209.

Dobash, R. and Dobash, R. (eds) (1998). *Rethinking violence against women.* Thousand Oaks, CA: Sage.

Dolan, P. (1997). Modelling valuations for EuroQol health states. *Medical Care, 11,* 1095–1108.

Dressler, J. (2002). Why keep the provocation defense? *Minnesota Law Review, 86,* 959–1002.

Drigotas, S. M. (2002). The Michelangelo phenomenon and personal well-being. *Journal of Personality, 70*, 59–77.

Duck, S. (1994). *Meaningful relationships: Talking, sense, and relating.* Thousand Oaks, CA: Sage.

Dunn, J. L. (1999). What love has to do with it: The cultural construction of emotion and sorority women's responses to forcible interaction. *Social Problems, 3*, 440–459.

Dutton, D. G. (1995). Intimate abusiveness. *Clinical Psychology: Science and Practice, 2*, 207–224.

Easteal, P. (1995). Homicide-suicides between adult sexual intimates: An Australian study. *Suicide and Life-Threatening Behaviour, 24*, 140–151.

Easton, D. and Liszt, C. A. (1997). *The ethical slut.* San Francisco, CA: Greenery Press.

Ellsworth, P. C. and Smith, C. A. (1988). Shades of joy: Appraisals differentiating among positive emotions. *Cognition and Emotion, 2*, 301–331.

Emerson, R. M., Ferris, K. O. and Gardner, C. B. (1998). On being stalked. *Social Problems, 45*, 289–314.

Etcoff, N. (1999). *Survival of the prettiest: The science of beauty.* New York: Doubleday.

Evans, M. (2004). A critical lens on romantic love: A response to Bernadette Bawin-Legros. *Current Sociology, 52*, 259–264.

Fehr, B. (1988). Prototype analysis of the concepts of love and commitment. *Journal of Personality and Social Psychology, 55*, 557–579.

Felson, R. and Messner, S. (1998). Disentangling the effects of gender and intimacy on victim precipitation in homicide. *Criminology, 36*, 405–423.

Finkel, E. J. and Campbell, W. K. (2001). Self-control and accommodation in close relationships: An interdependence analysis. *Journal of Personality and Social Psychology, 81*, 263–277.

Fisher, H. (2004). *Why we love?* New York: Holt.

Fitness, J. (2001). Betrayal, rejection, revenge and forgiveness. In M. R. Leary (ed.), *Interpersonal rejection.* Oxford: Oxford University Press.

Fitness, J. and Fletcher, G. (1993). Love, hate, anger and jealousy in close relationships: A prototype appraisal analysis. *Journal of Personality and Social Psychology, 65*, 942–958.

Forste, R. and Tanfer, K. (1996). Sexual exclusivity among dating, cohabiting and married women. *Journal of Marriage and the Family, 56*, 33–47.

Frank, R. H. (1999). *Luxury fever: Why money fails to satisfy in an era of excess.* New York: The Free Press.

Frankfurt, H. G. (1988). Equality as a moral ideal. In *The importance of what we care about.* Cambridge: Cambridge University Press.

Frankfurt, H. G. (2004). *The reasons for love.* Princeton, NJ: Princeton University Press.

Fredrickson, B. L. (1998). What good are positive emotions? *Review of General Psychology, 2*, 1–20.

Freedman, J. L. (1978). *Happy people.* New York: Harcourt Brace Jovanovich.

Frijda, N. H. (1988). The laws of emotion. *American Psychologist, 43*, 349–358.

Fromm, E. (1956). *The art of loving.* New York: HarperCollins.

Frye, V. and Wilt, S. (2001). Femicide and social disorganization. *Violence Against Women, 7*, 335–351.

Galeano, E. (1992). *The book of embraces.* New York: Norton.

Gauthier, D. K. and Bankston, W. B. (1997). Gender equality and the sex ratios of intimate killing. *Criminology, 35*, 577–600.

Gaver, W. W. and Mandler, G. (1987). Play it again, Sam: On liking music. *Cognition and Emotion, 3*, 259–282.

Gelles, R. J. (1997). *Intimate violence in families.* Thousand Oaks, CA: Sage.

Gert, B. (2004). *Common morality: Deciding what to do.* New York: Oxford University Press.

Giddens, A. (1992). *The transformation of intimacy: Sexuality, love and eroticism in modern societies.* Cambridge: Polity.

Gilbert, D. (2007). *Stumbling on happiness.* New York: Vintage.

Gladue, B. A. and Delaney, J. J. (1990). Gender differences in perception of attractiveness of men and women in bars. *Personality and Social Psychology Bulletin, 16*, 378–391.

Goetting, A. (1995). *Homicide in families and other special populations.* New York: Springer.

Goleman, D. (1996). Happiness may lie in your stars. *International Herald Tribune*, 18 July.

Goussinsky, R. (2002). Was the handwriting on the wall?! The meanings perpetrators attribute to intimate murder. Ph. D. dissertation, University of Haifa.

Grandjean, D. (2005).

Greene, R. (2001). *The art of seduction.* New York: Penguin.

Hatfield, E. and Rapson, R. (1993). Historical and cross-cultural perspectives on passionate love and sexual desire. *Annual Review of Sex Research, 4*, 67–98.

Hendrick, C., and Hendrick, S. S. (1988). Lovers wear rose-colored glasses. *Journal of Social and Personal Relationships, 5*, 161–183.

Henton, J., Cate, R., Koval, J., Lloyd, S. and Christopher, S. (1983). Romance and violence in dating relationships. *Journal of Family Issues, 4*, 467–482.

Higgins, E. T. (1997). Beyond pleasure and pain. *American Psychologist, 52*, 1280–1300.

Hite, S. (1988). *Women and love.* London: Viking.

Holland, D. and Eisenhart, M. (1990). *Educated in romance.* Chicago, IL: University of Chicago.

Holmberg, D. and Mackenzie, S. (2002). So far, so good: Scripts for romantic relationship development as predictors of relational well-being. *Journal of Social and Personal Relationships, 19*, 777–796.

Holtzworth-Munroe, A., Bates, L., Smutzler, N. and Sandin, E. (1997). A brief review of the research on husband violence. Parts 1–3. *Aggression and Violent Behavior, 2*, 65–99, 179–213, 285–307.

Hopkins, A. (1994). *The book of courtly love: The passionate code of the troubadours.* San Francisco, CA: Harper.

Hui, C. H. and Triandis, H. C. (1986). Individualism-collectivism: A study of cross-cultural searchers. *Journal of Cross-Cultural Psychology, 17*, 222–248.

Hunter, J. F. M. (1983). *Thinking about sex and love.* New York: St. Martin's.

Illouz, E, (1997). *Consuming the romantic utopia: Love and the cultural contradictions of capitalism.* Berkeley, CA: University of California.

Illouz, E, (2007). *Cold intimacies: The making of emotional capitalism.* Cambridge: Polity Press.

Jones, J. and Cunningham, J. (1996). Attachment styles and other predictors of relationship satisfaction in dating couples. *Personal Relationships, 3*, 387–399.

Kahneman, D., and Miller, D. T. (1986). Norm theory: Comparing reality to its alternatives. *Psychological Review, 93*, 136–153.

Kayser, K. (1993). *When love dies: The process of marital disaffection*. New York: Guilford.

Keats, J. (1958). *The letters of John Keats*. Cambridge: Cambridge University Press.

Kenrick, D. T., Gutierres, S. E. and Goldberg, L. (1989). Influence of erotica on ratings of strangers and mates. *Journal of Experimental Social Psychology*, *25*, 159–167.

Kim, S. and Smith, R. (1993). Revenge and conflict escalation. *Negotiation Journal*, *9*, 37–43.

Kinder, M. (1995). *Mastering your moods*. New York: Simon and Schuster.

King, L., Hicks, J. A., Krull, J. L., Del Gaiso, A. K. (2006). Positive affect and the experience of meaning in life. *Journal of Personality and Social Psychology*, *90*, 179–196.

Kipnis, L. (2003). *Against love: A polemic*. New York: Pantheon.

Kipnis, L. (2006). *The female thing*. New York: Pantheon.

Klohnen, E. C. and Mendelsohn, G. A. (1998). Partner selection for personality characteristics: A couple-centered approach. *Personality and Social Psychology Bulletin*, *24*, 268–278.

Koss, M. P., Goodman, L. A., Browne, A., Fitzgerald, L. F., Keita, G. and Russo, N. (1994). *No safe haven: Male violence against women at home, at work and in the community*. Washington, DC: American Psychological Association.

Landis, D., and O'Shea, W. A. (2000). Cross-cultural aspects of passionate love: An individual differences analysis. *Journal of Cross-Cultural Psychology*, *31*, 752–777.

Lazarus, R. S. (1991). *Emotion and adaptation*. New York: Oxford University Press.

Lazarus, R. S. and Lazarus, B. N. (1994). *Passion and reason: Making sense of our emotions*. New York: Oxford University Press.

Leary, M. R., Koch, E. J. and Hechenbleikner, N. R. (2001). Emotional response to interpersonal rejection. In M. R. Leary (ed.), *Interpersonal rejection*. Oxford: Oxford University Press.

Lederer, W. and Jackson, D. (1968). *The mirages of marriage*. New York: Norton.

Lerner, M. J. and Miller, D. T. (1978). Just world research and the attribution process: Looking back and ahead. *The Psychological Bulletin*, *85*, 1030–1051.

Levinas, E. (1998). *On thinking-of-the-other*. London: Althlone Press.

Levinger, G. A. (1976). A social psychological perspective on marital dissolution. *Journal of Social Issues*, *32*, 21–47.

Luo, S. and Klohnen, E. C. (2005). Assortative mating and marital quality in newlyweds: A couple-centered approach. *Journal of Personality and Social Psychology*, *88*, 304–326.

Marano, H. E. (2008). *A nation of wimps: the high cost of invasive parenting*. New York: Broadway Books.

Medora, N. P., Larson, J. H., Hortacsu, N. and Dave, P, (2002). Perceived attitudes towards romanticism: A cross-cultural study of American, Asian-Indian and Turkish young adults. *Journal of Comparative Family Studies*, *33*, 155–178.

Merino, N. (2004). The problem with 'we': Rethinking joint identity in romantic love. *Journal of Social Philosophy*, *35*, 123–132.

Metts, S., Sprecher, S. and Regan, P. C. (1998). Communication and sexual drive. In P. A. Andersen and L. K. Guerrero (eds.), *Handbook of communication and emotion*. San Diego: Academic Press.

Michael, R. T., Gagnon, J. H., Laumann, E. D. and Kolata, G. (1994). *Sex in America*. Boston, MA. Little, Brown.

Miller, W.I. (2003). *Faking it*. Cambridge: Cambridge University Press.

Milroy, C. (1998). Homicide followed by suicide: Remorse or revenge? *Journal of Clinical Forensic Medicine, 5*, 61–64.

Mitchell, S. A. (2002). *Can love last? The fate of romance over time*. New York: Norton.

Mullen, P. E., Pathe, M., Purcell, R. and Stuart, G. W. (1999). Study of stalkers. *The American Journal of Psychiatry, 156*, 1244–1249.

Murphy, C. M., Meyer, S. and O'Leary, K. D. (1994). Dependency characteristics of partner-assaultive men. *Journal of Abnormal Psychology, 24*, 1367–1386.

Murray, S. L. and Holmes, J. G. (1997). A leap of faith? Positive illusions in romantic relationships. *Personality and Social Psychology Bulletin, 23*, 586–604.

Murray, S. L., Holmes, J. G. and Griffin, D. W. (1996a). The benefits of positive illusions: Idealization and the construction of satisfaction in close relationships. *Journal of Personality and Social Psychology, 70*, 79–98.

Murray, S. L., Holmes, J. G. and Griffin, D. W. (1996b). The self-fulfilling nature of positive illusions in romantic relationships: Love is not blind but prescient. *Journal of Personality and Social Psychology, 71*, 1155–1180.

Neff, L. A. and Karney, B. R. (2002). Judgments of a relationship partner: Specific accuracy but global enhancement. *Journal of Personality, 70*, 1079–1112.

Neff, L. A. and Karney, B. R. (2003). The dynamic structure of relationship perceptions: Differential importance as a strategy of relationship maintenance. *Personality and Social Psychology Bulletin, 29*, 1433–1446.

Neff, L. A. and Karney, B. R. (2005). To know you is to love you: The implications of global adoration and specific accuracy for marital relationships. *Journal of Personality and Social Psychology, 88*, 480–497.

Neu, J. (2000). Odi et amo: On hating the ones we love. In Neu, *A tear is an intellectual thing*. Oxford: Oxford University Press.

Norton, M. I., Frost, J. H. and Ariely, D. (2007). Less is more: The lure of ambiguity, or why familiarity breeds contempt. *Journal of Personality and Social Psychology, 92*, 97–105.

Nozick, R. (1991). Love's bond. In R. C. Solomon and K. M. Higgins (eds), *The philosophy of (erotic) love*. Lawrence, KS: University Press of Kansas.

Nussbaum, M. C. (1986). *The fragility of goodness: Luck and ethics in Greek tragedy and philosophy*. Cambridge: Cambridge University Press.

Nussbaum, M. C. (2001). *Upheavals of thought: A theory of the emotions*. Cambridge: Cambridge University Press.

Oatley, K. (1992). *Best laid schemes: The psychology of emotions*. Cambridge: Cambridge University Press.

Oatley, K. and Jenkins, J. M. (1996). *Understanding emotions*. Cambridge, MA: Blackwell.

Orr, A. (2004). *Meeting, mating and cheating: Sex, love and the new world of online dating*. Upper Saddle River, NJ: Reuters.

Ortega y Gasset, J. (1941). *On love … Aspects of a single theme*. London: Jonathan Cape.

Ortony, A., Clore, G. L. and Collins, A. (1988). *The cognitive structure of emotions*. Cambridge: Cambridge University Press.

Overall, N., Fletcher, G. J.O, Simpson, J. A., (2006). Regulation processes in intimate relationships: The role of ideal standards. *Journal of Personality and Social Psychology, 91*, 662–685.

Palermo, G. (1994). Homicide-suicide: An extended suicide. *International Journal of Offender Therapy and Comparative Criminology, 38*, 205–216.

Parker, R. N. (1989). Poverty, subculture of violence and types of homicide. *Social Forces, 67*, 983–1007.

Parker, R. N. and Toth, A. M. (1990). Family, intimacy and homicide: A macrosocial approach. *Violence and Victims, 5*, 195–210.

Patrick, H., Knee, C. R., Canevello, A. and Lonsbary, C. (2007). The role of need fulfillment in relationship functioning and well-being: A self-determination theory perspective. *Journal of Personality and Social Psychology, 92*, 434–457.

Perlman, D. (2007). The best of times, the worst of times: The place of close relationships in psychology and our daily lives. *Canadian Psychology, 48*, 7–18.

Persson, I, (2005). *The retreat of reason: A dilemma in the philosophy of life.* Oxford: Oxford University Press.

Pines, A. M. (1996). *Couple burnout: Causes and cures.* New York: Routledge.

Pitcher, G. (1965). Emotion. *Mind, 74*, 326–345.

Polk, K. (1994). *When men kill: Scenarios of masculine violence.* Cambridge: Cambridge University Press.

Portmann, J. (2004). *Bad for us: The lure of self-harm.* Boston, MA: Beacon Press.

Portmann, J. (2007). *A history of sin.* Lanham, MD: Rowman and Littlefield.

Posner, E. (2001). Law and emotions. *Georgetown Law Journal, 89*, 1977–2012.

Prins, K. S., Buunk, B. P. and VanYperen, N. W. (1993). Equity, normative disapproval and extramarital relationships. *Journal of Social and Personal Relationships, 10*, 39–53.

Prioleau, B. (2003). *Seductress: Women who ravished the world and their lost art of love.* New York: Viking.

Regan, P. R., Kocan, E. R. and Whitlock, T. (1998). Ain't love grand! A prototype analysis of the concept of romantic love. *Journal of Social and Personal Relationship, 15*, 411–420.

Roese, N. J. and Olson, J. M. (eds) (1995). *What might have been: The social psychology of counterfactual thinking.* Mahwah, NJ: Erlbaum.

Rohlfing, M. E. (1995). 'Doesn't anybody stay in one place anymore?' An exploration of the under-studies phenomenon of long-distance relationships. In J. Wood and S. Duck (eds), *Understudied relationships.* Thousand Oaks, CA: Sage.

Rosenbaum, M. (1990). The role of depression in couples involved in murder-suicide and homicide. *American Journal of Psychiatry, 147*, 1036–1039.

Rosenberg, E. L. (1998). Levels of analysis and the organization of affect. *Review of General Psychology, 2*, 247–270.

Rothbaum, F. and Tsang, B. Y. (1998). Lovesongs in the United States and China: On the nature of romantic love. *Journal of Cross-cultural Psychology, 29*, 306–319.

Rougemont, D. D. (1956). *Love in the Western world.* New York: Pantheon.

Rusbult, C. E., Verette, J., Whitney, G., Slovik, L and Lipkus, I. (1991). Accommodation processes in close relationships: Theory and preliminary empirical evidence. *Journal of Personality and Social Psychology, 60*, 53–78.

Salovey, P. and Rodin, J. (1989). Envy and jealousy in close relationships. In C. Hendrick (ed.), *Close relationships.* Newbury Park, CA: Sage.

Salovey, P. and Rothman, A. J. (1991). Envy and jealousy: Self and society. In P. Salovey (ed.), *The psychology of jealousy and envy.* New York: Guilford Press.

Schaum, M. and Parrish, K. (1995). *Stalked: Breaking the silence on the crime of stalking in America*. New York: Pocket Books.

Schnarch, D. (1997). *Passionate marriage: Love, sex and intimacy in emotionally committed relationships*. New York: Norton.

Schopenhauer, A. (1969). *The world as will and representation*. New York: Dover.

Schwartz, B. (2000). Self-determination: The tyranny of freedom. *American Psychologist, 55,* 79–88.

Schwartz, R. M. (1997). *The curse of Cain*. Chicago, IL: The University of Chicago Press.

Seelau, E. P., Seelau, S. M., Wells, G. L. and Windschitl, P. D. (1995). Counterfactual constraints. In N. J. Roese and J. M. Olson (eds), *What might have been: The social psychology of counterfactual thinking*. Mahwah, NJ: Erlbaum.

Sharp, E. A. and Ganong, L. H. (2000). Raising awareness about marital expectations: Are unrealistic beliefs changed by integrative teaching? *Family Relations, 49,* 71–76.

Shaver, P. R., Schwartz, J., Kirson, D. and O'Connor, C. (1987). Emotion knowledge: Further exploration of a prototype approach. *Journal of Personality and Social Psychology, 52,* 1061–1086.

Shaw, G. B. (1952). *Don Juan in hell*. New York: Dodd, Mead.

Shaw, J. (1997). Treatment rationale for Internet infidelity. *Journal of Sex Education and Therapy, 22,* 29–34.

Sher, G. (1987). *Desert*. Princeton, NJ: Princeton University Press.

Simmel, G. (1987). *On women, sexuality and love*. New Haven, CT: Yale University Press.

Simon, H. (1957). 'A Behavioral Model of Rational Choice', in *Models of Man, Social and Rational: Mathematical Essays on Rational Human Behavior in a Social Setting*. New York: Wiley.

Sinclair, H. C., Frieze, I. H. (2000). Initial courtship behavior and stalking: How should we draw the line? *Violence and Victims, 15,* 23–40.

Skolnick, A. (2006). Beyond the 'M' word: The tangled web of politics and marriage. *Dissent,* Fall, 2006.

Snyder, C. R. (1994). *The psychology of hope*. New York: Free Press.

Sokolon, M. K. (2006). *Political emotions: Aristotle and the symphony of reason and emotions*. Dekalb, IL: Northern Illinois University Press.

Sprecher, S. and Metts, S. (1999). Romantic beliefs: Their influence on relationships and patterns of change over time. *Journal of Social and Personal Relationships, 16,* 834–851.

Srivastava, S., McGonigal, K. M., Richards, J. M., Butler, E. A., Gross, J. J. (2006). Optimism in close relationships: How seeing things in a positive light makes them so. *Journal of Personality and Social Psychology, 91,* 143–153.

Stack, S. (1997). Homicide followed by suicide: An analysis of Chicago data. *Criminology, 35,* 435–453.

Stafford, L. and Reske, J. R. (1990). Idealization and communication in long-distance premarital relationships. *Family Relations, 39,* 274–279.

St. Claire, O. (1996). *Unleashing the sex goddess in every woman*. New York: Harmony books.

Stark, E. and Flitcraft, A. (1996). *Women at risk: Domestic violence and women's health*. Thousand Oaks, CA: Sage.

Starzomski, A. and Nusssbaum, D. (2000). The self and the psychology of domestic homicide-suicide. *International Journal of Offender Therapy and Comparative Criminology, 44,* 468–479.

Stephen, T. (1986). Communication and interdependence in geographically separated relationships. *Human Communication Research, 13,* 191–210.

Sternberg, R. J. (1988). *The triangle of love.* New York: Basic Books.

Stout, K. (1993). Intimate femicide: A study of men who have killed their mates. *Journal of Offender rehabilitation, 19,* 81–94.

Strack, F., Schwarz, B., Chassein, B. Kern, D. and Wagner, D. (1990). The salience of comparison standards and the activation of social norms: Consequences for judgments of happiness and their communication. *British Journal of Social Psychology, 29,* 303–314.

Suzuki, S. (1970). *Zen mind, beginner's mind.* New York: Weatherhill.

Swann, W. B., Jr., De La Ronde, C. and Hixon, J. G. (1994). Authenticity and positivity strivings in marriage and courtship. *Journal of Personality and Social Psychology, 66,* 857–869.

Swidler, A. (2001). *Talk of love: How culture matters.* Chicago, IL: The University of Chicago Press.

Taylor, C. (1989). *Sources of the self: The making of the modern identity.* Cambridge, MA: Harvard University Press.

Taylor, C. (1991). *The ethics of authenticity.* Cambridge, MA: Harvard University Press.

Taylor, S. E. (1989). *Positive illusions: Creative self-deception and the healthy mind.* New York: Basic Books.

Tennov, D. (1979). *Love and limerence.* New York: Stein and Day.

Thomas, L. (1991). Reasons for loving. In R. C. Solomon and K. M. Higgins (eds.), *The philosophy of (erotic) love.* Lawrence: University Press of Kansas, 477–491.

Toulmin, S. (1981). The tyranny of principles. *The Hastings Center Report, 11,* 31–39.

Tversky, A. and Kahneman, D. (1982). Judgments of and by representativeness. In D. Kahneman, P. Slovic and A. Tversky (eds.), *Judgment under uncertainty: Heuristics and biases.* Cambridge: Cambridge University Press.

Tversky, A. and Kahneman, D. (1983). Extensional versus intuitive reasoning: The conjunction fallacy in probability judgment. *Psychological Review, 90,* 293–315.

Twenge, J. M. (2006). *Generation me.* New York: Free Press.

Vaihinger, H. (1935). *The philosophy of 'As if'.* London: Routledge and Kegan Paul.

Van Sommers, P. (1988). *Jealousy.* London: Penguin.

Veroff, J., Douvan, E. and Hatchett, S. J. (1995). *Marital instability.* Westport, CT: Praeger.

Waite, L. J. and Gallagher, M. (2001). *The case for marriage: Why married people are happier, healthier and better off financially.* New York: Broadway Books.

Wallerstein, J. and Lewis, J. M. (2004). The unexpected legacy of divorce: Report of a 25-year study. *Psychoanalytic Psychology, 21,* 353–370.

Watson, D., Klohnen, E. C., Casillas, A., Nus Simms, E., Haig, J. and Berry, D. S. (2004). Match makers and deal breakers: Analyses of assortative mating in newlywed couples. *Journal of Personality, 72,* 1029–1068.

Weaver, S. E. and Ganong, L. H. (2004). Romantic beliefs scale for African Americans and European Americans. *Journal of Social and Personal Relationships, 21,* 171–185.

Westheimer, R. K. and Mark, J. (1996). *Heavenly sex: Sexuality in the Jewish tradition.* New York: Continuum.

Wilding, R. (2003). Romantic love and 'getting married': Narratives of wedding in and out of cinema texts. *Journal of Sociology, 39,* 373–389.

Wilson, D. and Daly, M. (1993). Spousal homicide risk and estrangement. *Violence Against Women*, *8*, 3–16.

Wilson, M and Daly, M. (1998). Lethal and nonlethal violence against wives and the evolutionary psychology of male sexual proprietariness. In R. E. Dobash and R. P. Dobash (eds), *Rethinking violence against women*. Thousand Oaks, CA: Sage.

Wilson, M., Daly, M. and Daniele, A. (1995). Familicide: The killing of spouses and children. *Aggressive Behviour*, *21*, 275–291.

Wilson, M., Daly, M. and Wright, C. (1993). Uxoricide in Canada: Demographic risk patterns. *Canadian Journal of Criminology*, *35*, 263–291.

Wittgenstein, L. (2001). *Philosophical investigations*. Oxford: Blackwell.

Zentner, M. R. (2005). Ideal mate personality concepts and compatibility in close relationships: A longitudinal analysis. *Journal of Personality and Social Psychology*, *89*, 242–256.

Index

Printed and bound by CPI Group (UK) Ltd, Croydon, CR0 4YY